G Purnell

HOBBES and ROUSSEAU

A Collection of Critical Essays

Modern Studies in Philosophy is a series of anthologies presenting contemporary interpretations and evaluations of the works of major philosophers. The editors have selected articles designed to show the systematic structure of the thought of these philosophers, and to reveal the relevance of their views to the problems of current interest. These volumes are intended to be contributions to contemporary debates as well as to the history of philosophy; they not only trace the origins of many problems important to modern philosophy, but also introduce major philosophers as interlocutors in current discussions.

Modern Studies in Philosophy is prepared under the general editorship of Amelie Oksenberg Rorty, Livingston College, Rutgers University.

Richard S. Peters is professor of the philosophy of education at the University of London. Maurice Cranston is professor of political science at the London School of Economics.

MODERN STUDIES IN PHILOSOPHY

Amelie Oksenberg Rorty, General Editor

HOBBES and ROUSSEAU:

A Collection of Critical Essays

EDITED BY
MAURICE CRANSTON
AND
RICHARD S. PETERS

ANCHOR BOOKS
DOUBLEDAY & COMPANY, INC.
GARDEN CITY, NEW YORK
1972

This anthology has been especially prepared for
Anchor Books and has never before appeared in
book form.

Anchor Books edition: 1972

Library of Congress Catalog Card Number 77–168283
Copyright © 1972 by Richard S. Peters and Maurice Cranston
All Rights Reserved
Printed in the United States of America
First Edition

CONTENTS

ROUSSEAU

Contents

HOBBES and ROUSSEAU

A Collection of Critical Essays

INTRODUCTION

There has been a great deal of expository work done on Hobbes in recent times both in books and in articles. Schools of thought have developed which differ in the type of interpretation which they give of Hobbes' ideas. This can present problems to students who read books about Hobbes, for such readers may be unaware of the point of view which lies behind the commentator's interpretation. It was thought desirable, therefore, to open this collection of articles with W. H. Greenleaf's essay on "Hobbes: The Problem of Interpretation," which attempts to set out explicitly these main points of view.

This is followed by a recent article by Brian Barry on "Warrender and His Critics," which continues the controversy about Hobbes' theory of obligation with which several articles in Keith Brown's recent collection, entitled *Hobbes Studies*, were concerned. A different point of view on these matters is also represented by K. R. Minogue's article on "Hobbes and the Just Man." In an essay specially written for this volume on "Hobbes on the Knowledge of God" Ronald Hepburn attempts to assess differing interpretations of Hobbes' philosophy of religion and to arrive at a balanced judgment about what he actually thought.

These three articles continue controversies about Hobbes by drawing mainly on internal evidence from Hobbes' writings. They are followed by two articles which approach current controversies by introducing different types of consideration. Quentin Skinner contributes an article, based on some earlier work of his own, in which he confronts a prevailing interpretation of Hobbes' theory of political obligation with a careful examination of the ideological context in which it was written. This is followed by an article specially written by William Letwin on "The Economic Foundations of Hobbes' Politics," in which C. B. Macpherson's interpretation of Hobbes, as put forward in *The Political Theory of Pos-*

sessive Individualism, is discussed in the light of Hobbes'
views about economic matters seen in a context of economic theory and economic history.

The next three articles in the collection are not much
concerned with current controversies about interpretation, but they have a certain unity in that they attempt
to show the connexion between Hobbes' metaphysical
ideas and his approach to problems of human behaviour
—in particular his theory of power and liberty. Richard
Peters and Henri Tajfel attempt to demonstrate the similarity between Hobbes' mechanistic theory of human behaviour and that of Clark Hull, a recent and highly influential exponent of a mechanical theory of man. Stanley
Benn, in an article specially written for this volume,
meticulously examines Hobbes' theory of "power" and
causality and its link with his theory of political domination. John Watkins examines Hobbes' theory of "endeavour" and its influence on Leibnitz and shows the
connexion between this metaphysical theory and Hobbes'
theory of liberty. These are all examples, perhaps, of
what W. H. Greenleaf, in the opening article, calls "the
traditional theory," in which great emphasis is placed on
Hobbes' mechanistic type of metaphysics and the influence which it had on his theories about man in society.
A transition to the second part of this volume is provided by Peter Winch's essay on "Man and Society in
Hobbes and Rousseau."

There has been a marked revival of interest in recent
years in Rousseau as a political philosopher. Whereas it
was the fashion before the war to dismiss him as a sinister
romantic, a forerunner of fascism and communism, a man
unsound in mind and body, he has more recently been
read with greater respect. A leading article in the *Times
Literary Supplement* in June 1970 suggested that this
new interest in Rousseau might be dated from two publishing events: Bertrand de Jouvenel's edition of *Du
Contrat Social,* which came out in Geneva in 1947, and
Leo Strauss's essay on Rousseau's "Discours sur les Sciences et les Arts," which appeared about the same time

in *Social Research*, New York. Both Baron de Jouvenel
and Professor Strauss are contributors to this present volume: Jouvenel is represented by an essay on "Rousseau's
Theory of the Forms of Government" which develops
ideas first adumbrated in his introduction to the *Social
Contract*, and Strauss's paper on the "First Discourse" is
reproduced in its original integral form.

The other essays printed here are for the most part by
younger scholars. Some are reproduced from learned
journals, others have been specially commissioned for
these pages. Apart from Jouvenel, all the contributors are
British or American. The editors decided, with some re-
luctance, to exclude for reasons of space essays written
in French or other foreign languages. The contribution
to Rousseau studies since the war by continental specialists such as Starobinski, Burgelin, Polin, and above
all, Robert Derathé, is unquestionable; and numerous
references to their writings will be found in the articles
which follow. Nevertheless, it was not possible to give
adequate representation in this book both to continental
scholars and to English-speaking scholars, and it seemed
reasonable therefore to include only papers written originally in English.

Among the American contributions are an essay each
by the two leading Rousseau scholars of the younger
generation in the United States, Roger D. Masters and
Judith N. Shklar. Professor Masters' book *The Political
Philosophy of Rousseau* was published as recently as
1968, Mrs. Shklar's *Men and Citizens: A Study of Rousseau's Social Theory* came out in 1969; they have already
made a considerable impact. Masters has specially written for this volume an essay on the structure of Rousseau's political thought, and Mrs. Shklar is represented
by a paper on "Rousseau's Images of Authority," which
first appeared in the *American Political Science Review*.
Both in their different ways belong to the new tradition
of Rousseau scholarship initiated by Jouvenel and
Strauss.

The British contributors have perhaps more in common with the methods of contemporary analytic philosophy, at least in singling out one particular problem for scrutiny in depth. Thus, in essays previously unpublished, William Pickles considers Rousseau's notion of time and John Charvet discusses Rousseau's conception of individuality, while John Plamenatz, in a paper originally written for a conference of the Institut International de Philosophie Politique, provides a commentary on Rousseau's notorious remark about the possibility of a man being "forced to be free." Breadth of interest is not, however, lacking in the English contributions: John McManners joins Mrs. Shklar in seeking to relate Rousseau's political theory to his problems as a moralist and a man, and Ronald Grimsley, whose books have made a notable contribution to our understanding of Rousseau's epistemology and Rousseau's religion, writes here about Rousseau's theory of happiness.

We believe that these essays afford, within a relatively small space, a rich and varied measure of current scholarship in the two fields of Hobbes and Rousseau studies.

Richard Peters
Maurice Cranston

HOBBES: THE PROBLEM OF INTERPRETATION

W. H. GREENLEAF

The late J. L. Austin, observing that work of original merit tends to produce a flow of interpretative studies which, in their turn, are themselves elaborately glossed, described this process as The Law of Diminishing Fleas. What follows begins indeed simply with comment on the commentaries which have been written about Hobbes, but I want to use this parasitical survey to raise some issues of methodological interest.[1] First of all, then, I describe what I take to be the main lines of interpretation of Hobbes's theories which have emerged and the relationship between them; and, after this, I discuss some of the problems raised for intellectual history by this diverse exegesis.

I

There seem to be three main types of interpretation of Hobbes's ideas. I call them the 'traditional case', the 'natural-law case', and the 'individualist case'. Of course, these are (in a way) artificial categorisations and each encompasses a range of internal variation. But none is a mere abstraction and their distinctive characters can be discerned in the actual history of Hobbes scholarship.[2] And in describing these points of view, my object is not

---

From *Hobbes-Forschungen*, edited by Reinhart Koselleck and Roman Schnur. Duncker & Humblot, Berlin, 1969. Reprinted by permission of the author and publishers.

[1] In any event, Hobbes is a most apposite case to exemplify Austin's Law: See Swift's 'On Poetry: A Rhapsody', ll. 319 ff.

[2] For purposes of this discussion I draw specifically, and somewhat narrowly, on the literature in English. It would be most interesting and useful to learn whether a similar pattern of interpretation occurs in the commentaries on Hobbes by scholars writing in other languages.

to explain each in detail but simply to outline their main and contrasting features.

The *traditional case*, or orthodox interpretation of Hobbes, is that he is a materialist imbued with the ideas of the 'new' natural science and that he methodically applies its themes and procedures (the laws governing bodies in motion and their deductive elaboration) to the elucidation of a civil and ethical theory cast in the same mould. Thus, on this view, Hobbes's notion of obligation is founded on his egoistic psychology which itself rests on the naturalistic presuppositions. Duty is a matter of prudence, the rational pursuit of self-interest, the motion of appetite and aversion. Of course, this is hardly a genuinely moral theory at all; it is a descriptive rather than a normative account of human behaviour.[3]

Now, this is certainly something like the interpretation put upon Hobbes's thought by a good many of his contemporaries. Most of them believed that such naturalism and materialism necessarily involved a demeaning view of mankind, condoned cynical and selfish behaviour, and led directly to atheism, determinism, ethical relativism and a host of other evils all of which were destructive of the very foundation of Christian society.[4] At the same time, it is now clear that there was a substantial body of opinion which found a good part or all of Hobbes's ideas wholly congenial and did so precisely because of their uncompromising naturalistic character.[5] Cowley lauded

---

[3] The argument that obedience to the Leviathan is a duty because his commands have been authorized by individuals through the covenant suffers from the difficulty that the moral obligation thus attached to observance of the covenant is itself unexplained in ethical terms.

[4] J. Bowle, *Hobbes and His Critics* (London, 1951) and S. I. Mintz, *The Hunting of Leviathan* (Cambridge, 1962) describe in detail this contemporary reaction to Hobbes's writings, the former dealing largely with the political, the latter with the metaphysical and moral, aspects of criticism.

[5] Mr. Quentin Skinner has done much recently, and with a wealth of learned reference, to establish this wider perspective. See his "History and Ideology in The English Revolution", *Historical Jour-*

Hobbes as the 'great Columbus of the golden lands of new philosophies' and, in particular, many continental *savants* and *philosophes* acknowledged their debt to him. This company includes figures such as Spinoza, Leibniz, Diderot and d'Holbach; while Bayle openly recognized Hobbes as 'the greatest genius of the seventeenth century'. In this country, the utilitarians found his writings a major and most authoritative source of ideas, not least because of the vigour with which his naturalistic manner was applied to the elimination of philosophical nonsense. It was not an accident that Grote and Molesworth initiated a scheme for the publication of Hobbes's complete works: the project was an indication and acknowledgment of their school's indebtedness.[6] And, in a positivist dominated age, it would be natural for Hobbes to be regarded as one of the earliest and greatest forerunners of the scientific attitude to things in general, as a thinker who provided a magnificent expression of the naturalist doctrine. For Marx and his followers, Hobbes is a pioneer materialist and mechanist (as well as one who expounds the principles of bourgeois society).

The traditional Hobbes has, then, never been without influence. Yet it is an interesting feature of the modern literature that it would have been difficult (until fairly recently) to find a clear and complete acceptance of this view outside the text-books or similarly brief analyses. However, it is obvious enough that some of the general historians of philosophy and political thought do expound the traditional picture of Hobbes in their synopses. Two instances must suffice. Höffding says that Hobbes 'instituted the best thought-out attempt of modern times to make our knowledge of natural science the

nal, VIII (1965), pp. 151–78 esp. pp. 170–1; "The Ideological Context of Hobbes's Political Thought", *ibid.*, IX (1966), pp. 286–317; "Thomas Hobbes and his Disciples in France and England", *Comparative Studies in Society and History*, VIII (1966), pp. 153–67.

[6] G. Grote, *Minor Works* (ed. Bain; London, 1873), pp. 59–72, esp. p. 67.

foundation of all our knowledge of existence. The system which he constructed is the most profound materialistic system' of the modern world and effected a break with 'Scholasticism similar to that instituted by Copernicus in astronomy, Galilei in physics, and Harvey in physiology'. Thus he put the study of ethics and politics on a 'naturalistic basis'.[7] Again, Sabine suggests that Hobbes's formal conceptions of man, ethics and politics are intended to be part of 'an all-inclusive system of philosophy formed upon scientific principles'; so that political philosophy is treated 'as part of a mechanistic body of scientific knowledge' and elaborated by the application of the general principles of mathematical thinking.[8] And there are numerous other short or very short studies which to a great degree express the same point of view.[9]

Furthermore, this traditional interpretation has of late been asserted in two full-length works on Hobbes. Possibly these books constitute a deliberate reaction against

[7] H. Höffding, *A History of Modern Philosophy* (tr. Meyer; London, 1900, repr. 1924), I, 264.

[8] G. H. Sabine, *A History of Political Theory* (London, 1949), ch. XXIII.

[9] e. g. W. J. H. Campion, *Outlines of Lectures on Political Science Being Mainly a Review of the Political Theories of Hobbes* (Oxford, 1894), pp. 11–12; W. A. Dunning, *A History of Political Theories from Luther to Montesquieu* (New York, 1905, repr. 1961), pp. 264–5; J. Dewey, "The Motivation of Hobbes's Political Philosophy" in *Studies in the History of Ideas* (New York, 1918), I, 88–115 esp. pp. 103, 107; A. G. A. Balz, *Idea and Essence in the Philosophies of Hobbes and Spinoza* (New York, 1918), pp. 4–5, 7; B. Willey, *The Seventeenth Century Background* (1934, repr. London, 1962), p. 91; G. N. Clark, *The Seventeenth Century* (Oxford, 1947), p. 221; G. P. Gooch, "Hobbes and the Absolute State" (1939) repr. in *Studies in Diplomacy and Statecraft* (London, 1942), esp. pp. 343, 344, 362, 370; P. Zagorin, *A History of Political Thought in the English Revolution* (London, 1954), ch. XIII esp. p. 167; C. Hill, "Thomas Hobbes and the Revolution in Political Thought" in *Puritanism and Revolution* (London, 1958), ch. 9; K. Minogue, "Thomas Hobbes and the Philosophy of Absolutism" in D. Thomson (ed.), *Political Ideas* (London, 1966), p. 49; Q. Skinner, "The Ideological Context of Hobbes's Political Thought", *loc. cit.*, pp. 313–7.

the various criticisms of the traditional view which, as
we shall see, have become more frequent in recent years.
The first of these works is R. S. Peters's *Hobbes*,[10] the
other is M. M. Goldsmith's *Hobbes's Science of Politics*[11]
which is the most recent work on the subject to appear
in this country.[11a] Professor Peters holds that Hobbes's
'great imaginative idea' was 'the geometrical deduction
of behaviour of man in society from the abstract principles of the new science of motion'. He thus tried 'to
explain the behaviour of men in the *same sort of way*
as he explained the motion of bodies'.[12] He was, therefore, what he claimed to be, a revolutionary, because he
tried to free political philosophy from orthodox theological and moral trammels and to see man 'as part of
the mechanical system of nature'.[13] Professor Goldsmith
also cleaves very closely to the traditional point of view.
'Hobbes attempted to create a scientific or philosophical
system on the assumptions and methods of Galilean science. He attempted to show that a science of natural
bodies, a science of man, and a science of political bodies could all be elaborated systematically.' And, on these
fresh methods and assumptions, Hobbes 'proposed a new
understanding of political society'.[14]

However, a number of the works which expound
Hobbes's ideas broadly in terms of this traditional approach only do so with important reservations. For example, neither G. C. Robertson nor Sir Leslie Stephen
wholly sustained the view that Hobbes (whatever he
may have intended) was in fact a completely systematic
naturalist in his approach to morals and politics. They
both accepted that it was Hobbes's explicit purpose (as
Robertson put it) to 'bring Society and Man . . . within

---

[10] Harmondsworth, 1956.
[11] New York and London, 1966.
[11a] Written in 1968.
[12] Peters, *op. cit.*, pp. 22, 78 (italics in original).
[13] *Ibid.*, p. 81. Cf. p. 86.
[14] Goldsmith, *op. cit.*, pp. 228, 242.

the same principles of scientific explanation as were found applicable to the world of Nature'.[15] Yet they also believed that, whatever Hobbes's intentions, there were important discontinuities in the system so that the supposedly all-embracing natural philosophy did not completely hold together. In particular, they felt that the whole thing was a somewhat *ex post facto* affair and that Hobbes's political ideas at least were likely to have been formed before he knew of or espoused the scientific philosophy of motion. Further, it seemed likely that these political notions were considered by Hobbes more in terms of their practical relevance than their theoretical adequacy.[16] The same general attitude is reflected in Frithiof Brandt's crucial study. It is argued there that while Hobbes may have been the first and most consistent philosopher of mechanism, there were nevertheless clear limits to the completeness of his argument. Brandt stresses the significant admission made by Hobbes that civil philosophy could be treated independently of the physical doctrine of motion (and indeed more certainly) by building on an introspective basis, on a direct analysis of the mental phenomena known to every man.[17]

In sum, then, the nature of the traditional case is clear; but it has rarely been accepted by serious scholars in anything like a complete form. It was recognized that

---

[15] G. C. Robertson, "Hobbes", in *Encyclopaedia Britannica* (9th ed., 1881), XII, 39 b. Cf. *ibid.*, p. 33 a–b, also his *Hobbes* (Edinburgh and London, 1886), pp. 43–4, 45, 76; Leslie Stephen's *Hobbes* (London, 1904), pp. 27, 71, 73, 79–81, 139, 143, 163, 173.
[16] e. g. Robertson's *Hobbes*, pp. 57, 65, 138, 209, 216 and in *Enc. Brit.*, XII, 33 a, 34 a; Stephen, *op. cit.*, pp. 112–3, 125, 127, 173–5, 194–5, 208–9. Cf. also Peters, *op. cit.*, p. 138. J. W. N. Watkins has recently pointed out that Robertson, at least, did not know of Hobbes's *Short Tract on First Principles* until the text of his commentary was complete (Watkins, *Hobbes's System of Ideas* [London, 1965], pp. 29, 40).
[17] *Thomas Hobbes's Mechanical Conception of Nature* (Copenhagen and London, 1928), p. 244. Cf. A. Child, *Making and Knowing in Hobbes, Vico and Dewey* (Berkeley and Los Angeles, 1953), pp. 271–83.

Hobbes's explicit purpose and his achievement do not tally; and it has been felt necessary to point out how far and in what ways he fell short of a thoroughgoing scientific philosophy. He attempted the impossible in trying to combine an ethical with a naturalistic approach;[18] moreover, his political ideas were probably not deduced from the mechanical-materialist premisses;[19] and he admitted that, in the case of the study of man, this was not necessary or even desirable.

Yet it is a tribute to the strength of the traditional case that such difficulties did not, for so long, lead to any generally recognized conceptual revision. Hobbes was usually seen as an unsuccessful positivist rather than as a thinker who was not really of this kind at all. People were prisoners of the established view. It was not perhaps until the 1930's and after that there emerged in Britain substantially revised interpretations which pictured Hobbes's way of thinking in a quite different light.

What I call the *natural law case* is the first of these reformed attitudes. Its theme may be summarized in two propositions. First, that the apparently scientific cast and mechanical-materialist basis of the entire range of Hobbes's mature thought are quite misleading as indications of its real character. Secondly, that the true nature of his ethical and political thinking derives essentially from the Christian natural law tradition. There are, indeed, two major variations on this point of view. The less radical version (usually called the Taylor thesis after the well-known Platonic scholar A. E. Taylor who first confidently expounded it in this country) holds that there are two independent, incompatible, and (so to

---

[18] Cf. T. H. Green, *Lectures on the Principles of Political Obligation* (repr. London, 1948), §§ 46–7.

[19] C. B. Macpherson, in his *The Political Theory of Possessive Individualism* (Oxford, 1962), an interesting marxist variation of the traditional case, suggests that it is not possible to move from Hobbes's view of man as a mechanical system to the political theory without further assumptions tenable only in respect of bourgeois society, *ibid.*, pp. 15–16, 18.

say) equally basic elements in Hobbes's thought: his ethical ideas and his scientific philosophy. The other version suggests that the naturalistic philosophy and language are simply the fashionable guise in which Hobbes dressed up those aspects of his basically Christian and medieval ideas which lent themselves to such expression. On neither view is the naturalist philosophy everything or even the major part.

The Taylor thesis, then, rests on the suggestion of a basic dichotomy in Hobbes's thought between his scientific and ethical ideas. This notion springs from the impression that there are passages in Hobbes's works, especially those dealing with ethical issues, in which he uses language wholly at odds with his supposed naturalism and egoism and which reflect a genuinely moral (and not merely prudential) theory of obligation.[20] Taylor thinks Hobbes's conception of the laws of nature is central and argues that he sees them not as rules of expediency but as moral imperatives deriving from divine command.[21] So 'a certain kind of theism is absolutely necessary to make the theory work'.[22] Taylor says the point he is really anxious to make is that 'Hobbes's *ethical* theory is commonly misrepresented and unintelligently criticized for want of sufficient recognition that it is, from first to last, a doctrine of duty, a strict deontology'.[23]

In general, Professor Warrender follows the Taylor

---

[20] A. E. Taylor, "The Ethical Doctrine of Hobbes", reprinted in K. C. Brown (ed.), *Hobbes Studies* (Oxford, 1965), p. 37. Cf. Taylor's much earlier discussion *Thomas Hobbes* (London, 1908), pp. 44–5.

[21] Taylor's suggestions are: (I) Hobbes always describes the natural laws as dictates, as having an imperative character, and as obliging even in the state of nature. The obligation to obey the sovereign derives from the prior obligation to keep covenants. (II) The civil sovereign is himself subject to a "rigid law of moral obligation" though answerable in this respect only to God. (III) Natural law is the command of God which is the basis of obligation to that law. See Brown, *op. cit.*, pp. 40–50.

[22] *Ibid.*, pp. 49–50.

[23] *Ibid.*, p. 54 (italics in original).

thesis: that, in addition to the theory of prudential motivation, there is a concept of moral obligation running
through Hobbes's whole account and applicable to man
both in the state of nature and in civil society. And this
duty is itself based on an obligation to obey God in his
natural kingdom, an obedience based on fear of divine
power.[24] In sum:

> Hobbes's theory of political society is based upon a
> theory of duty, and his theory of duty belongs essen-
> tially to the natural law tradition. The laws of nature
> are eternal and unchangeable and, as the commands
> of God, they oblige all men who reason properly, and
> so arrive at a belief in an omnipotent being whose sub-
> jects they are . . . Thus the duties of men in Hobbes's
> State of Nature, and the duties of both sovereign and
> subject in civil society are consequences of a continuous
> obligation to obey the laws of nature in whatever form
> the laws apply to the circumstances in which these
> persons are placed.[25]

---

[24] H. Warrender, *The Political Philosophy of Hobbes: his Theory
of Obligation* (Oxford, 1957), pp. 7, 10. Warrender's view of the
role of God and so of the basis of the obligation to obey natural law
seems to have varied somewhat. A point of view which is, in many
significant respects, very similar to Warrender's had been put forward earlier by S. P. Lamprecht, "Hobbes and Hobbism", *American Political Science Review*, XXXIV (1940), pp. 31–53. Cf. the
introduction to his edition of *De Cive* (New York, 1949), pp. xv–
xxx. Similarly, there is an interesting anticipation of Warrender's
suggestion that the natural law exists before civil society but only
obliges when certain sufficient validating conditions prevail, in
R. Falckenberg, *History of Modern Philosophy from Nicholas of
Cusa to the Present Time* (tr., London, 1895), p. 78. At Bochum,
Warrender denied that, because he sees Hobbes as a natural law
theorist, he is committed to associating him with the medieval
Christian tradition: he would stress rather Hobbes's acceptance of
prescriptive and universal principles derived from Stoic and Roman
Law thinking. Professor Villey suggested a similar affinity. And it
might be better to subclassify the "natural law case" according to
the kind of emphasis given and the type of natural law in mind.
[25] Warrender, *The Political Philosophy of Hobbes* (ed. cit.), p. 322.
It is an essential part of Warrender's argument that the laws of

Hobbes's ethical theory is not, therefore, merely one of self-centred prudence. The 'reason why I *can* do my duty is that I am able . . . to see it as a means to my preservation; but the reason why I *ought* to do my duty is that God commands it'.[26] To Warrender, then, 'Hobbes was essentially a natural-law philosopher', even though he may also have criticized many aspects of this type of thinking as traditionally established, especially in respect of the vagueness or abstractness of its tenets and of the problems of interpretation thereby involved.[27]

Of course, this interpretation makes at least the apparently ethical aspect of Hobbes's doctrines more orthodox and medieval than was possible in terms of the traditional case. Taylor's paper was first published in 1938. But it would be wrong to suppose that recognition of Hobbes's affinity with medieval styles of thought had gone unrecognized before then. In fact, it had been remarked many times. Very early in the history of modern Hobbes commentary, Sir James Fitzjames Stephen observed that his manner was half-old and half-modern.[28] And in 1914, in a most interesting though (I think) little known paper, J. E. G. de Montmorency argued that Hobbes's major claim to pre-eminence was his revival of the 'whole medieval conception of the Law of Nature' the obligation to obey which is attributed to the force of 'a religious and external power'.[29] But I suppose the most extensive analysis of the suggestion that Hobbes's thought has medieval foundations was carried out by J.

---

nature only oblige to action in circumstances of "sufficient security", *ibid.*, pp. 58 ff.

[26] *Ibid.*, pp. 212–3 (italics in original); cf. pp. 97–100.

[27] *Ibid.*, pp. 323–8. Cf. Warrender's "Hobbes's Conception of Morality", *Rivista Critica di Storia della Filosofia*, XVII (1962), pp. 436–7. On Hobbes's innovations in natural law theory see also F. A. Olafson "Thomas Hobbes and the Modern Theory of Natural Law", *Journal of the History of Philosophy*, IV (1966), pp. 15–30.

[28] *Horae Sabbaticae* (2nd series; London, 1892), pp. 3, 14.

[29] This paper is printed in *Great Jurists of the World* (ed. Mac-Donnell and Manson; Boston, 1914), pp. 195–219.

Laird,[30] whose conclusion was that, in fighting his political and philosophical battles, Hobbes invented and employed no new weapons but only re-arranged and to a small extent refashioned the old. 'In matters of metaphysics, it is permissible to suggest that while Hobbes's voice had all the modernity of the new mechanics, his hands—that is to say, his technique—were scholastic, and even Aristotelian. In ethical and political theory, however, voice and hands were both medieval . . . The truth is that his fundamental notions on these matters were those of the Civil and of the Common Law . . . .'[31] And even Hobbes's erastianism, utilitarianism and the like may be discerned in the traditional ethics, stoic, civilian, canonical and scholastic.[32] The ground was well prepared, then, when Taylor published his now well-known paper.

But it is one thing to suggest that Hobbes's ideas are partly or from some aspects conventional in this way. It is to take a somewhat longer step in this direction to argue that his position is throughout basically medieval and essentially Christian and scriptural in an orthodox sense. But this seems to be suggestion of Professor F. C. Hood in his recent *The Divine Politics of Thomas Hobbes*.[33] Hood thus takes the step which Warrender delicately declines. Hood's argument is that Hobbes's

---

[30] *Hobbes* (London, 1934). In 1922 G. E. G. Catlin, in his *Thomas Hobbes as Philosopher, Publicist and Man of Letters* (Oxford), had remarked on the conventional nature of much of Hobbes's work and material; and in 1930 the importance of Hobbes's early scholastic training was stressed by Z. Lubienski, "Hobbes's Philosophy and its Historical Background", *Journal of Philosophical Studies*, V (1930), pp. 175–90.

[31] Laird, *op. cit.*, pp. 57–8. Cf. de Montmorency, *loc. cit.*, pp. 205–7, 209–12, 217–9.

[32] Laird, *op. cit.*, pp. 58, 79. Hobbes's concern with traditional metaphysical problems and his indebtedness to scholastic styles of thought has, too, been recently reaffirmed by J. Jacquot "Notes on an Unpublished Work of Thomas Hobbes", *Notes and Records of the Royal Society*, IX (1952), 188–95.

[33] Oxford, 1964.

scripturally-based belief in a divine moral law was logically and biographically prior to his naturalistic concerns,
and that his civil philosophy and mechanical conception
of nature were simply the expression, in the scientific
terms then coming into fashion, of only those parts of his
religious moral thought which were susceptible of such
translation.[34] It is only natural, therefore, that there
should be a basic problem or contradiction in Hobbes's
thought: for his construction of the commonwealth in
mechanistic terms depends in fact on 'an obligation of
conscience which cannot itself be put on a naturalistic
basis'.[35]

It is obvious, then, that this natural law revision involves a radical transformation of the traditional view of
Hobbes. From being a modern in the naturalistic style he
becomes, in essential respects, a medieval of the great
tradition. His thought is seen as moral and not scientific
in character.

At the same time, the natural law case has not gone
uncriticized. One obvious point is that Hobbes's own deliberate intention, repeatedly stated, was to present a
political and ethical theory firmly based on the principles
of nature scientifically conceived and thus (he assumed)
unchallengeable. Further, a good many of his contemporaries seem to have understood only too well that
Hobbes was proceeding in the naturalistic manner. Indeed, if an orthodox stress on moral law and divine command was an essential feature of his ethical doctrine, why
was such a critical and horrified fuss raised when he published his views? Again, if (as Warrender specifically
holds) the operation of the moral law depends on the
existence of certain validating conditions why are these
not embodied in the law? And does not their necessity
rather dilute its moral character?[36] Moreover, it may be

---

[34] *Ibid.*, pp. 4–5, 13, 14, 23, 32, 40–1, 253.

[35] *Ibid.*, pp. 229–30.

[36] J. W. N. Watkins, *Hobbes's System of Ideas: a Study in the
Political Significance of Philosophical Theories* (London, 1965),
pp. 88–9.

suggested that Hobbes cannot be conceived to have thought of the natural law as a divine command binding on all mankind, because this necessitates knowledge of God as author of this law and it is difficult to see how, on Hobbes's terms, this knowledge could be acquired. Natural knowledge (i.e. knowledge of hypothetical causal relations) cannot give it for natural reason leads only to recognition of a first cause; and faith is not something given to all. In any case, it is not God's omnipotence but *acceptance* of His authority which makes His commands binding. And where are the authentic accounts of His precepts?[37]

Finally, there is the third type of Hobbes interpretation, *the individualist* or *nominalist case* which also appears in two different but related forms. One version may be associated with the work of Professor Leo Strauss, the other with that of Professors Oakeshott, Watkins[38] and Glover. But each point of view shares, as common ground, a rejection of both the traditional and natural law attitudes. There is agreement with the natural law revisionists that the modern naturalistic appearance of Hobbes's thought is deceptive and that his political and moral theory was not dependent on his materialism or developed mainly by the use of scientific method. At the same time, however, exponents of this third sort of understanding do not accept the positive side of the natural law case, that Hobbes's political and ethical thought is only properly seen in the great natural law tradition; indeed, they regard Hobbes as having explicitly and

---

[37] M. Oakeshott, "The Moral Life in the Writings of Thomas Hobbes", in *Rationalism in Politics and Other Essays* (London, 1962), pp. 273–283. There are many other detailed discussions of some of the problems about obligation and the role of God in Hobbes's thought e. g. S. M. Brown Jnr., "The Taylor Thesis: Some Objections", in *Hobbes Studies* (ed. cit.), pp. 57–71; T. Nagel, "Hobbes's Concept of Obligation", *Philosophical Review*, XVIII (1959), pp. 68–83; D. D. Raphael, "Obligation and Rights in Hobbes", *Philosophy*, XXXVII (1962), pp. 345–52; J. Plamenatz "Mr. Warrender's Hobbes", in *Hobbes Studies* (ed. cit.), pp. 73–87.
[38] See n. 50 below.

firmly repudiated that tradition. But here the difference of historical perspective between the two branches of this individualist case emerges.

Professor Strauss argues that Hobbes's political and ethical philosophy breaks completely with the great tradition (of Aristotle, scholasticism and natural law) but not because his philosophy was basically naturalistic. If his viewpoint had been of this latter kind he would have seen all inclinations and appetites as morally indifferent. But, on the contrary, he singles out two passions for crucial emphasis of a moral kind: vanity, the fundamentally unjust force which makes men blind; and fear of violent or shameful death, the basically just force which makes men see a way out of the predicament created by their pride.[39] It is in his stress on the 'right of nature' of each individual, the right of self-preservation dictated by the fear of violent death, that Hobbes both breaks with moral orthodoxy and makes a stand against naturalism. For him, justice is embodied in the rational defence and pursuit of this basic right; and it is this 'specific moral attitude' which is the real, and very original, foundation of his thought.[40] In this light, Hobbes may indeed be said to be making an important contribution because it is precisely the assumption that the starting-point is natural right (the primacy of an absolutely justified subjective claim) and not, as hitherto, natural law (the primacy of obligation to an objective order) which distinguishes modern from earlier political thought.[41] Fur-

---

[39] L. Strauss, *The Political Philosophy of Hobbes: its Basis and Genesis* (Oxford, 1936), pp. 27–9, 130.

[40] In the second edition of his book Strauss gives priority in this respect to Machiavelli. But this is simply a prefatory observation which is not there elaborated at all. Though see Strauss's remarks in "On the Spirit of Hobbes's Political Philosophy", *Revue Internationale de Philosophie,* IV (1950), esp. pp. 414–8.

[41] Strauss, *Political Philosophy of Hobbes,* pp. xiv, 5, 6–7, 155–160. Cf. Sir Ernest Barker's foreword, *ibid.,* p. viii; also Strauss's "Quelques remarques sur la science politique de Hobbes à propos du livre récent de M. Lubienski", *Recherches Philosophiques* (1932), esp. pp. 613–4.

ther, Strauss argues that the scientific mode of discussion and presentation, so characteristic of Hobbes's major and later works, is misleading insofar as it obscures this real basis of his thought, his new moral point of view about 'right' and the passions. Moreover, Strauss suggests that this ethical attitude was formed before Hobbes discovered Euclid and modern science; it can be discerned in his early writings and, in diminishing strength, beneath the layers of the essentially alien naturalism with which he clothed his mature works. In fact, the way Hobbes uses scientific ideas depends on his essentially humanist premiss; while, at the same time, these ideas also come to act as an intellectual mould which forces the basic moral insight and what flows from it into a difficult shape causing discrepancies and logical defects.[42] Hobbes's attitude depends, then, on neither modern scientific naturalism nor the metaphysics of natural law. It is based on a notion of individual right which itself rests on an understanding of the human passions derived from a knowledge of men and confirmed by self-examination.

Strauss's thesis is clearly very important but does involve difficulties of both an analytical and historical kind.[43] The main point in respect of the former centres on criticism of Strauss's discussion of right and moral obligation. It is asked, for instance, why the felt need

---

[42] Strauss, *Political Philosophy of Hobbes,* pp. xiv, xv, 12, 29–43, 74, 79–81, 166–7, 170, ch. VI passim.

[43] Strauss's later discussion of Hobbes, in *Natural Right and History* (1963), is in some significant ways different from his earlier view. In particular, his perspective is wider and more satisfactory, largely, I suppose, as a result of the comments of critics such as Oakeshott. Yet he has specifically rejected the suggestion that Hobbes's political ideas are best seen in the context of the "anti-idealistic" medieval tradition: see "On the Spirit of Hobbes's Political Philosophy", pp. 406–8, 411, 421–2. Oakeshott's original criticisms are to be found most fully stated in "Dr. Leo Strauss on Hobbes", *Politica* II (1936–7), pp. 364–79. See also his later discussion, "Moral Life in the Writings of Thomas Hobbes", in *Rationalism in Politics* (ed. cit.). Another brief critical examination is to be found in Watkins, *op. cit.,* pp. 30–4.

to preserve one's self is also a duty; why rational conduct (i. e. conduct which is consistently compatible with self-preservation) is morally obligatory. The cause or motive of a man's endeavouring to secure peace may be a desire for self-preservation; but such a cause cannot be a justification of a moral kind for so acting, because in itself a motive of this sort has no ethically prescriptive force.[44] Some of the historical comments are also of the same critical type. For example, it is suggested that the evidence available to determine Hobbes's pre-scientific view is rather scanty; also that Strauss does not take sufficient note of the implications of Hobbes's *Short Tract on First Principles* (c. 1630) and fails to see that Hobbes's view of man's passions and will is, even at this early date, closely bound up with his views about nature and causation.[45]

However, more important than this negative type of observation is the main historical criticism of Strauss's 1936 discussion: that it rests on a faulty perspective. It is largely suggestions about how this defect may be remedied (so as to achieve a more historically satisfactory picture of Hobbes) that constitute the positive contribution of the second version of the individualist case. And basically the idea is that Strauss has a defective view of both the scientific and philosophical traditions, and generally of the intellectual environment in which Hobbes lived and the manner of his mental development.

Those who may be categorised as contributing to the second version of the individualist case accept, with Strauss, that neither the traditional nor the natural law interpretations is satisfactory. But these writers do not agree simply with the Strauss thesis that Hobbes's basic position rests on an essentially modern moral attitude to the will and passions of man, an insight which is to be

44 Oakeshott, "The Moral Life in the Writings of Thomas Hobbes", *loc. cit.*, pp. 265–6.
45 Oakeshott, "Dr. Leo Strauss on Hobbes", p. 371; Watkins, *op. cit.*, pp. 239–41, 250–1.

distinguished from or even contrasted with his use of scientific ideas and methods. Instead, the alternative suggestion is made that Hobbes draws on medieval notions of a particular kind, indeed on a long-established and essentially philosophical manner of thinking in terms of which his moral views and his understanding of the natural world are alike comprehensible. So the tension that Strauss detects in Hobbes is no more than a flaw in his own analysis deriving from an unsatisfactory historical viewpoint and a failure to appreciate the philosophical style which Hobbes employs. This defect leads, for instance, to a false equation between Hobbes's interest in the natural world and his discovery of modern science,[46] while another of its misleading aspects is the idea that there was only one medieval tradition of thought, that based on natural law, and that if Hobbes does not think in its terms then he belongs to no tradition at all.

The question that arises at this point is obvious. What is the nature of Hobbes's tradition, of this conception of philosophy and reasoning in terms of which every one of his characteristic doctrines is said to be formulated? In fact, this tradition is variously described. For example, Oakeshott refers at different times to the revival of Democritean-Epicurean thought, late scholastic nominalism, the averroism of Scotus and Occam, fideism and the philosophical scepticism of the libertins, certain brands of medieval and early modern theology with their roots in Augustine, and the Hebraic tradition of creative will.[47]

---

[46] As Oakeshott points out, at no stage of his intellectual career did Hobbes have any patience or sympathy whatsoever for experimental science: "Thomas Hobbes", *Scrutiny* IV (1935–6), p. 268; "Dr. Leo Strauss on Hobbes", *loc. cit.*, pp. 373–4.

[47] e. g. "Thomas Hobbes", *Scrutiny* IV (1935–6), pp. 267–9, 255 n. 1, 291. On Oakeshott's general theme that the only true contrast in *Philosophy*, XII (1937), pp. 240–1; intro. to *Leviathan* (Oxford, [1946]), pp. xiv–xvii, xx–xxi, xxv–xxvii, xlv, lii–liii, lv; "Moral Life in the Writings of Thomas Hobbes", *loc. cit.*, pp. 255 n.1, 291. On Oakeshott's general theme that the only true context in which to see a masterpiece such as *Leviathan* is the unity

And it must be said that his discussion of this vital matter is similarly somewhat fragmentary and scattered. But the basic suggestion is obvious: that the nature of Hobbes's ideas and whatever unity and system they achieve is best seen in the context of a long-established and still extant tradition of philosophical thinking.[48] This will be found to lie behind the concept of individual right and the theory about the will and passions of man (especially the role of pride and fear) correctly emphasized by Strauss. This tradition can also be seen as the foundation of his interest in and understanding of the natural world so that it is wrong simply to relate his view of things in this respect to modern science. For instance, he sees things on the analogy of a machine not because he is a scientific mechanist but because his conception of causal reasoning unavoidably turns whatever he looks at (including man and society) into a mechanism. And he is an individualist not because he chooses to begin with the sanctity of individual right but because his nominalism involves the view that only substantive individuals exist as subjects of philosophical inquiry.[49] J. W. N. Watkins's recent book seems to adopt a similar standpoint arguing specifically that the essentials of Hobbes's political theory are logically related to his philosophical way

---

of the entire history of philosophy and a specific strand or tradition of this history, see intro. to *Leviathan* (ed. cit.), pp. viii–xiii.

[48] I suppose that this tradition as it flourished in Hobbes's time is best described by Hiram Haydn in his *The Counter-Renaissance* (New York, 1950). On the background see also M. H. Carré's *Phases of Thought in England* (Oxford, 1949); his *Realists and Nominalists* (Oxford, 1946), esp. ch. IV on Occam; and G. de Lagarde's *La Naissance de l'esprit laïque au déclin du moyen age* (2nd. ed., Paris, 1956 ff.). At Bochum, Professor Watkins rather took exception to my speaking in this way of Hobbes and a tradition of thought as though the latter had a life of its own and Hobbes was only to be seen as an exemplar of this "suprapersonal phenomenon". But, of course, a tradition of thought is not like this at all: it is simply a category of interpretation and explanation that emerges from a study of individual writers between whom affinities may be detected.

[49] *Leviathan* (ed. cit.), pp. xix–xxi, lv.

of thinking and that, in this respect, Hobbes was firmly placed in the late medieval tradition of Paduan Aristotelianism.[50] And in the (so far) most satisfactorily documented and well-argued account of this sort of theme, Professor W. B. Glover has suggested that Hobbes's thought is best seen as a version of Christian philosophy and theology in the Augustinian and Reformist tradition which had strong fideist, nominalist, sceptical and voluntarist elements of the kind we associate with Hobbes.[51] And there have been numerous other discussions of Hobbes's works which have, in part at least, seen him in a similar sort of context and which, taken together, constitute an impressive, if scattered, array of evidence and argument to support this type of interpretation.[52]

---

[50] Watkins, *op. cit.*, e. g. pp. 9, 13, 66. Cf. Watkins's essay in *Hobbes Studies* (ed. cit.) p. 238 n. 2. It should be noted that during discussion of this paper at Bochum, Professor Watkins said he thought I had misconceived his point of view by categorising it in this way: he felt (as I understood him) that Hobbes's affinity was rather with the naturalistic style of thought, the traditional case as I have called it here.

[51] "Human Nature and the State in Hobbes", *Journal of the History of Philosophy*, IV (1966), pp. 293–311; also his essay in *Hobbes Studies* (ed. cit.), pp. 141–168.

[52] D. Krook, in "Mr. Brown's Note Annotated", *Political Studies*, I (1953), pp. 216–227, and "Thomas Hobbes's Doctrine of Meaning and Truth", *Philosophy*, XXXI (1956), pp. 3–22, stresses Hobbes's radical and uncompromising metaphysical materialism; L. I. Bredvold brings out Hobbes's fideism, scepticism and nominalism and the medieval and classical origins of these doctrines in his *Intellectual Milieu of John Dryden* (Ann Arbor, 1934), esp. chs. 2 and 3, also pp. 25, 37, 47, 50–3, 58, 73 ff.; F. A. Lange saw Hobbes primarily as a bold nominalist, *The History of Materialism and Criticism of its Present Importance* (1865; 3rd ed., London, 1925), I, 270–1; Phyllis Doyle argued some years ago that many of Hobbes's central conceptions belong to an established Augustinian-Scotist-Calvinistic tradition of theology and philosophy and derived, specifically, from the Arminian controversies of the sixteenth century; that is, that his views were formed *within* the Christian fold but were not wholly orthodox, "The Contemporary Background of Hobbes's 'State of Nature'", *Economica*, VII (1927), pp. 336–55; W. J. Ong has noted Hobbes's indebtedness to Ramism and suggested that he owed much more to the rigorous opera-

In sum, then, there are at least three different types of Hobbes interpretation. One which sees him in terms of modern science, another which asserts instead his link with the Christian or Stoic natural law tradition, while the third rests effectively on the view that his entire range of thought derives from scholastic nominalism. These are points of view which in turn emphasize Hobbes as positivist, as moralist, and as philosopher.

II

There are two main questions raised by this variety of interpretation. Clearly one is about the adequacy of these different views of Hobbes's thought and, I suppose, must lead to asking which is the most satisfactory. But there also arises a broader issue concerning the lessons that can be learned from this diversity of opinion about the study of political ideas generally and, indeed, about intellectual history as a whole. This second matter is best taken first because it raises the perspective necessary to deal with the initial question. And this general problem really concerns what is involved in the study and interpretation of a political 'text' (this being either a single book or series of writings by one man, or a whole body of work produced by, say, a given school or period of thought).

The first thing to recognize is that political thought

---

tions of this doctrine than to Galileo and Euclid, "Hobbes and Talon's Ramist Rhetoric in English", *Trans. Cam. Bibl. Soc.*, I (1949–53), pp. 260–9; Olafson, art. cit., pp. 27–8 suggests that Hobbes's views of God and the Law of Nature are like those of the "voluntaristic theologians of the fourteenth century" and put him in the tradition that stems from Scotus and Occam. One of the difficulties of the natural law case is that if Hobbes was orthodox in natural law terms why was there such an outcry against him by his contemporaries? This reaction is explicable if it is realized that views belonging to this other medieval tradition of philosophy and theology were themselves often regarded in Hobbes's time with horror, described as "atheism" and so on. See e. g. the account of Alexander Rosse's criticisms in Bowle, *op. cit.*, pp. 64, 70–1.

(like any other kind) exists at many different levels of articulation and generality. At the lowest (though not necessarily the least complex) plane there is the apparently unreflective following of a customary or habitual procedure where the rationale is present but not worked out or consciously in the mind of the agent. Then there is action that is intended, say someone deciding how to vote so as to serve his interests best; an official taking a decision in a particular case or, more widely, discussing alternative courses of action and recommending a broad line of policy. And the process proceeds to wider and more abstract levels of generality. A politician, in a parliamentary debate, considers a question in the context of national or group traditions and purposes or of party ideology. A commentator or pamphleteer reviews a current issue in terms of political principles of some kind or other; and this sort of discussion tips over into what we call political theory, that is, the examination of general concepts such as 'obligation', the 'state', 'rights', 'common good' and so on. Finally, at the highest level of abstraction, politics is seen in the context of a philosophy, a recommendation about how to look at the world as a whole; though (as at all the other levels) the degree of articulation and completeness which is achieved may vary considerably.[53]

Of course, these are notional distinctions: any given thinker may run up and down the scale as suits his purpose, ability or inclination. Burke's writings, for instance, spread over a large part of the continuum. Sometimes he plays the role of political analyst dealing realistically with a specific issue, then he invokes broad constitutional principle, then he is the party ideologist, while, at other times, he takes flight into the ethereal regions of transcendent moral law and divine purpose immanent in the history of the world. If he never tries to reach the highest level of abstraction, he is, in the history of political

---

[53] Cf. Oakeshott, intro. to *Leviathan* (ed. cit.), pp. viii–ix. The general view I adopt here is a common one among idealist thinkers.

thought, one of the masters of the middle range. Those who have achieved and consistently maintained themselves on the ultimate height are relatively few in number. But clearly Hobbes is one of them and what we now have to ask is how to interpret and assess political thought when it is expressed with this degree of abstraction.

And I take it as undeniable that what is sought is, in some way, unity, system, coherence, for this is what explanation is (in this context); a method which (as I see it) is a perfect exemplification of the principle of economy: one seeks the simplest possible overall account. Bacon has this in mind when he says somewhere that knowledge is worthiest when charged with the least multiplicity. Moreover, it seems obvious that, because it is thought which is being studied by thought, we can never in the end rest content with either an uncritical chronology or an unorganised congeries of ideas. Take the history of thought in any of its forms: this can itself never be satisfactory so long as it is presented as a mere succession of intellectual events, an unresolved variety. A more general and permanent entity has to be found. And such a history must itself be logical, assume and discern the existence of some form of order in what may at first sight appear chaotic. It must tell a credible story. The perhaps unlikely shade of Wittgenstein may be invoked to this Hegelian effect. For in the *Tractatus* he says that thought can never be of anything illogical for, if it were, we should have to think illogically.[54] It is not, of course, that any order or pattern discerned in the history of ideas is necessary independently of the process in which it is implicit or preordained in any teleological or purposive sense. There is no element of inevitability which will enable the logic of the past to be projected into future. But if intellectual history does not reveal its story as systematic, it is not itself thought: 'contingency must vanish' on the appearance of this kind of

---

[54] § 3.03 Cf. §§ 3.031–2 and Popper, *The Open Society and its Enemies* (4th ed., London, 1962), I, 246 n. 45.

inquiry.[55] Of course, we know (at the commonsense level) that people thinking out problems vary in the degree of success they achieve, get confused, contradict themselves, and so on. This is obvious. But the object of the student of this thought is not only to report these deficiencies but to account for them and so to transcend them.

It might be urged that this view is misleading, that the test of any historical picture is whether it conforms to the facts (e. g. of society) not whether it is consistent and credible merely. But this objection itself rests on a misconception. Consistency alone is, I agree, not enough; it can exist in a shadow world of mere ideas. The coherence sought must be a coherence which we are obliged to believe by the nature of the evidence. Yet this evidence is not something given, autonomous, objective. There is no such thing as an historical 'fact' in and of itself independent of 'interpretation', and used to judge an interpretation. A fact presupposes a world of ideas, an existing interpretation, something achieved in such a context and not something merely given. Any historian begins not with brute, objective facts about the past but with a body of present material seen in a certain light but which, thus seen, seems to lack coherence. And what he tries to do is to give this material a greater relative degree of coherence by looking at it in a different way, a process which will necessarily involve altering the manner in which the so-called facts have hitherto been regarded. The only historical facts *are* the interpretations. So to talk about the historical task as seeing influences and the connexions between two given events, ideas or persons, *may* be misleading.[56] This is because there *are*

---

[55] Hegel's *Lectures on the History of Philosophy* (tr. Haldane and Simson; London, 1963), I, 36–7.
[56] Cf. Q. Skinner, "The Limits of Historical Explanations", *Philosophy*, XLI (1966), 199–215. This is also why I find rather odd the suggestion often made that political philosophy is an answer given to the challenge of contemporary political problems and can only be understood as the outcome of a given social situation. There are

no independent entities to be connected in this way. Further, if the possibility of their relation is seen then its nature is already determined. To think of the possible influence of Hobbes on Locke (if this is a feasible thing to do) is to see both as belonging already to the same or a cognate world of ideas: they share something in common, a certain intellectual ambience. Not *influence* but *affinity* is the key word here. And I utterly fail to see why this view should be regarded as 'simply without content'.[57] It is wholly concrete and proper to say, for example, that there is a connexion between the general outlook of Sir Robert Filmer and Edward Forset; or Hooker and Locke, or (to be outrageous perhaps) Burke and Rousseau. No question of influence need arise: it is simply that there are certain similarities in manner of thought which appear to the mind of the observer. And it is merely pejorative to say this arises from ignorance of the detail concerned; though I suppose the critic might give the lie direct and say, 'But this is quite unhistorical'. So be it: but it is a curiously confined view of intellectual history that such a critic sustains.

And, of course, it is not that one is always driven to more and more tenuous frameworks of interpretation—at least not in any individual case. One does not say that, for instance, Burke was a political philosopher—but that his ideas (which never achieve this level of systematic abstraction) may, perhaps, be best seen reflected in the mirror of such a philosophy. One constructs this reflecting element, this abstraction, oneself, but does not suppose that Burke did.

And I tend more and more to the opinion that, in this pursuit of coherence, in the end one never criticizes. If one gets the cultural context right, if ways of thinking are recreated sympathetically, then one never refutes but always sustains. I belong to the 'tout comprendre' school

---

no given social or political "facts" which can be used to explain or assess the (merely epiphenomenal) ideas.
[57] *Ibid.*, p. 211.

of thought. It is, no doubt, a satisfying exercise to some (Professor Plamenatz provides a most sophisticated example) to detect in a political text apparent inconsistencies and dubious argument. But I feel that anyone possessed of a genuine historical sense could not rest content at this often complex but nonetheless historically superficial level of analysis. He would feel it necessary to go beyond the supposed defects, to transcend them by fuller investigation. We might take as motto one of the maxims of Vauvenargues: 'pour décider qu'un auteur se contredit, il faut qu'il soit impossible de le concilier.'[58] And Hobbes himself, interestingly enough, makes some most cogent remarks about this kind of question in the 'little treatise' of 1640, *The Elements of Law*.[59] He is discussing how men worked upon one another's minds by the use of language and says that, though words are the signs we have of other people's opinions and intentions, it is, nevertheless, often difficult to interpret them correctly because of what he calls 'diversity of contexture, and of the company wherewith they go'. So it follows, he thinks, that 'it must be extreme hard to find out the opinions and meanings of those men that are gone from us long ago, and have left us no other signification thereof but their books; which cannot possibly be understood without history enough to discover those aforementioned circumstances, and also without great prudence to observe them'. Moreover, Hobbes goes on, whenever there appears to be a contradiction of some sort in a man's writings (and assuming he is no longer 'present to explicate himself better') then the reader is properly to assume that the opinion signified most clearly and directly by the author is the one intended and that any apparently contradictory view arises either from an error of interpretation on the reader's part or from the writer's not seeing any reason to suppose a contradiction at all.[60]

---

[58] II, 279.
[59] (ed. Tönnies; Cambridge, 1928), pp. 52–3; cf. p. 98.
[60] *Ibid.*, English Works (ed. Molesworth), IV, 75. Cf.: "If you will be a philosopher in good earnest, let your reason move

I think that in principle these are sound words and ought to be taken to heart by all who practise the art of intellectual history.

We must, then, search for coherence or system in the ideas or ways of thinking that we study, both in particular cases or 'texts' and in the general continuum we call the history of thought as a whole. Yet although we are always looking for coherence or system, we are not always searching for the same kind of thing. And I would distinguish two main ways of achieving the object, one which can be called a 'biographical' and the other a 'rational' way of making thought intelligible.

The appropriate understanding of the role of biographical factors may often be a way in which system can be introduced into varied expressions of thought. It may be that in a man's work a series of inconsistencies or even contradictions exist which appear unresolvable at the intellectual level, but it is sometimes possible to reach a lower degree of coherence by taking account of the author's personality or situation. This is, I suppose, the only way to achieve a unity in the political and philosophical works that Locke produced; and, again, Professor Oakeshott suggested (in one place) that some of the difficulties in Hobbes's writings are perhaps to be put down to the same sort of factor.[61] But, of course, this kind of explanation will be invoked only when any more 'rational' mode of making thought intelligible fails.

So far as this latter mode is concerned, I would like to

---

upon the degree of your own cogitations and experience; those things that be in confusion must be set asunder, distinguished and every one stamped with its own name set in order; that is to say, your method must resemble that of the creation." (E. W. vol. I, p. xiii).

[61] "Moral Life in the Writings of Thomas Hobbes", *loc. cit.*, p. 287. Cf. J. F. Stephen, *op. cit.*, pp. 14, 34; Strauss, *Natural Right and History* (Chicago, 1953), p. 199. Of course, if it was Hobbes's purpose to equivocate then he did not cover up very well so it may be just as reasonable to suppose that he was not simply trying to be circumspect but expressing a view which was known to be heretical. On this see Mintz, *op. cit.*, p. 44.

suggest, tentatively, that there are three different types of system which may be in view.

The first might be called the synthetical or syntactical type of system, by which I mean a completely connected set of ideas linked by an overall method of explanation or analysis. This could be deductive in form, an attempt being made to derive a consistent set of conclusions or propositions from a given series of axioms, and this is done, classically, in the geometrical mode. Hobbes (or rather the traditional Hobbes) is a good example. Another instance, reflecting a related but different way of doing the same sort of thing, is Aquinas with his massive, architectonic structure of thought. On the other hand, this kind of system could be pursued by a method of classification, resting on the apparent recurrence of common features in what is observed and enabling the coherence of species and genera to be introduced. To this may be added some notion of a dynamic relationship between the types. Such are the comparative analyses of different systems of government which may also be seen succeeding one another in ordered succession (monarchy into tyranny into aristocracy into oligarchy and so on).

The next type may be called the discrete mode of systematization. This involves the application to different areas or topics of a given style of analysis and discussion without attempting to relate the conclusions achieved in each case into a whole. Plato is a good example of this. In each of the Socratic dialogues a similar method of analysis is applied to different topics (justice in the *Republic*, pleasure in the *Philebus*, knowledge in the *Theaetetus*) but there is no explicit attempt to unite all this together as part of a general metaphysic. It is the persistent application of a given understanding of philosophical thinking which gives whatever unity or system is achieved to a body of writings framed in this way.

The third type of system I call dialectical and what I mean is, I expect, clear from the name. This kind of system emerges when a manner of argument proceeds progressively by what may appear to be contradictory

conclusions to higher levels of understanding which also
encapsulate what is already achieved. Hegel and a number of the idealists provide obvious instances. A variation of this type of system may assume an historicist
form when the progressive pattern of development is
seen, not in terms of the understanding, but is discerned
in nature or in history itself, as in Augustine, Comte or
Marx. And it may be the case that one looks for some
sort of unity in the progressive unfolding of ideas or different levels of consideration in the books of a particular
writer whose early works seem not to conform with those
that come later.

Obviously, this classification is only a suggestion: I cannot insist on it. But the real point I am trying to make
is twofold: that if we are studying the history of thought
then, first, what we pursue is coherence of some sort;
and, secondly, that we must get the kind of system we
look for right. We will be in dreadful error if we suppose
a writer who had one sort of system in mind to be attempting a coherence of another sort. This kind of mistake is one of the most insidious forms of anachronism.
We must beware, too, of a constant danger in this kind
of analysis and reconstruction, that of adding to a corpus
of work assistance of our own. A man may never fulfil
his intentions as to systematic thinking, may not climb
as far up the scale of abstraction as he intended. But we
have to be content with what he actually did, with the
evidence as it is. The system (whatever it is) lies in what
is there, not in what we might want to supplement it
with. And, in all this, the right sort of context is everything. The probing categories we use have to be appropriate; we have to avoid the backward-look; we must not
think that 'Truth' is more important than belief; and so
on. It follows that it is *never* enough to read specific
original sources and then indulge in a lot of critical
analysis. The sources themselves and this kind of discussion can be awfully misleading. A text is, in any
case, something achieved, not something given. And it
can only be understood if we see it in the right frame-

work. We have to do a considerable amount of work of, so to say, a secondary kind, to get the context right, before the text (or document or whatever it is) is assessable in any historically satisfactory way. Nor is it ever sufficient to study only the great works. What is primarily needed for this sort of exercise is to deal with the host of the relatively obscure who fill in the intervals between the men of genius and who are probably more characteristic of the age.[62]

III

Now how does all this bear on the matter of Hobbes interpretation? In this particular case, I do not think there is any problem about the level of abstraction concerned: it is, unambiguously, the highest, the philosophical. This is a rare situation in the history of political thought, but (I feel) quite clear. So the question really is, How successful was Hobbes in his philosophical enterprise? And this means asking, as a logically previous question. What sort of systematization did he have in mind? Let us look at this in terms of the three types of interpretation earlier outlined.

The traditional case clearly looks for consistency of a synthetic kind and in the deductive mode: everything is supposed to follow from the naturalistic assumptions about matter and motion. The 'absolute presuppositions' of Hobbes's system (on this view) include, for instance, that bodies exist and that the world operates by causes and effects. So his natural philosophy begins with definitions of such concepts (body, cause, effect, motion, space, etc.) from which he derives the principles governing the different kinds of body and motion and their properties.[63] And human and political activity are to be seen

---

[62] Cf. my *Order, Empiricism and Politics* (London, 1964), pp. 12–13, where I follow a remark of Oakeshott's. See the *TLS* (1949), review of Butterfield's *The Origins of Modern Science*.
[63] Goldsmith, *op. cit.*, pp. 46, 47.

in these terms. Yet the coherence sought on this basis is elusive, and if this is indeed the kind of consistency that Hobbes intended then there are undoubtedly a number of loose ends. The political and ethical views do not seem to flow easily from the basic assumptions; and Hobbes himself indicates that these views may in fact be pre-meditated on quite another basis, that of introspection and self-knowledge. Further, Hobbes's view of the passions is (as Strauss points out) decidedly non-naturalistic. And, to say the least, Hobbes's language about the moral and divine law is most ambiguous in this respect. So if this naturalistic framework of ideas is really the correct one to have in mind when considering Hobbes's work then his philosophical enterprise is clearly faultily or un-successfully carried out. This is a conclusion which does not, however, end the matter but itself raises further problems which centre around the issue, why did not Hobbes himself see these difficulties? One answer may be that he did see them but chose to ignore them. A reason that has been suggested for this view is of the 'biographical' kind. Hobbes knew his materialist doctrine would be unpalatable to many of his contemporaries so he cunningly left ambivalences and incompatibilities that would enable him, in defending himself against detrac-tors, to point to sufficient evidence of his real orthodoxy. This image of timid Hobbes who artfully presents two quite different doctrines side by side as a means of equiv-ocation has a certain appeal and ring of truth. The diffi-culty is not simply that the stratagem was unsuccessful but that a number of the inconsistencies involved do not seem to be relevant to the supposed end. To say, for instance, that the political ideas may be derived intro-spectively and do not need to be established on the me-chanical, materialist premises is to little purpose if these ideas are in themselves likely to be found objectionable. But, in any case, this kind of explanation, or rather ex-cuse, for some obvious difficulties in the traditional pic-ture of Hobbes becomes unnecessary if it can be shown that what appear as loose ends and ambiguities are themselves the product of misinterpretation. And this would avoid the necessity for another possible line of escape which is that Hobbes simply got confused or made a great number of bad mistakes and omissions in developing his argument. This is not only a very different assessment of Hobbes from that which sees him as clever enough to make deliberate errors, but also is, on the evidence, unreasonable. At the very least, it would mean that if some sort of naturalistic, deductive system is Hobbes's intention then the performance is, in some important respects, an inferior one: a conclusion it is hard to accept.

There are ways, too, in which the natural law case seems unacceptable because it rests on an unexplained dichotomy in Hobbes's thought, between the ethical deontology on the one hand, and the scientific materialism, egoistic psychology and prudential morality on the other. The Taylor thesis is precisely that Hobbes's ideas are basically inconsistent, riven into two incompatible parts. Even if this were true, it would be a matter to be explained rather than a view satisfactory in itself. Again, did Hobbes not see this inconsistency? Is it possible that, in some way, he did not see the matter as an inconsistency at all? If not, why not? Yet if he did see it, why did he leave things as they were? I feel myself that, as a matter of principle basic to the study of intellectual history, it is not possible to accept as final a bifurcated understanding of this kind. The exploration of discontinuity is always to be rejected in favour of the search for a satisfactory consistency, even if this has to be sought in biographical data. Professor Hood's thesis about Hobbes's 'divine politics', the essentially religious foundation of his thought, avoids to some extent a defect of this kind, finding in the naturalistic aspects of Hobbes's ideas simply a concession to intellectual fashion. Yet little, very little, is said about the historical background of the kind of thinking thus attributed to Hobbes. Moreover, the presence of two very different, if not incompatible, elements is admitted. And it is not even suggested that the elements at least reflect a common manner of thinking.

Strauss's interpretation is open to the same sort of criticism. He stresses the non-naturalistic basis of Hobbes's political and ethical thought but fails to explore its genesis adequately enough. Here lies the strength of the line of inquiry indicated by Oakeshott, Watkins and Glover. They suggest (as I follow their discussion) that many or most of the apparent difficulties found in Hobbes's thought may be resolved by seeing him in the right sort of historical context, in particular, the context of a particular style of philosophical thinking. And the way in which this greatest possible degree of coherence is to be found in Hobbes's thought is to see it, in effect, as an instance of discrete systematization i. e. that what holds all Hobbes's ideas together is the continuous application of a particular mode of thought. Yet it is true to say that here a line of inquiry has been pointed out rather than that it has been explored in anything like the requisite degree of historical detail. This is partly due to the mistaken notion (unfortunately held by so many students of political ideas) that examination of the 'internal' evidence of the texts is all that is required. It follows that if the present state of Hobbes scholarship intimates any specific avenue of advance, it is likely to go in the direction of an attempt to show in detail what this nominalist tradition of thought involved (in particular the kind of systematic thinking it envisaged), how Hobbes was influenced by it, how it affected the development of his ideas and constituted the base and framework of whatever degree of coherence he achieved in his philosophical politics. What is most needed now is not more insight or textual exegesis but simply more research.[64]

---

[64] I am sustained in this view when I note it is persuasively urged by Mr. Skinner, e. g., "The Ideological Context of Hobbes's Political Thought", p. 317.

WARRENDER AND HIS CRITICS[1]

BRIAN BARRY

The decade of criticism directed at *The Political Philosophy of Hobbes*[2] has found the critics united in rejecting many of Warrender's conclusions, but it has not produced a generally accepted alternative interpretation. I shall argue in this paper that this has happened because the critics have not been searching enough in their criticism. Often they have taken over without discussion two crucial but highly questionable features of Warrender's book: first, his ignoring the definition of 'obligation' given in *Leviathan*; and, second, his presentation of logically independent conclusions about Hobbes's theory as if they were related. As a result of the first, Warrender's critics have sometimes followed him into error; and, as a result of the second, they have sometimes been led to dismiss correct conclusions in the belief that these were logically bound up with other conclusions that really were wrong. Too often they have thrown out the baby and kept the bathwater.

The first point, then, on which I maintain the critics have been less than properly critical, is the provenance of Warrender's definition of 'obligation'. We should notice at the start Warrender's claim that his interpretation of Hobbes is based on the *Leviathan*, and that everything he attributes to Hobbes can be found there. Quotations from elsewhere are used, he says, only where they make more clearly the same points as can be found in *Leviathan*. (Warrender, vii–viii.) Now, in *Leviathan* Hobbes gives the reader a single unequivocal definition of 'obligation', as follows:

> Right is laid aside, either by simply renouncing it; or by transferring it to another. . . . And when a man hath in either manner abandoned, or granted away his right; then he is said to be OBLIGED, or BOUND, not to hinder those, to whom such right is granted, or abandoned, from the benefit of it . . . [*Lev.*, 86].[3]

Warrender, however, makes little use of this definition.[4] Instead, he constructs a definition of 'obligation' from a passage in *De Cive* and another in *Liberty and Necessity*. In the first, Hobbes speaks of a kind of 'natural obligation'

> according to which the weaker, despairing of his own power to resist, cannot but yield to the stronger.

In this sense, Hobbes says, we are 'obliged to obey God in his natural kingdom' (*De Cive*, XV, 7; *E.W.* II, 209). The second passage runs thus:

> Power irresistible justifies all actions, really and properly, in whomsoever it be found; less power does not, and because such power is in God only, he must needs be just in all actions . . . [*E.W.* IV, 250].

According to Warrender, the basic concept of obligation in Hobbes's political theory, which can be derived from these quotations, is one which makes the relation rest on unequal power, and especially the disparity of power between God and man. But if we follow Warrender in taking our task to be the interpretation of *Levi-*

---

[3] References in this form are to the pages of the edition of *Leviathan* edited by M. Oakeshott (Oxford: 1960).

[4] He does quote Hobbes as saying that when a man has given up a right he is under an obligation, but loses the point of it by taking it to mean simply that being obliged is 'suffering impediment' (Warrender, 101). But giving up a right is not merely one among a number of possible ways of coming under an obligation, it is (by definition) the only way.

athan (as against the *Elements of Law* or *De Cive*) we
need to be sure that the passages are relevant to *Leviathan*; even more fundamentally, of course, we need to
be sure they are about obligation. I think it can be shown
that the first passage fails the first test and the second
fails the second test.

Let us begin with the first passage, from *De Cive*, according to which we have a 'natural obligation' to obey
God because 'the weaker . . . cannot but yield to the
stronger'. The striking fact here is that, in the parallel
passage of *Leviathan*, the reference to 'natural obligation' is dropped. In Chapter 31 of *Leviathan*, Hobbes
again speaks, as in *De Cive*, of God's 'natural kingdom',
and again explains that God is able to get men to do
what He wants. But at no point does he now say that
God's operations in His 'natural kingdom' lay obligations
upon men.[5] This, we can be sure, is not mere carelessness
on Hobbes's part. Very few substantial points in the earlier workings of Hobbes's political theory are omitted in
Leviathan.[6] Now, it is not essential to my case to be able
to show why Hobbes chose to delete any reference to
'natural obligation' from *Leviathan*; it is enough that he

---

[5] In *De Cive* Hobbes in fact distinguishes two kinds of 'natural obligation'. The first is exhibited by God's attaching unpleasant consequences to certain kinds of behaviour and thus controlling the
rational members of His creation through their ability to foresee
these consequences and take appropriate avoiding action. This is
the kind of 'natural obligation' already discussed, and the kind
which Warrender proposes to make central to his interpretation of
the *Leviathan*. The second kind of 'natural obligation' is exhibited
by God's making stones fall and planets revolve. In the *Leviathan*
this kind of 'natural obligation' gets even shorter shrift than the
other; so far from being an example of 'obligation', God's operations in this manner are only metaphorically allowed to be even an
example of 'reigning'.

[6] M. M. Goldsmith, in his *Hobbes's Science of Politics* (New York
and London: 1966), has been very thorough in giving footnote
references to the parallel passages; the quotation from *De Cive*
(which he gives on p. 112) is one of the few which are not given
with a cross-reference to *Leviathan*.

did. But I do not doubt that Hood[7] is right in suggesting
that the explanation lies in Hobbes's controversy with
Bramhall about liberty and necessity. Since he now held
that liberty is not taken away by the fear of consequences, and wanted to contrast liberty with obligation,
he no longer had room for a concept of 'natural obligation' based on fear of consequences.

Luckily, Hobbes has given us a comment on the doctrine of *De Cive*, XV, 7, in his *Answer* to Bramhall's
Catching of the Leviathan, and this is of great interest.
Bramhall quotes Hobbes as saying that men are obliged
to obey God because of their weakness, and accuses him
of impiety (*E.W.* IV, 290). In his reply, Hobbes coolly
replaces the sentence quoted by Bramhall with a quite
different one, writing:

'to the same sense I have said in my *Leviathan*, that
the right of nature whereby God reigneth over man,
is to be derived not from his creating them, as if he
desired obedience, as of gratitude; but from his irresistible power'. [*E.W.* IV, 295.]

And then he argues that this is not discreditable to
God. But notice that by his maneouvre of citing *Leviathan*, Hobbes has neatly avoided having to defend the
words quoted by Bramhall, which spoke of *obligation*.
(Indeed it is hard to see any other point in making the
substitution.) As if this were not enough evidence that

---

[7] 'The argument of *De Cive* is based upon a concept of arbitrary
impediment to liberty which Hobbes had abandoned by 1646. . . .
The most important point regarding the paragraph on natural obligation in *De Cive* [i.e. the passage quoted by Warrender] is that
Hobbes had to jettison it when he wrote *Leviathan*. His first species
of natural obligation, whereby the liberty of all created things is
limited by the laws of their creation, had to disappear, because lack
of intrinsic power does not restrict liberty. His second species of
natural obligation, whereby the liberty of God's subjects is taken
away by fear and hope aroused by His irresistible power, had to
disappear, because there could no longer be arbitrary impediments
to liberty; fear and hope, too, do not restrict liberty.' F. C. Hood,
The Divine Politics of Thomas Hobbes (Oxford: 1964), 45 and 50.

Hobbes found the quotation from *De Cive* awkward, he added: 'But see the subtilty of his disputing. He saw he could not catch *Leviathan* in this place, he looks for him in my book *De Cive*, which is Latin, to see what he could fish out of that . . .' (*E.W.* IV, 295.)[8] How ironical that Warrender, by making the same passage the cornerstone of his analysis, should have laid himself open to exactly the same charge!

Now let us turn to Warrender's second passage, from *Liberty and Necessity*, which says that 'power irresistible justifies all actions . . . and because such power is in God only, he must needs be just in all actions'. There is no problem about the relevance of this passage to *Leviathan*, since it occurs there, too, almost word for word. But there is a serious question about its relevance to obligation. It should be noticed that the word 'obligation' does not occur in the passage, so at best its relevance to the concept of obligation must be an inferential one. I shall now try to show that no inference can in fact be made from anything in this passage to an implied definition of 'obligation'.

There is an obviously apparent connecting link in the word 'just', which does occur in the passage. If all God's actions are just, doesn't this entail that we are obliged to obey him? The answer is that Hobbes's definition of 'just' does not allow us to make any such inference.

> When a covenant is made, then to break it is *unjust*: and the definition of INJUSTICE is no other than *the not performance of covenant*. And whatsoever is not unjust, is *just*. [*Lev.*, 94.]

Hobbes equivocates on the interpretation of the last sentence, so that saying someone is acting justly sometimes means that he is keeping a covenant and sometimes merely that there is no covenant which he is breaking—the latter of course including situations that are not cov-

---

[8] Notice that Hobbes here effectively admits that there *is* something in *De Cive* to be 'caught' that does not recur in *Leviathan*.

ered by a covenant at all. In this latter sense of 'justice' there need be no connection with obligation at all. If we know that someone is behaving justly we can infer that he is not breaking an obligation, but we are not entitled to infer that he is keeping an obligation either.

In the *Leviathan*, Hobbes usually operates with this second, wider, sense of 'just', as when he says in the 'Review and Conclusion' that if a man lives in a country secretly (and has therefore not tacitly promised to obey the government)

> he is liable to anything that may be done to a spy, and enemy of the state. I say not, he does any injustice, for acts of open hostility bear not that name; but that he may be justly put to death. [*Lev.*, 462.]

'Justly' here means simply 'not unjustly'; Hobbes is not suggesting that the sovereign is carrying out a covenant, merely rejecting the idea that he might be breaking one. The sovereign and the man living secretly are in a state of nature with one another. Now, God's actions with respect to men are 'just' in exactly the same sense, and for the same reason.[9] Leaving aside the Israelites, who had a covenant with God (and were therefore in God's *prophetic* kingdom) men's relation to God is that of a state of nature. Nobody has covenanted with God so therefore God cannot behave unjustly with respect to men. Nor, by the same token, can men behave unjustly with respect to God; breaking God's law may be foolish but Hobbes does not describe it as unjust. Thus, everything God does with respect to men is just; but this sort of

---

[9] Hobbes actually took up the interpretation of his phrase about 'power irresistible' in his reply to Bramhall; and he clearly rejected the construction put on it by Warrender (and, as we shall see below, Plamenatz). 'He would make men believe, I hold all things to be just, that are done by them who have power enough to avoid the punishment. . . . I said no more, but that the power, which is absolutely irresistible, makes him that hath it above all law, so that nothing he doth can be unjust.' (*E.W.* IV, 146.)

'justice' does not entail the existence of any obligation upon anybody.[10]

A slight variation on the suggestion that God's commands oblige because they are just is the suggestion that God's commands oblige because they are laws; but this is equally baseless. Warrender quotes Hobbes's statement that the 'dictates of reason' which he has been calling laws of nature are, strictly speaking, properly called *laws* only in so far as they are considered as 'delivered in the word of God, that by right commandeth all things'. (Warrender, 98, quoting *Lev.*, 104–105.) And he then comments:

> Thus, if the laws of nature in the State of Nature are considered as the commands of God, they may properly be regarded as laws, *and it is this factor which is responsible for constituting their obligatory character.* [Warrender, 98.][11]

---

[10] In the other sense of 'justice', which presupposes the existence of a relevant covenant, there *is* a necessary connection between justice and obligation, but even if we supposed that this *was* the relevant sense here, the obligation that would follow from it would unfortunately come in the wrong place to help Warrender. For, in this sense of 'justice' what we can infer if we know that someone is behaving justly is that he himself is carrying out an obligation; we still cannot say that anybody else has obligations. At the *most* then, saying that God behaves justly in commanding men might entail that in so doing God is carrying out His own (contractual) obligations.

[11] Note may also be taken of Hood's view that the laws of nature oblige *qua* commands of God *delivered in Scripture*. This is repeated at least five times (4, 49, 227, 228 and 253—the last sentence in the book) each time without any reference. This compounds Warrender's illicit move from 'law' to 'obligation' with a groundless denial of God's being able to give laws without resorting to revelation. Hobbes makes it clear that the 'word of God' includes the 'dictates of reason and equity' (*Lev.*, 275), so that there is a 'triple word of God, rational, sensible and prophetic'. (*Lev.*, 233). It is true that in *De Cive* Hobbes says that the laws of nature are properly *laws* 'as they are delivered by God in holy Scriptures'. But, quite apart from the fact that this is altered in *Leviathan* to the more general formulation of 'the word of God', Hobbes immediately adds, in

Now, the clause which I have italicised, and which is essential to Warrender's argument at this point, has absolutely no foundation. To say that God commands 'by right' does not entail, in the terminology of *Leviathan*, that men have an obligation to obey His commands. God's 'right' to rule over men is merely the 'right of nature'. It 'is to be derived from his irresistible power' (*Lev.*, 234). Men, Hobbes says, need to come out of the state of nature with respect to one another (by covenanting to obey a sovereign) because otherwise their approximate equality of strength results in their all getting hurt. But God has no need to come out of the state of nature with respect to men, for, being omnipotent, He cannot be hurt by them. God's 'right' over men is exactly on a par, Hobbes makes it clear, with the 'right' of one man to club another in the absence of an effective sovereign.[12]

De Cive, that the 'laws of nature are divine laws as well because reason, which is the law of nature, is given by God to every man for the rule of his actions; as because [they occur in Scripture]'. (Both passages from *E.W.* II, 50–51.) A more general point against Hood is that Hobbes sometimes maintains that the Bible is a law to us only on the authority of the sovereign: 'How came it then to be a law to us? Did God speak it *viva voce* to us? Have we then any warrant for it than the word of the prophets? Have we seen the miracles? Have we any other assurance of their certainty than the authority of the Church? And is the authority of the Church any other than the authority of the commonwealth . . . ?' (*Liberty and Necessity*, *E.W.* V, 179.) Even if we discount this as a polemical excess, the fact that Hobbes was willing to put it forward at all suggests that he did not regard it as undermining the thing closest his heart—the obligation to obey the sovereign. Yet this it would certainly do if (as Hood maintains) that obligation depended ultimately on the Scripturally-based obligation to obey the laws of nature. For the obligation to keep (or even endeavour to keep) the laws of nature could not be valid until (*per impossibile*) a sovereign had already been brought into existence. And even if this difficulty could be circumvented, there could be no obligation to obey infidel sovereigns (since, by definition, they would not underwrite the Bible); yet Hobbes holds that there is in general such an obligation.

[12] As originally defined, the 'right of nature' was a right to act in self-defence only; you could hurt another man legitimately only if you sincerely believed him a threat to your existence. It was a 'right

Warrender, however, ignores Hobbes's account of the
way in which God commands man 'by right'. Instead, he
seizes on a statement made by Hobbes while defining
civil law, that 'law in general, is command; nor a command of any man to any man; but only of him, whose
command is addressed to one formerly obliged to obey
him'. (Warrender, 97, quoting *Lev.*, 172.) Hobbes is saying here that among men law is the result of covenant:
a command of *A* is a law for *B* only if *B* is 'formerly
obliged' (that is, if he has already covenanted) to obey
A's commands. Hobbes's use of the expression 'formerly
obliged' shows clearly that he is using the concept of
obligation in the way in which he defines it in *Leviathan*
—to refer to the result of giving up a right. If we try to
apply the concept of natural obligation from *De Cive*,
the expression 'formerly obliged' makes no sense at all,
for natural obligation depends on power relations at the
moment of action, and not (as contractual obligation
does) on anything that has occurred in the past.[13]

As an illustration of the tendency for Warrender's

---

to all things' only in the sense that there was no general category
of action (e.g. killing) that it ruled out. But thus limitation is soon
dropped. For example, God's 'natural right' is 'to afflict men at his
pleasure' (*Lev.*, 234); but obviously He has no need of self-defence.
It is easy to see why Hobbes drops the restriction. He wants to say
that the covenant setting up a sovereign simply leaves him to exercise his 'right of nature' without impediment, but to restrict the
powers of the sovereign to acting in his own self-defence would
obviously defeat Hobbes's whole purpose. The 'right of nature'
must therefore be unlimited to save the sovereign's absolute authority; God is an incidental beneficiary.

[13] Even if we accepted for the sake of argument that the definition
of law quoted by Warrender applied to God's law as well as civil
law, we should get the conclusion that men have a contractual
obligation to obey God's laws, which is something that Hobbes
explicitly denies, and in any case is not what Warrender wants to
maintain. Warrender quotes the passage to prove that men have a
natural obligation (in the *De Cive* sense) to obey God's laws, but
the passage would not support this even if it were about God. And
since, if it were about God, it would have to mean that every man
has covenanted with God to obey Him, we can add that it certainly
is not about God.

critics to take over some of the more questionable aspects
of his treatment, let me cite John Plamenatz, one of the
earliest and shrewdest critics. In his review of *The Political Philosophy of Hobbes*, Plamenatz, while dissent-
ing from many of Warrender's interpretations, nevertheless agrees that the laws of nature oblige *qua* commands
of God, uses the tag about 'power irresistible justifying
all things' in the context of obligation, and follows Warrender in ignoring Hobbes's definition of 'obligation' as
the logical consequence of a contract. 'Men are said to
be *obliged*, when they stand in such a relation to someone that, if they see that relation clearly, they cannot
choose but do what is commanded of them.'[14] This leads
him to construct a theory in which one is obliged to
obey the sovereign because of his ability to inflict pun-
ishments. But this was never Hobbes's view of the basis
of political obligation, and, as we have seen, even the
premise—natural obligation—was eliminated in the writing of *Leviathan*.

The other point on which Warrender's critics have
failed to take up a sufficiently critical stance is a more
general one. They have, I suggest, tended to take over
uncritically his way of setting out the problems and connecting the issues. It will be recalled that Warrender begins his book by saying that there are three possible ideas

---

[14] J. Plamenatz, 'Mr Warrender's Hobbes' (*Political Studies*, vol.
V, No. 3 [1957], 297; reprinted in K. C. Brown (ed.) *Hobbes
Studies* (Oxford: 1965), 75). The same view is expressed in *Man
and Society* (London: 1963), vol. I, 130. In a subsequently written
account, he suggests that this sort of obligation to obey someone can
be treated as a special case of a more general concept such that
'when Hobbes says a man is obliged . . . to do something he implies that, if he saw his advantage clearly, he would necessarily do
it'. (Introduction to *Leviathan* [Fontana paperback, London:
1962], 32.) The obligation to keep covenants is still treated as
logically on a par with (say) the obligation to kill another man;
it is obligatory when it pays and all that is meant by saying it is
obligatory in some situation is that it does pay. (Incidentally, the
idea that the laws of nature are obligatory *qua* commands of God,
and the move from God's 'irresistible power' to man's obligation to
obey Him, recur on pages 28 and 30.)

about obligation in Hobbes: some people have said, he claims, that there is no such concept and that the theory is descriptive only, others that

> when civil society is established, a new type of obligation is created; and still others that obligation, as Hobbes understood it, is essentially the same in civil society and out of it.[15]

Warrender espouses the third view, and thus commits himself to showing that for Hobbes: (a) there can be obligations in the state of nature and (b) that no new kind of obligation is added with the formation of a state.

However, in the body of the book he spends most of his time trying to establish a number of quite different propositions, including the following:

(c) the laws of nature do not rest on individual self-interest either for their demonstration or for their effectiveness,

(d) the laws of nature oblige (in the primary Hobbesian sense of the word 'obligation') in the state of nature and *a fortiori* under a sovereign, and

(e) the obligation to keep the covenant by which a sovereign is set up (or equally any other covenant) depends on, and is merely a special case of, the obligation to obey the laws of nature.

Now if (c), (d) and (e) are true, then certainly (a) and (b) are true, for (d) entails (a) and (e) entails (b). But the falsity of (c), (d), (e) or any combination of them does not entail the rejection of either (a) or (b). It is logically possible for (c), (d), and (e) all to be false while yet (a) and (b) are true; and I shall argue later that it is this combination which Hobbes in fact espouses in the *Leviathan*. Subsequent writers, however, have tended to follow Warrender's way of grouping the possible relationships. Watkins, in *Hobbes's System of Ideas* (London, 1965) rejects (c) explicitly and (d) and

---

[15] Summary by Plamenatz, *Political Studies*, vol. V, No. 3 (1957), 296; Brown (ed.), 73–4.

(e) implicitly.[16] But he goes on to put a negative sign in front of *all* Warrender's assertions by rejecting (a) and (b) too. He claims that the sovereign is 'himself responsible for the creation of obligations, where there were none before' (p. 68) and says that '*pace* Warrender, the sovereign's role *is* to create a public system of moral rules out of a moral vacuum' (p. 138). Thus, the sovereign not merely creates a new kind of obligation; he creates the only kind there is.

Hood, on the other hand, accepts all five propositions in his *The Divine Politics of Thomas Hobbes*. That is, he accepts the structure laid down by Warrender without question, and differs only on the content: where Warrender took the obligatory force of the laws of nature to depend on their being commands of God, Hood adds 'as delivered in Scripture'; and where Warrender leans towards saying that the sort of obligation the laws of nature have is Hobbesian 'natural obligation', Hood rejects this and says that it is a special sort of 'moral obligation' based on Scripture.[17]

---

[16] (c) is dealt with on pages 89–94 of *Hobbes's System of Ideas*. With (d) and (e) we must be more inferential since Watkins employs the concept of 'obligation' very little in his exposition. (There is no entry in the index.) However, on 87–9 he denies that the laws of nature are morally obligatory without suggesting they are obligatory in some other way; and in dealing with the reasons for obeying the sovereign he mentions only two: firstly that he 'bears the person' of the subjects (160–1) and secondly that he can 'cause men, by threat of punishment' to obey the law (162).

[17] Hood also calls this 'natural obligation', but it is clearly not the 'natural obligation' of the *De Cive* passage. He does not, in my view, produce any textual evidence for believing that Hobbes at any time recognised any form of obligation except those resulting from physical manipulation, fear of consequences, and contract. Obligations to God are not an additional *form* of obligation; they must take one or more of these three forms. Incidentally, Warrender seems to have set the fashion for speaking of 'moral obligation' as if this were a Hobbesian category—both Watkins and Hood do it. As far as I am aware, the term 'moral obligation' appears nowhere in Hobbes. He does sometimes say that the laws of nature are (among other things, such as natural and positive divine law)

I have pointed out that Warrender and his critics are alike in placing little store by Hobbes's explicit definition of 'obligation' in *Leviathan*, but I have not yet shown that they are wrong to do so. I have also asserted that Warrender's conclusions (a) and (b) are true while (c), (d) and (e) are false, but again substantiation needs to be provided. In the rest of this paper an attempt will be made to meet both points at once by showing that, starting from Hobbes's definition of 'obligation', we can develop a consistent theory—more consistent than either Warrender or his critics have given Hobbes credit for—in which Warrender's first two conclusions are true and the others false.[18] First I argue that there can, for Hobbes, be obligations in the state of nature, in the sense of 'obligation' defined by him. That is to say: in certain circumstances a man may create a binding obligation upon himself to perform a certain act as a result of his having given up a right, even where there is no 'common power set over' both parties. If this is accepted then the truth of (a) will have been demonstrated. I shall then try to prove (b) by arguing that the obligation to obey the sovereign is not a different kind of obligation from that given in Hobbes's definition—a citizen is obliged to obey the sovereign because he has given up his right not

---

moral laws, 'because they concern the manners and conversation of men, one towards another'. (*Elements of Law*, 5-1.) But just as divine law does not entail divine obligation neither does moral law entail moral obligation. (The sovereign's laws do, of course, involve an obligation, which we may if we like call political or legal obligation, though as far as I know Hobbes does not. But if we do, we must be clear that it is not a new *form* of obligation, but one of the three forms mentioned—in fact, the contractual form—applied to certain special covenants.)

[18] It is perhaps worth noting that C. B. Macpherson's essay in Marxist psychoanalysis, *The Political Philosophy of Possessive Individualism* (Oxford: 1962), which aimed to supply the 'hidden premises' allegedly needed to make Hobbes's theory work, took its warrant from the consensus among commentators on Hobbes that his political theory is incoherent. But if the theory is in fact coherent already, the case for an elaborate reconstruction to *make* it coherent immediately collapses.

to obey him. Finally, reasons will be given for rejecting
the three propositions culled from Warrender about the
basis and status of the laws of nature.

To be under an obligation means to have given up a
right; that is, to have given up some part of one's 'right
to all things'. Simply giving up a right is 'renunciation';
giving it up in favour of a particular person is 'transfer';
and mutual transfer is contract. 'Covenant' or 'pact' is a
particular kind of contract, namely a contract to perform
some time in the future. *A* may covenant to perform later
in return for *B*'s present performance (in this case *B*
does not covenant, though he does enter into a contract); or *A* and *B* may both covenant to perform in the
future (*Lev.*, 85–7). Hobbes later distinguishes the second kind of situation as one of 'covenants of mutual trust'
(*Lev.*, 89) or 'promises mutual' (*Lev.*, 95).

Can there be obligations (in the sense defined) in the
absence of a 'common power set over both' parties, that
is to say 'in the condition of mere nature'? This does not
reduce to the question whether in the state of nature
covenants are ever obligatory; still less to the question
whether covenants of mutual trust can be obligatory.
The question is whether *any* form of renouncing or
transferring rights can create an obligation to perform in
the state of nature. Now, contracts, Hobbes tells us, are
only conditionally beneficial; it only pays me to do my
part given that you do yours as well. Therefore, it is not
obligatory for one party to perform his part if he has a
'reasonable suspicion' that the other party will fail to do
his.[19] The key is trust; in the absence of a 'common
power' over the contracting parties, the larger the element of trust involved, the less chance there is that a

---

[19] Incidentally, to say that a promise obliges only when keeping
it conduces to your security does not entail saying that everything
which conduces to your security is obligatory. If an action conduces
to your security, then it would indeed be contrary to 'that reason,
which dictateth to every man his own good' (*Lev.*, 95), not to do
that action; but doing it is *obligatory* only if you have promised to
do it.

contract will create an obligation to perform. As Hobbes points out (see especially *E.W.* II, 20), where both parties perform their part of the contract 'instantly' (by, for example, exchanging physical goods), there is no need for either party to trust the other. There is no room for one party to harbour a 'reasonable suspicion' of the other party's good faith, so that a contract providing for both parties to perform together must always give rise to a firm obligation to carry it out.

If one end of the scale is represented by the case where both parties perform simultaneously and the other end consists of the case where both parties have yet to perform at separate or undetermined times, the intermediate case is where one party has already performed while the other has still to do so. Hobbes is quite explicit about this—in these circumstances the second party is obliged to do his part, too. Covenants are binding, he tells us, 'either where one of the parties has performed already; or where there is a power to make him perform' (*Lev.*, 92). The absence of a common power is, of course, the defining characteristic of the state of nature; thus Hobbes is saying here that even in the state of nature there is an obligation to perform your side of a covenant if the other party has already performed his. For example,

> if I covenant to pay a ransom, or service for life, to an enemy; I am bound to it: for it is a contract, wherein one receiveth the benefit of life; the other is to receive money, or service for it; and consequently, where no other law, as in the condition of mere nature, forbiddeth the performance, the covenant [i.e. the promise to pay] is valid. [*Lev.*, 91.]

Once the enemy has released me, I can obviously no longer plead mistrust of his good faith, and this would be the only acceptable excuse for not carrying out my part of the bargain. I am therefore obliged to do so.

Finally, there are covenants of mutual trust. The element of trust is at a maximum here; if you perform first you have no assurance that the other party will do his

part. Hobbes is undecided as to whether this means that
there is never an obligation to perform first or whether
it is merely rare.[20] But, as we have seen, this does not
entail that there can be no obligations in the state of nature. Even in the case of covenants of mutual trust,
Hobbes never denies that there is an obligation to perform *second*. Thus, the enemy holding prisoners would
never (or hardly ever) be obliged to carry out a promise
to release them in return for a mere promise that they
would pay a ransom when they get home. But if the
prisoners *were* released (however quixotically) in return
for a promise, they would be obliged to pay up.

The obligation to obey the sovereign's commands, or
laws, is a special case of the obligation to keep one's
word. Hobbes puts it neatly in *De Cive*: 'A contract
obligeth of *itself*; the *law* holds the party obliged by virtue of the universal *contract* of yielding obedience'.
(*E.W.* II, 185. Italics in original. Cf. *Lev.*, 112–3, 462.)
Of course, the sovereign creates new obligations by his
commands but he does not create a new *kind* of obligation.[21] An analogy would be this: if I sign a contract to
teach 'under the direction of the professor' and the pro-

---

[20] First, Hobbes says that 'on any reasonable suspicion it is void',
and adds discouragingly that 'he which performeth first, does but
betray himself to his enemy'. But a little later, he stipulates that
'the cause of fear, which maketh such a covenant invalid, must always be something arising after the covenant made'. (*Lev.*, 89–
90.) Cf. Goldsmith, *op. cit.*, 135–7.

[21] To say, as Warrender does, that the sovereign operates 'in a
system of rights and duties that he does not himself control or create except in the most trivial sense' (Warrender, 28), is surely to
overstate the point. The sovereign's commands obviously do create
'a system of rights and duties' which is new, though the obligation
to observe them is not of a new kind. Watkins quite properly objects to Warrender here (Watkins, 154–7) but he again rejects too
much. It is quite true that 'what the legislator commands, must be
held for *good*, and what he forbids for *evil*' (Watkins, 155), but it
does not follow from this that nothing is generally agreed on as
good or evil until the sovereign commands it. 'All men agree on
this, that peace is good, and therefore . . . the laws of nature are
good' (*Lev.*, 104).

fessor then says 'Teach *x*' the obligation to teach *x* is a contractual obligation. I now have an obligation that I did not have before but its basis is just the same as that of a contract to deliver a sack of potatoes. 'Obligation' is for Hobbes the result of giving up a right; and the obligation to obey the sovereign is the result of transferring to him all one's natural rights, except, of course, the inalienable right to defend oneself again 'death, wounds and imprisonment' (*Lev.*, 91; cf. *Lev.*, 86–7). In other words, and employing Hobbes's explanation of what it is to transfer one's rights, we can say that a man gives up all those rights that can be given up by means of a covenant (either with his fellow subjects or with the sovereign) in order that the sovereign should be less hindered in exercising his own natural 'right to all things'. The object in so doing is, of course, peace: even if the sovereign is oppressive he is better than the state of nature, and any attempt to guarantee against oppression invites a return to the state of nature.

Why does the covenant to transfer one's natural rights to a sovereign create a real obligation? The general answer is that the sovereign operates in such a way as to remove the excuses for not performing which can so easily be maintained in the absence of a coercive power. It is not so much that the sovereign makes it pay to keep your covenant by punishing you if you don't, but that it always pays anyway to keep covenants provided you can do so without exposing yourself, and the sovereign ensures that you will not be exposing yourself by keeping your covenant. Exactly how this works out in detail is not shown by Hobbes, but it would seem that the precise formulation must differ between a commonwealth by institution and a commonwealth by acquisition.

A sovereign by institution is set up by a 'covenant of mutual trust' among the prospective subjects of the sovereign, in which they all promise, roughly speaking, blanket obedience in perpetuity to whatever commands (including standing commands, i.e. laws) the sovereign may see fit to give. 'Covenants of mutual trust' are defective in the state of nature because one party cannot be reasonably sure that the other party will perform in due course when his turn comes.

> But in a civil estate, where there is a power set up to constrain those who would otherwise violate their faith, that fear [of being double-crossed by the others] is no more reasonable; and for that cause, he which by covenant is to perform first, is obliged to do so. [*Lev.*, 89.]

Hobbes does not argue that the covenant obliges you because 'there is a power set up to constrain' *you*; he says that the covenant obliges you because 'there is a power set up to constrain' the *other* parties to it, thus taking away the 'reasonable suspicion' of being double-crossed that would otherwise invalidate such a covenant. Of course, Hobbes does not discount the fear of punishment as a motive encouraging people to obey the law; but it is not the probability of having a sanction applied to oneself that makes one's obedience to the laws *obligatory.*[22]

A 'commonwealth by acquisition' comes about when a person or group of persons

> for fear of death, or bonds, do authorize all the actions of that man, or assembly of men, that hath their lives and liberty in his power. [*Lev.*, 129.]

Exactly the same 'natural rights' have to be given up as before, but the covenant this time is with the powerful man or assembly (that is to say, with some already existing sovereign).

> So that *conquest*, to define it, is the acquiring of the right of sovereignty by victory. Which right, is acquired in the people's submission, by which they con-

---

[22] In *De Cive*, Hobbes makes the point by saying that 'a man is obliged by his contracts' but the law 'ties him being obliged' (*E.W.* II, 185). Contrast Austin's view that legal obligation *consisted in* the chance or likelihood of suffering an 'evil' at the hands of the sovereign.

tract with the victor, promising obedience, for life and liberty. [*Lev.*, 463.]

Now this is not in fact a 'covenant of mutual trust', for the victor lets you go (or refrains from killing you) now, whereas you promise to obey him in the future. (The victor cannot give you any guarantees about your 'life and liberty' *in the future*, because this would be a derogation of his sovereignty.) The case is, in fact, precisely analogous to that of the men released by their captors in return for the promise of a future ransom; and it will be recalled that even 'in the condition of mere nature' that promise was held to be obligatory, because the other party had already performed its part of the bargain. The logical role of the state's coercive power is thus a little different with sovereignty by acquisition. There is no need (as there is with sovereignty by institution) of a guarantee that the other party will perform, for he performs at once and once for all. But there may well still be a need for a guarantee that you can perform your part safely, and that is where the coercive power of the state comes in. Hobbes illustrates this a little after the ransom example:

> If a weaker prince, make a disadvantageous peace with a stronger, for fear; he is bound to keep it, unless . . . there ariseth some new, and just cause of fear, to renew the war. [*Lev.*, 91.]

The sovereign can use his coercive power to make sure as far as is humanly possible that the covenant to obey him will not be undermined by any 'new and just cause of fear'. Again, it is not that the sovereign obliges you to obey him by threatening sanctions if you don't, but rather that the sovereign removes the usual excuses which prevent promises from being obligatory.

To reduce Hobbes to saying, 'Obey the sovereign, or he'll punish you', is to miss the core of his doctrine, which is that you are obliged to obey wherever certain nullifying conditions are absent. Obedience pays because it helps to secure peace, which is the only sure means to personal survival. It pays, *other things being equal*, and it is the state's job to make them equal. If Hobbes's 'message' were that we ought to obey for fear of the police, why should he have thought that having his doctrine taught in the universities and preached in the pulpits would make England a less turbulent country? It was precisely because he had seen the fragility of régimes resting only on bayonets that he wrote *Leviathan*.[23] If we have to reduce Hobbes to a slogan, it must be something like this: 'Obey even when there isn't a policeman, because this contributes to peace: only provided that there are enough policemen around to give you more security than you would get in a free-for-all'. And it may be added that since a free-for-all is very, very insecure, the critical level of police protection need not be very high to make it preferable for you to cast your vote for peace by obeying the government's commands.

So far I have been in effect defending Warrender's theses (a) and (b), *viz*. that there can be obligations in the state of nature and that the sovereign does not create a new kind of obligation. Of course, my version of (a) is different from Warrender's in that I have been following Hobbes's definition of 'obligation' in *Leviathan* as the consequence of renouncing or transferring a right, whereas he takes obligation to be primarily connected with the laws of nature—that is to say, with all the laws of nature, and not just the third, which deals specifically with covenants. But I have still been holding, as War-

---

[23] 'The ground of these rights [of the sovereign] have the rather need to be taught diligently, and truly taught; because they cannot be maintained by any civil law, or terror of legal punishment.' (*Lev.*, 220.) And in *Behemoth*, Hobbes wrote, 'If men know not their duty, what is there that can force them to obey the laws? An army, you will say. But what shall force the army?' (*E.W.* VI, 237.) Thus Hobbes, like Hume in the well-known opening of the essay 'Of the First Principles of Government', is clear that it is 'on opinion only that government is founded'. (*Hume's Essays* [Oxford: 1963, edn.], 29.)

render does, that (a) and (b) are true. The other three
theses, which I called (c), (d) and (e), I maintain to be
false; I believe that the laws of nature *do* rest on the requirements for individual self-preservation, that they do
not oblige (in the main sense of the 'oblige' used by
Hobbes) and in particular that the obligation to keep
covenants does *not* depend on there being an obligation
to obey the laws of nature.

Since all these propositions involve the laws of nature
it is worth asking where these come into Hobbes's theory. It seems to me that Hobbes gives three different,
though not inconsistent, reasons why (to put it deliberately vaguely) it is a good idea to obey the commands
of a sovereign. First, you are obliged to do so in that you
have covenanted to, and not to keep covenants is injustice. Second, because the sovereign is your 'representa-
tive' who 'bears your person', you are the 'author' of his
acts and you thus 'own' them. Since nothing done to a
man, by his own consent, constitutes 'injury' (*Lev.*, 98),
you cannot complain that any act of the sovereign in-
jures you. And third, the 'reason which dictateth to every
man his own good' tells you (i) to enter into a covenant
setting up a sovereign and (ii) to keep the covenant.
Note that these are not to be regarded as 'three theories
of obligation'; obligation arises from having covenanted,
and is thus relevant only to the first of these three points.
The second point takes up a logical consequence of the
precise *form* taken by the covenant, and the third point
emphasises the personal gain from undertaking and adhering to an obligation to obey a sovereign.

The case against Warrender's view that Hobbesian
laws of nature are not rules for individual self-preservation is a familiar one but none the worse for that. It consists, on the positive side, of citing Hobbes's numerous
statements to that effect (including his definition of a
law of nature); and, on the negative side, of showing
that Warrender misapplies the quotations he uses to support his position. Thus, for example, Hobbes defines a
law of nature as 'a general rule, found out by reason, by

which a man is forbidden to do that, which is destructive
of his life. . . .' (*Lev.*, 84); and, although he does at one
place say that the laws of nature that he has put forward are necessary for 'the conservation of men in multitudes', he goes on at once to say that these laws are
only a selection, namely those that are politically relevant, and that there are others which conserve men
singly.[24]

I come now to the case for saying that the laws of nature do not constitute obligations for men, in the primary
sense of 'obligation' which is employed in *Leviathan*. By
'the primary sense' is meant simply that sense of 'obligation' which seems to make sense of the word in most of
the contexts in which it occurs in *Leviathan*. It is easy
to see that if we take 'obligation' as the result of giving us
a right we are in accord with Hobbes's own definition of
'obligation', which is in precisely these terms. Of course,
it may be that Hobbes failed to stick to his definition in
most of his subsequent uses of the word 'obligation', but
it seems on the face of it unlikely that a man so emphatic
about the importance of using words in clearly defined
ways would have treated his own definition of an absolutely central concept in so cavalier a way. Whether the
unlikely is nevertheless true can only be decided by reading *Leviathan* with alternative definitions of 'obligation'
in mind. My own conclusions are, first, that the *Leviathan*
hangs together intelligibly when 'obligation' is read in the
way proposed, and second, that (with the exceptions to
be mentioned) all occurrences of 'obligation' fit this reading—that is, people are said to be obliged only when they
have renounced or transferred a right.

In particular, I think it is true to say that, subject to
the same exceptions, Hobbes does not refer to the laws

---

[24] What makes rules for collective conservation a means to individual conservation is the fact of virtual equality. Since no man can
hope to dominate others securely by a sheer superiority of natural
strength everyone must accept terms which are equally favourable
to all (i.e. which will conserve men in multitudes) if there is to be
peace. (See *Lev.*, 100–1.)

of nature as creating obligations. There is, indeed, a slight complication here in that the third law of nature is 'that men perform their covenants made'. Thus the third law of nature underwrites the obligation to keep covenants, by making it a 'dictate of reason'. But it does not, of course, follow from this that the obligation to keep covenants is derived from an obligation to obey the laws of nature. Covenants create obligations by virtue of what they are—having given up a right is what being obliged *means*. Hobbes establishes this many pages before even introducing the third law of nature. How absurd, then, to maintain (and this is point (e), taken out of turn) that the obligation to keep covenants is merely a special case of an obligation to obey the laws of nature!

We must now, as promised above, look at the exceptions, the deviant uses of 'obligation' which do not fit Hobbes's own definition. These are mostly clustered together in a familiar passage which begins with the comment that the laws of nature

> oblige in *foro interno*; that is to say, they bind to a desire they should take place: but in *foro externo*; that is, to the putting them in act, not always. For he that should be modest, and tractable, and perform all he promises, in such time, and place, where no man else should do so, should but make himself a prey to others, and secure his own certain ruin, contrary to the ground of all laws of nature, which tend to nature's preservation. And again, he that having sufficient security, that others shall observe the same laws towards him, observes them not himself, seeketh not peace, but war; and consequently the destruction of his nature by violence. [*Lev.*, 103.][25]

Hobbes is here saying that *all* the laws of nature oblige, so we must concede that a new, non-contractual, sense of obligation is being introduced. The only way of avoiding such a conclusion would be to maintain that, for

---

[25] The laws of nature are also said to 'oblige' at *Lev.*, 219–220.

Hobbes, the laws of nature oblige in virtue of men's voluntarily 'giving up the right' to do what is forbidden by them. This unlikely solution has actually been put forward, in an article by A. G. Wernham entitled 'Liberty and Obligation in Hobbes'. According to him, a man *makes* a law of nature obligatory for himself by 'willing to adopt it'. He thus 'gives up his right' to do actions of that kind, unless of course he believes such an action necessary to save his life (Brown [ed.] *Hobbes Studies*, p. 135). But there is no reason for supposing that Hobbes either held this view or would have wished to. 'It is manifest that the *divine laws* sprang not from the consent of man, nor yet the *laws of nature*.' (*E.W.* II, 184.)[26]

The whole point of the laws of nature is that they are the means by which each person increases his own chances of staying alive; and on Hobbes's psychological premises trying to stay alive is not a matter of choice but (under normal conditions) a necessity of every human being's nature. Failure to act on the laws of nature is not due to a defect of will but a defect of reasoning akin to an inability to put two and two together. 'The whole breach of the laws of nature consists in the false reasoning, or rather folly of those men, who see not those duties they are necessarily to perform towards others in order to their own conservation.' (*E.W.* II, 16.)[27]

---

[26] A covenant is the giving up of a right, so that the third law of nature, 'that men perform their covenants made', means that when you have given up a right it should stay given up. Now, according to Wernham one adopts a law of nature by 'giving up the right' to do what it forbids, but then where does this put the adoption of the third law of nature? On Wernham's view, adopting the third law of nature would have to consist in giving up the right to go back on one's word when one had given up a right. But this is absurd. If the man's giving up rights is already effective in controlling his actions, his giving up the right to break the third law of nature is redundant; but if it is not already effective then giving up the right to break the third law of nature is ineffective, too, and we have an infinite regress.

[27] M. M. Goldsmith also tries to reconcile the ideas 'that all obligations are self-imposed' and that the laws of nature are obligatory. He writes: 'If these natural regularities [the laws of nature] apply

If we reject Wernham's suggestion, then, we have to conclude that Hobbes is using 'obligation' in the passage cited in a way other than that defined. He does not seem to be saying anything different about the status of the laws of nature from what he has already said; the innovation lies in using the term 'oblige' where he has previously been using 'dictate'. It may be significant that the terminology of 'dictation' would have been rather awkward for making the point Hobbes wants to make here. This is that although 'reason dictates' the laws of nature as 'convenient articles of peace' they will not tend to a given individual's self-preservation unless others follow them, too. Reason does not therefore dictate that one should always put the laws of nature 'in act' but only one should always be ready to do so when others will, too. If we analyse what is being said with 'obligation' here it appears that '*A* is obliged to do *x*' is equivalent to '*x* is a means to *A*'s self-preservation'. It should be noticed that in this sense of 'obligation'—which is 'natural obligation' slipping in again—it is not just the laws of nature that are obligatory, but any action which genuinely tends to the agent's self-preservation. Thus even actions carried out

---

whether they are known or not, how can a man be obliged to obey them only by his own act? In the sense of physical necessity [i.e. the actual regularities themselves], surely no one has a choice. Nevertheless, there is another sense in which these laws oblige only by a man's own act; it is by his own discovery of their existence and their necessity that he realizes that he is bound to respect them in the sense of taking account of them in his deliberations.' (*Hobbes's Science of Politics*, 132–3.) If this kind of tortured reasoning is necessary to reconcile the two ideas, this is equivalent to their being irreconcilable; to say that the 'act' which puts a man under an obligation is discovering a regularity is, at best, a rather weak joke. The laborious attempt is especially perverse because the phrase quoted—that there is 'no obligation on any man, which ariseth not from some act of his own'—is perfectly clear in its context. (*Lev.*, 141; reference on 134 of Goldsmith.) Hobbes is arguing that the obligation of the citizen depends on the terms of the covenant setting up the sovereign; thus the 'act of his own' by which alone a man undertakes obligations is the act of making a covenant.

under the 'right of nature', where the agent had correctly assessed the situation, could also be obligatory in this sense.[28]

Since, on the 'self-preservation' definition of 'obligation', laws of nature (among other things) are obligatory, it follows that covenants—whose keeping is enjoined by the third law of nature—are obligatory too in this sense of the word. Thus, covenants are obligatory on either definition of 'obligation'. The question is: when Hobbes speaks of covenants 'obliging' does he simply mean that keep-

---

[28] Perhaps a comment is unavoidable at this point on Hobbes's statement (*Lev.*, 84) that 'obligation and liberty . . . in one and the same matter are inconsistent'. If Hobbes had wanted to make obligation and liberty strict contradictories he could have done it by two alternative pairs of definitions. One pair would be that obligation in a matter is having given up a right to do it, and liberty is not having given up a right to it; the other pair would be that liberty is not suffering corporal impediment (chains, imprisonment, etc.) and obligation *is* suffering them. Unfortunately, in *Leviathan* he picked his definition of 'obligation' from the first pair and his definition of 'liberty' from the second pair. But in practice he brings his use of 'liberty' in line with his definition of 'obligation': in his chapter on 'The Liberty of Subjects' he sticks at the beginning to saying that 'in the proper sense for corporal liberty' it is 'freedom from chains and prison' (*Lev.*, 138), but he then uses the word to cover (a) those matters where there is no command of the sovereign (i.e. no law) so no contractual obligation, and (b) those matters (e.g. self-destruction) where no covenant can give rise to obligations. Hobbes would have been much better off if he had couched his formal definition of freedom in terms of the absence of contractual obligation. His actual definition produces absurd results when substituted for occurrences of the word 'liberty'. For example, substitute it in his definition of 'laying down a right' as 'divesting yourself of the liberty of hindering someone else's right'; the latter would then read, 'divesting yourself of the absence of external impediments [e.g. chains or prison] to hindering someone else's right'. Thus undertaking an obligation would entail literally, not metaphorically, chaining yourself up! This point is worth making because it is as well to be clear that the correlative of 'corporal liberty' is not 'natural obligation', for 'natural obligation' is not physical restraint but fear of consequences. So Hobbes's misjudgment in clinging to 'corporal liberty' is no encouragement to those who wish to read 'natural obligation' into a central position in *Leviathan*.

ing covenants sometimes tends to self-preservation? Reasons have already been given for rejecting this view, but there is another which seems very difficult to meet. It is this. On the 'self-preservation' definition, keeping covenants represents only a small proportion of all the actions that are obligatory. Saving your skin by the 'right of nature' and keeping all the laws of nature are also obligatory. If Hobbes had intended to use this definition widely in *Leviathan* we would expect to find the word 'obligation' occurring wherever the right of nature or laws of nature were under discussion. Instead we find that exercising the right of nature is never described as obligatory, and that of the many references to the laws of nature only a tiny proportion call them obligatory. Aside from this small number of cases, what are said to give rise to obligations are invariably covenants, contracts and the like. Why would Hobbes have confined the term 'obligation' to renunciations and transfers of right so exclusively if what he normally wanted to convey by using the word was that keeping your word was a means to self-preservation? Surely he would then have used 'obligation' freely when talking about the many other means to self-preservation.

If we were to suppose, then, that Hobbes intended the 'self-preservation' sense of 'obligation' to be read into his talk of the obligatory nature of covenants, etc., we should be faced with this insuperable mystery: why did he restrict the employment of such a wide-ranging concept to such a limited part of its field of application? The mystery disappears at once if we take it that the relevant sense of 'obligation' when Hobbes speaks of covenants, etc., is the sense defined by him in terms of having given up a right. From this perspective, the passages where the laws of nature are said to oblige are to be regarded as isolated instances of a secondary sense of 'obligation'. In reworking *De Cive*, Hobbes cut out the definition of 'natural obligation' (which would otherwise have occurred in Chapter 31 of *Leviathan*), but he was not entirely successful in eradicating all uses of it from the revised version. The suppressed passage from *De Cive* and the occasional slips in *Leviathan* have been made the basis of an analysis, which, as I have tried to show, has been accepted in this vital respect even by its critics.

Finally, does it all matter? Perhaps the whole question is not of earth-shaking importance to human welfare; but, taking as given the narrower focus of appreciating Hobbes, I think it matters quite a lot. Hobbes, as everybody knows, was an early exponent of the 'command theory of law' which received its classic statement from Austin. However, if I am right, Hobbes's version is free from the most fundamental logical objections to Austin's theory. We do Hobbes not credit but discredit by reading Austin back into him. As Hart has pointed out, Austin assimilates the legal situation to a stick-up by a gunman;[29] but Hobbes is clear that legal obligation is different from merely being in someone's power.[30] 'He [Bishop Bramhall] thinks, belike, that if a conqueror can kill me if he please, I am presently obliged without more ado to obey all his laws. May I not rather die, if I think fit? The conqueror makes no law over the conquered by virtue of his power; but by virtue of their assent, that promised obedience for the saving of their lives.' [*E.W.* V, 180.]

To put the same point linguistically: Austin assimilates 'being under an obligation [to keep a promise, obey a law, etc.]' with 'being obliged to [hand over the money to the gunman, throw the goods overboard in a storm, etc.]'.[31] The temptation to a tough-minded theorist to run the two together is manifest: 'to many later theorists [than Austin] this has appeared as a revelation, bringing down to earth an elusive notion and restating it in the

---

[29] H. L. A. Hart, *The Concept of Law* (Oxford: 1961), 80.

[30] Plamenatz would attribute to Hobbes the view that the state obliges *qua* gunman; Warrender that God, *qua* super-gunman, obliges you to obey the state.

[31] See Hart, *op. cit.*, 79–88.

same clear, hard, empirical terms as are used in science'. (*The Concept of Law*, 81.) But, although Hobbes dabbled with a type of 'natural obligation' in *De Cive*, he never took the short cut of reducing legal obligation to 'being obliged' in that sense. We may well think that 'having an obligation to do x' cannot always be reduced to 'having previously promised (contracted, etc.) to do x', as Hobbes suggested it should. But we must acknowledge that he had picked on the clearest, we might even say the paradigm, case of 'having an obligation' *as distinct from* 'being obliged'.

HOBBES AND THE JUST MAN

K. R. MINOGUE

I.

Like most who write about Hobbes, I cannot resist laying a few methodological cards on the table at the beginning. There are many different kinds of interest we may have in the philosophy of times past. One kind of interest is historical, and has its own very strict presuppositions. For example, historians do not correct their characters; it is only a bad historian who pauses to say of one of his characters: "He shouldn't have done that" or "here he is contradicting himself". To this extent, it is true that "in the end one never criticises". But there are other things one may do with a text besides take it historically. One may, for example, argue with it, as if the author were speaking directly to any reader, at any time. Or, one might go to a writer such as Hobbes for help in answering a question like: what kind of philosophy might we generate if we assume that men are fundamentally anti-social. One may treat a philosophy as a storehouse of arguments, or one may simply read it for the pleasure of its prose. In many of these cases, what we take from it may be historically corrigible; and we may have to defer to the historian who shows us that we have misunderstood what our author was saying. But this should not be taken to allow the historian to legislate about everything we may or may not do with a text.

The pleasure which we may get from absorption in a writer like Hobbes resembles an addiction. One has entered a complex world of ideas which is, like any world, full of dark corners and concealed places, ready for exploration. And the work of commentators often consists

From *Hobbes-Forschungen*, edited by Reinhart Koselleck and Roman Schnur. Duncker & Humblot, Berlin, 1969. Reprinted by permission of the author & publishers.

in giving an account of these places, or of showing connections between this world and some other world tangential to it. A philosophy like that of Hobbes is, among other things, the product of a man, and one activity we may pursue is to explore his intentions, as they emerge in the work, and perhaps also with the aid of biographical or other non-philosophical information. But a philosophy is also a creation in some degree independent of its originator; there will be things in it which he did not realise. With each generation, new philosophical questions come to be asked, and consequently the philosophy appears in a new light which could not have been evident to its creator. This is particularly true of a political philosophy. Any philosophy is a body of assertions and implications; there are always further implications which may be drawn. But it is also a body of nuances: it has an artistic character, which cannot be ignored, and which may often reveal areas of this philosophical world not illuminated by direct assertion.[1]

Alongside the recognition that the philosophy of Hobbes is a single world, both by virtue of having one creator, and also by virtue of having a rational coherence which affects all the parts, we may also observe that it is in many respects a profoundly miscellaneous body of thought. It contains many diverse elements which are often hard to fit together. The result is that there are a number of causes of ambiguity in Hobbes and I would like briefly to consider two of them.

The first arises from the fact that Hobbes is discussing an abstractly specified set of subjects. The first Part of *Leviathan* is concerned with Man, a subject who in the course of the first hundred pages or so acquires a puzzling variety of predicates. Man, for example, is bent on self-preservation and seeks power after power without end except in death. He never laughs but with a feeling of pleasure in his own power and in the weakness of

---

[1] Dorothea Krook has done some useful work of this kind: *Three Traditions of Moral Thought* (Cambridge, 1959).

others. There have been readers of Hobbes who do not find this a convincing account of each and every human being. Those who find this kind of problem in Hobbes generally cast around for a more specific subject such that the predicates may be truly asserted. It has been Professor Macpherson's enterprise, for example, to demonstrate that "man" is too wide a subject, and should be replaced by "bourgeois man". Again, the philosophy of the *Leviathan* particularly fascinates those who study international relations, and find connections between the mechanistically conceived entity called Man and the states about whose relations they theorise. There are various other possible candidates for the job of subject: when we learn, for example, that sons are not in the state of nature,[2] we might be inclined to restrict "man" to those patriarchal heads of families who seem to have bulked so large in the political thought of the seventeenth century. Similarly, the state of nature is an ambiguous subject which may be construed in a variety of ways.

The second kind of ambiguity arises from the fact that Hobbes's political philosophy is a variety of different sequences in which terms follow each other according to different principles. How do we explain the way in which one thing follows from another? The most evident principle of continuity is an expository one, and Hobbes suggests this when he claims that he has performed the supremely difficult task of setting down "his own reading (of mankind in himself) orderly, and perspicuously". But again, Hobbes has been his own best propagandist in suggesting that the dominant sequence is deductive, and that the *Leviathan* represents the compositive stage of an entire resolute-compositive analysis of the state. It has often been noticed that this is not really so. Again, a good deal of the early part of *Leviathan* consists in translating ordinary words into Hobbes's conceptual idiom. As he proceeds to build up his picture of man, he pauses to pluck from current discourse the terms he now claims

---

[2] *De Cive*, I 10 n.

have been explained. The introduction of the laws of nature is a good example of this. We are told that men are curious about the causes of their own fortune and misfortune.[3] Death being the greatest misfortune, men are inclined to peace, and reason suggests convenient articles of peace upon which men may be drawn to agreement. These articles are then asserted to be none other than what "otherwise are called the Laws of Nature".[4] The validity of this equivalence has been one of the battlefields of Hobbes scholarship. Then, in rapid succession, Hobbes plucks concepts like that of covenant, and of person, out of his environment, explores their implications, and sets them to work in his system. And in this process other sequences arise.

For example, there are at least three sources of psychological generalisation in Hobbes. One of them is deductive and arises from his account of natural man: the "general inclination of all mankind, a perpetual and restless desire of power after power, that ceaseth only in death"[5] seems to belong in this sequence. A second source of psychological generalisation is the casual remark of the *moraliste* in Hobbes, the kind of remark based upon common experience which reminds us that he was a contemporary of La Rochefoucauld. There is no doubt that Hobbes as an observer of man was extremely sensitive to hypocrisy. Sometimes the deductive and the empirical coalesce, as when Hobbes suggests[6] that one reason a man may transfer his right is "to deliver his mind from the pain of compassion"—a remark which reminds one of the story of Hobbes and the beggar, reported by Aubrey. Sometimes, however, Hobbes is not being cynical, but

---

[3] *Leviathan*, Ch. XII, p. 69. Page references to *Leviathan* refer to the Blackwell edition edited by Professor Oakeshott.
[4] *Leviathan*, Ch. XII, p. 84.
[5] *Leviathan*, Ch. II, p. 64. But it should be observed that Professor Macpherson thinks this does not follow from the account of natural man. See: *The Political Theory of Possessive Individualism*, Oxford, 1962.
[6] *Leviathan*, Ch. 14, p. 87.

rather using empirical generalisations to support the deductive sequence. He has a vivid sense of those moments when a contemporary reader might look up from *Leviathan* muttering "zounds" or "pshaw", or perhaps "by God, this is impossible". At these moments he appeals to the commonsense of the reader, the most familiar occasion being when he says "It may seem strange to some man, that has not well weighed these things; that nature should thus dissociate, and render men apt to invade, and destroy one another . . ." And he refers to locked chests and armed travellers.

There is a third, distinct, source of what at least look like psychological generalisations. It is derived from the concept of a contract. It is linked to the deductive sequence by the principle that "of the voluntary acts of every man, the object is some *good to* himself". Thus a man cannot "lay down the right of resisting them, that assault him by force, to take away his life; because he cannot be understood to aim thereby, at any good to himself".[7] When Hobbes uses this rationalistic psychology, he is usually careful to signal the fact by the use of copulae like "cannot be understood to", thus distinguishing it from his naturalistic observations. But the careless conflation of these three strands in Hobbes has led many readers to attribute to him a doctrine of psychological egoism, which he did not hold, and which vulgarises his philosophy.[8]

II.

Hobbes was a man of strong moral feeling who produced a philosophy whose ethical content is obscure. The moral feelings, as approvals and disapprovals, slip out throughout his writings, and as such they have been bril-

---

[7] *Leviathan*, Ch. XIV, p. 87.
[8] Cf. Bernard Gert, "Hobbes, Mechanism, and Egoism", *Philosophical Quarterly*, 1965.

liantly assembled by Keith Thomas.[9] On the other hand, Hobbes did not seem to be greatly interested in moral theory, by which I mean here the study of moral qualities, of good and evil. In a number of well-known passages, he dismissed "good" and "evil" as terms whose meaning is entirely dependent upon a man's current structure of appetites and aversions: "This is good", he argued, meant no more than "this is the object of my desire". Such pseudo-moral locutions were not, Hobbes argued, merely mistaken attributions of moral qualities to external things; they were positively iniquitous, in that their bogus objectivity was one reason for quarrelsomeness in the state of nature. Hobbes's moral interest appeared for the most part to have been absorbed by the deduction of binding rules of behaviour.

Such rules at least generate "oughts", and given that the moral field is difficult to demarcate, the copula "ought" might be taken as a sign that this was moral theory. But it is an elementary move to demarcate the field of morals from that of prudence, which also contains prescriptions; and most of the prescriptions found in Hobbes rest upon a solidly prudential base. Besides, another way of demarcating the field of morals is in terms of egoism and altruism; and Hobbes's philosophy is egocentric, if not consistently egoistic. One common view of Hobbes's work, then, was that it contained little that was genuinely moral. From this charge—if charge it be—Hobbes was rescued by those convinced by the Taylor Thesis. A. E. Taylor split off the psychology from the obligation, which was supposedly found in the divinely commanded laws of nature. God's moral sovereignty was based upon his irresistible power; and Taylor, advancing this view, confessed "to finding a real difficulty in understanding how Hobbes could hold that mere *irresistible power* can

---

[9] "The Social Origins of Hobbes's Political Thought", *Hobbes Studies*, Ed., K. C. Brown, Oxford, 1965, p. 185.

be the foundation of a moral *obligation*".[10] Could even
the fact of God's commandment turn the rational theo-
rems into *morally* obligatory laws? Stuart M. Brown Jr.
summed up the difficulty as follows: "For to say that natural law is the command of God is simply to say that a
set of rules, lacking in moral content, is law in the strict
sense".[11] To go beyond this would require additional
support, of a kind not open to Hobbes to provide, such
as the assertion that God is good. In these terms we are
forced back upon the view that there is no real moral
theory in Hobbes, and that, for example, the laws of nature are assertoric hypothetical imperatives, akin to "doctor's orders".[12]

But we cannot rest here. For in recent discussions of
Hobbes, increasing attention has been paid to a series of
hints, not only that Hobbes's moral opinions deserve more
prominence, but that they may be essential to the rational coherence of the work.[13] "Nay", he wrote in one
of the three key passages of this kind in *Leviathan*[14] "ex-
cepting some generous natures, (fear) is the only thing,
when there is appearance of profit or pleasure by breaking the laws, that makes men keep them". How do we
account for these "generous natures?" There is, furthermore, the problem arising from the fact that (to take the
formulation of *De Cive*, I 2) "he that first performs, by
reason of the wicked disposition of the greatest part of
men studying their own advantage, either by right or
wrong, exposeth himself to the perverse will of him with
whom he hath contracted. For it suits not with reason,

---

[10] Taylor, A. E., "The Ethical Doctrine of Hobbes", *Hobbes Studies*, p. 50, italics in text.
[11] Brown, Jr., Stuart M., "The Taylor Thesis; Some Objections",
Hobbes Studies, p. 63.
[12] Watkins, J. W. N., *Hobbes's System of Ideas*, London, 1965,
Ch. V.
[13] Strauss, Eg. Leo, *The Political Philosophy of Hobbes*, Oxford,
1936; Oakeshott, Michael, "The Moral Life in the Philosophy of
Hobbes", in: *Rationalism in Politics*, p. 248.
[14] *Leviathan*, Ch. 27.

that any man should perform first, if it be not likely that
the other will make good his promise after." The problem
is to understand the behaviour of the man who first performs the command of a newly instituted sovereign, and
one suggested solution to the problem is that he will be
one of those generous natures.[15]

If this is a correct solution to the First Performer problem, then Hobbes's theory of moral qualities must be allowed a greater importance than hitherto. But even if
the problem does not require the intervention of men
more generous than rational, we still have to account for
the fact that Hobbes gives an account of the just man as
one whose will is framed by justice, rather than by the
apparent benefit of what he is to do. If Hobbesian man is
simply determined by his desires modified by obligations,
then he is a calculating machine whose behaviour will
certainly be characterised by just action, but about whom
nothing more elaborate can be said. Yet we are told of a
class of human actions characterised by the relish of justice, which is attributable to "a certain nobleness or gal-
lantness of courage, rarely found, by which a man scorns
to be beholden for the contentment of his life, to fraud
or breach of promise".[16] Is this moral rarity inexplicable
within the terms of Hobbesian philosophy?

In discussing this question, we may discern four stages
by which natural man turns into a just citizen. These are
at least stages of exposition; whether they are stages of
any other sort we may consider later. The first stage is
that of natural man taken in isolation. As such, he is an
unreal figure, but his characteristics persist, though over-
laid, through to the final stage. Natural man is a creature in whom no artificial restraints have yet taken root;
he is a succession of thoughts and desires within a continuing body. There appears to be at this stage no questions of that distinction between the private thought and
the public face—a distinction to which Hobbes was ex-

---

[15] Oakeshott, op. cit., p. 294.
[16] *Leviathan*, Ch. 15, p. 97.

tremely sensitive. In discussing madness, he tells us: "For, I believe, the most sober men, when they walk alone without care and employment of the mind, would be unwilling the vanity and the extravagance of their thoughts at that time should be publicly seen; which is a confession, that passions unguided, are for the most part mere madness."[17] Here we have implicitly a picture of solitary man as a creature subject from moment to moment to internal and external pressures within which he lives. Later in the *Leviathan*, when Hobbes has described the whole process, he defines a natural person as "he whose words or actions are considered as his own", i. e. someone who has a stable identity in the world.[18] The description of the stages by which a man becomes a member of civil society is also, for Hobbes, an account of the generation of natural persons, and of the artificial person—the sovereign—who is one of their necessary conditions. A person is an artificial unity which has emerged from a natural plurality. At this first stage, there is nothing resembling a person, merely a succession of physical and psychological states.

The characteristics of man conceived abstractly at this first stage as a solitary creature may be gathered by implication from Hobbes's remarks. The second stage is the state of nature, and it is entirely explicit. It serves as a platform on which man's initial social dispositions may be displayed. What drives men into society? "All society" we learn "is either for gain, or for glory; that is, not so much for love of our fellows, as for the love of ourselves".[19] And supporting this, Hobbes turns the Aristotelian flank with a neat if superficial *reductio:* "For if by nature one man should love another (that is) as man, there could no reason be returned why every man should not equally love every man, as being equally man, or why he should rather frequent those whose society affords

[17] *Leviathan*, Ch. VIII, p. 48.
[18] *Leviathan*, Ch. XVI, p. 105.
[19] *De Cive*, I. 2.

him honour or profit." In this state of nature, a man by comparison discovers what he is like: because he looks up to most men, he finds he is short, and because they talk a lot, he discovers himself to be taciturn. But the purpose of intense comparing is not to make discoveries, but to indulge in the mind's most specific pleasure— glorying. Being a man of the word, Hobbes uses a talkative example: "But if it so happen, that being met, they pass their time in relating some stories, and one of them begins to tell one which concerns himself; instantly every one of the rest most greedily desires to speak of himself too".[20]

Here, then, are the impulses which drive men into social relations with one another. The effects are manifold, but one of them is to impose at least some element of social face upon the normally meandering mental processes. If men's thoughts are akin to madness "when they walk alone", they do at least attain some degree of order when others are present. Further, the split between inner and outer experience is widened. For conventions arise which impel man to repress certain of his natural tendencies: "The secret thoughts of a man run over all things, holy, profane, clean, obscene, grave, and light, without shame, or blame; which verbal discourse cannot do, farther than the judgment shall approve of the time, place, and persons".[21] In the state of nature, then, a man exists as a kind of social nucleus, distinguishing himself by contrast with other men, and becoming an individual in the contrast between his inner nature and his outward behaviour.

In the state of nature, furthermore, man's thoughts and feelings are additionally concentrated to a single point by the pervasiveness of fear. Being creatures impelled to explore the causes of their fortunes and misfortunes they are led to discover the desirability of peace, and also the ways in which peace might be secured. One aspect of

---

[20] *De Cive*, I. 2.
[21] *Leviathan*, Ch. VIII, p. 44.

man's misery in the state of nature is the diversity of his moral views. And in order to arrive at universally binding prescriptive conclusions, a moral philosopher must discover some universally agreed premise. Yet, as Hobbes insisted, the moral sphere in the state of nature is one of continual and radical disagreement, each moral judgement being merely the unstable creature of a passion. One common solution to this problem has been to suggest a fundamental circumstance in which all men *do* agree. Some theologians have thought that the imminence of death puts atheistical fancies to instant flight. And many philosophers have been tempted to believe that all men will agree on ethical fundamentals only provided that they reason in an entirely general manner. Hobbes uses this very argument in a subordinate role when he writes: "They therefore who could not agree concerning a present, do agree concerning a future good, which indeed is a work of reason; for things present are obvious to the sense, things to come to our reason only".[22] The state of nature, however, is for Hobbes the fundamental circumstance which unifies moral opinion: "All men easily acknowledge this state, as long as they are in it, to be evil, and by consequence that peace is good." Fear is, then, a highly philosophical passion, which on this subject inclines the minds of men to the same conclusions as those of a civil philosopher. The concluding however is unstable; the acknowledgement lasts "as long as they are in it" but may well be succeeded by other opinions if men are for a little time released from this fear.

This fact has interesting consequences for the status of the state of nature. We have seen that it is an expository device, and we have discussed it as a stage in the generation of the just citizen. It is much else. It actually exists among the Indians, and has existed in times past.[23] It remains a constant shadow over actual societies, for a long period of peace may, in an ill-governed society, re-

---

[22] *De Cive*, III, 31.
[23] *Leviathan*, Ch. XIII, p. 83; *De Cive*, I. 13.

lease vain-glorious passions which will tend to reconsti-
tute the state of war, men having to learn their lesson
all over again. Indeed, what is apparently a properly
ordered civil society may in actual fact be a society in
the condition of a state of nature. Hobbes is presumably
thinking of contemporary Europe, and especially England before the civil war, when he writes: "For those men
that are so remissly governed, that they take up arms to
defend, or introduce an opinion, are still in war; and their
condition not peace, but only a cessation of arms for fear
of one another; and they live, as it were, in the precincts
of battle continually".[24] The state of nature describes a
form of behaviour to which men are permanently liable.
And a prudent man will recognise it as a Damoclean
sword.

The transition from the state of nature to civil society,
from our second to third stage is obviously the hinge of
Hobbes's theory of the generation of the state. It is also
the point at which Hobbes appears to have generated a
moral character out of entirely naturalistic materials. In
considering this transition, we need to remember that
Hobbes has, by the terms in which he philosophises, forbidden himself the use of ideas like habit and custom. He
is in an intellectually difficult situation. He wishes to give
an account of the state as a structure of rational decisions; any suggestion of a temporal sequence is disad-
vantageous, because it immediately leads the reader to
think in irrelevantly realistic terms. On the other hand, a
philosopher who *does* employ narrative in explaining the
structure of civil society will be impelled by these realistic considerations to emphasise habit and the slow development of human institutions. In this latter case, the kind
of "snowball" account of society that we find in Hume is
likely to be produced. Now Hobbes is a man committed
both to a rationalistic account of society, and also to the
conventions of the social contract theory. Hence, at the
moment when civil society has been established, *all* the

---

[24] *Leviathan*, Ch. XVIII, p. 116–7.

relevant choices must be presumed to have been made, and all the requisite moral connections must have been asserted. But realism must then enter to emphasise that these choices have been quite unstable, and need to be converted into actual behaviour by the threat of the sword. For men will not abide by their decisions, particularly as the implications of these decisions come to seem increasingly remote.

For this reason, a split opens up between the naturalistic psychology and the moral obligations. The latter cannot at this point be allowed a causal status in holding Leviathan together. To this extent, those critics are justified who seek to cut through the apparently moralistic smokescreen and represent Hobbes simply as a power theorist; but what they describe is not Hobbes, but the result of an overloading of the Hobbesian system. Hobbes himself is drawn far enough in this direction to insist that the passion to be reckoned with is fear. The Sovereign is, in this rational system, a figure performing the same function as a Platonic philosopher-king: he supplies what is defective in the rationality of ordinary men. For the consequence of disobedience is the misery of the state of nature; but this may seem to many men a remote consequence of an impulsive disobedience. They will not reason that far. What is needed, then, is a power to inspire fear as an *immediate* consequence of disobedience, a sanction evident to the least rational of men. ". . . he that foresees what will become of a criminal, reckons what he has seen followed on the like crime before; having this order of thoughts, the crime, the officer, the prison, the judge, and the gallows. Which kind of thoughts, is called *foresight,* and *prudence,* or *providence*".[25] This is an altogether less taxing mental effort than the discovery and elaboration of the natural condition of men and the laws of nature.

A civil society can work, then, if we merely assume man's rational obligation to obey the state. Indeed,

---

[25] *De Cive*, I. 2.

Hobbes appears to think that this is the way most societies have worked, and do work; and it is also the reason why they are such ramshackle structures. For a body of men united in this way will never constitute a mortal god; it will never esteem iron as straw, and brass as rotten wood. Something more is needed; and that "more" is adumbrated in the complex of moral obligations, especially the implications of authorising the sovereign. But it cannot become effective unless it is fitted into the actual account of man's behaviour. And here the crucial point is what Hobbes does with the idea of obligation.

To be obliged is to be bound; and if I am physically obliged, then my behaviour is entirely determined. I do not have an alternative. This is the basic content of "obligation" and it must always be accommodated into any specification of the *kind* of obligation. When we talk of moral obligation, we mean similarly that I do not have a *moral* alternative to the behaviour described in the content of the obligation. But while I may not have a moral alternative, I do have a psychological one. Obligation is, consequently, a usefully ambiguous term, because it can simultaneously refer to acts which do, and which do not, have alternatives; corresponding to this ambiguity, it may have a naturalistic or a moral use.

Now for the establishment of civil society, as I have argued, "rational obligation" is a minimum but a sufficient condition. We simply require that men *are* miserable in the state of nature, that they *do* reason and agree that peace is good, that they actually work out the ways to peace, and that they authorize the sovereign. This is, on Hobbes's argument what men do, "by a certain impulsion of nature, no less than that whereby a stone moves downward".[26] This achieves the link Hobbes wished to make with the natural law tradition, which was powerfully persuasive. And it also supplied, as we shall see, a crucial link between the naturalistic argument and the moral conclusions.

---

[26] *De Cive*, I, 7.

This problem is faced in an interesting and difficult passage in Ch. 15 beginning, in a parody of Psalm 14, "The fool hath said in his heart, there is no such thing as justice . . .".[27] The point about this fool is that he exemplifies purely rational obligation, and believes that justice is *nothing more than* rational obligation, and goes on to conclude that he may act unjustly if he sees that it is to his advantage. The discussion proceeds somewhat obscurely to rather weak conclusions. It is argued out in terms of short-term and long-term interest: "when a man doth a thing, which notwithstanding any thing can be foreseen, and reckoned on, tendeth to his own destruction, howsoever some accident which he could not expect, arriving may turn it to his benefit; yet such events do not make it reasonably or wisely done." And again: ". . . he which declares he thinks it reason to deceive those that help him, can *in reason*[28] expect no other means of safety, than what can be had from his own single power. He therefore that breaketh his covenant, *and consequently declareth that he thinks he may with reason* do so, cannot be received into any society, that unite themselves for peace and defence, but by the error of them that received him; nor when he is received, be retained in it, without seeing the danger of their error; which error a man cannot reasonably reckon upon as a means of his security." Such behaviour is "against the reason of his preservation".[29]

Faced with such difficulties, it is not surprising that at this point Hobbes is tempted into switching his concept of reason from the servant and scout of earlier stages in the argument, to Reason the master of the passions, as found in the natural law tradition. On his usual view, reason is subordinate to a plurality of shifting passions, and what Hobbes requires is moral unification. Reason, as he has earlier conceived it, cannot supply that. And, in

[27] *Leviathan*, Ch. XV, p. 94.
[28] *Leviathan*, p. 96, my italics.
[29] *Ibid.*, my italics.

a sense, he does not need it. Yet he is still tempted in this passage to use "reason", in sentence after sentence, as a bludgeon to silence the fool. Such arguments would hardly convince a clever rogue who thought his contemporaries were gullible; and in fact, of course, (as the Psalms often complain) the wicked often flourish like the green bay tree.

It seems to me that these difficulties would disappear if we take moral obligation as a fourth stage in the emergence of the state, and that such an ordering is a submerged pattern in Hobbes's system. The term "obligation" refers to a determination of the behaviour, and is consequently linked to the sequence of hypothetical causes which preceded it. The term "moral" indicates the manner of the determination. What is this manner, and what generates it? It arises from the act of authorisation of the sovereign, an act which, properly understood, fixes the will of a man to the performance of those acts which the sovereign has commanded. This is a unity of the mind which runs counter to the passions of men; consequently it is a kind of second nature imposed upon men by their own wills. It can only become this second nature by a modification of man's passions, and particularly of those respects in which a man finds his self-esteem. And it must be self-imposed, rather than something held in place by such an external factor as the fear of punishment. This fourth stage is alike the emergence of ethics, of civilisation, and indeed of disinterestedness—and in a system like that of Hobbes, disinterestedness can only be a carelessness of consequences, resembling irrationality. In this respect, moral obligation is "beyond reason", at least as reason is defined in Hobbes's argument. Moral obligation is also non-rational in that where it operates men naturally are disposed to peaceable behaviour, and do not need reason to supply inducements to it. At this stage, the external unity of the law-abiding citizen—whose behaviour is determined by the sovereign and his punitive apparatus—has become the internal unity of the moral person.

Such behaviour is that of a paragon, and it would no doubt be unrealistic to look for it in any one man. In spite of this, Hobbes seems to have thought that such generous natures, though rare, did exist. Hobbes's account of moral obligation is, consequently, the description of a type of man. It is also, as we have arranged it, a stage in Hobbes's argument. Above all, however, it is a kind of behaviour. For the point of each of these stages is that they are never superseded, and each of them is a perfectly accurate description of some of the behaviour likely to be exhibited by any actual person. Moral obligation can be taught, and Hobbes believes that it ought to be taught and disseminated by the sovereign. But being a realist, he feels that most obedience to the sovereign, most of the time, will be rational rather than moral.

III.

My argument has been highly selective. It has, in particular, paid little attention to the prescriptive apparatus which is so prominent in Hobbes's political writings. But that prescriptive apparatus is itself difficult to sustain, and the two writers on politics who had most evidently digested Hobbes's philosophy—Spinoza and Hume—agreed in dispensing with it altogether. As Professor Oakeshott has written in another connection: "For, perhaps with some colour of paradox, it now appears that the power necessary to establish peace and to compel the keeping of covenants is generated not by making the covenant but only in the process of keeping it, that is, in dispositions and acts of obedience".[30] Intertwined with the social contract material is the sequence I have emphasised, in which the generation of the state is described as an intelligible series of kinds of behaviour. Can we discover any further principles which determine this sequence?

The main principle, it seems to me, is one of increas-

---

[30] Oakeshott, op. cit., p. 296-7.

ing unification. Solitary natural man is a plurality of passions; when desire is strong, any one of these can impose a temporary unity both upon the operations of his mind and of his behaviour. Man in the state of nature has as a further unifying element, the presence of other men, in whose eyes he wishes to construct a permanent social identity, one which others will recognise as superior. Rational fear projects him one stage further: To the extent that he recognises this fear as fundamental and overriding, a man will subordinate his other passions into a system of behaviour consistent with his survival. And to the extent that this does not happen internally, it is provided with an external focus in the artificial person of the sovereign. And when a man has recognised a moral obligation, pride and self-esteem will have been harnessed to a consistent line of behaviour whose immediate impulsion is entirely from within.

The identity of a moral person, as it appears in these stages, is a man's commitment to peace and civil obedience. And from this primary commitment stem the variety of subordinate agreements which a man can make in the situation of trust created by the state. The Hobbesian citizen can say: I am obliged, therefore I am. And in this way he has acquired a single mask by which he is recognised in society.

This argument suggests a second principle of the sequence we have discussed. At each stage, a man's grip on the reality of his human situation has broadened, until by the fourth stage, it is equivalent in many respects to that of the philosopher. We have here, in fact, an equivalence of knowledge and virtue which is almost inevitably found in philosophical accounts of goodness, but which the heavily rationalist apparatus of Hobbes's thought manages pretty effectually to conceal. Indeed, in *De Cive*, though not in *Leviathan* Hobbes is quite explicit about the connection, for there he adds a twentieth law of nature different from the twentieth which appears at the end of *Leviathan*. "Furthermore, forasmuch as the laws of nature are nought else but the dictates of reason, so as, unless a man endeavours to preserve the faculty of right reasoning he cannot observe the laws of nature, it is manifest, that he who knowingly or willingly, doth aught whereby the rational faculty may be destroyed or weakened, he knowingly, and willingly, breaks the law of nature . . . But they destroy and weaken the reasoning faculty, who do that which disturbs the mind from its natural state; that which most manifestly happens to drunkards and gluttons. We therefore sin, in the twentieth place, against the law of nature by drunkenness".[31]

Hobbes presents us with an account of the generation of civilised man by a steady refinement of what look initially like rather unpromising materials. Part of the plausibility of this process results from the fact that in many ways it parallels the way in which society manufactures citizens out of babies. In Hobbes we have a profound exploration of the pessimistic platitude that civilisation is merely a veneer over natural barbarism—and earlier generations commonly took children as barbarians who had to be civilised by the stick. The end product of this evolution resembles Spinoza's rational man who has released himself from the bondage of the passions, and is distinguished by the fact that he is active, not passive. Similarly, a generous nature is one with a firm and civilised character of his own, one not entirely at the mercy of the ceaseless pressure of passion and environment.

---

[31] *De Cive*, III, 25.

HOBBES ON THE KNOWLEDGE OF GOD

RONALD HEPBURN

Hobbes wrote copiously on the philosophy of religion:
so copiously that one would expect him to have made
his viewpoint and attitude about religion abundantly
clear. Yet there could not have been greater disagreement
among his interpreters and critics, from his own day to
the present. Many have seen him as a crypto-atheist,
and all he wrote on God's incomprehensible nature as
obliquely sceptical. It has been argued that, for all the
bulk of Hobbes's writing about religion, the grounding
of his moral and political philosophy in no way depends
upon theological beliefs. These beliefs are idling wheels
in his system, and we can eliminate them without loss.
But other commentators—some of them very recent writers—take an entirely different view and see Hobbes's
theology as integral to his thought as a whole. If Hobbes
had wanted to construct an essentially secular system,
they say, he would hardly have made his theology so ar-
resting and controversial a structure in its own right.

On the other hand, it is not so eccentric a structure
that we cannot find echoes in it of undoubtedly serious
and central theologians such as Tertullian, Aquinas, and
Calvin. Where Hobbes is agnostic, they are agnostic also.
The incompetence of natural reasoning about God's nature and the Christian's dependence upon scriptural revelation are themes common to late medieval fideism and
mid-twentieth-century biblical theology. There are post-
Wittgensteinian fideists: and even a Roman Catholic
philosopher like Peter Geach can seriously look for support for his religious moral philosophy to Hobbes's account of morality and divine command (*God and the
Soul*, 1969, pp. 117 ff).

This essay was written especially for this volume by R. W. Hepburn, Professor of Philosophy, University of Edinburgh.

To A. E. Taylor, "a certain kind of theism is absolutely necessary to make [Hobbes's] theory work," e.g., his theory of natural law (*Hobbes Studies*, ed. K. C. Brown, 1965, p. 50). What Hobbes's critics have often taken as "insincere verbiage" on the topic of deity was in fact a very proper repudiation of anthropomorphism.

With equal assurance, however, other writers have urged that such theologically solemn readings of Hobbes are misguided and naïve. It is often argued that Hobbes's laws of nature can perfectly well be taken as rational, prudential principles in need of no supernatural sanction. D. P. Gauthier argues (in *The Logic of Leviathan*, 1969) that Hobbes's philosophy is a "secular" philosophy: both its formal structure and its material content are independent of theological beliefs (pp. 204 f). All obligations are human creations: in general an obligation not to do X is created by laying down the natural right to do X (pp. 40 f). This is not to deny that Hobbes saw the laws of nature as divine laws; but it is not *as* divine laws that "the laws of nature enter into Hobbes's moral theory" (pp. 69 f).

F. S. McNeilly (*The Anatomy of Leviathan*, 1968) believes that "it is not of the least importance to Hobbes . . . to regard God as author of the laws of nature" (pp. 211 f). Hobbes could have denied God's existence altogether, without weakening his arguments in the least degree. More generally, "in Hobbes's philosophy, and in most of the philosophy of his time, God was kicked upstairs": he was "not assassinated, but retired into constitutional monarchy." He was like a machine maker who subsequently "keeps his finger out of the works" (p. 22).

Other writers have complained not simply that theism *idles* in Hobbes, but that it is, rather, a positive source of confusion. "Hobbes speaks strangely of God, if his purpose is to make use of him to explain why we obey our rulers"; strangely, because appeal to an avowedly "incomprehensible" being can hardly explain or clarify anything. And if it is by *revealed* doctrine that we learn of divine punishment hereafter (and thus that we should keep the covenant that creates sovereignty), that doctrine comes with the authority of the sovereign himself! (John Plamenatz, in *Hobbes Studies*, p. 80.)

On yet another view, Hobbes's system requires atheism, and only circumspection prevented him saying so. Leo Strauss sees Hobbes's theory of natural law as "deduced from the most powerful of all passions"—namely, "fear of violent death at the hands of others." This fear, however, is reliably the most powerful, only if it is not in competition with fear of *supernatural* powers. It is thus an "a-religious or atheistic society" that Hobbes's philosophy really requires, despite all his theological protestations (*Hobbes Studies*, pp. 12, 26 f).

These brief samplings may serve to indicate the range of disagreement over Hobbes's philosophy of religion. I am not going to engage in debate with those rival interpretations seriatim, nor argue in detail over the question of Hobbes's sincerity or insincerity. Rather, I shall concentrate on a small number of central themes in his philosophy of religion and ask the question *"How good or bad* is this part of Hobbes's writing?" The topics will be: (1) Hobbes's arguments for the existence of God; (2) the problem of our knowledge of God's nature: the incompetence of natural reasoning, and the incomprehensibility of God; (3) a tension between two moments in Hobbes's theology, the one making God sublimely remote and disengaged from the world, the other bringing him into a very close relation with nature; and (4) Hobbes's fideism.

It is easily shown that Hobbes constructed his philosophy of religion out of theological materials that had a thoroughly respectable, indeed distinguished history. Nevertheless, I want to argue, his peculiar way of *putting together* these materials, the roles he wanted them to play in his system, come very close to being self-stultifying or self-undermining. Because there is confusion at a fundamental level (in his discourse about God as such), Hobbes's theological claims cannot serve him as a foundation or grounding for morals or politics.

Does this not open the way to seeing Hobbes as indeed a sceptical propagandist, an oblique sceptic, who shows that a coherent theology cannot be fashioned? I am dubious about this, on two scores. First: the case against Hobbes's sincerity is much weaker than has often been supposed (see, e.g., W. B. Glover, in *Hobbes Studies*, Chapter 7). Second: if it was his consistent intention to show this incoherence, he had the wit, the subtlety, and certainly the courage to show it much more effectively than he did, even if still obliquely and under a "front" of theism. As it is, he missed many chances of sharpening the sceptically tending side of his theological writing: too many for this to be a convincing interpretation of his aim.

It is most reasonable to see Hobbes's philosophy of religion as an unsuccessful venture—unsuccessful either as construction or as destruction. One can pass that verdict upon the venture as a whole, but nevertheless see parts of it as retaining real philosophical interest.

1. Hobbes's Arguments for the Existence of God

Various versions of causal and teleological arguments are scattered about Hobbes's writings. A recent discussion of them appears in "Hobbes' Grounds for Belief in a Deity" by K. C. Brown (in *Philosophy*, 1962). Hobbes claimed we can know that God exists by the light of natural reason, and (according to Brown) he saw teleological reasoning as the more fundamental form of argument. Brown repudiates Strauss's claim that these arguments constitute only a "residue of tradition which contradicts the whole of Hobbes's philosophy." Hobbes in fact used teleological arguments at the beginning of their period of greatest popularity.

On the power of natural reason to show God's existence, Hobbes, it seems to me, has an equivocal position. There are places where he restricts the scope of philosophical reason to what is "generated." "The *subject* of Philosophy . . . is every body of which we can conceive any generation, . . . or which is capable of composition and resolution." Theology, in contrast, is concerned with the "doctrine of God, eternal, ingenerable, incomprehensible" (*English Works of Thomas Hobbes of Malmesbury*, Vol. I, p. 10. These volumes hereafter will be referred to as E.W.). Equally certainly there are places where Hobbes does allow philosophical reasoning the capacity to show God's existence. K. C. Brown quotes Hobbes's words in *De Cive*, that "by the light of nature it may be known that there is a God" (E.W., Vol. II, p. 27). In its context this is a very unstressed and incidental remark—within a discussion of *oaths*; but it is not unique. Hobbes wrote to Bramhall: "It is agreed between us, that right reason dictates there is a God" (E.W., Vol. IV, p. 293; also noted by Brown, loc. cit.).

Could not God's *nature* be incomprehensible, and yet the question of his *existence* be within the scope of reason? This is a familiar and tempting reconciling formula, and one expressly relied upon by Hobbes (e.g., E.W., Vol. IV, pp. 59 f). But it is not a satisfactory view. Something does have to be knowable about his nature before we could even meaningfully identify the being whose existence reason is investigating. It is true that Hobbes admits the existence of countless beings whose nature he declares is unknowable to us by natural reason.

> In this natural kingdom of God, there is no other way to know anything, but by natural reason, that is, from the principles of natural science; which are so far from teaching us any thing of God's nature, as they cannot teach us our own nature, nor the nature of the smallest creature living. [E.W., Vol. III, pp. 353 f.]

Hobbes's scepticism about our knowledge of God's nature, nevertheless, runs far more deeply than his scepticism about "generated" beings: so deeply that it is a real problem whether he can say enough to conduct an argument about the divine existence.

In some contexts Hobbes does not make a contrast between God's existence, knowable by reason, and God's

attributes, incomprehensible. He includes existence
among the divine attributes, and the contrast becomes
one between attributes that are and are not accessible
to reason. This carries Hobbes at least to the borders of
the Ontological Argument. "It is manifest, we ought
to attribute to him *existence*. For no man can have the
will to honour that, which he thinks not to have any
being." ". . . There is but one name to signify our conception of his nature, and that is, I AM" (E.W., Vol.
III, pp. 350 f, 353; cf. E.W., Vol. II, p. 216). Hobbes's
language hesitates between offering a *clarification* of natural religious thinking about God, and an ontological
argument in the proper sense, whereby God's existence
is demonstrated from the conception of supreme perfection itself. Hobbes does not elaborate the latter possibility—consistent though it would be with his great emphasis on thinking worthily enough about God: it was
very much *less* consistent with the empiricist side of his
thought.

Even if it were true that teleological argument is, on
the whole, more important to Hobbes than purely causal
argument, he nevertheless does deploy some arguments
to God as the ultimate *causal power*. God is "the first
power of all powers and first cause of all causes" (E.W.,
Vol. IV, pp. 59 f). In order to explain the various effects
"we acknowledge naturally," we must presuppose "something existent that hath [the] power" to produce them;
and this in turn, "if it were not eternal, must needs have
been produced by somewhat before it . . . till we come
to an eternal, that is to say, the first power of all powers
and first cause of all causes; and this it is which all men
conceive by the name of God" (E.W., Vol. IV, pp. 59 f).

This type of argument is an integral part of Hobbes's
necessitarianism. God is the "first link" in the chains of
causality. "By the word *God* we understand the *world's
cause*" (E.W., Vol. II, pp. 213 f). He does sound a possible teleological note three sentences later, where he defends God's "government of the world of mankind"; but
this is an *a priori* argument from divine perfection, not

an *a posteriori* argument from the design we find in the world. In *Leviathan,* causal and teleological arguments do indeed appear together in one sentence. "By the visible things in this world, and their admirable order, a man may conceive there is a cause of them, which men call God" (E.W., Vol. III, p. 93: cf. Brown, p. 342). But it is hard to see Hobbes as giving any priority to the teleological aspect, since many more words, earlier in the same paragraph, are given to the argument from the regress of causal dependence. This regress leads "of necessity . . . to this thought at last, that there is some cause, whereof there is no former cause, but is eternal; which it is men call God." And in the next chapter Hobbes returns again to the specifically causal version. "The acknowledging of one God eternal [etc.] may more easily be derived" from desire to know "causes of natural bodies," than from fear (E.W., Vol. III, p. 95).

Two other teleological reflections are quoted by K. C. Brown. One is in *Decameron Physiologicum* (E.W., Vol. VII, pp. 175 ff): ". . . it is very hard to believe, that to produce male and female, and all that belongs thereto, as also the several and curious organs of sense and memory, could be the work of anything that had not understanding." Then in *De Homine* (*Complete Latin Works of Thomas Hobbes of Malmesbury,* Vol. II, p. 6; hereafter referred to as L.W.) Hobbes declares how evident it is that the mechanisms of generation and nutrition are "constructed by some mind [*a mente aliqua*]." The topic reappears on pp. 106 f: When men contemplated the vastness of heaven and earth and the "*organorum ingeniosissimam fabricam,*" they were moved both to a sense of their own insignificance and to marvel at the "*incomprehensibile illud, a quo condita sunt maxima.*"

While Hobbes certainly alludes in these places to teleological argumentation, and presents such an argument in *outline*, his allusions are much too perfunctory and incidental to provide a philosophical foundation for theism. He makes no attempt, for instance, to show that one could identify a designer ("some mind") with the one, infinite, eternal deity, perfect in his attributes. If one looks at the contexts of the allusions to teleology, the impression of perfunctoriness is confirmed. The passage in *Decameron Physiologicum* occurs in a discussion of whether the earth has retained the power of producing new living creatures. The teleological argument is brief, naïvely presented, and in no way defended against possible objections. Nor is it any more fully treated in L.W., Vol. II, p. 6, where it occupies part of one sentence only, though it is forceful in expression. The later reference in *De Homine* (L.W., Vol. II, pp. 106 f) occupies at least one long sentence; but here Hobbes's main concern is with tracing the origin of the sense of "natural piety" (in a chapter entitled "De Affectionibus"), not with advancing grounds for theistic belief.

Does the specifically causal argument fare any better? It involves a formidable *religious* difficulty—namely, whether a being who is involved in the series of causes and effects (even if as "first member") can have sufficient transcendence to be the God of Christian theism.

The most serious *philosophical* question to ask about Hobbes's causal argument is whether he completely undermined his own use of it, in the well-known passage in *De Corpore*, Chapter 26, "Of the World and the Stars." In that chapter Hobbes states that only a very few questions can be investigated about the world as such, "and those we can determine, none." Considering the world's duration, we ask "whether it had a beginning or be eternal"; and "if it had a beginning, then by what cause . . . and again whence that cause . . . till at last we come to one or many eternal cause or causes" (loc. cit.). Now, knowledge of the infinite is unattainable by a "finite enquirer." And though a man can

> ascend continually by right ratiocination from cause to cause; yet he will not be able to proceed eternally, but wearied will at last give over, without knowing whether it were possible for him to proceed to an end or not.

From "Nothing can move itself" it may rightly be inferred that there was some first eternal movent; yet it can never be inferred . . . that that movent was eternally immoveable, but rather eternally moved [*aeternum motum*—L.W., Vol. I, p. 336]. For as it is true, that nothing is moved by itself; so it is true also that nothing is moved but by that which is already moved. The questions, therefore about the magnitude and beginning of the world, are not to be determined by philosophers, but by those that are lawfully authorized to order the worship of God.

Hobbes therefore cannot commend people who "boast they have demonstrated" that the world had a beginning (E.W., Vol. I, pp. 411–13).

How much damage, then, does Hobbes do here to his own use of causal arguments to God? K. C. Brown argues that Hobbes is primarily concerned to chasten those who claim to "demonstrate" the existence of God in a very strong sense. Where demonstration is impossible, the mind may yet be "inclined" to belief rather than to unbelief. Hobbes does indeed inveigh against would-be demonstrators. But he also denies that we can "*determine*" any of the ultimate cosmological questions by philosophical reasoning. "Determining" is a broader notion than that of quasi-mathematical demonstration—as is evident from the fact that those cosmological questions are to be "determined" by religious authorities. These latter will certainly not demonstrate them *more geometrico*.

Hobbes is surely expressing a deep scepticism about our ability to infer from given causal dependences to an eternal mover, not itself moved. Fatigue rather than logic prevents the regress of causal explanation being indefinitely pursued. Even if we are able to postulate a "first eternal movent," that being cannot without more ado, be identified with God: for the eternal mover may eternally owe its motion to another. Hobbes does not go on to argue that a regress of eternally moved

movers is impossible; reason cannot, here, decide between "one or many eternal cause or causes" (E.W., Vol.
I, pp. 411, 412). K. C. Brown states that in the last resort "Hobbesian matter cannot create itself by its own
motions, nor determine its own basic characteristics." Nor
indeed, one wants to say, can anything else. If we want
to reach theism, we have to rule out what Hobbes denies we can rule out, viz., the possibility that the eternal
cause of the world (whatever it was) might itself be a
movens, only because it is also, eternally, a *motum*.

In *Human Nature*, as we saw, Hobbes did claim that
the causal regress led reliably to "an eternal, that is to
say, the first power of all powers, and first cause of all
causes . . . which all men conceive by the name of God"
(E.W., Vol. IV, pp. 59 f); and in *Leviathan* he claimed
"that which is eternal has no cause" (E.W., Vol. III,
p. 351). Here Hobbes ignores the possibility that what is
eternal might, even so, be still moved itself, a *motum*.
To accept the *De Corpore* passage cannot fail to undermine these versions of the causal argument.

A rejoinder might be offered on these lines. Hobbes
is no more sceptical than St. Thomas Aquinas; for St.
Thomas also denied that we can know by natural reason
whether or not the world had a temporal beginning. We
can learn this by revelation alone. And that did not prevent St. Thomas from making his First and Second
"Ways" versions of causal argument. Only they were not
arguments from the impossibility of infinite *temporal*
causal regresses, but from the impossibility of an infinite
regress of *simultaneous* causal conditions. "A thing
which exists always is not exempted from needing another in order to exist" (*Disputations* III, *De Pot.*, 13,
ad 1: trans. T. Gilby).

In the causal arguments we have sampled from
Hobbes, however, we do not find him exploiting this distinction. The regress of causes leads to some existent
which, "if it were not eternal, must needs have been produced by somewhat *before* it"; and so back to God as
first cause (E.W., Vol. IV, pp. 59 f): or, in *Leviathan*, to

"some cause whereof there is no *former* cause, but is eternal . . ." (my italics in both quotations).[1]

Furthermore, if Hobbes wished seriously to defend the logic of argument from world to God, it is hard to understand why he made no attempt in the *De Corpore* passage to restrict its obviously sceptical implications: either on St. Thomas' lines—even if the world were eternal, it would be eternally insufficient without God—or else by arguing that although causal argument is unreliable, the *design* argument is unaffected. If Hobbes saw teleological considerations as fundamental to his theism, and saw theism as fundamental to his whole system, it is extraordinary that he made no extended allusion to teleology in a chapter on what can be known by reason about "the world and the stars."

In a word, Hobbes's natural religious arguments for God's existence are not well presented or well defended. On the other hand, there is no strong case for seeing them as consistently ironical and obliquely sceptical—though the *De Corpore* passage does make it hard to see him as caring whether his reader retains belief in arguments from the world to God.[2]

---

[1] I stress the temporal reference in these contexts, in view of K. C. Brown's remark (itself looking back to A. G. Wernham) that "Hobbes's concept of 'a cause' had *no* necessary connection with antecedent motion, or with temporal antecedence at all" (op. cit., p. 341). Brown may well be right that the ambiguities of Hobbes's concept of cause made it difficult for him clearly to distinguish between First Mover and Teleological types of argument.

[2] K. C. Brown wrote: "the Argument from Design is immune to the objections raised against 'proofs' of the beginning of the world in the *De Corpore* passage . . . since its whole assumption is that one recognizes the possibility that the world might have had no Creator, but decides that the wonders of nature make this incredible" (op. cit., p. 341).

Three comments: (i) I have not wished to deny that Hobbes could consistently appeal to the Design Argument, in a dispute over the scope of the sceptical arguments in *De Corpore.*

(ii) I do wish to claim, however, that the *De Corpore* passage (which I have quoted more fully than Brown) is more potentially sceptical than Brown brings out, or than Hobbes himself may have

2. God's Nature as "Incomprehensible"

We may know *that* God is, not *what* he is; for we have
no knowledge of infinites. Attributes we do apply to God
are expressions either of our inability to comprehend him
or of our desire to honour him. To speak, for instance, of
God's *wisdom* is to speak of "an incomprehensible attribute given to an incomprehensible nature, for to honour
him" (E.W., Vol. V, p. 212). To *philosophize* about such
attributes necessarily results in deeper obscurity, not in
clarification. What we say about God must be limited
to what the Scriptures authorize us to say. This is a perplexing position, for if God's nature is altogether incomprehensible, what meaning can our discourse about him
possess—whether or not the words we use of him are the
words of Scripture?[3]

The basic difficulty about divine attributes is nicely
expressed by Hume in the *Dialogues*. Demea argues that
"if it appear more *pious and respectful* (as it really is)
still to retain these terms, when we mention the supreme
Being, we ought to acknowledge, that their meaning, in
that case, is totally incomprehensible." To which Cle-

---

realized. The Argument from Design is *not* "immune" to the critique it presents in outline. It is not till Hume that these difficulties are vividly seen and expressed (though Hume drew upon Strato
and Bayle): the chief problem being how to prevent a regress of
designing minds, if any move beyond the world is ventured at all.
(Cf. *Dialogues* IV.) But, once more, I am not following those writers who see Hobbes as deliberately and systematically sabotaging
his own theism, argument by argument.

(iii) Brown has not really persuaded me that although the First
Mover Argument is "an important supporting argument," the Argument from Design is "the more fundamental" to Hobbes.

[3] Cf. A. G. N. Flew, "Hobbes," in *A Critical History of Western
Philosophy*, ed. D. J. O'Connor, 1964, p. 169: "Revelation is at
most a way of learning that something is true; this problem is one
of understanding." Cf. also J. S. Mill (against Mansel): "all trust
in a Revelation presupposes a conviction that God's attributes are
the same, in all but degree, with the best human attributes" (*Examination of Sir William Hamilton's Philosophy*, Chapter 7).

anthes replies: "If our ideas . . . be not just and adequate, and correspondent to [God's] real nature, I know not what there is in this subject worth insisting on. Is the name, without any meaning, of such mighty importance?" (*Dialogues Concerning Natural Religion*, ed. Kemp Smith, pp. 157 f).

Hobbes certainly saw the pertinence of this question, where the doctrines of schoolmen were concerned. Scholastic writings abounded in names without meaning. "Incorporeal spirit" and "eternal now" were precisely that. Hobbes did wish, however, to accept many propositions about God—namely the propositions of Scripture—while himself acknowledging that many of those too were incomprehensible! He relied, in doing so, on a distinction between two sorts of incomprehensibility—"of words" and "of the thing." "When the nature of the thing is incomprehensible, I can acquiesce in the Scripture: but when the significance of words is incomprehensible, I cannot acquiesce in the authority of a Schoolman" (*An Answer to Bishop Bramhall*, E.W., Vol. IV, p. 314). He relied also on a distinction between what is "*contrary*" to reason and what is "*above*" reason (E.W., Vol. III, p. 360). Can these distinctions, as Hobbes presents them, bear the weight he required them to bear?

God is described, for instance, as speaking to Moses on Mount Sinai. "To say God spake and appeared as he is in his own nature, is to deny his infiniteness, invisibility, incomprehensibility. . . ." Therefore, Hobbes concludes, "in what manner God spake . . . is not intelligible" (E.W., Vol. III, pp. 419 f). Here is Hobbes taking his own advice to "captivate our understanding to the words [of Scripture]" (E.W., Vol. III, p. 360). *Without* such captivating, Hobbes could have made as good a case for this scriptural claim as being *contrary* to reason as he did with any scholastic metaphysical paradox.

But we have seen that the incomprehensibility is not limited to particular cruces: it affects virtually all discourse about God. How do we know that it is due to "the incomprehensibility of the thing" and not mere "incom-

prehensibility of words"? I do not think this *can* be
known, on Hobbes's account. In order to know it, we
should have to have some kind of independent access
to, or experience of, the "thing," by virtue of which we
could then say, "Our words fall short of their target; but
our aim and direction are at least roughly correct." Such
an account may be open to a writer who accepts a hier-
archical ontology, and admits enough continuity between
predication in the human and in the divine spheres for
a doctrine of analogy to be possible. In most contexts,
however, Hobbes so emphasizes *dis*continuity that this
route is quite barred to him. Moreover, the whole bias of
Hobbes's philosophy of human nature runs against his
admitting any range of distinctively religious experiences
from which one could extrapolate so as to obtain some
inkling of a divine mode of being, freed from the limiting
conditions of human existence. The task is to have "faith
reposed in him that speaketh" (in the Scriptures),
"though the mind be incapable of any notion at all from
the words spoken" (E.W., Vol. III, p. 360). Discourse
about God seems, in such a view, to break down altogether.

Hobbes might reply by repeating his claim that the
force of such discourse is to "honour," not to describe,
God; it signifies "neither true nor false . . . but the reverence and devotion of our hearts" (E.W., Vol. V, p. 6).
Honouring and revering are certainly intelligible performances. But on what *grounds* is it said that God should
be honoured and revered? This relevant question carries us back again, inevitably, to scriptural narrative. The
scriptural authors testify to God's mighty acts, to revealing events. Some at least of these crucial narratives, however, rely upon language that is avowedly incomprehensible. It is hard, therefore, to see how we can find a
basis here for judging whether or not honorific epithets
are the appropriate ones. While it makes sense to speak
of relying on witnesses of events remote from us in space
or in time, it does not make sense to speak of this when

both the events and the possibility of their being witnessed are *inconceivable*.

Hobbes does, on occasion, try to mitigate the problem. "It is to be noted," he wrote, "that when God speaks to men concerning his will and other attributes, he speaks of them as if they were like to those of men, to the end he may be understood" (E.W., Vol. V, p. 14). But this claim that we do understand, at least sometimes, is hard to reconcile with the other and repeated claim that in revealed discourse about God the mind is "incapable of any notion at all from the words spoken." It implies, once again, a continuity between ordinary and theistic senses of words, which elsewhere Hobbes emphatically repudiates. Besides, it introduces a new logical problem. If we are to accept that God speaks of his attributes as if they were like human attributes, we must already be able to attach sense to the proposition "God speaks"—i.e., we must understand personhood and speech as attributes of the infinite God. But since this prior condition is not in fact fulfilled, we are not in a position to take anthropomorphic discourse as a reliable guide to understanding God's nature and will.

In many contexts Hobbes looks for guidance about what can and cannot be said of God to the notion of *divine perfection*. Leaving aside the question of justifying this procedure, let us consider what Hobbes in fact does with this important notion. The logic of religious discourse is a logic of superlatives: "we honour not God worthily, if we ascribe less *power* or *greatness* to him than possibly we can" (E.W., Vol. II, p. 214). We have to eliminate all attributions that "signify some finite and limited thing" (ibid.). We cannot say, therefore, that God has *shape*, or *parts*. Such concepts as *sight, knowledge*, or *understanding*, in any sense we can understand, involve the ideas of passivity and dependence. What they could be in Deity we have no conception whatever (E.W., Vol. II, pp. 214–16).

A reader might well wonder whether Hobbes is slyly

exploiting the theme of divine perfection, in the interests, ultimately, of scepticism. Bearing in mind that Hobbes also claimed that God was *corporeal* spirit, his corporeality is (to say the least) on the brink of being qualified to nothing: no parts, no shape. But I do not see internal or external evidence to show that Hobbes himself meant his reader to take his writing in this way. Such a reading would, I dare say, be compatible with Hobbes's use of the perfection argument to support his "corporeal spirit" doctrine itself. "Immaterial" or "incorporeal substances" were postulated by Plato and Aristotle, "heathens, who mistook those thin inhabitants of the brain they see in sleep for so many *incorporeal* men. . . . Do you think it an honour to God to be one of these?" (E.W., Vol. IV, pp. 426 f).

Nonetheless, Hobbes does not consistently and cunningly seize upon any and every use of the perfection argument to increase the offence to reason—whether by piling up the paradoxes or by reducing theological claims to nullity. He will not allow, for instance, that God is "infinite in all his attributes," though such a claim has the *prima facie* ring of a perfection argument. It is in fact unscriptural nonsense (E.W., Vol. V, p. 344). So too is the "*nunc stans*" account of God's eternity, with which it is logically connected.

It looks, once again, as if an increase in "honour" is paid to God when a theologian says that God is not just, but justice itself; not eternal, but eternity itself; not wise but wisdom itself. On the contrary, Hobbes claims, these are

> unseemly words to be said of God, that he is not just . . . eternal . . . wise; and cannot be excused by any following *but*, especially when the *but* is followed by that which is not to be understood. Can any man understand how justice is just, or wisdom wise? [E.W., Vol. V, p. 342.]

3. A Tension in Hobbes's Account of God

One of the chief problems for any theism is to develop the themes of divine transcendence and perfection to the fullest possible extent—yet without allowing discourse about God to become sublimely empty. As already noted, Hobbes has been seen by some critics as wanting precisely that: to escort God safely upstairs, to "sky" him, or assert so radical a discontinuity between world and God that his existence makes no difference to us and can be altogether discounted. Certainly, the skying movement is present in Hobbes's writing: but I have argued that it is not consistently directed to this end. It needs to be added that the whole transcending, skying, movement of Hobbes's theology is in tension with another movement, no less important to him—in which God is attached firmly to this world, let us say, "earthed." These are in tension, because although one could easily enough reconcile the two movements in a verbal formula, "God is both transcendent and immanent," Hobbes gives no real help in bringing them into a convincingly unified account. Rather, his concept of God splits into two irreconcilable parts, the one transcendent to the point of sheer incomprehensibility; and the other involving God too closely with nature, as part of nature itself.

Hobbes argues expressly against the total disengagement of God from his creation; and he invokes, interestingly, a perfection argument to make his point.

> They . . . have a wretched apprehension of God, who imputing idleness to him, do take from him the government of the world and of mankind. . . . If he mind not these inferior things, [then] . . . what is above us, doth not concern us.

God would be to men "as though he were not at all" (E.W., Vol. II, p. 214).

What, then, does the "earthing" movement amount to? God, once more, is *corporeal*, since nothing other than

body exists. So God acts as body upon body. Although
the most thoroughgoing qualification is required when
concepts like wisdom, knowledge, love are applied to
God, Hobbes speaks much more directly and assuredly
about God's *power*. It does have its mysterious aspects,
since God's "irresistible power," unlike any limited
power, is held to justify all God's acts. But this power
is clearly exerted (as we saw in section 1) as *causal
agency*. In addition, God's "immediate hand" is at work
in miracles (E.W., Vol. III, p. 432); and he will causally
act in the setting up, upon earth, of his final kingdom.
Man, at the resurrection, "shall be revived by God, and
raised to judgment" (E.W., Vol. IV, p. 353). God can
"raise a dead carkasse to life again, and continue him
alive for ever" (E.W., Vol. III, p. 615). "The *power of
the agent* and the *efficient cause* are the same thing"
(E.W., Vol. I, p. 127).[4]

This "earthing" movement does constitute an important part of Hobbes's theology; for there are close connections among his claims that God is corporeal spirit,
that his eternality is endless existence in time rather than
timeless being, that the world is a deterministic structure
with God as its first cause, and that eschatology is to be
read in terms of a this-worldly kingdom of God. Continuity between God's action and the events of the universe is purchased, however, at a high price.

To put it another way, Hobbes seems to have bur-
dened himself with the drawbacks of both the defences
of theism in Hume's *Dialogues*: with the insufficient
transcendence of Cleanthes' designer, and with the excessive transcendence of Demea's sublimely incomprehensible Deity. It is only fair to add that although the
difficulty is particularly glaring in Hobbes, it confronts

---

[4] Cf., yet again (in general drift, if not in detail), Mill against
Mansel: "the doubt whether words applied to God have their human signification is only felt when the words relate to his moral
attributes; it is never heard of in regard to his power" (op. cit.,
Chapter 7).

any version of theism, and may possibly be intractable for theism as such.

4. Hobbes's Fideism

"When our reasons, for which we assent to some proposition, derive not from the *proposition itself*, but from the *person propounding* . . . our assent . . . is called *faith*" (E.W., Vol. II, pp. 304 f). "Acknowledgment of Scripture to be the Word of God is not evidence, but faith, and faith consisteth in the trust we have of other men; . . . the men so trusted are the holy men of God's church, succeeding one another from the time of those that saw the wondrous works of God Almighty in the flesh" (E.W., Vol. IV, p. 65). The authors of the Bible, being imbued with one and the same spirit, can be trusted as giving "true registers" of the acts of prophets and apostles (E.W., Vol. III, pp. 375 f).

The criteria for authentic prophecy, to Hobbes, are the performance of miracles and teaching in conformity with religion already established (E.W., Vol. III, p. 362). As both criteria are necessary, it is difficult to imagine how a religion could be first established, or (once established) reformed. But the question is idle, since "miracles now cease" and prophets likewise (E.W., Vol. III, p. 365). We are to rely solely upon the Holy Scriptures. To raise questions about scriptural authority is ultimately to raise questions about *law*.

> He . . . to whom God hath not supernaturally revealed that [the Scriptures] are his . . . is not obliged to obey them, by any authority, but his whose commands have already the force of laws

—i.e., the sovereign (E.W., Vol. III, p. 378). For "in Christian cities, the judgment both of *spiritual* and *temporal matters* belongs unto the civil authority" (E.W., Vol. II, p. 297). The question about scriptural authority is the question: "*By what authority they are made law*" (E.W., Vol. III, p. 378).

We cannot here adequately sample Hobbes's biblical theology in action. Against "School-argument" Hobbes persistently sets his "Scripture-argument" (E.W., Vol. IV, p. 306). The corporeality of God, for instance, can be defended by appeal to Scripture. St. Paul wrote: "In [Christ] *dwelleth all the fullness of the Godhead bodily*" (E.W., Vol. IV, p. 306). "The word incorporeal is not found in Scripture" (Ibid., p. 305). The concreteness of biblical language is Hobbes's touchstone, and his lever against the abstract and ill-formed formulae of scholasticism. Even Hobbes's own physiologically centred account of human nature, though certainly belonging to his own day as an extension of explanation in terms of matter-in-motion, is at the same time reminiscent of Old Testament psychology with its unabashed stress on the physical ("bowels," "heart," "reins," as seats of the emotions). To Hobbes, delight is "motion about the heart," which helps the "vital motion"; pain is "motion [that] *weakeneth* or hindereth the vital motion" (E.W., Vol. IV, p. 31).

Serious though fideism is as a theological approach, Hobbes himself cannot be said to have made strenuous efforts to ground and justify his version of it, far less to have succeeded. Consider again the question of scriptural authority. "Have we seen the miracles?" Hobbes rhetorically asks. "Have we any other assurance of their certainty than the authority of the Church?" And the authority of the Church? It is one with "the authority of the commonwealth." That authority, in turn, rests with the "head of the commonwealth," and it is an authority "given him by the members" (E.W., Vol. V, p. 179). This is an extraordinary account. For the ultimate authority is traced to citizens who have *not* seen the miracles, and who can be credited with no peculiar wisdom for discriminating authentic from inauthentic claims to revelation.

I quoted, however, that other derivation of scriptural authority, which lodges authority in the "holy men of God's church, succeeding one another from the time of

those that saw the wondrous works of God Almighty in
the flesh" (E.W., Vol. IV, p. 65). There is a problem,
already noted earlier, as to how anyone could be said
to have "seen," witnessed, those wondrous works, like
God's speaking to Moses, which Hobbes declares to be
incomprehensible. Some scriptural teaching, on the
other hand, refers to what is at least *prima facie* intelligible. The law apart, have we good reason to accept the
scriptural authors as *reliable* witnesses? Hobbes sees no
reason to believe substantial distortion of the record has
occurred (E.W., Vol. III, pp. 375 f); but, overall, his
treatment of alleged ancient authorities may well leave
his reader's confidence diminished rather than augmented. He fails effectively to insulate the claims of
Scripture from two sorts of sceptical challenge. Hobbes
himself characterizes these types of challenge eloquently
and incisively—with reference, of course, to ancient
"authorities" other than the scriptural authors: but the
way is left open for challenging these also on similar
lines. This possibility is, of course, particularly disturbing
for a Hobbesian theology, since the overwhelming weight
of its apologetic has been left to rest on scriptural authority alone.

One challenge is to the authenticity of alleged claims
by individuals to have had divine revelations. Such
claims are, to put it mildly, difficult to sustain. "For if a
man pretend to me, that God hath spoken to him supernaturally and immediately, and I make doubt of it, I
cannot easily perceive what argument he can produce,
to oblige me to believe it" (E.W., Vol. III, p. 361). Still
bolder is the famous remark: "To say [God] hath spoken
to [someone] in a dream, is no more than to say he
dreamed that God spake to him; which is not of force to
win belief from any man" who knows possible naturalistic
explanations (E.W., Vol. III, p. 361). "He . . . to whom
God hath not supernaturally revealed that [the Scrip-
tures] are his . . . is not obliged to obey them, by any
authority, but" the civil sovereign (E.W., Vol. III, p.
378). Ostensibly, Hobbes has expressed doubts about the

possibility of vindicating to *others*, and convincing others, that one has had a supernatural revelation: in fact the same reflections may equally well prompt scepticism in any person about the authenticity of what he has taken as a revelation to himself. So we should be thrown back on the sovereign's "authorizing" the Scriptures.

If we are dubious about grounding the authority of Scripture either upon individual revelation or upon the decree of the civil power, presumably we consider the Bible as an ancient document among other documents. Hobbes, however, has the harshest things to say (at the very end of *Leviathan*) about claims to authority on behalf of ancient writings in general. He tells his reader that he has

> neglected the ornament of quoting ancient poets, orators, and philosophers. . . . For all truth of doctrine depends on reason or upon *Scripture*. . . . There is scarce any of those old writers that contradicteth not sometimes both himself and others. . . . Such opinions as are taken only upon credit of antiquity, are not intrinsically the judgment of those that cite them, but words that pass, like gaping, from mouth to mouth. [E.W., Vol. III, p. 711 f.]

We need more reason than Hobbes ever provides us for not permitting that last-quoted sentence to erode confidence in the supposed authority of the Scripture itself. For scriptural claims, again, were transmitted, by the holy men of God's Church, passing their words from mouth to mouth and from pen to pen.

Hobbes reverenced those ancient writers "that either have written truth perspicuously, or set us in a better way to find it out ourselves; yet to the antiquity itself," he wrote, "I think nothing due. For if we reverence the age, the Present is the Oldest" (E.W., Vol. III, p. 712). Hobbes has repeatedly admitted, however, that Scripture is *not* perspicuous, since it speaks often incomprehensibly of an incomprehensible being; and our minds are "incapable of any notion at all from the words

spoken" (E.W., Vol. III, p. 360). And he does not see
the Scriptures as setting us in a better way to find out the
nature of God by ourselves—so that we may in the end
"intrinsically" judge of the matter. We are to remain dependent on Scripture.

Hobbes speaks, and has to speak, of the Scriptures as
"the Word and Commandment of God" (e.g., E.W., Vol.
V, p. 12). But how God can command, how he can com-
municate through a "Word," is entirely incomprehensible, according to Hobbes's account itself. If Scripture
speaks of God as speaking, willing, commanding, then
these expressions are authorized as appropriate. But we
cannot *presuppose* their propriety when we are trying
to decide what to make of the Scriptures themselves *in
toto*: for this is a question of how to relate the Scriptures
to reality *outside* the domain of Scripture itself. Hobbes
needs, therefore, to mitigate once again his doctrine of
divine incomprehensibility, not merely in order to give
more scope for a natural theology, but even to allow for
the establishing of his fideism itself: or at the very least
to save it from extreme arbitrariness. This problem too
is not at all unique to Hobbes; any theology will encounter it, which tries to combine a biblical fideism with
scepticism over the meaningfulness of religious discourse.
I doubt if Hobbes had a clear view of the extent and
gravity of the problem.

A thorough study of Hobbes's philosophy of religion
demands discussion of many topics not touched upon in
this chapter: his detailed and idiosyncratic interpretation
of Scripture; his account of miracles; his treatment of
natural law as divine command; his moral philosophy in
relation to Christian ethics; his philosophy of man in relation to the Christian doctrine of man; and (perhaps most
important of all) his treatment of the relation between
Church and state.

The topics this chapter has explored are fundamental
ones; and I think Hobbes's treatment of them supports
the appraisal I suggested at the outset. There are unex-
ceptionally orthodox ingredients in Hobbes's philosophy

of religion; yet, although this should check extravagant attempts to see Hobbes as an out-and-out sceptic, it certainly does not mean that his own reworking and combining of these ingredients are either orthodox or successful. He does present arguments for God's existence, but they are not adequately defended against sceptical reflections that Hobbes himself records elsewhere. He writes of God as a being whose transcendence of our experience is so thoroughgoing that we can only bow the knee and utter words without truth-value; but he writes of God also as a being whose immanence, whose continuity with the world, is so thoroughgoing that he becomes a natural cause among causes. Hobbes does not show us how to accommodate our vision so as to bring these two images into a single focus. Lastly, the philosophical scepticism about God is to be compensated for by the biblical fideism: but that scepticism is so intense that it gets in the way of establishing the fideism itself; and so far-reaching that it carries incomprehensibility into the very content of revelation. A writer who is struck by this self-undermining character of Hobbes's writing on religion may readily be tempted to see that character as precisely what Hobbes aimed to insinuate. This is a just conceivable reading, but neither the internal nor external evidence is strong enough to make it a likely one. A writer with no anti-religious intent whatever might have argued in basically the same fashion as Hobbes. And quite a number of features of Hobbes's theology would appear quite gratuitously and bafflingly controversial if his consistent aim had been to sabotage traditional Christian theism by displaying it as a self-stultifying structure.

THE CONTEXT OF HOBBES'S THEORY
OF POLITICAL OBLIGATION[1]

QUENTIN SKINNER

I

Two assumptions about the original reception of
Hobbes's political theory seem to be generally accepted.
The first is that the theory bore virtually no relation to
any other political ideas of its time.[2] It was "an isolated
phenomenon in English thought, without ancestry or posterity."[3] The second is that the theory proved completely
unacceptable. Hobbes's "boldness and originality" merely
provoked "intense opposition,"[4] so that "no man of his
time occupied such a lonely position in the world of
thought."[5] My aim in what follows is to show that both
these claims are mistaken. One reason for producing this
evidence is of course to provide an historically more accurate picture of Hobbes's intellectual milieu. In particular, I wish to suggest that the intentions of Hobbes's
critics, as well as the positive ideological purchase of
his own theory, have been somewhat misunderstood. My
main reason, however, is to suggest that a knowledge

---

[1] An abbreviated and much altered version of an article which appeared in *The Historical Journal*, IX, 3 (1966), pp. 286–317. For
providing me with extra references I am most grateful to Conrad
Russell, Keith Thomas, and J. M. Wallace. For discussions about
the original essay I am particularly indebted to John Dunn, as well
as to Peter Laslett and J. G. A. Pocock. Note: in all citations from
seventeenth-century sources, any translations are mine, and all
spelling and punctuation have been modernised.
[2] E.g., C. Hill, *Puritanism and Revolution* (London, 1958), p. 91.
[3] H. R. Trevor-Roper, "Thomas Hobbes," in *Historical Essays*
(London, 1957), p. 233.
[4] S. I. Mintz, *The Hunting of Leviathan* (Cambridge, 1962),
p. 155.
[5] G. P. Gooch, *Political Thought in England: Bacon to Halifax*
(London, 1915), p. 23.

of this intellectual milieu is not merely of historical but also of exegetical significance for the student of Hobbes's political thought. In particular, I wish to argue that to understand the ideological context in which Hobbes's political theory was written is to be in a position to cast decisive doubts on one prevailing interpretation of Hobbes's theory of political obligation.

II

The view that Hobbes was simply "the bête noire of his age,"[6] and made his impact "almost entirely by rousing opposition"[7] itself seems to derive from placing too much emphasis on the fulminations of Hobbes's many clerical opponents. There is no doubt, of course, that Hobbes was particularly singled out for his originality, particularly denounced for his heterodoxy. But there is equally no doubt that during his own lifetime Hobbes began to receive a serious and to some extent sympathetic hearing as a philosopher of politics. This was particularly true on the Continent. By the end of the century Hobbes was being hailed by Bayle in his *Dictionary* as "one of the greatest minds of the seventeenth century."[8] And within his own lifetime he had gained an extensive following in France (a fact reflected in the correspondence he kept up after his return to England[9]), he had seen his political works extensively translated,[10] he

---

[6] Mintz, op. cit., p. vii.

[7] Leslie Stephen, *Hobbes* (London, 1904), p. 67.

[8] Pierre Bayle, *Dictionnaire Historique et Critique*, 4 vols. (Rotterdam, 1697), Vol. III, pp. 99–103.

[9] For a special study of this group and its correspondence with Hobbes, see my article "Thomas Hobbes and his Disciples in France and England," *Comparative Studies in Society and History*, VIII (1966), pp. 153–67.

[10] Samuel Sorbière translated *De Cive* (*Elements Philosophiques du Citoyen* [Amsterdam, 1649]), as well as *De Corpore Politico* (*Le Corps Politique* [Amsterdam, 1652]). Du Verdus also translated *De Cive* (*Les Elements de la Politique de M. Hobbes* [Paris, 1660]).

had been seriously studied and discussed by a number of jurists,[11] and he had even gained something of a popular following in Holland as well as France.[12] As Hobbes was fond of pointing out himself,[13] his serious influence on the Continent during his own lifetime is in fact well attested.[14] Nor did he entirely lack a similar reputation in England. Again, by the end of the century his works had come to be accepted as authoritative even by theorists of avowedly opposed temperament. Blount cites him as "the great instructor of the most sensible part of mankind,"[15] and even Shaftesbury concedes that "Tom Hobbes I must confess a genius, and even an original among these latter leaders in philosophy."[16] Again, this element of sympathetic as well as serious appraisal dates from the decade in which *Leviathan* had first been published. As early as 1654, Webster had warned in his *Academiarum Examen* against overrating ancient theories of statecraft, specifically on the grounds that "our own

---

[11] E.g., see J. C. Beckman, *Meditationes Politicae* (Frankfort, 1679), p. 7; N. H. Gundling, *De Jure Oppignorati Territorii* (Magdeburg, 1706), p. 16; S. Pufendorf, *Of the Law of Nature and Nations* (London, tr. 1710), Bk. II, Ch. IV; Bk. V, Ch. II; Bk. VII, Ch. VII; J. W. Textor, *Synopsis of the Law of Nations* (1680), in *The Classics of International Law*, ed. L. von Bar, 2 vols. (Washington, 1916), Vol. II, pp. 9, 82.

[12] For Holland, see Johan de la Court *Consideratien van Staat* (n.p., 1661); *The Correspondence of Spinoza*, ed. A. Wolf (London, 1928), p. 446; L. Velthuysen, *Epistolica Dissertatio* (Amsterdam, 1651), p. 2. For France, see E. Merlat, *Traité du Pouvoir Absolu* (Cologne, 1685), pp. 219–22; see also the discussions in Lionel Rothkrug, *Opposition to Louis XIV* (New Jersey, 1965), pp. 116–30 (on Lartigne) and pp. 315–28.

[13] E.g., in "Considerations," *The English Works*, ed. W. Molesworth, 11 vols. (London, 1839–45), Vol. IV, p. 435.

[14] There is a good survey, such that no more need be said of this here, in G. Sortais, *La Philosophie Moderne*, 2 vols. (Paris, 1920–22), Vol. II, pp. 456–516. Sortais's analysis of Hobbes's influence in England is of little value.

[15] Charles Blount, *The Oracles of Reason* (London, 1693), p. 104.

[16] *The Life, Unpublished Letters and Philosophical Regimen*, ed. B. Rand (London, 1900), Letter to Stanhope, p. 414.

countryman Master Hobbes hath pieces of more exquisiteness and profundity in that subject than ever the Grecian wit was able to reach unto."[17] Selden and Osborne, both of whom arguably reveal Hobbesian traits in their own political works, were also (according to Aubrey) amongst the earliest sympathetic students of Hobbes's political theory. Selden is known to have sought Hobbes's acquaintance on the strength of reading *Leviathan*,[18] while Osborne was writing of Hobbes as early as 1659 as one of the men who had most "embellished the age."[19] Similarly James Harrington, in working out his own political theory during the 1650's, was to treat Hobbes's *Leviathan* as the only serious rival to his own concept of the need for a balanced Republican constitution. And although, as he said himself, he totally disagreed with the form of "balance" for which Hobbes had argued, yet he agreed "that Mr. Hobbes is and will in future ages be accounted the best writer at this day in the world."[20]

Hobbes's serious reputation amongst "the solemn, the judicious," as Eachard mockingly called them,[21] was conceded at the time even by Hobbes's opponents. It is clear, moreover, that what disturbed them was not merely the alarming content of Hobbes's doctrines, but the alarming extent to which they were gaining serious attention. This point has tended to get submerged under the weight which has been given to these contemporary attacks. There is no doubt, however, that the popular acceptance of Hobbes's views was a point which weighed with his critics from the start. Within two years of the publication of *Leviathan*, Rosse claimed to be expecting to be denounced himself for denouncing so fashionable a

---

[17] J. Webster, *Academiarum Examen* (London, 1654), p. 88.

[18] John Aubrey, *Brief Lives*, ed. A. Clark, 2 vols. (Oxford, 1898), Vol. I, p. 369.

[19] Francis Osborne, *A Miscellany* (London, 1959), Sig. A.

[20] J. Harrington, "The Prerogative of Popular Government," *Works* (London, 1771 edn.), p. 241.

[21] See J. Eachard, *Some Opinions of Mr. Hobbs Considered* (London, 1673), Sig. A, 4a–b.

work.[22] By 1657 Lawson was noting how much *Leviathan* was "judged to be a rational piece" both by "many gentlemen" and by "young students in the Universities."[23] By 1670 Tenison felt obliged to admit that "there is certainly no man who hath any share of the curiosity of this present age" who could still remain "unacquainted with his name and doctrine."[24] Clarendon noted at the same time how readily Hobbes's reputation seemed to weather every attack, how much his works continued "still to be esteemed as well abroad as at home."[25] By the time of his death Hobbes had grown "so great in reputation," as Whitehall angrily remarked, that even apparently "wise and prudent" men had come to accept his political views, which "are daily undertaken to be defended."[26] Doubtless Hobbes's enemies wished to emphasise the menace. But there is certainly independent evidence of Hobbes's continuing popularity. A catalogue of "the most vendible books in England" which happens to survive for the year 1658 included all Hobbes's works on political theory, and showed him one of the most popular of all the writers listed under "humane learning," surpassed in the number of his entries only by Bacon and Raleigh.[27] The printing histories of all Hobbes's political works certainly bear this out. *Leviathan*, for example, went through three editions in its first year of publication, and by 1668 the book was "so mightily called for" (as Pepys noted) that he had to pay three times the original price to get a copy,[28] even though there had in

---

[22] Alexander Rosse, *Leviathan Drawn out with an Hook* (London, 1653), Sig. A, 4b.

[23] George Lawson, *An Examination of the Political Part of Mr. Hobbes his Leviathan* (London, 1657), Sig. A, 2b.

[24] Thomas Tenison, *The Creed of Mr. Hobbes Examined* (London, 1670), p. 2.

[25] Edward Hyde, Earl of Clarendon, *A Brief View and Survey of . . . Leviathan* (Oxford, 1676), Sig. A, 3a.

[26] John Whitehall, *Leviathan Found Out* (London, 1679), p. 3.

[27] W. London, *A Catalogue . . .* (London, 1658), Sig. T, 3a to Sig. Z, 1b.

[28] Samuel Pepys, *Diary*, ed. H. B. Wheatley, 8 vols. (London, 1904–5), Vol. VIII, p. 91.

fact been two further editions of the book that year.[29]
Ten years later, the figure of Hobbes in Eachard's dialogue is still able to taunt his detractors with the fact
that, despite their denunciations, his works "have sold
very well, and have been generally read and admired."[30]

The failure to stress this element of popularity has
tended to give a misleading impression of the intentions
of Hobbes's contemporary critics. They have been pictured as attacking a single source of heterodox opinion.
Hobbes was trying, it has been said, "to sweep away the
whole structure of traditional sanctions," but this was a
single-handed effort, which merely provoked "a wide-
spread re-assertion of accepted principles."[31] This was
not what his critics felt at the time. They rather saw themselves as attacking merely the ablest presentation of a
political outlook which had itself gained alarmingly in
acceptance. To the more hysterical it even seemed possible to believe that "most of the bad principles of this
age are of no earlier a date than one very ill book, are
indeed but the spawn of the *Leviathan*."[32] Certainly it
was widely believed that "Hobbes his *Leviathan* hath
corrupted the gentry of the Nation."[33] Indeed this
sense that Hobbes had played a leading part in what one
opponent called "the debauching of this generation"
moved even Hobbes's most statesmanlike critics. Cumberland excused his long philosophical attack on Hobbes
with the hope that it might help to limit the increasing

---

[29] For printing histories of this and other of Hobbes's political
works, see H. Macdonald and M. Hargreaves, *Thomas Hobbes:
a Bibliography* (London, 1952), pp. 10–14, 16–22, 30–36, 76–77.
The "three editions" of *Leviathan* in 1651 may of course be slightly
misleading due to the use of false imprints.

[30] J. Eachard, *Mr. Hobbes's State of Nature Considered*, ed. P.
Ure (Liverpool, 1958), p. 14.

[31] John Bowle, *Hobbes and His Critics* (London, 1951), pp. 13,
43.

[32] Charles Wolseley, *The Reasonableness of Scripture-Belief*
(London, 1672), Sig. A, 4a.

[33] See *The Life and Times of Anthony Wood*, ed. A. Clark, 5 vols.
(Oxford, 1891–1900), Vol. II, p. 472—cf. also Vol. II, p. 116.

acceptance of Hobbes's political views.[34] And even Clarendon, from the bitterness of his second exile, claimed to be able to trace "many odious opinions" back to *Leviathan*, "the seed whereof was first sowed in that book."[35] A more revealing (and realistic) assumption, however, was that the reason for Hobbes's doctrine being, as Baxter put it, "so greedily sought and cried up"[36] was the existing "prevalence of a scoffing humour" in "this unhappy time."[37] This was Atterbury's diagnosis when he came to reflect, a generation later, on the evil influence of Hobbes's reputation.[38] This was also Burnet's judgment on Hobbes in his *History of My Own Time*.[39] And the same point had already been made by several earlier critics. According to Lucy, *Leviathan* had merely crystallised "the genius that governs this age."[40] And according to Eachard, Hobbes's rudest and shrewdest critic, the age itself had thrown up so many "resolved practicants in Hobbianism" that they "would most certainly have been so, had there never been any such man as Mr. Hobbes in the world."[41]

To some Hobbes was the leading symptom, to others the sole cause, of the increasingly sceptical and rationalist temper of political debate. But the point on which all the critics agreed was that it was not merely Hobbes but the new and apparently increasing phenomenon of "Hobbism" which had to be denounced. It is true of course that "Hobbism" was often applied as little more than a general term of alarm and abuse. The "Hobbist" villain

---

[34] Richard Cumberland, *A Treatise of the Laws of Nature* (1672; tr. London, 1727), Introduction, Sect. XXX.

[35] Clarendon, op. cit., Sig. *, 3a.

[36] Richard Baxter, *The Second Part* . . . (London, 1680), p. 8.

[37] Anonymous *Inquiry* cited in Mintz, op. cit., p. 136.

[38] Francis Atterbury, *Maxims, Reflections and Observations* (London, 1723), p. 66.

[39] Gilbert Burnet, *History of My Own Time*, ed. O. Airy, 2 vols. (Oxford, 1897–1900), Vol. I, p. 334.

[40] William Lucy, *Examinations, Censures and Confutations* . . . (London, 1656), Sig. A., 3b.

[41] Eachard, *Some Opinions*, Sig. A., 3b.

became a familiar parody on the Restoration stage: Vizard in *The Constant Couple*, for example, comes on reading what appears to be *The Practice of Piety*, but is in fact *Leviathan* under plain cover.[42] "Hobbism" in this type of context was usually used to mean nothing more than "wild atheistically disposed" attitudes to the powers that be,[43] coupled with the presumed desire to "subvert our laws and liberties and set up an arbitrary power."[44] It is also true, however, that the concept of "Hobbism" was also applied more precisely and seriously than this, to describe a quite specific political outlook. When Newton confessed to Locke, for example, that "I took you for a Hobbist," it is clear that both of them attached a specific meaning to the charge, as well as regarding it as a serious accusation, for which Newton was subsequently most anxious to apologise.[45]

When the concept of "Hobbism" was seriously applied by contemporaries in this way, it was generally used to refer to two specific political doctrines. The first and most important was a theory of political obligation. The "Hobbist" was recognised as a man for whom the obligation to obey a given government derived not from any religious sanction, but merely from a self-interested calculation made by each individual citizen. To be a "Hobbist" was to regard all men as concerned above all with their own self-preservation, and with the consequent desirability of obeying any government capable of affording them protection. The "Hobbists," it was thus claimed, believed that God had left it "arbitrary to men (as the Hobbeans vainly fancy)"[46] to establish political societies

---

[42] G. Farquhar, *The Constant Couple* (London, 1700), p. 2. See L. Teeter, "The Dramatic Uses of Hobbes's Political Ideas," *E.L.H.*, III (1936), pp. 140–69.

[43] R. F., *A Sober Enquiry* (London, 1673), p. 51.

[44] John Crowne, *City Politics* (London, 1683), p. 50.

[45] Newton to Locke, 16 September 1693, in *The Correspondence of Sir Isaac Newton*, ed. W. H. Turnbull, (Cambridge, 1961) Vol. III, p. 280.

[46] Anonymous, *A Letter to a Friend* (London, 1679), p. 6.

"upon the principles of equality and self-preservation agreed to by the Hobbists."[47] It is in exactly these terms, for example, that John Locke in the *Essay* contrasts the "Hobbist" with the Christian sense of obligation. The "Hobbist" justifies his keeping of "compacts" not by saying "because God, who has the power of eternal life and death, requires it of us," but "because the public requires it, and the Leviathan will punish you if you do not."[48] It followed, as Locke confided to his commonplace book in 1677, that "an Hobbist, with his principles of self-preservation, whereof himself is to be judge, will not easily admit a great many plain duties of morality."[49]

The second doctrine regarded by contemporaries as characteristic of the "Hobbists" was their "scheme of human nature."[50] It is clear that the "Hobbist" theory of political obligation does depend on being able to show that the citizen's *need* for protection is paramount, if it is to be argued that the capacity of any given government to protect its citizens is to count as a sufficient condition of political obligation. The "Hobbist" is thus recognised as the man whose theory of political obligation derives from the assumption that man's nature is basically anti-social, that he is "compelled into society merely for the advantages and necessities of life,"[51] and that the natural condition of men outside political society should be represented, as Shaftesbury sardonically put it, "under monstrous visages of dragons, Leviathans and I know not what devouring creatures."[52] This concept of man's

---

[47] Anonymous, *The Great Law of Nature* . . . (n.p., British Museum catalogue dates 1673), p. 6.
[48] John Locke, *An Essay Concerning Human Understanding* (London, 1690), Bk. 1, Ch. 3, para. 6.
[49] See the memorandum "Study" cited in *The Life of John Locke*, ed. Lord King, 2 vols. (London, 1830 edn.), Vol. 1, pp. 171–203, at p. 191.
[50] Anonymous, *Animadversions on a Discourse* (London, 1691), p. 16.
[51] Anonymous, *Confusion Confounded* (London, 1654), p. 9.
[52] A. A. Cooper, 3d Earl of Shaftesbury, *Characteristics*, ed. J. M. Robertson, 2 vols. (London, 1900), Vol. II, p. 83.

natural instinct to produce "a state of war"[53] passed into general currency as a characteristically "Hobbist" belief. In 1673, for example, Dryden is censured for representing men in one of his plays "in a Hobbian state of war."[54] In 1691 Sherlock justifies the right to change political allegiance when a ruler becomes incapable of governing on the grounds that society "would otherwise dissolve into a mob, or Mr. Hobbes's state of nature."[55] By 1694, Lownde was assuming that to write of man's natural sociability might be thought old-fashioned, as the assumption was at odds with the views of many "learned persons," amongst whom Hobbes is particularly mentioned.[56] Similarly, the Whig writers on political obligation—Locke, Sidney, Tyrrell, Mead—all allude to the fact that "some men" (as Locke put it), and notably Hobbes (as all the others mention) had been popularising the view that man's natural condition without government would be a state of *bellum omnium contra omnes*.[57]

The existence of such "Hobbists," so alarming to contemporaries, has been virtually ignored by modern commentators. The one analysis of the relations between "Hobbes and Hobbism" has claimed in fact that in Hobbes's own lifetime there was to be only one "favourable" as opposed to fifty-one "hostile" published reactions to Hobbes's own political theory.[58] It is evident, however, that a great deal of information has been missed here.

---

[53] Anonymous, *The Parallel* (London, 1682), p. 12.

[54] Anonymous, *The Censure of the Rota* (Oxford, 1673), p. 3.

[55] William Sherlock, *The Case of Allegiance* (London, 1691), p. 38.

[56] J. Lownde, *A Discourse concerning the Nature of Man* (London, 1694), Sig. A, 5a and 6b.

[57] See John Locke, *Two Treatises of Government*, ed. Peter Laslett (Cambridge, 1960), p. 298, and note to para. 19; Algernon Sidney, *Discourses Concerning Government* (London, 3d, edn., 1751), pp. 43, 342; James Tyrrell *Bibliotheca Politica* (London, 1692), pp. 153, 155–56, 169, 174, 181; Samueal Mead, *Oratio* (n.p., 1689), Sig. B., 3b–4a.

[58] Sterling P. Lamprecht, "Hobbes and Hobbism," *The American Political Science Review*, XXXIV (1940), pp. 31–53, at p. 32.

First, a considerable group of political writers, all contemporary with Hobbes, can in fact be shown to have adopted precisely the "Hobbist" views which so alarmed the more conventional critics. And second, it can be shown that several of these writers explicitly relied on Hobbes's authority in setting out their characteristically "Hobbist" views on political obligation.

III

The problem of political obligation became the central issue of ideological debate at two points in the English Revolution: at 1649, immediately after the execution of Charles I and the proclamation of the Republic; and again at 1689, immediately after the removal of James II and the acceptance of William and Mary. At both points the new governments themselves raised the issue in an acute form by requiring new oaths of allegiance to be sworn to their authority. This made the question of the grounds on which it might be appropriate to swear allegiance the central issue of political debate. One answer to the problem, offered both at 1649 and 1689, consisted of arguing that one ought to regard oneself as politically obliged on the grounds that the new government itself was based on an acceptance of the people's ultimate sovereign power, and on the grounds that it had successfully removed a ruler who had been tyrannously denying the people their right to this recognition. This was of course the implication of Milton's argument at 1649, in *The Tenure of Kings and Magistrates,* and of Locke's at 1690, in his *Second Treatise.* Another answer, however, which was also offered both at 1649 and 1689, consisted instead of trying to argue that the new government ought to be obeyed even if it could not be shown either to reflect the will of the people or to have been rightfully acquired. This answer has been much less studied than the first, but it was arguably of more importance at the time, since the adoption of the first answer—which in effect placed both the grounds and the limits of political obligation upon a theory of natural law and natural rights—was a highly sophisticated as well as politically radical step to take in a society which in general believed its government to be the direct gift of God's providence.

This second answer, the *de facto* view that political obligation might be owed to an unrightful or even a usurping power, was to be reached by two different forms of argument. One form consisted of placing an absolute stress on the providential origins of all government. The Pauline injunction to obey the powers that be was thus taken to cover *all* successfully constituted political authority, whether or not those in power could be shown to have a just or even a legal title to rule. Their title to rule was thus taken to lie simply in their capacity to rule, for this capacity, it was said, must itself reflect the will and be the gift of God. The credit for originating this ingenious compromise between passive obedience and active political change seems to be owed to the Presbyterian, Francis Rous. His brief pamphlet of April 1649, *The Lawfulness of Obeying the Present Government*, contained exactly this argument, and was followed by a considerable pamphlet literature concerned with the obligation to obey and the duty to "engage" with Cromwell's *de facto* government.[59] The revival of the same argument after 1689 was mainly the work of William Sherlock, Dean of St. Paul's, whose *Case of Allegiance* was published in 1691 to justify his decision to take the new oaths of allegiance "after so long a refusal." Again, this was followed by further pamphlet literature, the proponents of the argument being labelled on this occasion the "*de facto* Tories."

This form of argument in favour of the rights of *de facto* powers was in fact to be one of the theories of obligation regarded at the time as "Hobbist." The charge

---

[59] See the complete bibliography, which places Rous first, by John M. Wallace, "The Engagement Controversy 1649–1652," *Bulletin of the New York Public Library*, 68 (1964), pp. 384–405.

in this case is of course quite obviously unfair. The stress, however, on the need for submission rather than the rights of the people certainly suggests at least a parallel between this version of passive obedience and the "Hobbist" view of political obligation. And this comparison was certainly urged, particularly after 1689, by several proponents of the alternative view that governments can only be legitimated by the consent of the people. To accept this alternative, populist view of the 1689 settlement, it was thus urged, meant not only "that our Government is now thoroughly settled" but also "that we who submit to it cannot be charged with Hobbism, since we do not say that any Prince who has quiet possession of the throne can claim our obedience, but only such as are confirmed and settled in it by the determination of our representatives."[60] Several of the *de facto* Tories themselves, moreover, were sufficiently aware of the dangerous affinities of their argument to want to distinguish it with some care from the views of the "Hobbists." As Sherlock admitted, some have claimed "that it is Hobbism" to argue the rights of *de facto* powers at all. "But those who say this do not understand Mr. Hobbes or me. For he makes power and nothing else to give right to dominion, and therefore asserts that God himself is the natural lord and governor of the World not because He made it but because He is omnipotent. But I say that Government is founded in right, and that God is the natural lord of the World because He made it."[61] Such disclaimers, however, did not prevent both the "engagers" of the early 1650's and the "*de facto* Tories" of the early 1690's from being energetically charged by their enemies with "Hobbism." Sherlock and his followers might claim, it was said, to be endorsing the principles of the Church of England, but they were in fact reviving arguments from "the rebels in the year '42 and

---

[60] Anonymous, *Their Present Majesties' Government Proved to be thoroughly settled* [etc.] (London, 1691).
[61] Sherlock, op. cit., p. 15.

from the advocates of Cromwell's usurpation."[62] They
might claim to be corroborating the *Convocation Book's*
doctrine of obligation, but that work in fact "did but
little service" to them, while "there were other writings
that would have done the trick to an hair, such as
Hobbes, Baxter, Owen Jenkins, etc."[63] And Hobbes is
still seen as the major influence. Several of the attacks
on Sherlock ("the Doctor" to his opponents) tried to
establish by extensive textual comparisons that long before the Doctor's time "Mr. Hobbes hath taught the
same." "The question," as this critic put it, "is whether
Mr. Hobbes and the Doctor teach not the same doctrine
about the legal right and possession of sovereignty, and
the transferring of allegiance to usurpers?" And the answer, given after extensive textual comparison, was that
on political obligation Hobbes and Sherlock were *"fratres
fratrerrimi,* and it is not within the power of metaphysics
to distinguish them."[64] A similarly detailed textual comparison was provided by another critic, who claimed to
show that "Mr. Hobbes makes power and nothing else
give right to dominion. And pray does not the Doctor
do the same? I am much mistaken if this be not the design of his whole book."[65] Another less patient critic
concluded that Hobbes's principles had actually been
surpassed. For while "Mr. Hobbes taught the absolute
power of all Princes only as a philosopher, upon principles of mere reason," these latter-day Hobbists "by
adding the authority of scripture" also make themselves
"sure of a profitable office in the state."[66]

There was a second form of argument, however, by

---

[62] Anonymous, *An Answer to a Late Pamphlet* (London, 1691),
p. 1.
[63] Anonymous, *Providence and Precept* (London, 1691), pp. 4–5.
[64] Anonymous, *An Examination* [of Sherlock's *Case*] (London,
1691), pp. 14, 15.
[65] Anonymous, *Dr. Sherlock's Case of Allegiance Considered* (London, 1691), p. 73. Parallels with *Leviathan* cited pp. 80–82.
[66] Anonymous, *Dr Sherlock's Two Kings of Brainford* (London,
1691), p. 13.

which this conclusion (that political obligation might be owed to unlawfully gained power) was reached in both the major debates about political obligation during the English Revolution. This consisted of maintaining the authentically "Hobbist" claim that submission was due to the powers that be on the grounds of oblique self-interest. The consequences of refusing allegiance to any government capable of protecting its citizens, it was claimed, would always and necessarily be less desirable than the apparent inconveniences of ceding one's rights to that government. The capacity of any government, regardless of its title to rule, to offer this essential protection is thus treated as a sufficient reason for obeying and paying allegiance to it. This was the rationalist and utilitarian form of "engagement" and *"de facto"* theory, which was regarded by contemporaries both as being Hobbes's own view of political obligation, and as being the view of an authentically "Hobbist" following who adopted the same political outlook. And it is to this group of authentically "Hobbist" writers (hitherto virtually ignored)[67] that I now turn.

It is true of course that a list of the theorists who regarded themselves, and were regarded by their contemporaries, as being the authentic followers of Hobbes would be short and would contain no theorist of the front rank. The evidence from which such a list can be compiled, however, can only consist of unequivocal citations and sympathetic discussions specifically of Hobbes's political works. And it must be recognised at the outset that such tests—although they clearly provide the only unequivocal means of gauging the acceptance of one particular writer—are not only particularly rigorous when applied to the conventions of seventeenth-century politi-

---

[67] This was so when I originally wrote this article, but is less so now. See the admirable edition of Nedham's *Case of the Commonwealth of England, Stated,* ed. Philip A. Knachel (Charlottesville, 1969), and the excellent discussion of Ascham in John M. Wallace, *Destiny His Choice* (Cambridge, 1968).

cal debate, but will tend in themselves substantially to underestimate the evidence.

One reason why such tests must underestimate the evidence is simply that Hobbes's political theory *did* contribute to the attitudes of a larger group. There was thus no reason why such writers, in citing their authorities, should have focussed exclusively on the authority of Hobbes. Several of the writers who discussed Hobbes's views were themselves to be treated as authorities on points which were in fact common to the whole "Hobbist" group. It is thus not uncommon to find such "Hobbist" writers as Anthony Ascham, Marchamont Nedham, or Lewis du Moulin cited as authorities on points where an acknowledgment of Hobbes might have been equally appropriate.[68] Another reason why the evidence will tend to be underestimated is that all the conventions of political debate at the time were against the extensive citation of contemporary authorities. The trend was towards informality, even anonymity. There is no doubt that a failure to recognise the force of this convention has contributed something to the impression of Hobbes's lonely notoriety. Hobbes was not much cited in his own time, but nor was any other contemporary political writer. The fashion was to treat too much citation as slavish, too much reading as a waste of time. It was of course a famous boast with Hobbes himself that he had read few works by other men.[69] His friend Francis Osborne similarly pointed out his own emancipation from the citation of authorities, and even suggested cultivating the habit of reading sparingly, lest a man become diffident about his own views.[70] The same advice is given by another of Hobbes's friends, Sir William Petty,

---

[68] E.g., of Ascham cited, Anonymous, *A Combat between Two Seconds* (London, 1649), p. 5; of Nedham, K. Goodwin, *Peace Protected* (London, 1654), p. 75; of Du Moulin, Michael Hawke, *The Right of Dominion* (London, 1655), p. 136.

[69] Aubrey, op. cit., Vol. I, p. 349.

[70] Francis Osborne, "Conjectural Paradoxes," *Works* (London, 1689 edn.), pp. 538, 548.

in a letter to Sir Robert Boyle which assures him in extremely strong language that it is scarcely ever worthwhile to read the supposed authorities on any subject.[71] And John Selden, another of Hobbes's friends, actually laid it down as a maxim that "in quoting of books" one should cite only "such authors as are usually read. Others you may read for your own satisfaction, but not name them."[72]

It seems likely, moreover, that even amongst those writers who might have felt Hobbes worthy of citation as an authority, the number may have been further diminished by considerations about Hobbes's dangerous reputation. A man who had been named in Parliament[73] as the author of blasphemous and profane works was not a writer to cite without very good reason as an authority on anything. This type of suppression is of course impossible to prove. But it was certainly regarded at the time as beyond dispute that amongst those prudent men who would "scarce simper in favour or allowance" for Hobbes, there were many who were none the less "Hobbists" for that.[74] And it is certainly clear that in seventeenth-century England there were political opinions which a man might entertain, even discuss, but much prefer not to see printed. Many thought that Hobbes himself had acted too boldly in publishing views which "though he believed them to be true" were none the less "too dangerous to be spoken aloud."[75] And there are certainly signs that a man who sympathised with Hobbes's views was better able to say so in private than in any published form. "Hobbism" is anatomised without any sort of comment only in private commonplace

---

[71] Petty to Boyle, cited in Lord Edmond Fitzmaurice, *The Life of Sir William Petty* (London, 1895), pp. 45–46.

[72] John Selden, *Table Talk*, ed. Sir. F. Pollock (London, 1927), p. 24.

[73] See *The Journals of the House of Commons* (n.p. or d.), Vol. VIII, 1660–67, p. 636.

[74] Eachard, *Some Opinions*, Sig. A., 4b.

[75] Thomas Pierce, ΑΥΤΟΚΑΤΑΚΡΙΣΙΣ (London, 1658), Sig. *, 3b–4a.

books.[76] And Sir William Petty provides at least one further example of a contemporary writer on politics who
commends Hobbes in his private memoranda as the
leading writer on political theory, but never once mentions Hobbes in any of his published works.[77]

When such considerations about the conditions as
well as the conventions of political discussion are given
their due weight, it becomes by no means necessarily
tendentious to add that there may have been much more
silent reliance on Hobbes by contemporary writers than
ever appears explicitly in their published works. The
premise, for example, that political society must be based
on man's mediation of his own anti-social psychology
can also be found in many of the "engagement" tracts
of 1650,[78] in several discussions of the need for absolute
political power published under the Commonwealth,[79]
as well as in such "Hobbist" writers as Francis Osborne,[80]
Thomas White,[81] and Matthew Wren.[82] The deduction,
similarly, that the capacity to be given protection constitutes sufficient grounds for political obligation can
also be found in many of the "engagement" tracts,[83]

---

[76] E.g., see the commonplace book entries "Mr. Hobbes's Creed"
and "The Principles of Mr. Hobbes," in B.M., Sloane MSS, 904,
1458.

[77] For the private citations see *The Petty Papers*, ed. the Marquis
of Lansdowne, 2 vols. (London, 1927), Vol. II, p. 5.

[78] E.g., in T.B., *The Engagement Vindicated* (London, 1650),
pp. 5–6; Anonymous, *A Disengaged Survey of the Engagement*
(London, 1650), p. 20; John Dury, *Considerations Concerning the
Present Engagement* (London, 4th edn., 1650), pp. 13–14.

[79] E.g., in Anonymous, *Confusion Confounded* (London, 1654),
p. 9; John Hall, *Of Government and Obedience* (London, 1654),
pp. 13–14, 98.

[80] Francis Osborne, *A Persuasive to a Mutual Compliance* (London, 1652), p. 11.

[81] Thomas White, *The Grounds of Obedience and Government*
(London, 1655), pp. 44–45.

[82] Matthew Wren, *Monarchy Asserted* (London, 1659), pp. 49–50.

[83] E.g., Samuel Eaton, *The Oath of Allegiance* (London, 1650),
p. 8; Anonymous, *Conscience Puzzled* (London, 1650), p. 7; E.
Elcock, *Animadversions* (London, 1651), p. 47; N.W., *A Discourse
Concerning the Engagement* (London, 1650), p. 11.

expressed in exactly Hobbes's terminology of "mutual relationship" between protection and obedience, as well as in such claims as Du Moulin's that "possession is the great condition required for the duty of allegiance"[84] or John Hall's that the need for "peace and benefit" and the "necessity of submission" are the essentials of political obligation.[85]

My first point about this "Hobbist" group is thus that while only a small number of writers specifically acknowledged and followed Hobbes's authority, this test must considerably underestimate Hobbes's probable influence. My main point, however, is that several of these *de facto* writers on political obligation did in fact offer explicit acknowledgment of Hobbes's authority. The earliest citations are in an anonymous tract of 1649 on *The Original and End of Civil Power*,[86] and in John Hall's tract of 1650, *The Grounds and Reasons of Monarchy*.[87] Hobbes continues to be cited in a similarly familiar way at various points in the 1650's as an authority on political philosophy.[88] Such citations are of course somewhat cut off at the Restoration (from which point we may date Hobbes's merely evil popular reputation), although as late as 1660 he is still cited by John Heydon in *The Idea of the Law* as an authority both on the law of nature and the law of nations.[89] The most important citations of Hobbes, however, are as an authority on political obligation. These arise out of the "engagement" controversy

---

[84] Lewis du Moulin, *The Power of the Christian Magistrate* (London, 1650), p. 29.

[85] John Hall, *The True Cavalier* (London, 1656), p. 94.

[86] "Eutactus Philodemius," *The Original and End of Civil Power* (London, 1649), p. 15.

[87] John Hall, *The Grounds and Reasons of Monarchy Considered* (Edinburgh, 1650), Sig. A, 4a–b.

[88] E.g., Philip Scot, *A Treatise of the Schism of England* (London, 1650), p. 140; Harrington "Politicaster," *Works*, p. 559. See also Anonymous, *A Treatise of Human Reason* (London, 1674), pp. 44–45.

[89] John Heydon, *The Idea of the Law* (London, 1660), pp. 125, 151.

—that most "Hobbist" political debate—and are thus to be found very soon after the publication of Hobbes's *Philosophical Rudiments* and *De Corpore Politico* in 1650, and his *Leviathan* in the following year.

In these citations the first view associated particularly with Hobbes's name is that each man is capable of reckoning the necessity of submission, since each man is aware of his own paramount desire for self-preservation and protection. On the one hand, as Michael Hawke pointed out in his *Killing Is Murder*, "the natural state of man, before they were settled in a society, as Master Hobbes truly saith, was a mere war."[90] But on the other hand, as he had earlier pointed out in his *Right of Dominion*, the recognition of this fact means that "everyone hath sufficient power to rein and moderate his outward demeanour," so that "in this sense is Mr. Hobbes's saying true, that the law of nature is easily kept."[91] The basic point, as an anonymous writer put it, was that in Hobbes's view political obligation arises because men are "forced thereto by a kind of necessity for prevention of those evils which would necessarily be the consequents of having all things common."[92] In the *Right of Dominion* the same basic point is put in even more Hobbesian language. For as Hawke says, citing "Mr. Hobbes, *Philosophical Rudiments*" as his source, "it is the law of nature that men live peaceably, that they may tend the preservation of their lives, which whilst they are in war they cannot, and which is the first and fundamental law of nature." It is thus even possible, as Hawke rather dramatically adds, again citing Hobbes as his authority, to regard "human nature itself" as "the mother of the natural law."[93]

The "corollary" of this view, as Hawke puts it (following the organization of Hobbes's theory in his own argu-

---

[90] Michael Hawke, *Killing Is Murder* (London, 1657), p. 7.
[91] Michael Hawke, *The Right of Dominion* (London, 1655), p. 25.
[92] "Eutactus Philodemius," op. cit., p. 15.
[93] Hawke, op. cit., pp. 27, 29. Cf. also p. 30.

ment) is that "possession is the great condition for our
obedience and allegiance." For "as Mr Hobbes [says],
a sure and irresistable power confers the right of dominion."[94] The same conclusion is reached by Albertus Warren in his *Eight Reasons Categorical*. "The question"
during the revolution, he insists, "never was whether
we or any other people ought to be governed by an arbitrary power," for there must be some such power in
any state, if its citizens are to be protected. To know
who now has that power, moreover, is in Warren's view
equivalent to knowing whom one ought to obey. Thus,
as he insists, "our present governors, I say without more
ado, do not offend the letter of the law in rationally providing for the people, because they are above the law
of men and (taken collectively) to those ends aforesaid.
Else we should be in a hostile condition, as Mr. Hobbes
well observeth."[95] And the suggestion—much canvassed
by more recent commentators on Hobbes—that such a
view of political obligation is hard to square with
Hobbes's statements about natural law also seems to be
anticipated by one of these writers. The grounds of
political obligation, according to Heydon's account, evidently cannot be based on the law of nature, which cannot "actually and formally oblige a creature, until it be
made known." It may seem that obligations in society
are based on a "natural law" in cases "as Mr. Hobbes
describes" when people "bind themselves by general
compact to the observation of such laws as they judge
to be for the good of them all." But this would be to
mistake the nature of law, since "before all this can rise
to the height and perfection of a law, there must come
a command from superior powers, whence from will
spring a moral obligation also, and make up the formal-
ity of a law."[96]

---

[94] Hawke, *Killing Is Murder*, p. 12.
[95] Albertus Warren, *Eight Reasons Categorical* (London, 1653),
p. 5.
[96] Heydon, op. cit., p. 137.

Apart from such citations from his two or three avowed followers, however, there is a more important way in which the contemporary ideological relevance of Hobbes's theory of political obligation can be proved. Hobbes was also cited as an authority by several rationalist and "Hobbist" theorists of "engagement," who can be shown, however, to have arrived at these distinctively "Hobbist" conclusions independently of any study of Hobbes's own political works. Hobbes is cited not as the source of their opinions, but rather in corroboration of the "Hobbist" views they already held. They thus provide the most decisive evidence that Hobbes's theory was not an isolated phenomenon, but was itself a contribution (and conceivably intended as a contribution) to a particular strand of "engaging" theory in the ideological debates of the English Revolution.

The most important of these writers was Anthony Ascham, who published *A Discourse* in 1648, concerned (in the words of its own subtitle) with *What is particularly lawful during the confusions and revolutions of governments*.[97] Ascham's point of departure, in his preface, was with the Hobbesian fear that anarchy was the sole alternative as well as the ever-present threat to any given political order. His equally Hobbesian conclusion was thus that the will of a power "absolute without redress or appeal," and the virtues of passive obedience, provided the sole means of escape from the mutability of things. Part I of the *Discourse* argued for this conclusion from very Hobbesian claims about the "natural" laws of men's conduct in their basic and original social situation. The sole but essential right of all men in such a situation would be the right of self-preservation. This led to a history, in Chapter 3, of "first possessors," who could "without scruple of doing other wrong, place their bodies where they would." This discussion was then modified in Chapter 4, very much in the manner of Grotius,

---

[97] To maintain uniformity of citation, all page references are to the enlarged edition of 1649. See fn. 99.

by positing a situation of extreme need in which men would have to revert to a more communal system. It followed from these claims, in Ascham's account, on the one hand that appropriation has always served since primitive times as a sufficient basis for political societies. "Possession therefore is the greatest title." And on the other hand, it followed that even rights of possession cannot be absolute. Any such right must lose priority, in times of emergency, to the basic and Hobbesian right to life. The assumption governing the whole account is thus that necessity provides the only real guide to political rights. For, as in *Leviathan*, "tis necessity itself which makes laws, and by consequence ought to be the interpreter of them after they are made."

These assumptions about political power lead, in Part II of the *Discourse*, to the development of a completely Hobbesian argument about the "mutual relations between protection and obedience" as the grounds of political obligation. The specific issue which Ascham was naturally concerned to discuss was whether a man might take oaths and pay allegiance to a usurped power. Ascham showed complete and deliberate disregard in this discussion for any questions about either the rightful origins or the best forms of government. The only question was whether the possessors of governmental power are capable of protecting the lives of their citizens. If they cannot do this, the citizen's obligations are at an end, while he endeavours instead to protect himself. Since "nature commends me to myself for my own protection and preservation," so "he who hath sworn allegiance and fidelity to his Prince is absolved and set at liberty if his Prince abandon his kingdom." If the government does manage, however, to maintain the freedom and protect the lives of its citizens, then their duty can only be to obey, regardless of any questions that might be asked about the legal basis of the government's powers. The touchstone throughout the argument is necessity; as the final chapter concludes, citizens are bound to obey their governments "so long as it pleases God to give them the power to command us."[98]

The language as well as the assumptions throughout Ascham's work are of a strongly Hobbesian character. Hobbes is never mentioned, however, and his authority is never invoked; there is no evidence that Ascham had at this time read Hobbes's only published political work, *De Cive*. In 1649, however, Ascham reissued his book in a second edition, its length augmented by nine chapters, its title changed to *Of the Confusions and Revolutions of Governments*. Ascham now reverted (at the end of Part II) to his earlier discussion about the "natural" state and character of man. Here he not only expanded and corroborated his earlier account, but now justified it further by invoking the authority of Hobbes. Ascham first added a justification of his views on political obligation by considering the origins of magistracy and civil government in the state of nature. He now deduced the obligation of any citizen to obey any power capable of affording him protection from the typically Hobbesian assumption that without such protection, and thus such obligation, no society at all would be possible. Such liberty would be "a great prejudice to us; for hereby we were clearly left in a state of war, to make good this natural free state of the world, which referred all to the trial of force and not of law, against which no one could offend." The only solution was thus complete subjection to a single source of power, for (as Ascham now concluded) "Mr. Hobbes his supposition (if there be two omnipotents, neither could be obliged to obey the other) is very pertinent and conclusive to this subject." Ascham added finally a further justification of his views about the mutual relations between protection and obedience. He repeated the claim that a failure of the government automatically sanctions a change of allegiance. But he now called in two greater authorities to corroborate the point.

---

[98] Anthony Ascham, *A Discourse* (London, 1649 version), Part I, pp. 6, 10; Part II, pp. 21, 39, 45.

The change is now said to be justified whenever "(as Grotius and Mr. Hobbes say) there be a dereliction of command in the person of whom we speak, or if the country be so subdued that the conquerors can no longer be resisted."[99]

A further example of the use by a "Hobbist" of Hobbes's own authority to corroborate an already completed political argument can be found in the writings of Marchamont Nedham. So close indeed was Hobbes's own account of political obligation to the view which Nedham and the other *de facto* theorists used to justify the rule of the Commonwealth that in the pages of *Mercurius Politicus*, the official newspaper which Nedham edited, Hobbes's doctrines were to be given the somewhat invidious status of propaganda for the Republic of England. Twice during 1651 the serious editorials which prefaced Nedham's news-sheet consisted simply of unsigned extracts from Hobbes's *De Corpore Politico*. The first was a long quotation from Hobbes's characteristic discussion of the citizen's obligation to obey any power with the capacity to protect him. The second set out Hobbes's insistence on the congruence of the civil authority's commands with God's purposes.[100] And twice apart from this Hobbes was to be advertised in Nedham's paper as an authority on political theory.[101]

Nedham was to illustrate in his own writings as well as in his journalism how much his own political views could be sustained by the authority of Hobbes. This can best be seen in *The Case of the Commonwealth of England, Stated*, which Nedham published in 1650. The aim was to prove in general (in Part I) the "necessity and

---

[99] Anthony Ascham, *Of the Confusions and Revolutions of Goverments* (*sic,* in original) (London, 1649), pp. 108, 119.

[100] See *Mercurius Politicus*, No. 31 (2–9 January 1651), and No. 34 (23–30 January 1651).

[101] *Mercurius Politicus,* No. 29 (19–26 December 1650), p. 486, and No. 352 (5–12 March 1657), p. 7641. Cf. J. Frank, *The Beginnings of the English Newspaper* (Cambridge, Mass., 1961), p. 257.

equity" of submission to the powers that be; and to vindicate in particular (in Part II) the authority of the new Commonwealth government. The central contention in Nedham's as in Ascham's work was the Hobbesian claim that the basis of all government must lie in men's absolute need to protect themselves from themselves and each other by yielding their rights to some protecting power. The maintenance of such a power is at all times essential as the sole alternative to anarchy. In Part II of his book Nedham used this claim to denounce all changes proposed by Royalists, Levellers, and all other enemies of the Commonwealth. In the central chapter of Part I he simply states it as axiomatic that "there being a necessity of some government at all times, for the maintenance of civil conversation and to avoid confusion, therefore such as will not submit, because they cannot have such a government as they themselves like, are in some sense mere anarchists."[102]

Nedham is thus led, like Ascham, to the bleak and typically Hobbesian conclusion that since government is an absolute necessity, so political obligation must be absolutely owed to whatever government is in fact capable of sustaining good political order. Nedham has no doubts about the grounds of allegiance changing with events. The wheel of fortune, as his opening chapter is devoted to claiming, turns in an unpredictable but irrevocable manner. Once it has turned against a particular government, its citizens are merely building "castles in the air against fatal necessity" if they try to go on insisting on "a fantasy of pretended loyalty." There can be no question, moreover, of insisting on retaining one's allegiance to a rightful rather than a usurped power. Nedham endorses his Hobbesian conclusions by refusing to accept that there is any distinction to be made between

---

[102] Marchamont Nedham, *The Case of the Commonwealth of England, Stated* (London, 1650), p. 17. As with Ascham, to maintain uniformity of citation, all page references are to the enlarged 1650 edition. See fn. 104.

the obligation to obey *de jure* rather than *de facto* authority. As he insists in Chapter 2, there never has been an ancient or a modern state capable of surviving an examination of its original right to rule. All governments originally had "no other dependence than upon the sword." The only possible rule of obligation is thus to recognise and submit to the necessity of power itself, as the sole means for each citizen to be assured of the protection he needs.[103]

As in the case of Ascham's work, this Hobbesian defence of *de facto* power was completed without any reference to Hobbes. As with Ascham, however, the authority of Hobbes is subsequently used to corroborate these claims. When his book reached a second edition in 1650 Nedham added an appendix explaining that "notwithstanding that I have already . . . sufficiently proved" the claims it contained, yet "I thought meet to fasten them more surely upon the reader" by "inserting some additions" from Salmasius and "out of Mr. Hobbes his late book *De Corpore Politico*." The last five pages of the appendix accordingly consisted of extracts from Hobbes's discussion at both the points crucial to Nedham's own argument. "It may plainly be inferred" from Hobbes's account that there can be "no security for life, limbs and liberty" except "by relinquishing our right of self-protection." It may also be inferred from what "Mr. Hobbes saith" that "since there is no other possible way to preserve the well-being of the Nation" except "by a submission to the present power," it is entirely appropriate "to pay subjection to them," and to regard oneself as politically obliged, simply for "our own security."[104]

IV

When Sir Robert Filmer came to write his very shrewd critique of Hobbes's political doctrines, he thought of

---

[103] Nedham, ibid., pp. 5, 9.
[104] Nedham, ibid., 2d edn., with Appendix (London, 1650), pp. 103, 108, 109.

them not in isolation—as virtually all Hobbes's more recent exegetes have done—but rather as the views of "Mr. Hobbes, Mr. Ascham, and others of that party."[105] The appropriateness of this linkage of names (to which we can now add at least the names of Hawke, Heydon, Nedham, Osborne, and Warren) has, I hope, by now been vindicated. It remains to show, however, that the failure of more recent commentators to understand this context has had a damaging effect on the exegesis of Hobbes's own political thought, and notably his theory of political obligation.

One recent trend in the interpretation of Hobbes's theory of political obligation has consisted of increasing the emphasis on his connections with a more traditional political outlook. Hobbes's view of political obligation, on this account of his intentions, is detached from its apparently "scientific" psychological premises, and grounded instead on a traditional doctrine of natural law. Professor Warrender, in the most persuasive of these expositions, actually reformulates Hobbes's discussion in the language of a theory of duty. A subject is thus said to be obliged not primarily by means of his own calculations of oblique self-interest, but by his acknowledgment of his prior duty to obey the laws of nature, in virtue of recognising them to be the commands of God. Hobbes is thus treated as "essentially a natural law philosopher," believing that "the laws of nature are eternal and unchangeable and, as the commands of God, they oblige all men who reason properly, and so arrive at a belief in an omnipotent being whose subjects they are."[106] This view of the obligatory force of the laws of nature has been accepted by Professor Plamenatz,[107] and much extended by Professor Hood. Hood suggests a

---

[105] Sir Robert Filmer, *Patriarcha and other Political Works*, ed. Peter Laslett (Oxford, 1949), p. 231. Cf. also p. 188.

[106] H. Warrender, *The Political Philosophy of Hobbes* (Oxford, 1957), p. 322.

[107] J. P. Plamenatz, "Mr. Warrender's Hobbes," *Political Studies*, V (1957), p. 297.

dichotomy in Hobbes's account between an "artificial" and a "real" system of obligation, which is said not to be resolved until Hobbes "goes behind his philosophic fiction of command without a commander to the reality from which the fiction was derived, when he says that the second law of nature is the law of the Gospel."[108] The essential contention which all these accounts have in common can be summarised in the words of Professor Taylor, the first interpreter to suggest this view of Hobbes's theory of political obligation. Hobbes, we have to assume, "meant quite seriously what he so often says, that the 'natural law' is the command of God, and to be obeyed *because* it is God's command."[109]

I cannot in fact find a single place in *Leviathan* where Hobbes states the entailment which Taylor claims he "so often" asserts. But it is not my intention here to ask directly, as a matter of textual exegesis, whether this interpretation offers the best account of Hobbes's meaning. What I wish to point out is that the relations between Hobbes's statements and the context in which they were written can be shown to bear on this exegetical issue far more directly than has been supposed. For the view of Hobbes's intellectual relations implied by these accounts would in fact be historically absurd. My suggestion is that the weight of this testimony is perhaps sufficient in itself (somewhat as Hume argued in the case of miracles) for any such interpretation to stand discredited.

If Hobbes intended to ground political obligation on the prior obligation to obey the commands of God, then it follows, first of all, that every contemporary—every follower, every opponent, every sympathiser—all equally missed the point of his theory. All of them, moreover (surely an astounding coincidence), were mistaken in

---

[108] F. C. Hood, *The Divine Politics of Thomas Hobbes* (Oxford, 1964), p. 97.
[109] A. E. Taylor, "The Ethical Doctrine of Hobbes," *Philosophy* XIII (1938), p. 418.

exactly the same way. Consider first the position of the
"Hobbist" followers I have discussed. In the first place,
it certainly cannot now be argued (as some recent
commentators on Hobbes appear to have assumed) that
a purely rationalist and utilitarian theory of political
obligation would have been virtually impossible to artic-
ulate or understand in seventeenth-century England. The
"Hobbists" all unequivocally endorsed just such a doctrine—and far more crudely, of course, than ever appears in Hobbes's own political works. All of them, that
is, located the grounds of political obligation in the paramount need for protection, and located this need in turn
in their analysis of man's nasty and brutish nature. Many
of them, moreover, cited Hobbes specifically as an authority on both these crucial points. And there is no
doubt that this was also the popularly received impression of Hobbes's intentions amongst his contemporaries.
One contemporary commonplace book, for example, in
which "Mr. Hobbes's creed" is anatomised, summarizes
Hobbes as having taught "that the prime law of nature
in the soul of man is that of temporal self-love," and
"that the law of the civil sovereign is the only obliging
rule of just and unjust."[110] Another put it more tersely as
the view that "whatever the civil magistrate commands is
to be obeyed notwithstanding contrary to divine moral
law."[111] And when Daniel Scargill, the much discussed
"penitent Hobbist," recanted his "Hobbist" views before
the University of Cambridge in 1669, the views which
both he and they regarded as pre-eminently those of
Hobbes were that "all right of dominion is founded only
in power," and that "all moral righteousness is founded
only in the positive law of the civil magistrate."[112]

Consider next the position of Hobbes's contemporary

---

[110] British Museum, Sloane MSS, No. 1458, fo. 35.

[111] British Museum, Sloane MSS, No. 904, fo. 14.

[112] See James L. Axtell, "The Mechanics of Opposition: Restoration Cambridge *v.* Daniel Scargill," *Bulletin of the Institute of Historical Research*, 38 (1965), 102–11 and refs. there.

critics. These writers were themselves Christian moralists, who might have been expected to be particularly attuned to seeing any similar overtones in Hobbes's political works. Most of them, however, went out of their
way to emphasise what Clarendon called Hobbes's
"thorough novelty."[113] They could find in Hobbes no element of a traditional political outlook: they saw only a
complete iconoclast who (as Bramhall put it) "taketh a
pride in removing all ancient land-marks, between prince
and subject, father and child, husband and wife, master
and servant, man and man."[114] All of them agreed, moreover, on the form which Hobbes's iconoclasm took. They
associated Hobbes with two particular political doctrines,
both of which (as Clarendon remarked) would "over-
throw or undermine all those principles of Government
which have preserved the peace of this kingdom through
so many ages."[115] They assumed, in the first place, that
as Hobbes grounded political obligation on calculations
of rational self-interest, so he supposed that a man became obliged to any power with the capacity to protect
him. Hobbes's point of departure, in the eyes of these
critics, was not with the obligations of natural law but
merely with the fears and needs of natural man. When
the University of Oxford, for example, issued its famous
condemnation of heterodox books in 1683, Hobbes was
mentioned and denounced by name as the writer who
had invented the claim that "self-preservation is the fundamental law of nature and supersedes the obligation of
all others."[116] This was the view of all Hobbes's contemporary readers. Hobbes had taught that there was
a "right of nature" in every man, that society can only
"arise from necessity and fear" upon "the principles of

---

[113] Clarendon, *Brief View*, Sig. A, 1b.

[114] John Bramhall, *The Catching of Leviathan* (London, 1658),
p. 542.

[115] Clarendon, op. cit., Sig. A., 3b.

[116] "Judgment . . . of the University," in D. Wilkins, *Conciliae
Magnae*, 4 vols. (London, 1737), Vol. IV, pp. 610–12.

equality and self-preservation."[117] And in the second place, all the critics assumed that as Hobbes had made obligation depend on protection, so he had intended to teach that when a citizen is not adequately protected, then his obligations cease. Hobbes intended no less, as Clarendon put it, than to give subjects "leave to withdraw their obedience" from their ruler at the very time "when he hath most need of their assistance."[118] This was seen, indeed, as the final proof that Hobbes had abandoned any belief in "the obligation laid on us by fidelity (the law of God Almighty in our nature) antecedent to human conventions."[119] He had instead made "civil laws the rules of good and evil."[120] So far therefore from seeing in Hobbes any traditional elements of their own natural law doctrine, they regarded his account of political obligation as a most dangerous attack on it. "Where these principles prevail," as Bramhall concluded, "adieu honour and honesty and fidelity and loyalty: all must give place to self-interest."[121]

Some modern commentators have taken the heroic course of denying that any of this contemporary evidence matters, on the grounds that "any modern reader can see the general irrelevance" of Hobbes's critics.[122] But to concede this claim would only be to complete the paradox, and to make Hobbes's entire intellectual milieu impossible to understand. Hobbes himself is turned into the most incredible figure of all. He has to be represented as presenting a traditional type of natural law theory in a manner so convoluted that it was everywhere taken for the work of a complete utilitarian, a man prepared

---

[117] See respectively Filmer, op. cit., p. 242; Philip Warwick, *A Discourse of Government* (London, 1694), p. 55; Anonymous, *The Great Law of Nature*, p. 8.
[118] Clarendon, op. cit., p. 90.
[119] Tenison, op. cit., p. 147.
[120] Anonymous, *An Examination*, p. 15.
[121] Bramhall, op. cit., p. 519.
[122] K. C. Brown, "Hobbes's Grounds for Belief in a Deity," *Philosophy* XXXVII (1962), p. 337n.

(in Bramhall's memorable phrase) to "take his sovereign for better but not for worse."[123] And despite Hobbes's own predilection for the quiet life, his terror at being arraigned for heterodoxy, he must be represented as failing altogether either to disown the alarmingly radical writers who cited his authority, or to disarm his innumerable critics by pointing out their complete misconception of his intentions. It certainly becomes very extraordinary that Hobbes never in fact did any of these things. His followers and critics, moreover, are turned into scarcely less incredible figures. First, it becomes impossible to understand why Hobbes's opponents should have felt so threatened. A more careful reading (we are assured) would have reassured them that there is "nothing that is original in Hobbes's moral thought."[124] A reading of any of the writers who cited Hobbes's authority, however, would certainly have revealed to them a highly original view of political and moral obligation, of exactly the type which (mistakenly, we are assured) they claimed to find in Hobbes's own works. It certainly becomes hard to understand why it should have been Hobbes, rather than these evidently much more radical writers, on whom they continued to focus their attacks. And second, it becomes impossible to understand why any of Hobbes's avowedly "Hobbist" followers should have troubled to cite his authority. All of them had worked out a view of political obligation infinitely more radical than any exponent of natural law doctrine could ever attain or endorse. All of them (we are assured) must in any case have completely misunderstood the intentions of the writer whom they all continued (without eliciting any protest) to cite as their leading authority. It becomes clear, in short, that however plausible the deontological interpretation of Hobbes's theory of political obligation can be made to look as an account of Hobbes's *Leviathan*, the price of accepting it is to re-

---

[123] Bramhall, op. cit., p. 519.
[124] Hood, op. cit., p. 13.

move any meaningful points of contact between Hobbes
and his own intellectual milieu, and in general to purchase exegetical coherence at the price of historical absurdity.

V

My intention, in this very brief attempt to surround
Hobbes's theory of political obligation with its appropriate ideological context, has been to suggest a methodological as well as an historical and interpretative conclusion. I am suggesting that a knowledge of this sort
of historical information is not *merely* desirable as "background" to the study of a given writer. It can also be de-
ployed in effect as a further test of plausibility, quite
apart from the evidence of the writer's own works, for
any suggested interpretation of those works. I am suggesting, that is, that it has been a mistaken procedure
to assume, in the interpretation of Hobbes's political
works, that the "question of what his theory is" (as Professor Warrender puts it) can properly be regarded as
"prior" to and quite separate from the question of its
intellectual relations,[125] and the climate of opinion in
which it was formed and to which it contributed. Any
interpretation must imply some links (or the absence
of them) between a given theory itself and the exact
circumstances in and for which it was produced. My
general conclusion is thus that one of the conditions for
accepting any suggested interpretation of such a theory
should be that these historical links themselves must
be capable of being shown to be of an historically credible and plausible kind. My particular conclusion is that
this condition is so completely lacking, in the case of
the deontological interpretations of Hobbes's theory of
political obligation, that the validity of these interpretations themselves must for this reason be regarded at
least as very doubtful.

---

[125] Warrender, op. cit., p. ix.

THE ECONOMIC FOUNDATIONS
OF HOBBES' POLITICS

WILLIAM LETWIN

Hobbes' views about economic matters have not attracted much attention until recently. They do not catch the eye of the normally acute reader, nor have they forced themselves on the heightened sensitivities of scholars. Historians of political thought, until recently, passed them by in silence. Economic historians still do. And historians of economic ideas, notably assiduous hunters, have scarcely caught sight of this rare prey; Hobbes is mentioned only casually, and erroneously, in so wide-ranging a survey, for instance, as Myrdal's *The Political Element in the Development of Economic Theory* (1953).[1] For all this apparent neglect there is an obvious explanation: Hobbes said little, almost nothing, about economics. And this should not surprise us, for political philosophy was, and still can be, concerned with larger and broader questions than the economic organization of society or the economic agenda of the state.

More recently, however, interest has been awakened in Hobbes' economic views by a number of scholars who believe that political ideas are reflections of social facts and class interests. Most influential among those has been Professor C. B. Macpherson, who argued in *The Political Theory of Possessive Individualism* (1962) that *Leviathan* can be properly understood only by recognizing the close correspondence between the economic facts of England in his time and the basic ideas on which Hobbes

---

This essay was written especially for this volume by William Letwin, London School of Economics and Political Science.
[1] According to Myrdal (p. 70) "Hobbes introduced . . . into British political philosophy" the "natural law notion that property has its natural justification in the labour bestowed on an object." Myrdal gives no citation to Hobbes. On Hobbes' view of property rights, see below, pp. 160–1.

erected his system. Macpherson put forward three chief theses: (1) England at Hobbes' time was "essentially a possessive market society" (p. 62),[2] or as Macpherson put it elsewhere, a "bourgeois market society" (M.L., p. 12).[3] (2) Hobbes drew the premises of his political philosophy from the facts that prevail in such a society, with the result that his philosophy is "bourgeois"; it detects certain profound truths about bourgeois society, though Hobbes mistakenly supposed them to be true about every sort of society (p. 67; M.L., p. 12). (3) But because Hobbes underestimated the power of class, he made a basic mistake: overlooking "the centripetal force of a cohesive bourgeois class within the society" (M.L., p. 56), he concluded that chaos would result unless the sovereign (whether a natural person or an assembly) were self-perpetuating; and this mistaken doctrine explains why "the bourgeoisie" rejected the bourgeois teachings of Hobbes. Each of these theses is mistaken.

I

Macpherson's first thesis is that England at Hobbes' time, say in 1651, when he published *Leviathan*, was "essentially a possessive market society" (p. 62). A "possessive market society" he contrasts with two other types: a "customary or status society," which comprehends "ancient empires, feudal societies, and tribal societies"; and a "simple market society," which does not comprehend anything real—"it is less a model of any historical society than an analytical convenience." The three types are said to be exhaustive—"the fewest possible models to which all known kinds of society could be assimilated . . ."—even if not suitable for all purposes

---

[2] Citations to C. B. Macpherson, *The Political Theory of Possessive Individualism* (1962), are given throughout by page number without prefix.

[3] Hobbes, *Leviathan*, ed. C. B. Macpherson (Penguin, 1968); cited as "M.L."

of "general sociological or historical analysis" (p. 47). Despite this claim, however, the types are clearly not exhaustive. They make no provision for totalitarian societies, democratic socialist societies, or mixed economies. This defect might be shrugged off, for despite the great gaps in the scheme as a whole the separate categories might still be useful: it might be accurate or revealing to speak of England in 1650 as a "possessive market society." But, on the other hand, the gaps in the scheme, coupled with a general lack of logical symmetry in the categories it does set up, point to an arbitrary quality in Macpherson's method of analysis, an arbitrariness whose worst consequence is the conclusion that England in 1650 *must have been* a "possessive market society" because it was *not* a "status society" or a "simple market society." But this conclusion would hold only if the three types were exhaustive, and if, furthermore, an actual society at any given moment could not belong to more than one of the types. As I shall show, England in 1650 was not "essentially" a possessive market society: it had many characteristics that Macpherson allots to a "status society" and other characteristics that do not correspond to anything in Macpherson's categories.

By a "possessive market society," Macpherson explains, he means a bourgeois or capitalist society in the senses pictured by Marx, Weber, and Sombart, a society whose two essential features are "the pre-eminence of market relations and the treatment of labour as an alienable possession" (pp. 48–49). More particularly he defines a possessive market society by characteristics which may be summarized as follows:

Individuals are economically free agents.
They make contracts which are enforced by custom or law.
All individuals act rationally in the economic sphere.
Some individuals have unsatisfied appetites for pleasure or power.

Some men are better endowed than others. (pp. 53 ff; cf. pp. 46–53.)

These are in Macpherson's view the defining character-istics of "bourgeois" society today as well as of English society in the seventeenth century, and also the premises about man and society on which Hobbes erected his philosophy.

How well do Macpherson's attributes describe Hobbes' England? Beginning with the one that seems most ac-curate, is it true that men were unequal, or, in Macpher-son's words (p. 54), that "some individuals have more energy, skill, or possessions, than others"? Could any-body believe otherwise? Could anybody believe other-wise about *any* society? Curiously enough Macpherson does. He declines to include factual inequality among "the essential properties of a customary or status society," even while he discusses the presence in that kind of society of slaves and masters, superiors, "ruling classes" and "upper ranks" (p. 49). Again he excludes the fact of inequality from his model of a "simple market society" (p. 51). We are left to infer that although—as Macpher-son repeatedly implies—inequality exists in all three types of society, he regards it as an "essential property" only of a "possessive market society." Why? Apparently because he believes that a general struggle for pre-eminence takes place only in a bourgeois society. Only there is exploitation general, though he does not speak of "exploitation," preferring the more lurid metaphor of "invasion." Thus, he says, "a customary status society, while it permits perennial forcible invasion between ri-vals at the top, and occasional forcible invasion between classes or sections of classes, does not permit perennial invasion, either forcible or otherwise, of individuals by individuals throughout the society" (p. 50). Similarly with a "simple market society." Therefore "invasion" of a sort which is peaceable, lawful, and general—meaning the transfer of property from one person to another—is characteristic only of a possessive market society. "Competition," which is another name for such "invasion," is said to stem from inequality and to intensify inequality, and that is why we are to believe that although inequality holds in all societies it is "essential" only in bourgeois society. A strange and arbitrary chain of reasoning thus bypasses all the inequalities inherent in the notion of "status" and exhibited in the difference between a pharaoh and his field slave to arrive at the conclusion that inequality is "really" only possible when competition becomes general throughout a society. In fact, although there was plenty of inequality in England in 1650, there is no shred of evidence to suggest that it was greater than at any earlier time; on the contrary, individual differences in "energy, skill, or possessions" were quite possibly shrinking during the seventeenth century.

How true is it, secondly, that some men in Hobbes' time were moved by restless desire, or, to use Macpherson's formulation, that "some individuals want a higher level of utilities or power than they have" (p. 54)? Again, on the face of it, it would seem undeniable. All experience suggests that *all* kinds of society contain *some* men like that. If there had not been some men like that in the status society of the Old Testament, Moses need not have troubled to proclaim God's commandments against stealing and coveting. Indeed Macpherson concedes that in a status society *some* men do want a higher level of utilities or power than they have. "There is room in this model for men at the upper levels of power, who want more delights, to invade others at those levels forcibly. . . . But this is competition between rivals for the benefits already being extracted from the subordinate population. It cannot be general throughout the society . . ." (pp. 49–50). Therefore, since competition is not general throughout a status society, Macpherson refuses to regard the acquisitive drive of some members as an essential characteristic of status society. But although he very particularly insists that acquisitiveness is not general in a possessive market society either, he does identify it as an essential characteristic of that sort of society—

because, he maintains, the acquisitiveness of the few forces everyone in such a society to act similarly, whether they like to or not. "Since the market is continually competitive, those who would be content with the level of satisfactions they have are compelled to fresh exertions by every attempt of the others [individuals who want more delights than they have] to increase theirs" (p. 59).

Is there a particle of evidence that this hypothesis accurately portrays life in England when Hobbes lived? Let it be said in the first place that Macpherson gives none. Add that it is not easy to imagine how one could possibly find much solid evidence either for or against it. The inescapable conclusion is that Macpherson's hypothesis is an entirely unsubstantiated surmise. That is, although anybody might agree, on grounds of common experience, that *some* people in *any* society want more than they have—which is why Hobbes' premise is innately plausible as a universal generalization about man's nature—nobody need agree, or is offered by Macpherson any good reason for agreeing, that the ambitions of *some* men in a competitive market economy (and only in such a society) result in a general scramble to acquire continually more and more. It is just as likely that in modern economies most men desire more and more because of their own autonomous desires and not because competition in any sense "forces" them into this position; and it should be noted that intense desire for economic growth and higher incomes is not confined today to possessive market economies but is present also in non-competitive totalitarian economies. Further it is quite likely that many men in a possessive market economy are in fact content with what they have, and do not feel "compelled to fresh exertions" by the example of their more ambitious neighbors; this hypothesis is more consistent than Macpherson's with such facts of possessive economies today as the increasing length of holidays taken by workers and the increasing amount of voluntary early retirement—all of which shows that many people are content with less income than they could get.

Taking into account, then, what Macpherson really means by the statement that some men want more than they have, it can be recognized as a hypothesis that is neither substantiated nor plausible.

This becomes more evident when we consider the related proposition that in Hobbes' England "all individuals seek rationally to maximize their utilities" (p. 54), "that is, to get the most satisfaction they can for a given expenditure of energy or goods, or to get a given satisfaction for the least possible expenditure of energy or goods" (p. 51). To suppose that this describes any real society is sheer extravagance; to suggest that it "essentially" or even roughly represents England in the seventeenth century is false. Over half the people of England in 1650 earned their living from agriculture, much of it still carried on by old communal arrangements that restricted farming to traditional crops and ancient methods. Agricultural reformers kept urging farmers to break out of those restraints by enclosing the fields and adopting new crops and techniques; some farmers did, but only a few and slowly and against heavy resistance. One of the greatest innovators, Walter Blith, wrote—within a year of *Leviathan*'s appearance—to complain about the irrationality of the old-fashioned farmer: "He will toil all his days, himself and family, for nothing, in and upon his common arable field land; up early and down late, drudge and moil and wear out himself and family; rather than he will cast how he may improve his [lands] of imposturing [composturing?] and enclosing of it."[4] And the contemporary literature on every branch of trade and shipping provides further evidence that while some Englishmen were trying hard to achieve economic efficiency, many others continued in their customary and inefficient ways. Anything else would have been astounding. Macpherson's proposition can be salvaged as a his-

---

4 Quoted (spelling modernized) from Charles Wilson, *England's Apprenticeship, 1603–1763* (1965), p. 27; see Ch. 2 for an admirable summary of agricultural practices at Hobbes' time.

torical statement only by saying that the desire for economic efficiency was probably increasing during the seventeenth century, while the force of custom was diminishing somewhat. But one should instantly add that this process had been going on for centuries before Hobbes' time and is still going on now. So that though Macpherson's specification in its severely qualified sense has some validity for England in the seventeenth century, it does not apply to it distinctively and was not true of it generally.

How correct is it to assert, as Macpherson does, that contracts were authoritatively enforced in Hobbes' England? Here again the answer is that while true, the statement is not distinctively true. Contracts are an old matter. They have been made and honoured as long as there has been history. In Europe after the decline of Rome it was not always easy for an aggrieved party to find a public authority who would or could uphold the obligation. Nevertheless, according to Pirenne, contracts were enforced by custom "very early and at latest at the beginning of the eleventh century" and by law from the twelfth century on.[5] And in England statutes as early as 1283 and 1285 required mayors and sheriffs to seize the goods or bodies of persons who defaulted on commercial debts.[6] Long before the seventeenth century, then, contracts—that is, enforceable voluntary agreements—were familiar to many Englishmen. In the seventeenth century contracts were more frequent than they had been, customary arrangements were less common than they had been; both coexisted as normal practice, and their relative importance is not known. Macpherson offers no evidence on this point, beyond the flat assertion that "there is plenty of evidence that England approxi-

---

[5] H. Pirenne, *Economic and Social History of Medieval Europe* (1937), p. 53; and see the medieval authorities cited by O. Gierke, *Political Theories of the Middle Age* (1938), n. 279, p. 181.
[6] Bland, Brown, and Tawney, *English Economic History* (1914), pp. 161–62. S. F. C. Milsom, *Historical Foundations of the Common Law* (1969), Chs. 10, 11, 12.

mated closely to a possessive market society in the seventeenth century," buttressed by a statistic about the number of wage earners and a single quotation from a single historian who says that between *some* (apparently few) new landlords and their tenants "there was no personal tie—nothing except a cash nexus" (p. 61). It is far too thin a base to support Macpherson's conclusion, and indeed there *is* plenty of evidence that contracts were abundantly made and enforced both earlier and later than the seventeenth century.

How true, finally, is it to describe Englishmen contemporary with Hobbes as economically free agents? Were they in fact unrestrained by law and custom from exchanging their property as they liked and for whatever proceeds they could manage to get? The answer, very roughly, is that they were. Labour could be hired out, land could be rented and bought, so could goods of all sorts, and money could be borrowed at interest; markets existed in all these commodities and assets. It may well be, as Macpherson concludes from the contemporary population estimates of Gregory King, that about half the men were full-time wage earners and it seems certain that well over half earned wages at some time or other, especially at harvest time. But the magnitude of the labour force shows that the phenomenon was not, as Macpherson implies, new: the shift from feudal obligations to labour by voluntary agreement did not take place in a few years but over several centuries. As early as the fourteenth century, work for wages was common enough, in country and town, so that Edward III legislated to stem the rise in wages that followed the Black Death; "no man," he declared in the Ordinance of Labourers of 1349, a precursor of present Incomes Policy, "shall pay or promise to pay to any man more wages, liveries, hire or salaries than is accustomed. . . ."[7] So

---

[7] Bland, Brown, and Tawney, p. 165, and see pp. 167–76, 282–84, and 325–60 for other examples down to the seventeenth century.

once again it turns out that the condition which Macpherson attributes specifically to Hobbes' time had in fact existed for a long while.

The same is true about other aspects of economic freedom in the seventeenth century. Men could alienate land, and did; but there were also many severe limits on alienation, such as by entail, and on use, as by local ordinances, orders in council, and judgments of courts. Men could dispose of other sorts of property in trade, and did. But on the other hand, commerce was severely restricted by statutes and proclamations, guilds and trading companies, and the whole administrative weight described as the "mercantilist system." To say therefore that "land and resources are owned by individuals and are alienable" (p. 54) is no more than a half-truth.

To sum up, then, England in Hobbes' time was not "essentially" a "bourgeois" or "capitalist" or "possessive market" society. Of the characteristics that Macpherson mentions, some applied only partly, some applied because they apply to all societies, and some applied only in the sense that the opposite did not apply. Macpherson's logic is like assuming that all hats are either red or green, and then arguing that as this hat is not green it must be red, when in truth it is red and green and yellow decorated with black lace. England in fact was a mixture of status, custom, and innovation, of freedom and restraint, of efficiency and carelessness, and was not any simple thing fit to be summed up by a ragged and emaciated model.

II

According to Macpherson's second thesis, Hobbes drew his premises from the bourgeois society that existed around him, not perhaps altogether consciously, yet consistently, so that "it is clear that his model approximates most nearly to the model of the possessive market society" (p. 67).

For Macpherson one telling indication of this correspondence is that Hobbes regarded labour as a commodity; for a free market in labour is—according to Macpherson and many others—a vital attribute of capitalism. Unfortunately, however, Hobbes himself gives little help on this score, for only once, and then quite by the way, does he speak of labour "as a commodity." The unique passage occurs in the course of a comment on foreign trade which opens Chapter 24 of *Leviathan* (L., p. 188).[8] After distinguishing between native and foreign commodities, Hobbes observes that few countries are large enough to be self-sufficient economically and few do not produce surpluses. He goes on: "the superfluous commodities to be had within become no more superfluous, but supply these wants at home, by importation of that which may be had abroad, either by exchange, or by just war, or by labour; for a man's labour also is a commodity exchangeable for benefit, as well as any other thing: and there have been commonwealths that having no more territory than hath served them for habitation have nevertheless not only maintained but also increased their power, partly by the labour of trading from one place to another and partly by selling the manufactures whereof the materials were brought in from other places" (L., p. 189). Foreign goods can be acquired, Hobbes says, by exchange, by just war, and by labour; it is a curious trio, for exchange and seizure would seem to be exhaustive; where then does labour fit in, otherwise than as a component of both exchange and seizure? The answer, as the last clause indicates, is that labour has two additional roles, especially for a country too small to grow its own raw materials, let alone an exportable surplus, a country, Hobbes probably meant, like Holland or England: it supplies manpower for the carrying trade and for the manufacture of imported raw materials. In effect, then, there are four ways a nation can get goods

---

[8] Hobbes, *Leviathan*, ed. W. G. Pogson Smith (Oxford, v.d.); cited throughout as "L." When quoting Hobbes I have modernized the spelling and punctuation.

from abroad: by exporting its native materials, either raw or wrought; forcible seizure; earnings from the carrying trade; and re-exporting foreign materials that have been worked up at home. The last two methods, Hobbes is pointing out, involve the figurative export of native labour as distinct from the literal export of native materials, and in saying that "a man's labour also is a commodity exchangeable for benefit," he means that native labour is as capable as native commodities of earning imports from abroad. Macpherson, taking the passage out of context, misinterprets it as "presumptive evidence that [Hobbes] was taking for granted the normality of the wage relationship" (pp. 62–63).

There is no evidence that Hobbes took wage work as "normal," and indeed it was not then as "normal" as self-employment. There is evidence that he knew some people worked for wages. It occurs in a passage in *Behemoth* where Hobbes, after castigating merchants for being naturally sponsors of rebellion, rebuts the standard defense that they are public benefactors because they provide the poor with work. He answers:

> That is to say, by making poor people sell their labour to them at their own prices; so that poor people, for the most part, might get a better living by working in Bridewell, than by spinning, weaving, and other such labour as they can do; saving that by working slightly they may help themselves a little, to the disgrace of our manufacture. [*Behemoth*, (1889, 1969) p. 126.]

This is no more, in spirit, than a caustic rejoinder that nobody ought to be considered a public benefactor for suiting himself. Taken at the letter it says that poor workers would live better in the workhouse than they could on their piecework wages *except that* they increase their total earnings by working too fast, so skimping on quality: "working slightly" meant working shoddily, which is why it "disgraces" goods manufactured in England—a common complaint in mercantilist literature. Taken any way at all this passage cannot support the heavy weight

Macpherson loads on it. In his view it shows that
Hobbes believed "Labour is a commodity, and there is
such a large supply of it that its price is driven down, by
the buyers, to a level of bare subsistence" (p. 66). It
shows nothing of the sort, but only that Hobbes shared
an entirely traditional skepticism about the motives of
merchants, as blunt as that expressed a century earlier by
one who wrote that "All merchants . . . liveth by other
men's work, and . . . riseth to great riches, intending
nothing else but only to get riches. . . ."[9] A complaint
old as time and as persistent should not be read as a
specific allusion to capitalism.

Another indication, and in Macpherson's view a more
important one, that Hobbes was talking about a capitalist
society is his treatment of commutative and distributive
justice. Taken in isolation from its immediate context,
as Macpherson takes it, it does seem an unmotivated
attack, perverse and even sneering, on the distinction
established by Aristotle and transmitted by Aquinas (cf.
Summa Theologica, Ia, xxi.I). "Writers," as Hobbes describes his philosophical ancestors, tell us that justice
of actions is "divided into commutative and distributive"
(L., p. 115). And commutative justice, they say, consists
in "the equality of value of the things contracted for."
But, says Hobbes, they are wrong. It is not unjust to exchange things of unequal value. More precisely, it is not
proper for an onlooker, setting himself up as an objective
judge of a transaction, to assert that it is unjust because
the things exchanged are not equal *in his eyes.* The only
true measure of the value of things exchanged is the
"appetites," the subjective tastes, of the parties to an
agreement; "and therefore the just value is that which
they be contented to give." Is there any objective standard by which the justness of an agreement can be
measured? The old tradition said, Yes; Hobbes says, No.
There is only one, formal standard in Hobbes' view:

[9] Tawney and Power, *Tudor Economic Documents* (1924), Vol.
III, p. 126; spelling modernized.

justice requires that men carry out their contracts, that they honour their pledges and keep their covenants. So he redefines commutative justice in accordance with this governing principle: "To speak properly, commutative justice is the justice of a contractor, that is, a *performance of covenant*, in buying and selling, hiring and letting to hire, lending and borrowing, exchanging, bartering, and other acts of contract" [L., p. 115; italics added].

Macpherson, seeing all these commercial images—which had always been relevant to the idea of commutative justice, for from its beginning it was meant to explain justice *in exchange*—seizes on them as signs that Hobbes is speaking of things as they are in a "market society." "And what has made the old concepts an object of scorn" to Hobbes, he says, "is one of the attributes of the market model, namely, that the value of anything is simply its price as established by supply and demand" (p. 63). It is worth pausing for a moment to note the sophomoric proposition that "value" has only one meaning in a "bourgeois society." If that were so, what would "we" mean when we speak of the "value" of friendship, or of a poem, or of things such as liberty that we regard as "priceless"? Macpherson persists in his view, however: "In treating commutative and distributive justice in this way, Hobbes is drawing the logical conclusions from his model of society: where all values are reduced to market values, justice itself is reduced to a market concept" (p. 64).

Macpherson's view of the matter quite misses the point of Hobbes' attack on traditional ideas. Justice, according to Hobbes, is the third law of nature, which commands "That men perform their covenants made" (L., p. 110). This is, obviously, the only definition that can do Hobbes' work: an absolute sovereign who results from a *covenant* must rationally be obeyed because justice requires men to perform in accordance with their covenants, and the sole rational ground, if any, for disobeying the sovereign is that he has failed to provide the satisfaction he was authorized to provide. If any other, substantive notion of justice were allowed to stand, men might apply it to the actions of the sovereign, might conclude that any one of his particular commands was unjust, and might regard themselves as rationally justified in disobeying the sovereign or even in overthrowing him. So Hobbes, in Chapter 15, which bears the innocuous title "Of Other Laws of Nature," deals with justice and sets out on the insidious and philosophically revolutionary task of destroying every idea which would establish an objective and rational ground for assessing the justice of agreements and actions other than only this one, that justice means sticking to one's agreements. And it is in the course of this clearance operation that Hobbes shoves aside the idea of "commutative justice," which as we have seen he redefines as nothing more than "a performance of covenant" in acts of contract. It has nothing whatever to do with a market society, except possibly in the eyes of one who supposed that covenants, contracts, and agreements exist—conceptually and legally—in no society but a "market" society.

And so it is as to other basic postulates of Hobbes' system: that men can reason and make rational, efficient choices; that men exhibit "a perpetual and restless desire of power after power, that ceaseth only in death"; that they can make agreements. These, as I have shown, though it is hardly necessary to prove at length, were not distinctively true of the society in which Hobbes lived or more true of it than they have been of all societies. Hobbes may have drawn on his own immediate experience; he could not have helped doing that; but he knew enough about other times and places—a knowledge of which was and is available in any society which remembers some history and meets some foreigners—to draw on their experience as well. His premises, in short, are universal statements about the nature of man. Insofar as they are true at all, they are more or less equally true of all men at all times.

III

Macpherson's third thesis is that Hobbes failed to persuade the bourgeoisie because he made a theoretical mistake: he overlooked the role of classes in a bourgeois society (M.L., pp. 53–60). He did not offend the bourgeoisie in advocating an absolute sovereign, because "There was no reason why the bourgeoisie should have objected to a supreme legislative and executive body consisting of themselves or their nominees . . ." (M.L., p. 53). What did offend them was his insistence that "the sovereign, whether a single person or an assembly, should have the power to name its successors" (M.L., p. 54). And the reason this offended them is that it could not satisfy any "group or class which wanted to keep some control over the supreme legislative and executive body . . ." (M.L., p. 54). It would seem that their rather reasonable objection might apply, *a fortiori*, to an absolute sovereign, since absolutism means nothing other than that the sovereign is uncontrollable by any "group or class." Macpherson's response is that "the bourgeoisie" would quite endorse absolutism if it were in "their" hands but would object violently to any that were not. Everything turns on "their" sense that what any of "them" wants is much the same as what the rest of "them" want. In short, Macpherson charges Hobbes with having missed "the possibility that there might be a substantial group or class, such as the bourgeoisie itself, with a sufficient sense of its common interest . . ." (M.L., p. 55). Macpherson, contrary to Hobbes, does not overlook the social cement of the "common interest" of a "ruling class."

This is not the place to raise the large question of whether the hypotheses embodied in the category of "class" reveal anything very illuminating about politics. Nor need I expand here the assertion that the "common interest" of any broad class is always far less compelling than "special interests," the diverse desires and conflicting proposals that divide presumed "classes" into separate and shifting parties, factions, alliances, associations, companies, sects, societies, clubs, movements, cliques, and leagues. Leaving those larger questions aside, what of Macpherson's allegation that Hobbes committed an oversight? Why did Hobbes overlook "the bourgeoisie as a class" (M.L., p. 57)? The answer is simple. There was no such thing. That there were rich men and poor men Hobbes certainly knew and said (e.g., L., p. 266). But to treat "rich" and "poor" as "classes," as Macpherson does (M.L., p. 60), makes little sense about a society in which Gregory King—on whom Macpherson relies heavily (pp. 279–92)—easily distinguished twenty-two different "ranks, degrees, titles and qualifications," *most of which* were neither rich nor poor. If rich and poor defined class, then all societies would be class societies. And, in any event, Macpherson's assertion that "the bourgeoisie" would not have objected to absolute government if "they" controlled it, flies directly in the face of the whole constitutional history of England from 1650, which exhibits continual objections from all sorts of Englishmen against everything that suggested absolutist pretensions or rule. Among those who objected were merchants—who deserve, if anybody does, to be called "bourgeois"—and the more important thing is that among their chief opponents were always other merchants.[10] So little is the bourgeoisie bound together by common interests.

If one needs an explanation of why Hobbes did not please the bourgeoisie the most likely is that he could not easily please anybody but an absolute ruler, and could not even please any particular absolute ruler, because his doctrine did not endorse any particular one as against any other. In any event, intellectual audacity is not a popular taste.

---

[10] Letwin, *Origins of Scientific Economics* (1963), Ch. 1, espec. pp. 41–47, and passim.

IV

It still remains to digest properly the little that Hobbes said about economic policy. Most is set out in a short chapter, "Of the Nutrition and Procreation of a Commonwealth" (L., Ch. 24, pp. 188–95), which tells us what a proper sovereign should do about the economic activity of its subjects. First, it arbitrarily distributes land among the subjects, thus setting up property rights, which it enforces on behalf of each subject as against all others; but as the subject has no property right as against the sovereign, the sovereign may tax or dispossess him whenever public need requires (L., pp. 190–91). Second, it licenses foreign trade, both as to the places with which subjects may trade and the goods they may export and import (L., pp. 192–93; cf. L., pp. 177–79). Third, it establishes and regulates the modes of contract, that is their legal forms, though not their substance (L., pp. 192–93). Next it establishes money and regulates the value of coin (L., pp. 193–94). And, finally, it takes charge of "procreation" by licensing the founding of colonies, which can of course have no rights except those granted in their charters (L., pp. 194–95). A few other functions of a distinctly economic character Hobbes discusses elsewhere. The sovereign should provide a certain minimum of public instruction, chiefly such as will make the subject more obedient (L., pp. 258–65); provide public charity to the unemployable (L., p. 267); and eliminate unemployment among the able-bodied by forcing them to take work while encouraging others to provide work (L., p. 267). And that fundamentally is all. As to the rest of his economic activities the subject is to be free, he is to enjoy liberty by pretermission: "The liberty of a subject lieth therefore only in those things which, in regulating their actions, the sovereign hath praetermitted: such as is the liberty to buy and sell and otherwise contract with one another; to choose their own abode, their own diet, their own trade of life; and institute their children as they themselves think fit; and the like" (L., p. 163).

Everything considered, it is a fairly moderate program of economic intervention. Most of the economic functions that Hobbes allocates to the absolute state have nothing to do with absolutism. Any state may levy taxes. Any state, however liberal, regards itself as responsible for guaranteeing private property, administering the law of contracts, creating a coinage, and licensing the founders of colonies. Adam Smith regarded these as normal and so does the Constitution of the United States. Most states, liberal or not, also administer some public charity and some public instruction, though liberal states do not put the chief emphasis in public education on teaching people to obey the sovereign. Almost all the items in Hobbes' agenda for economic policy, therefore, would suit almost any modern state; it does not go too far for a liberal state and, if anything, it leaves the subject too much economic freedom to suit a totalitarian state.

On only one point in the economic agenda did Hobbes take an extreme position, a position of the sort commonly labelled Hobbesian. This was his view that the private property of the subject could claim no immunity as against the sovereign. In asserting this he was contradicting one of the chief conclusions of political liberalism, and one of the main contentions of the liberal constitutionalists of his own time. The Constitution of the United States, for instance, ordains that no person shall "be deprived of . . . property, without due process of law; nor shall private property be taken for public use, without just compensation." In writing this provision the framers of the Constitution were deliberately following Chapter 39 of the Magna Carta, which held that "No free man shall be . . . disseised [dispossessed] . . . except by the lawful judgment of his peers or by the law of the land." To this provision their attention had been drawn by Sir Edward Coke, Hobbes' contemporary, who repeatedly cited it as a reason why the English sovereign had no authority to take his subject's property.[11] When Charles I imposed the forced loan of 1626, Coke was one of the leaders of the opposition, and during the ensuing crises—the dissolution of the two Parliaments, the trial of the Five Knights, and the bringing in of the Petition of Rights—he kept saying "Magna Carta is such a fellow he will have no sovereign," in other words, that royal prerogative could not override the guarantee that private property would be taken only after fair trial or after the subjects consented to a tax. This resistance by Coke and his colleagues Hobbes later identified as the first beginning of "the attempt of popular government," the first step toward chaos.[12] And by flatly denying Coke's theory, Hobbes knowingly took a special, extreme, and violently unpopular position.

Yet leaving aside this one great exception, the whole rest of the economic agenda that Hobbes set out for the state is remarkably neutral. Most states follow, in one way or another, most of the economic policies he proposed, though many go considerably further. It might seem therefore that Hobbes drew up his list by reflecting, in the abstract, on what most or all states do in the economic sphere, and then adding one sharp drop of absolutism to give the mixture its required flavour. And perhaps that is what he did.

There is, however, a different and more plausible source on which he could have drawn: England as it had been down to the beginning of the Civil War, or, more exactly, England as Hobbes understood it to have been. The correspondence between what Hobbes required of the sovereign and the actual economic policies practiced by English government down to 1640 is rather close. That many subjects considered their landed property to be open to seizure by the Crown is clear, and sometimes it was seized, though the rights and wrongs of seizure

---

[11] See A. E. Dick Howard, *The Road from Runnymede* (1968), espec. pp. 117–25.
[12] *Behemoth* (1889, 1969), p. 27.

without conviction (or of taxation without consent) were hotly disputed. The licensing and regulation of foreign trade was always regarded as part of the royal prerogative, and though some fraction of it passed gradually into the hands of Parliament, the East India Company still turned to the Privy Council for a charter in 1600 and to Charles II in 1661. That English sovereigns down to 1650 established and enforced the law of contract, coined money, and chartered colonial adventures goes without saying. As to the poor, the policies of Elizabeth fitted exactly Hobbes' prescription, as can be seen from the title of a piece of legislation in 1572, "An Act for the punishment of vagabonds, and for the relief of the poor and impotent."[13] As for setting the able-bodied but unemployed to work, that was the aim of the Statute of Artificers[14] and of the "Act for setting of the poor on work, and for the avoiding of idleness"[15] and of the many laws and policies earlier and later. And, finally, the economic liberties of the subject that Hobbes instanced were in fact liberties not merely pretermitted by English sovereigns but regarded well before Hobbes' time as having become common law "rights." It might be concluded from this close correspondence that Hobbes based his conspectus of economic policy largely on the actual practice and some current theories of the English constitution as of, say, 1610 to 1630, that is, from the time he became an adult until the time when the constitutional order in which he grew up began to crumble.

From this summary of Hobbes' economic attitudes one may draw a perplexing summary of his underlying political attitude. As to the constitution of the state he was an absolutist. As to the economic policy of government he was a conservative, if by conservative we mean someone generally disposed to have things go on as he be-

---

[13] 14 Eliz., c.5, 1572.
[14] 5 Eliz., c.4, 1563.
[15] 18 Eliz., c.3, 1576.

lieves they have been going for a long time. And as to the economic scope of government he was a liberal, if by liberal we mean someone generally disposed toward a government that governs little. Meeting so complex a position, expressed with such great intellectual boldness, the reader of Hobbes oscillates between extremes of irritation and enlightenment.

HOBBES AND HULL—METAPHYSICIANS
OF BEHAVIOUR

R. S. PETERS AND H. TAJFEL

1 The Idea of a Universal System of Behaviour

It is sometimes instructive to compare modern systems
of thought with those of the past not simply for the sake
of pointing out what startling similarities can be found,
but also because the past systems are usually less clut-
tered up with details and it is easier to see the logical
difficulties they involve. This is particularly the case with
mechanical systems for explaining human behaviour; for
in such systems there are certain crucial logical difficulties which can too easily be covered up by the intricacy
and subtle devices of the latest machine.

There are many candidates to the title of 'the father of
modern psychology'. But the claims of Thomas Hobbes
can be pressed very strongly in that he was not only the
first to suggest that human beings are machines, but also
the first to attempt a systematic explanation of *all* human
actions in terms of the same principles as were used to
explain the behaviour of inanimate bodies. Descartes
and others thought that animal behaviour and the *involuntary* actions of men could be mechanically explained,
but not distinctly human actions, involving reason and
will. Hobbes ruthlessly extended Galileo's assumptions
into the innermost sanctuaries of human thought and decision. He claimed originality for his civil philosophy on
this account. Indeed, he hoped that his name would be
as famous in the history of psychology and social science
as that of Harvey who extended the new science of motion to physiology.

Hobbes sketched a Grand Plan for the explanation of

From *British Journal for the Philosophy of Science*, Vol. 8 (1957–
58). Reprinted by permission of the authors and publishers.

human behaviour—starting with simple motions in geometry and proceeding via mechanics, physics, and physiology to psychology and social science. A more limited version of this deductive dream is to be found in recent times in the work of C. L. Hull. The title of Hull's latest book is *A Behavior System*.[1] The aims of the enterprise are explicitly stated both in the latest book and in its predecessor, his *Principles of Behavior*,[2] published some ten years earlier. Thus, 'the objective of the present work is the elaboration of the basic molar behavioral laws underlying the "social sciences" '.[3] Elsewhere, it is said that:

> An ideally adequate theory even of so-called purposive behavior ought, therefore, to begin with colorless movement and mere receptor impulses as such, and from these build up step by step both adaptive behavior and maladaptive behavior. The present approach does not deny the molar reality of purposive acts (as opposed to movement), of intelligence, of insight, of goals, of intents, of strivings, or of value; on the contrary, we insist upon the genuineness of these forms of behavior. We hope ultimately to show the logical right to the use of such concepts by deducing them as secondary principles from more elementary objective primary principles.[4]

In the concluding pages of the *Principles of Behavior*, the Grand Plan is given an even more ambitious and more detailed expression. Through a 'systematization of the behavior sciences' based on the consistent use of certain methodological rules, Hull hopes that ultimately treatises 'on the different aspects of the behavior sciences will appear'. These treatises will be based on systematic primary principles, and will present general or specific theories of individual and social behaviour, of 'communi-

---

[1] C. L. Hull, *A Behavior System* (New Haven, 1952).
[2] C. L. Hull, *Principles of Behavior* (New York, 1943).
[3] Hull, op. cit., p. 17.
[4] ibid., p. 25–26.

cational symbolism or language', of 'social or ritualistic symbolism', of economic, moral, and aesthetic valuation,

of familial behavior; of individual adaptive efficiency (intelligence); of the formal educative processes; of psychogenic disorders; of social control and delinquency; of character and personality; of culture and acculturation; of magic and religious practices; of custom, law and jurisprudence; of politics and government; and of many other specialised fields of behavior.[5]

Now it would be very welcome to have a deductive system in which statements about human behaviour could be deduced from more general laws—e.g. of mechanics or physiology. But it may well be that this programme is a pipe-dream—especially if the model is based on mechanics. For the difficulties in developing such a system may not be empirical ones connected with the complexity of human behaviour, as is often thought, but *logical* ones connected with the categories of description appropriate to human action.

It used to be held that man was a rational animal and that his reason was of a different ontological status from the rest of his body—not subject to the laws of nature. As often, this metaphysical thesis may well have enshrined an important logical truth, namely that man is a rule-following animal and that adequate explanations in terms of efficient causes *alone* cannot be given for actions which are in accordance with rules, conventions, criteria, canons, and so on. The old time-honoured gulf between nature and convention may well have far more general application than is often realised.

It is our thesis that there are certain logical difficulties about *any* mechanical system of human behaviour. These exhibit themselves in a deductive system as gulfs

(*a*) between motions at a physiological level and hu-

---

[5] ibid.

man actions which are goal directed and usually conform
to certain criteria or conventions,

(*b*) between motions of the body and consciousness—
especially rational thought.

These gaps may well all be connected with man's pe-
culiarity as a rule-following animal. Our hope in this
paper is to exhibit the rather surprising similarity between the systems of Hobbes and Hull, and to substantiate, in places where the similarity between the systems
is most apparent, the general thesis that mechanical explanations can never be *sufficient* for actions falling under the concept of rule-following.

2 Motions and Human Actions:
The Similarity between the Theories
of Hobbes and Hull

The basic presupposition of mechanistic explanation is
that all causes are antecedent motions. As Hobbes put it,
there can be no action at a distance, 'no cause of motion, except in a body contiguous and moved'.[6] Now a
great many things happen for which there is presumably
some cause, yet it is difficult to see any motion in a contiguous body which could have caused it. Recourse is
therefore made to the notion of unobservable motions
either within or between bodies. Hobbes exploited this
move with considerable ingenuity. He managed to bridge
the gap between the movements in external bodies,
which were transmitted by means of a medium to the
sense-organs, and the movements of the body in appetite
and aversion by introducing the concept of 'endeavour'
or 'conatus', which he defined as 'motion made in less
space and time than can be given; that is motion made
through the length of a point and in an instant or point

---

[6] T. Hobbes, *E.W.*, Vol. I, p. 124 (*E.W.* stands for *English Works*
and is the standard way of referring to the Molesworth edition of
Hobbes' Works. Similarly *L.W.* stands for *Latin Works*).

of time'.[7] It was a term for *infinitely small* motions which he took over from the physical scientists and generalised to bridge the gap between physics, physiology, and psychology. It was a peculiarly subtle move; for although the term was used as a physical construct at the molecular level, it conveyed the suggestion of striving and direction which was so apt for the transition to psychological happenings at the molar level. So wherever there was a gap in observable motion—e.g. between the object and the sense-organ or between the stimulation of the sense-organ and the movements of the muscles in appetite and aversion, Hobbes postulated 'endeavours' which transmitted the motion.[8] For, according to his theory, motions from the external world not only move to the brain and produce images; they also affect the vital motions of the body which are manifest in the circulation of the blood, breathing, excretion, nutrition, and other such processes. When these incoming motions impede the vital motions, this is felt as pain and the parts of the body are acted on by the muscles 'which is done when the spirits are carried now into these, now into other nerves, till the pain, as far as possible, be quite taken away'.[9] Similarly in the case of pleasure, the spirits are guided by the help of the nerves to preserve and augment the motion. When this build-up of endeavours tends towards things known by experience to be pleasant, it is called an appetite; when it tends to the avoidance of what is painful, it is called an aversion. Appetite and aversion are thus 'the first endeavours of animal motion'. Even in the case of a few appetites and aversions which are born with men, such as those for food, excre-

---

[7] T. Hobbes, *E.W.*, Vol. I, p. 206.

[8] The concept of 'endeavour' also enabled Hobbes to give a substantial interpretation of dispositional terms. On his view, when we ascribe a 'power' or capacity to anything, we are making a statement about an actual build-up of minute motions. Even habits were explained as *actual motions* made more easy and more ready by perpetual endeavours.

[9] T. Hobbes, *E.W.*, Vol. I, p. 407.

tion, etc. (which sound very much like the modern 'primary drives'), initiation of movement is from without.

Hull's system is surprisingly similar; he starts, as Hobbes did, from the simplest possible elements. An adequate theory of behaviour, he says, ought 'to begin with colorless movements and mere receptor impulses as such, and from these build up step by step both adaptive and maladaptive behavior'.[10] For Hobbes action was an outcome of an interplay between internal and external motions. Hull's analysis of the initiation of action is also based on an interplay of assumed minute motions within the 'neural structures'. Observable actions of the organism are for him, in most cases, the result of existing 'habit structures' slowly built up on the basis of previous experience, according to certain principles specified in his postulates. There is no direct cause-and-effect sequence, as in Hobbes, between the properties of the present stimulation and the consequent actions. But Hull's picture, made much more complex by the intervention of the past through learning, remains nevertheless an essentially mechanical picture. The extrapolation from minute occurrences to behaviour, while not based on a direct link between sensation and action, or external and internal motions following each other in a simple manner, is based on 'habit structures' built into the nervous system during the past, and active at the time of stimulation. The main difference here between Hobbes and Hull is not a difference of principle: it consists in the fact that Hull specifies the conditions of the past motions (learning) which led to the pattern of motions as it is observed in the present. The passing of the organism into action is the result of the preponderance of the 'strongest' of these motions. The concepts used by Hull at this stage of his analysis are stated in mechanical terms. A threshold is 'a quantum of resistance or inertia which must be overcome by an opposing force before the latter can pass

---

[10] T. Hobbes, *E.W.*, Vol. I, p. 25.

over into action'.[11] The 'competition of reaction potentials' is basically a conflict of 'motions', the strongest of which 'wins', and thus determines action. The 'behavioral oscillation', a concept introduced in order to account theoretically for those unpredictable movements of the organism which could not be entirely explained by the momentary status quo between the competing 'reaction potentials', is conceived as an outcome of an infinite number of minute motions.

The basic principles concerning the inner workings of motives and incentives are very similar in both systems. Hobbes is concerned with a mechanical explanation of pain and pleasure. Hull is in need of simple assumptions, which would allow him to describe the 'mechanism' by which successful (i.e. rewarded) responses remain a part of the organism's habit equipment, while the unsuccessful ones are eliminated. Hobbes assumes an increase and decrease in vital motions. Hull's reductionism goes one step further. In his simplified scheme the nature of reinforcement consists essentially in a reduction in the internal stimulation (e.g. in hunger, thirst, fear) which follows the successful response. The locus of this reduction must, by necessity, remain vague. It is applied to primary drives by assuming, in each case, some specific internal pattern of stimulation to be reduced. More complex forms of motivation are reducible to the basic mechanism by a transition in which both the incentive nature of previously rewarded situations, and the intervention of some kind of stimulation to be reduced (e.g. anxiety) play their part.

The 'drive-reduction hypothesis' is the equivalent of Hobbes' decrease in vital motions. But Hobbes was content with the statement of the general principle, which then allowed him to go on talking about motivation in terms of efficient mechanical causes. Hull attempts to be more specific: the 'minute unobservable' finds its way into an explanation of 'secondary motivation'. The most

---

[11] ibid., p. 323.

explicit attempt at generalising the principle to various forms of human endeavour can be found in a recent paper by Brown,[12] in which anxiety reduction is made the basis of assigning to the 'reduction principle' the capacity of explaining a very wide range of human motivational phenomena.

As a matter of fact Hobbes did something rather similar in his theory of the passions, though at the molar level and without any pretence of relating his theory of 'passions' to his physiological theory; for all the 'passions' are represented as manifestations either of the desire for power or of the fear of death. Laughter, for instance, is explained as an expression of sudden glory when we light upon some respect in which we are superior to others; courage is aversion with hope of avoiding hurt by resistance; and pity is grief for the calamity of another rising from the imagination that a like calamity may befall ourselves. The reduction of all passions to the desire for power and the fear of death provided Hobbes with an exciting psychological analysis of politics and with great opportunities for coining epigrams; but it had a tenuous connection only with the physiological details of his theory of motivation. The Hullian reduction of complex behaviour, on the other hand, sketches a simplified 'picture' of our internal workings and transfers physiological description to behaviour at the molar level. And the use of 'avoidance behaviour' (such as behaviour due to anxiety) to redescribe other forms of motivation in terms of its negative forms is due, to a large extent, to the fact that 'avoidance behaviour' can be quite easily described in terms of reduction of internal stimulation. It can thus be linked with a vague physiological 'picture'; but, apart from this dubious advantage, its merits as an explanation are very questionable.[13]

---

[12] J. S. Brown, 'Problems Presented by the Concept of Acquired Drives', *Current Theory and Research in Motivation: A Symposium*, 1953.

[13] See, for instance, Harlow's comments on Brown's paper: Ibid., pp. 22–23.

3 The Illegitimacy of the Transition from Motions to Human Actions

The link with physiology, which we have described as 'a dubious advantage' is regarded by Hull as the chief strength of his theory. For he claims that eventually descriptions of actions at the molar level will be deducible from physiological postulates at the molecular level. But surely the link cannot be that of *deducibility*. Hamlyn[14] has recently discussed the confusion existing in some psychological theories, in which activities have been described in terms of movements, observable or unobservable. The distinctive features of activity, or behaviour, will be left out in such a description. For no fixed criterion can be laid down which will enable us to decide what series of movements constitutes a piece of behaviour—e.g. getting a treaty signed or winning a girl's affection. Descriptions of behaviour imply standards, which are loosely defined and which are interpretations at quite a different level from descriptions of movements. Of course behaviour involves movements; but it cannot be described simply in terms of movements. For similar pieces of behaviour can involve quite different movements.[15] *Some* movements in the body and brain, for instance, are necessary conditions for passing an examination, but it has yet to be shown that any *particular* movements are either necessary or sufficient. Now if behaviour cannot ever be *described* purely in terms of movements, how much less can it be *deduced* from a theory which is concerned only with 'colourless movement'.

By his analysis of motivation Hobbes hoped to substantiate his claim that: 'A final cause has no place but

---

[14] D. W. Hamlyn, 'Behaviour', *Philosophy*, 1953, 28, pp. 132–145.
[15] A similar distinction between behaviour and physical movements was drawn in a different context by J. O. Wisdom, 'Mentality in Machines', *Proc. Arist. Soc.*, Sup. Vol. 26, 1952, pp. 10–15.

in such things as have sense and will; and this also I shall prove hereafter to be an efficient cause.'[16] And, of course, he was right in saying that human actions have efficient causes—external stimuli, movements of the sense-organs, internal motions, and so on. But this does not mean that a list of any such movements could ever be *sufficient* to explain actions. For actions are distinguished by the goals towards which movements are directed; the goal makes the movements part of an action of a certain sort. And since we cannot specify which movements *must* be involved in attaining the goal, so also we cannot specify *precisely* which antecedent movements are sufficient to initiate behaviour. This general logical difficulty holds against Hull's more complicated theory as well as against Hobbes' simpler one.

This kind of logical difficulty is even more glaring in Hobbes' theory of the passions. For most of our terms at this level of description are either like 'ambition' in assigning a certain kind of objective to an action or like 'honesty' in classifying an action as being in accordance with a certain rule or convention. It is most implausible to suggest, as Hobbes did, either that such terms imply anything specific about the efficient causes which initiate behaviour of this kind,[17] or that such behaviour could be *deduced* from a theory concerned only with colourless movements. For a gross muddle of explanatory models is involved. Terms like 'ambition' and 'honesty' derive their meaning from a model of behaviour peculiar to goal-directed and rule-following activities, which is of quite a different logical type from that of mechanics. In this explanatory model an agent is assumed to have an objective (like being a professor, in the case of 'ambition'), and to have information about means which will lead to this objective in a manner which is both efficient and in accordance with certain conventions of appropriateness (as in the example of 'honesty'). This model

---

[16] T. Hobbes, *E.W.*, Vol. I, p. 132.
[17] See R. Peters, *Hobbes*, Penguin Books, 1956, pp. 144–147.

forms a kind of explanatory ceiling in understanding human behaviour just as the mechanical model of bodies pushing other bodies formed an explanatory ceiling in the seventeenth-century understanding of nature. And all our psychological explanations are related to this model just as all explanations in classical economics presupposed the model of a rational man.

Now physiological descriptions can state *necessary* conditions for behaviour conforming to this model; for it is a truism to say that we cannot plan means to ends or be sensitive to social norms unless we have a brain. Similarly physiology, like psycho-analysis, can state conditions under which this type of behaviour breaks down. A man with a brain injury may well be insensitive to social pressures just as a man with an obsession may be incapable of taking the means necessary to bring about a desired objective. Obviously physiological theories are extremely *relevant* to explanations of action at the molar level of behaviour. But this does not mean that there is a *deductive* relation between them—that behaviour can be deduced from the physiological description *alone*. Our contention is that Hobbes and Hull were mistaken in assuming that the relation was of this sort.

But surely, it might be objected, Hull had much more rigorous standards of scientific method than Hobbes. Surely he must have introduced subsidiary hypotheses to bridge the gap between physiological and psychological descriptions. On the contrary, our case is that neither Hobbes nor Hull saw that these types of explanations were of logically different types. Hull's ultimate aim is a 'truly molecular theory of behaviour firmly based on physiology.'[18] As this is at present impossible because of the inadequacy of our knowledge, a molar approach based on the use of 'quasi-neurological principles' must serve for the time being. There are, however, 'degrees of the molar, depending on the coarseness of the ultimate causal segments or units dealt with. Other things equal,

---

[18] Hull, op. cit., p. 20.

it would seem wisest to keep the causal segments small, to approach the molecular, the fine and exact substructural details, just as closely as the knowledge of that substructure renders possible.'[19]

This makes explicit Hull's assumption that the difference between physiology and psychology is only a difference in the 'coarseness of the ultimate causal segments or units'. There is no *logical* difference, on his view, between these explanations; it is merely a matter of the 'fineness' of the 'substructural details'. Yet as soon as he starts developing explanations instead of just making programmatic pronouncements, the logical gulf immediately appears. For instance, as Koch points out, 'stimulus' is conceptually defined by Hull either in terms of physical energy, or in terms of neural impulses. R is 'reaction or response in general (muscular, glandular, or electrical)'; but when Hull refers to stimuli or responses in his description of the behaviour of experimental rats, R comes to mean *actions* such as 'biting the floor bars', 'leaping the barrier', and so on.[20] Stimuli, to quote Koch again, 'are certainly not being specified in terms of independent physical energy criteria'. The symbols which previously referred to the 'substructural detail' are kept unchanged, but even at this low level of behavioural complexity, they acquire new meanings: they refer to *actions* classified in terms of their end-results.

This reference to the 'substructural detail' also occasions another query. What sort of description is appropriate to it? Is it in fact described in physiological terms? Or could it be that Hull, like Hobbes, makes a plausible transition from physiology to psychology by according the 'logically more primitive elements' a sort of twilight status? Hobbes found the elements on which he constructed his system in motions of particles of all sizes. When a jump into the unobservable became necessary,

[19] ibid., p. 21.
[20] S. Koch, *Clark L. Hull* in *Modern Learning Theory* (New York, 1954), pp. 24–25.

motions became shadowy 'endeavours' which belonged
to minute particles of matter. The 'reality status' of minute motions in Hobbes' system was obvious and explicitly affirmed. Hull's position, however, is more ambiguous. The data for both sides of his formulae are
stimuli and responses, or molar movements of the organism. Between these two classes of observables, a
series of 'theoretical constructs' serves the attempt to
express the infinite variation at both ends in some uniform, lawful, and communicable manner. The constructs are not meant to be observable, and are, or
should be, unequivocally defined without reliance on
'substance'. Discussions about the doubtful status of these
supposedly abstract links are a familiar feature of the
recent psychological literature, and need not be invoked
here in detail.[21] The main objection levelled against
them is that they are not abstract, but have an implicit
existential status. 'Habit strength' may well be an abstract
quantifiable concept, but 'habit' or 'reaction potential' are
for Hull not only theoretical constructs. They are also
'neural organisations', they form pseudo-physiological
'pictures' of what happens inside the organism. These
events are described, as in Hobbes' system, in terms of
minute motions. And just as Hobbes' 'endeavours' enabled him to slip unobtrusively from mechanical to
psychological descriptions, so also Hull's language
shuffles between that appropriate to a description of the
physiology of the central nervous system and that which
is used to describe observable molar events. But it is
not definitely committed to either. A peculiar use of
terms (e.g. 'reaction-potential') bridges the gap in both

---

[21] See, for example, F. H. George, 'Logical Constructs and Psychological Theory', *Psychol. Rev.*, 1953, pp. 1–6; S. Koch, *Clark L.
Hull* in *Modern Learning Theory* (New York, 1954); K. Mac-
Corquodale and P. E. Meehl, 'On a Distinction between Hypothetical Constructs and Intervening Variables', *Psychol. Rev.*, 1948, 55,
pp. 95–107. Koch's paper especially contains a very detailed discussion of the logical difficulties raised in Hull's system by the ambiguous, pseudo-physiological character of the 'theoretical constructs'.

systems: language describing the 'primary elements' is still used in the description of behaviour, and the transition is achieved because its difficulties are ignored.

It is this which renders untestable an important aspect of Hull's theory. System-builders who aim at an 'explanation of human behaviour' and find their point of departure in any form of atomism must state clearly the steps which enable them to hope for such an achievement. It is true that many of Hull's hypotheses have been tested in a number of severely limited experimental situations. Indeed it is often said that testability is one of the main virtues of Hull's theory; for he was 'the first psychologist who could be proved to be wrong'.[22] But these tests only establish certain regularities of behaviour in extremely simple situations without showing how these regularities can be deduced from the underlying principles of internal motion. Neither do these tests in any way establish the applicability of such simple laws to forms of behaviour such as are outlined in his ambitious scheme which we have described above.

4 Consciousness and Rational Thought

If we can trust Hobbes' autobiography, his psychology was developed in part as an answer to a problem that haunted him for years. He had once been present at a gathering of learned doctors who were discussing problems connected with sensation. One of them asked what, after all, sensation was, and how it was caused. To Hobbes' astonishment not one of them was able to suggest an answer. Hobbes pondered over this for years until, after his meeting with Galileo, a solution suddenly occurred to him. He looked at the familiar process of sensation in the unfamiliar way he had learnt from Galileo.

---

22 Derek Pugh, Review of *A Theory of Social Control*, *British Journal of Psychology*, 1955, 46, p. 153.

It occurred to him that if bodies and all their parts were to be at rest, or were always to be moved by the same motion, our discrimination of all things would be removed, and (consequently) all sensation with it; and therefore the cause of all things must be sought in the variety of motion.[23]

Sensation, which was but 'some internal motion in the sentient', was a meeting place of motions. Deductions from a general mechanical theory were all that were required both to explain the peculiarities of sensation itself and the initiation of actions in response to external stimuli. These Hobbes proceeded to provide.

The selectivity of perception was explained by suggesting that while the organ retains motion from one object, it cannot react to another; similarly in attention the motion from the root of the nerves persists 'contumaciously', and makes the sense-organ impervious to the registering of other motions. The explanation of imagination is a straight deduction from the law of inertia:

When a body is once in motion, it moveth, unless something else hinder it, eternally; and whatsoever hindreth it, cannot in an instant, but in time, and by degree, quite extinguish it; and as we see in the water, though the wind cease, the waves give not over rolling for a long time after; so also it happeneth in that motion, which is made in the internal parts of man, then, when he sees, dreams, etc. . . . Imagination therefore is nothing but decaying sense.[24]

The decay, of course, is not a decay in motion. For that would be contrary to the law of inertia. Rather it comes about because the sense-organs are moved by other objects. This explains the vividness of dreams. For in sleep there are no competing motions from the external world. When sense-impressions are constantly crowding in on

[23] T. Hobbes, *L.W.*, Vol. I, p. 21.
[24] T. Hobbes, *E.W.*, Vol. III, p. 4.

us, the imagination of the past is obscured and 'made weak as the voice of a man in the noise of the day'. Thus the longer the time that elapses after sensing an object, the weaker our imagination.

There is something almost incredibly hard-headed and naive about Hobbes' gross materialism. To say that sensation and the conceptual processes are *nothing but* motions is rather like saying that kissing is simply a mutual movement of the lips or that work is moving lumps of matter about. Hobbes, too, is aided in this rather monstrous piece of metaphysics by using terms like 'agitation', 'celerity', 'disturbance', and 'tranquillity' to describe mental processes; for these terms have meaning as descriptions both of physical and psychological happenings. Hobbes could thus talk like a physiologist and preserve the common touch of everyday psychological description. But at any rate he did openly, not to say brazenly, make the transition from mechanics to psychology. He did not, however, seem to be sufficiently aware of the *sort* of gap that he is bridging. For just as he developed a *causal* theory of imagery and thought also that he was answering questions about the reference or *meaning* of images, so also he thought that differences between activities like perceiving, imagining, and remembering could be explained solely in terms of their efficient causes. But the distinction between sense and imagination is not *simply* that imagination is *decaying* sense any more than the distinction between imagination and memory is that the latter involves only the addition of a sense of pastness. For these activities have different names because they imply different logical criteria. Psychologically speaking, perceiving may be the same as imagining in a given case. When we say, in spite of this that we did not *imagine* something, we are making a logical point, not a psychological one. Human actions imply criteria of distinction which are at quite a different logical level from that appropriate to stimuli, movements, and other such mechanical concepts.

Hobbes, then, leapt openly, if recklessly, from me-

chanics to psychology. Hull, who deals very little with
sensation, either ignores the gap or bridges it by implied
assumptions. He ignores problems connected with the
status of consciousness and his assumptions about sensation are implicit in his development of a theory of
learning rather than explicitly stated. Hobbes assumed
that identical motions from the external world will lead
to identical counter-motions in the organism; in other
words, discrimination between various stimuli, and generalisation of responses to stimuli varying quantitatively
and qualitatively will be a function of the degree of
difference between the motions imposed on the organism
from the outside. Hull, preoccupied with learning rather
than with problems of perception, is interested only in
the influence of past events on present perception. But
again the conclusions reached in both systems are almost
identical, as the common assumption is that, in the last
analysis, it is the degree of identity of patterns of minute motions which determines the degree of identity of
perceptions. And no doubt there are such differences in
minute movements. But it is questionable whether a
knowledge of these alone would ever enable us to explain
the differences in the descriptions of what we see. For
such descriptions involve the use of conventions and
standards of correctness which we impose on what we
see. Man is a rule-following animal in perceiving as well
as in moral behaviour, and it is this characteristic which
makes all such causal theories unplausible as *sufficient*
explanations of his activities.

Hobbes saw that it was man's capacity for using symbols in deductive reasoning and in descriptive languages
which distinguishes him from animals, together with the
theoretical curiosity that goes along with it. But he even
suggested a mechanical explanation of language in his
crude causal theory of signs. This was a grotesque failure because he never properly distinguished logical
questions of the reference of signs from causal questions
of their origin. Similarly he gave a mechanical explanation of choice. Will, he held, simply *is* the last desire in

deliberating which emerges after an oscillation of impulses. Here again, in his writings on free-will, he never properly distinguished questions about the justification of actions (their reasons) from questions about their causes. Indeed, he seemed to think that *all* reasons for actions are rationalisations—a smoke-screen concealing the underlying thrust and recoil of a pleasure-pain calculating machine. But this is inadequate. For there is a manifest difference between compulsive and rational behaviour. A person who deliberates rationally about means to an end will be influenced by logically relevant considerations. For him there is a difference between good and bad reasons for a course of action. But for a compulsive there is no such similar distinction. No reasons will make any difference to what he does. Like a man under post-hypnotic suggestion he will only 'reason' to find excuses for what he is going to do anyway. Now any mechanical theory, even if it has recourse to minute motions, must face the glaring inappropriateness of giving causal explanations of transitions in terms of logical dependence. In what sense can a physiological theory of the brain be said to *explain* a geometer's conclusions or a move at a game of chess?

Hull suggests in his opening chapter that all sorts of formalised procedures like those of law, ritual, and government, can be explained by means of his mechanical theory. But, needless to say, he never gives an inkling of how this can be done. Is there much point in elaborating a system in such detail and making such far-reaching claims for the derivations which one day might be made from it, if the grave logical problems of applying such mechanical explanations to distinctively human behaviour are completely ignored? Hobbes saw the crucial gaps and audaciously, if unconvincingly, attempted to leap them. Could it not be said that the detail and alleged logical rigour of Hull's system, far from putting psychology on a truly scientific path, merely serve to conceal important logical difficulties in his system?

In his last book Hull wrote:

> It is clear from the foregoing discussion that natural-science methodology presumably will be able, ultimately, to deduce from its principles all kinds of behavior of organisms, whether generally characterised as good, bad, or indifferent. Moreover, since the passing of a moral judgement is itself a form of verbal behavior, either overt or covert, it is to be expected that natural-science theory will be able to deduce the making of moral judgements along with other forms of behavior.[25]

Now it is understandable that Hobbes should also have shared this methodological pipe-dream; for he lived before Hume and Kant had shown the logical impossibility of deducing statements about what ought to be from statements about what is the case. But any modern philosopher, who read this extract from Hull, would marvel at the naiveté of a man who thought that normative judgments could be deduced from a physiological theory. Our case, however, has not been a laboured exposition of this obvious logical lapse. It has been, rather to stress that the logical leap occurs in a much more interesting transition—in that from movements to actions. Misled by the obvious fact that physiological theories are extremely *relevant* to explanations of human actions, Hull, like Hobbes, thought that descriptions of human actions could be *deduced* from a physiological theory alone. This, in our view, is the basic logical mistake in mechanistic theories which both Hobbes and Hull commit in a surprisingly similar manner.

---

[25] T. Hobbes, *E.W.*, Vol. III, p. 338.

HOBBES ON POWER

S. I. BENN

I cannot hope to add anything illuminating to the already extensive literature on Hobbes's view of *potestas*, the right by virtue of which some men control others. Not so much has been written, however, of *potentia*, of power not as right but as possibility, natural faculty, or *de facto* control (whether by right or otherwise).[1] My purpose in this paper is to examine what Hobbes had to say about *potentia* in five different kinds of contexts: the account of natural power that we find in *De Corpore*; the account of human faculties of body and mind, for instance in *Human Nature*; the account of the relation of power and will, in the polemics on Liberty and Necessity; and the accounts of power as means to desired ends, and of social power, the power that is "compounded" of the powers of other men, to be found in *Leviathan* and elsewhere. I shall try to establish that the accounts given of "power" in the later contexts are incompatible with the strictly causal, actualist analysis of *De Corpore*, and that the shifts are required because the analysis of the concept offered in *De Corpore* would make it unfit for the work it has to do in contexts concerned with voluntary action and interpersonal relations.

This essay was written especially for this volume by S. I. Benn, Senior Fellow in Philosophy, Australian National University.

NOTE: I am greatly indebted to my colleague, Geoffrey Mortimore, for the time he has generously given to reading and arguing over this paper. I have benefited both from his criticisms, and from his suggestions as to how I might avoid at least some of them.
[1] R. Polin, *Politique et philosophie chez Thomas Hobbes* (Paris: 1952); and R. Peters, *Hobbes* (Harmondsworth and Baltimore: 1956), are unusual among recent studies of Hobbes in putting what he has to say about the power of men against the broader setting of his views on the nature of possibility and of the powers of objects.

I—The Identity of Power and Cause

The analysis of "power" and "act" in *De Corpore* follows hard on the account of cause and effect; "nay," says Hobbes, "those and these are the same things; though, for divers considerations, they have divers names."[2] Hobbes takes as his causal paradigm an agent *imparting* an effect to a patient,[3] the effect and the cause being of the same kind, "some certain accident or accidents, with which both . . . [the patient] and the agent are affected."[4] Moreover, since all change consists of changes in motion, an agent acts upon a patient by imparting motion to it, mediately or immediately; it does so by virtue not of its being a body (for then all agents being alike bodies would have the same effects on a patient), but of possessing a specific accident, which is to be understood as a motion of some specific sort. "Fire . . . does not warm, because it is a body, but because it is hot."[5]

Accidents qualify as causes only if they are conjoined appropriately for an effect to follow;[6] for where there is no effect it is absurd to speak of a cause. When Hobbes speaks therefore of a cause as "entire," he is referring to some situation in which an agent is actually imparting motion to a patient; he is referring, that is, to an event. So accidents are causes only as they figure in explanations of events. For the imparting of motion to occur, both agent and patient must possess the necessary accidents; there must be not only an efficient but also a material cause, sufficient for the effect—not only

---

[2] *De Corpore*, X.1. *English Works*, ed. W. Molesworth (London: 1839–45) (hereafter cited as E.W.), Vol. 1, p. 127.
[3] Ibid., IX.1, p. 120.
[4] Ibid., IX.3, p. 121.
[5] Ibid.
[6] "The cause, therefore, of all effects consists in certain accidents both in the agents and in the patients; which when they are all present, the effect is produced" (Ibid.).

must the agent be moving but the patient moveable. But though Hobbes distinguishes between these "partial causes," it is a division only within one "entire" cause with an actual effect; one cannot argue

If r, p would have caused q
But not r
∴ p is a partial cause of q;

for p is no cause at all, the expected effect q being frustrated.[7] Nor will Hobbes allow it to be a potential or possible cause; for he maintains that no effect is possible for which the cause will never be entire. So a thing is possible only if it will *at some time* occur; what will never happen is for ever impossible.[8] To say p *was* a possible cause would have required Hobbes to admit counterfactual conditional statements as truth conditions for statements of possibilities. I shall suggest reasons later for his believing this unsatisfactory.

---

[7] Ibid., IX.4, p. 122.

[8] It might be argued, perhaps, that the view Hobbes is expressing is no more extreme than that which E. Gilson attributes to St. Thomas and Maimonides, that "as far as individuals are concerned, a possible may or may not be realized, but what is possible for a species, whose duration is eternal, must inevitably come to pass, otherwise the word possibility is vain" (*The Christian Philosophy of St. Thomas Aquinas* [London: 1957], p. 69). I am indebted to my colleague Mr. John Kilcullen for drawing my attention to this passage, and suggesting this as a possible interpretation of Hobbes.

It seems unlikely to me, however, that this would be a correct interpretation of Hobbes, given his opinion that "that is an impossible act, for the production of which there is no power plenary. . . . [If] there will always be wanting some of those things, without which the act cannot be produced . . . that act shall never be produced; that is, that act is IMPOSSIBLE: and every act, which is not impossible, is POSSIBLE. Every act, therefore, which is possible, shall at some time be produced; for if it shall never be produced, then those things shall never concur which are requisite for the production of it; wherefore that act is *impossible*". (*De Corpore*, X.4; E.W., Vol. I, p. 129). Since Hobbes identifies "act" and "effect" (Ibid., X.1, p. 127), it seems to follow that when he says "where there is no effect, there can be no cause" (Ibid., IX.4, p. 122), he means to deny any meaning to "possible but unrealized" causes. An accident does not qualify for consideration as a cause, unless it is an actual part of an entire cause.

Hobbes's analysis of cause as a total situation, sufficient for the effect, leads him to the rather embarrassing conclusion that "in whatsoever instant the cause is entire, in the same instant the effect is produced."[9] It is only at the moment of impact, when a moving ball sets a stationary ball actually in motion, that the cause is entire. Neither the precedent motion of the approaching ball—the efficient cause—nor the mobility of the stationary one—the material cause—is enough on its own. Now aside from the question of the correct characterization of material causes, there is a difficulty for Hobbes arising from the simultaneity of the entire cause and the effect. Can these be different events, or should they be considered as a total situation that might be viewed either under the aspect of cause or of effect, the whole amounting, as it were, to a still taken from the moving picture of universal change? The difficulty with the latter interpretation is that to sustain his determinist model of the universe, Hobbes needs to present later stages as *necessitated* by earlier; causes must be *antecedent* to their effects, if the chain of necessitating causal conditions, "the progress of causation"[10] is not to turn out to be a series of disconnected moments. Any event ("action"), says Hobbes, may be viewed either as cause or effect according as one looks forward or backward from it; but it must surely be the cause of the next succeeding, or the effect of the next preceding event—it cannot be simultaneously cause and effect in respect of itself.

All this bears directly on power, since according to Hobbes, the relation of cause to effect is identical with that of "power" to "act":[11]

For whensoever any agent has all those accidents which are necessarily requisite for the production of some effect in the patient, then we say the agent has

---

[9] Ibid., IX.5, p. 123.

[10] Ibid., IX.6, p. 124.

[11] "Correspondent to *cause* and *effect*, are POWER and ACT; nay, those and these are the same things; though for divers considerations, they have divers names." Ibid., X.1, p. 127.

power to produce that effect, if it be applied to a patient. . . . [T]he same accidents, which constitute the
efficient cause, constitute also the *power* of the agent
[i.e., active power]. . . . [But] *cause* is so called in
respect of the effect already produced, and power in
respect of the same effect to be produced hereafter;
so that *cause* respects the past, *power* the future
time.[12]

"Efficient cause" corresponds therefore to "active power,"
"material cause" to "passive power"; "effect" corresponds
to "act." When the active power, the heat, say, of a
lighted match, is brought together with the hitherto inert
but combustible barrel of gunpowder (combustibility
being, I suppose, its passive power), the resulting act is
the barrel's explosion. And this act will undoubtedly
impart motion to other things, which is precisely what
Hobbes would lead us to expect: ". . . all active power
consists in motion . . . and that power is not a certain
accident which differs from all acts, but is indeed an
act, namely motion, which is therefore called power,
because another act shall be produced by it afterwards."
If A moves B, which in turn moves C, B's motion is the
effect of A's; it is also an act produced by the active
power of A; but this act of B is also an active power in
respect of C.[13]

I am inclined to think, however, that there is some
equivocation here. Hobbes clearly wants to avoid a
scholastic account of *potentia* and *actus*, whereby a
substance B has the *potentiality* for assuming a form q,
which issues in act (i.e., is actualized) by the operation
of an efficient, or trigger cause A. According to that view,
the active power itself can exist in potentiality; so an
unlighted match would have the potential power to
ignite the gunpowder, which in turn has the potential
passive power to be ignited. For Hobbes, however, to

---

[12] Ibid., X.1, pp. 127–28.
[13] Ibid., X.6, p. 131.

ascribe a power to a body is to ascribe to it an accident
with a *future* (not a hypothetical and possibly counterfactual) role as cause. And he gives no meaning to "potentiality" beyond power.[14] So a potential power would
be a power to be a power, which for Hobbes would mean
the cause of a thing's being a cause, at some future date.
Hobbes was clearly of the opinion that a determinist
could not intelligibly employ the concept "other possible
worlds"; so counterfactual or subjunctive conditional
propositions could not be of use in explicating true
propositions attributing powers to things as they actually
are. If the manifestation of a power is conditional on
an event which will never occur, it is conditional upon
an impossibility. But a power, or possibility of action
which it is impossible to exercise, is no power at all. The
argument would go thus:

Suppose: A had the power to q = If, but only if, Z,
                                 A would have q-ed;
           But not Z; i.e., conditions were not sufficient
                 for Z.
       ∴ Z was impossible.
       ∴ It was impossible that A should q.

And Hobbes takes this as equivalent to:

It was impossible for A to q (A had no power to q).

But if Hobbes repudiates the concept of a hitherto
unrealized potentiality—a mere possible cause—what are
we to make of his concept of "passive power," which for
the scholastics meant the capacity to assume a given
form? "All active power," says Hobbes, "consists in motion"; so to attribute active power to an agent is to ascribe to it some accident that is a form of motion to be

---

[14] Cp. *An Answer to Bishop Bramhall*, E.W., Vol. IV, p. 299: "I
understand . . . [potentiality] to be the same with *potentia*, which
is in English power. . . . [Potentiality] is found only in School-
divinity, as a word of art, or rather as a word of craft, to amaze
and puzzle the laity."

communicated in due course to a patient. But what is ascribed when we attribute passive power to a patient? What kind of an accident is mobility? Should this also be understood as motion? Can the patient be both at rest and in motion at one and the same time?[15] So far as I am aware, Hobbes does not expressly deal with this problem; but he might possibly have answered it, using the ingenious concept of "endeavour," which he defines as "motion made through the length of a point, and in an instant or point of time"[16]—an infinitesimal motion, having direction and, it seems, velocity, though operating through no considerable space or time. A moving body, exercising an active power, will encounter *resistance* in another body—"the endeavour of one moved body either wholly or in part contrary to the endeavour of another body, which toucheth the same."[17] The mobility of a body—its passive power to be moved—might then be characterized as a lack of a contrary endeavour equal to or greater than the active power. It would be this that distinguished a stationary cow from a cliff, such that a moving car colliding with the former will move it, but with the other will not. But are we to say, then, that the patient that resists motion was in motion—endeavouring —prior to the impact, or that the endeavour was set off by the impact? If the former, then we should have to conceive of the body at rest as having an endeavour in every direction at once, ready, as it were, for any impact. If the latter, we should have to conceive of the endeavour not as a passive power (material cause), but as the *effect* of the impact of the agent.

But this is merely conjecture. For Hobbes does not

---

[15] Hobbes cites a stone that "lieth still" as a case of an object lacking the power to move. But this would be consistent with his general view of power, provided he conceded that a stone *about to be moved*, e.g., by a torrent, possessed the (passive) power to move. Cf. *Leviathan*, XXI, E.W., Vol. III, p. 196.

[16] *De Corpore*, XV.2, E.W., Vol. I, p. 206.

[17] Ibid., p. 211.

claim explicitly that passive power is motion; only that

> whensoever any patient has all those accidents which it is requisite it should have, for the production of some effect in it, we say it is in the *power* of that patient to produce that effect, if it be applied to a fitting agent.[18]

There is no ground for supposing that Hobbes considered every accident a form of motion; indeed, it would be strange had he done so, since accidents like spatial dimension and position are logically prior to mobility. Accordingly, it may be enough to say that passive powers are those accidents *whatever they may be* that are sufficient for the effect, given a fitting agent. So in ascribing to a patient the passive power of combustibility, one would not necessarily be ascribing motion to it; one might be asserting rather that the body possessed some *unspecified* accident or accidents needful for its being burned at some future time. The passive power would be identifiable, then, only in terms of the outcome, though its existence *might* be inductively inferred from a knowledge of the patient's other properties, together with an expectation of its future encounter with a fitting agent.

If Hobbes meant to offer no more than an analysis of the concept of a power, this would be good enough. Indeed, a mechanical account of mobility, or a chemical account of the combustibility of gunpowder or the solubility of salt, would not explain what it *means* to attribute such passive powers to objects. At best it might suggest a property or accident contingently identical with the power, or capable of explaining it. For a theory about combustibility could be wrong, without affecting the truth of the proposition that gunpowder is combustible. And, of course, there may be no one specific accident corresponding to the power, active or passive, of y to q. The power to extinguish a flame is possessed alike

---

[18] Ibid., X.1, p. 128.

by a bucket of water, a cold wind, or a quantity of pyrene foam, each possessing the same power by virtue of quite different properties (or accidents); and one may know the power without being able to specify the property. None of this amounts to an objection, then, to Hobbes's analysis of passive power, providing analysis is all Hobbes had in mind. In the case of active power he clearly intended something more—a theory claiming that every accident contingently identical with an active power was also a form of motion. There seems to be no corresponding theory in respect of passive powers.

Powers, both active and passive, are, says Hobbes,

> but conditional, namely, *the agent has power, if it be applied to a patient; and the patient has power, if it be applied to an agent;* otherwise neither of them have power, nor can the accidents, which are in them severally, be properly called powers.[19]

So for Hobbes, "the fire can burn you, if you get too close to it" really *is* a conditional,[20] since it certainly won't, and can't, unless you do; it has the power if and only if you do (or, more strictly, if you will). This is much stronger than to claim, for instance, that "the fire has the power to burn you" *means* "there is some condition under which it would burn you."[21] For that would ascribe the power categorically, whether or not the condition were fulfilled. For Hobbes an accident like heat may be ascribed categorically, but not the corresponding power to burn; that depends on the presence of a nearby burnable patient.

Hobbes could persist with his conditional account, perhaps, if "power" were needed only to refer to par-

---

[19] Ibid., X.3, p. 129.
[20] Cf. J. L. Austin, "Ifs and Cans," *Proceedings of the British Academy*, XLII (1956), pp. 109–32.
[21] Cf. M. R. Ayers's proposed analysis of "natural powers" in *The Refutation of Determinism* (London: 1968), pp. 68–75. Ayers's treatment of Hobbes is useful and suggestive.

ticulars: "This x has the power to burn this y now"—or "will have the power to burn y when, in five minutes time, y comes close to it." But what conditions need to be satisfied for it to be true that x's have the power to burn y's? It is surely not necessary that every x shall, at some time, burn every y. Following the analysis of "natural power" suggested by M. R. Ayers, the present case might be analysed along these lines: there are *some* (unspecified) circumstances, not involving a change in the essential or intrinsic properties of the x and the y in question (e.g., *not* like "Any fire would have the power to burn asbestos, if asbestos readily combined with oxygen"), in which any x would burn any y. This is more promising than Hobbes's account; but I doubt whether even this would do for negative instances. Consider

"Lead cannot (has not the power to) float on water."

"It can, if it is supported by an air-filled float of appropriate volume and density."

"That is true; but those are not the kind of conditions I had in mind."

General negative power propositions may be true, it seems, but defeasible; moreover, the defeating conditions need not alter the intrinsic properties of their subject. Rather, such a proposition contextually presupposes a set of standard conditions, and its truth claim may be defeated by denying that these conditions hold in some particular relevant case. The truth or falsity of the proposition would then be contextually relative.

Hobbes is barred from any analysis of this kind, however, by his insistence that, time reference apart, power and cause are identical; "having a power" entails "exercising a power" in the conditions actually obtaining; so relations to context are beside the point. Since some instances of class x will, and some will not, cause a y to q, it is impossible to ascribe a general power to either class. But, of course, one continually needs to do this. The imagined dialogue concerning the powers of lead might very well have arisen in a discussion concerning the best material for some practical purpose, a context where we characteristically need a conception of a thing's powers, to know how alternatives might perform, and under what variable conditions, in order to decide between competing courses.

Hobbes is led to his actualist analysis of power by the following reasoning. Every event is both sufficiently caused and necessitated by antecedent events. To say x was possible, but did not occur, or that y had the power to produce it, but did not, is to say that the necessary conditions for it might have existed, but did not. Yet, the actual conditions being necessitated, these others were *not* possible. So there can be no possibles that are not (or will not be) actuals; and we shall not *know* (though we may hope, guess, or infer) that they are possible, until they become actual.

The powers of a thing are whatever it is possible that it will do—consequently, according to Hobbes, if we know all the conditions, we know precisely what it will do, and know, therefore, that it is impossible that it will do anything else. But supposing this to be true, it might still make sense to say of a runaway car: "Admittedly, it was impossible that it should have been stopped, since there was no guard rail or anything else to stop it; still, up to point P, it was possible for something (say, a guard rail) to stop it, had anything been there; beyond P, nothing could have made any difference." This would be to isolate certain features of a total situation (the car's mass and acceleration, perhaps), considering these as given or of its essence, the rest (the presence of a guard rail) being considered as contingent or conceivably otherwise. To show that there were sufficient causes for there being no guard rail would not make the statement of contingent possibility either untrue or meaningless, though it might deprive it of certain kinds of point (e.g., it *might* affect ascriptions of responsibility). But it would not affect statements of power and possibility with a point of a different kind.

Suppose, for instance, we were interested in preventing other runaway cars getting completely out of hand; to identify the point up to which the actual runaway could (contrary to fact) have been stopped, would be important for deciding, say, where to place a guard rail. Hobbes does not deny that deliberation has a causal role, or that the powers of things are inferred from past performance;[22] yet deliberation directed to avoiding the recurrence of disasters necessarily involves ascribing powers to things, precisely to ensure that they will *not* be exercised. Hobbes was mistaken, then, in the belief that to show that it was impossible *that* something should have happened is to show that it was impossible *for* it to have happened; moreover, he was further mistaken if he believed, as I think he did, that a determinist could not consistently make use of counterfactual propositions in attributing possibilities.

II—Powers as Personal Capacities

So far I have worked with the Hobbesian paradigm of an agent—say, a lighted match—exerting active power to produce an effect, the act of a patient—say, the explosion of a barrel of combustible powder. But Hobbes often uses "power" as a synonym for "faculty."

> Man's *nature* is the *sum of his natural faculties and powers*, as the faculties of *nutrition, motion, generation, sense, reason,* etc. These powers we do unanimously call *natural,* and are contained in the definition of man, under these words, *animal* and *rational.*[23]

He gives little attention, however, to the general nature of such powers, though he analyses very carefully certain specific cognitive powers. In the *Little Treatise*,[24]

---

[22] *Human Nature*, VIII.3, E.W., Vol. IV, p. 37.

[23] Ibid., I.4, E.W., Vol. IV, p. 2. See also Ibid., VIII, 4, p. 38.

[24] I.e., *A Short Tract on First Principles*, included by F. Tönnies as Appendix I of his edition of *The Elements of Law* (London:

however, he does claim explicitly that sense, understanding, and appetite are passive powers of the Animal Spirits "to be moved" by external objects. Hobbes believed that the Animal Spirits flowed through the channels of the nervous system, stimulating or retarding the circulation of the blood, digestion, and other "vital motions," stimulating images in the brain, and activating the muscles, thereby inducing actions of the limbs. Now, when Hobbes refers to a man's power to walk, he cannot allow the action of walking to be self-generating, for "nothing can move itself."[25] It must be excited, therefore, by an external agent.

This conclusion is in keeping with Hobbes's account of voluntary action, which, he says, is always the outcome of an appetite or an aversion. In the *Little Treatise*, he declares that

> The Act of Appetite is a Motion of the Animal Spirits towards the object that moveth them. The object is the Efficient cause, or Agent, of desire, . . . and the Animal Spirits the Patient. . . . Appetite therefore is the Effect of the Agent. . . . [T]he effect of power attractive . . . is Motion towards the Agent indued with that power. . . .

> *Corollary*—Appetite, as a power, is a passive power in the Animal Spirits, to be moved towards the object that moveth them.[26]

The motion set up in the Animal Spirits constitutes an appetite or aversion. Only the last appetite in deliberation issues in bodily action, tensing muscles, initiating steps, and so on. Earlier appetites will have been overborne by succeeding and opposing motions. But *every*

1889), reissued with "An Introduction to the Second Edition" by M. M. Goldsmith (London: 1969).
[25] *Little Treatise*, I, Concl. 10; loc. cit. (1969), p. 196.
[26] Ibid., pp. 209, 210.

appetite (and aversion) is an "endeavour," an infinitesimal motion towards, or away from, its object.

This account of appetite highlights the problem of faculties as passive powers. "Appetite," it seems, refers sometimes to a power, sometimes to an act. The motion actually induced by an agent in the animal spirits is an appetitive *act*; the endeavours excited by a succession of such agents are all acts of the same kind. Appetite *as a power* is a passive power or capacity—that in the Animal Spirits (whatever it may be) by virtue of which they can be attracted and repelled by objects exerting active powers. So the efficient cause of some past appetitive action would be the attraction exerted by an object; its material cause, that (whatever it may be) about the Animal Spirits that made them susceptible to that kind of attraction; and the appetitive act itself would be the effect produced by these conjoined causes.

Hobbes aspired to give both a physiological and a mechanistic account of human faculties. In pursuance of this programme, acts of appetite, deliberation, sense, and imagination are all taken to be diverse instances of fluid motion, each with its characteristic channels. But such an explanation at best shifts the problem of the nature of the passive powers only one step backward. For though the faculty of perception might be explained by the aptitude of the Animal Spirits to be moved in whatever ways characterize that kind of an act, Hobbes has no theory about the accidents by virtue of which these spirits have different aptitudes from, say, whisky or gin. Again, Hobbes restricts the faculty of sensation to those bodies that have "organs, as living creatures have, fit for the retaining of such motion as is made in them," since "sense . . . hath necessarily some memory adhering to it."[27] But by virtue of what accidents do such organs possess this passive power or "fitness"? I suspect that, by identifying perceptive and appetitive acts with physiological motions, Hobbes thought he had

---

[27] *De Corpore*, XXV.5, p. 393.

offered an account of the corresponding faculties without employing dispositional or subjunctive conditional propositions. But this clearly cannot be the case; for one needs to use subjunctive conditionals just as much to explicate the "fittingness of an organ" or the "aptitude of spirits to flow," as to explicate "the faculty of a man to perceive." Nor could the scientific programme that Hobbes had adopted be fulfilled without a theory cashing the promissory note that the passive powers in question could be identified with specific accidents of the patient.

Hobbes does not explicitly insist on the actualist account of human faculties that his general theory of powers would require of him. To do so would commit him to saying that a man is incapable of all those acts he never performs. Yet we clearly need the distinction between non-performance on account of lack of desire or occasion, from non-performance on account of lack of capacity. And there is no difficulty about ascribing the capacity to do things that are never actually done, or in justifying the ascription; we can know from past experience what conditions warrant such an ascription. Indeed, Hobbes himself makes the point that

> *beauty* of person, consisting in a lively aspect of the countenance, and other *signs* of *natural heat* are . . . signs precedent of power *generative*, and much issue.[28]

To possess "power generative" is not to be actually engaged in generating children. Neither is taking a vow of chastity like submitting to sterilization; a nun does not lose her power when she takes her vows, nor regain what she has lost when she breaks them. The accident that is the ground of the power is a physiological structure that remains unchanged by whatever vows she takes; having the one, she has the other. Yet the structure is not what is *meant* by the power; their identity is con-

---

[28] *Human Nature*, VIII.5, E.W., Vol. IV, p. 38.

tingently dependent upon a physiological theory; it is not a conceptual necessity.

III—Power, Will, and Freedom

The actualist restriction that Hobbes puts on "power" is closely related, I have suggested, to his brand of determinism. He is anxious to leave room for deliberation, intentional action, and choice, to be able to say that a man is free to do what he has a will to do, yet still to deny that he has the power to do what he has a will not to do, or that he is free to will anything other than he does will. Men, unlike stones, have the power to will.

> In things inanimate, the action is always according to the extent of its power; not taking in the power of willing, because they have it not. But in those things that have will, the action is according to the whole power, will and all.[29]

What distinguishes objects that have the "power of willing" is that an appetite is among their causes of action. It is not, as might appear from a casual reading of this passage, that the action of inanimate agents is according to the extent of their power, whereas appetitive agents have the *further* power to choose whether to exercise their full powers or not. The difference lies rather in what constitutes their full power; the voluntary agent's powers including also the will, as a causal accident not present in the inanimate agent. So

> God doth not all things that he can do if he will; but that he can *will* that which he hath not *willed* from all eternity, I deny.[30]

Clearly, God has the power to do x if and only if he wills to do x. "I can if I will" is a genuine conditional.

---

[29] *Liberty, Necessity and Chance*, E.W., Vol. V, p. 246.
[30] Ibid., E.W., Vol. V, p. 246.

What then is "the power of willing"? In *Leviathan*, Hobbes declares:

> In *deliberation*, the last appetite, or aversion, immediately adhering to the action, or to the omission thereof, is that we call the WILL; the act, not the faculty, of *willing*. And beasts that have *deliberation*, must necessarily also have *will*.[31]

A similar account in *De Corpore* concludes:

> if by liberty we understand the faculty or power, not of willing, but of doing what they will, then certainly that liberty is to be allowed to both [i.e., men and beasts]. . . .[32]

Hobbes seems to deny (though not by strict implication) in these last two passages what he affirms in the passage quoted from *Liberty, Necessity and Chance*, that willing *is* a power. The explanation lies, I think, in his desire, in the one case, to distinguish appetitive or intentional action from the action of inanimate creatures; in the other, to deny that this distinction implies a kind of free-ranging, uncaused power that is different from and capable of controlling appetites and aversions. We have the power of willing, but not of willing to will. If appetites are powers, as he elsewhere asserts, then action in accordance with the last appetite in deliberation—willing—is the exercise of that power. But it is not a power *distinct* from the appetite. So the causal account of appetite is also a causal account of will: where appetite enters into the causal aggregate, we have voluntary action—an exercise of the power of willing.

Yet loose ends remain. In *Human Nature* he characterizes "deliberation" as the

> *alternate succession of appetite and fear* during all the time the action is in our power to do or not to do . . .

---

[31] *Leviathan*, Ch. 6, E.W., Vol. III, p. 48.
[32] *De Corpore*, XXV.13, E.W., Vol. I, p. 409.

which name hath been given it for that part of the definition wherein it is said that it lasteth so long as the action, whereof we deliberate, is in our power: for, so long we have liberty to do or not to do; and deliberation signifieth a taking away of our own liberty.[33]

A similar passage is to be found in *De Corpore*, where deliberation is said to last as long as deliberating agents

> have it in their power to obtain that which pleaseth, or to avoid that which displeaseth them.[34]

But how can Hobbes, the actualist, consistently claim that doing something is, or ever was, in a man's power, if he never actually does it? Yet what account could he give of choice, were he to deny that what appeared as competing options were truly all within the agent's power?

Hobbes might have argued that the power to do or not to do x is the same as the power to do [either x or not-x]; and if the agent eventually does x, this is ground enough for saying he had *that* power. But his having *that* power would hardly be ground enough for saying he made a choice; for even a paralysed man has the power [either to walk or not to walk], since he does not walk. But this is precisely the kind of example Hobbes gives of a man "wanting the power to walk."[35] For a man to deliberate, he must at least *believe* that so long as he has not done x (or anything irrevocably committing him to x), it is in his power to do each of x and not-x (but not both). But how could Hobbes imagine that any man, with at least his own intelligent understanding of the relations of will, power, and act, could believe such a thing? Perhaps, then, he would have to say that a man deliberating is really trying to discover which act he is

---

[33] *Human Nature*, XII.1, E.W., Vol. IV, p. 68.
[34] *De Corpore*, XXV.13, E.W., Vol. I, p. 408.
[35] *Liberty, Necessity and Chance*, E.W., Vol. V, p. 265.

going to do, and which therefore he has the power to do. When inclined to x, he would believe he had the power to do x; when inclined to not-x, the power to not-x; believing each proposition, however, would entail denying the other.

Now, this is farfetched, but it would be at least consistent with Hobbes's general actualist account of power. For the agent will not have the power to x if, in fact, he will never actually do x; yet if all that stands in his way is his lack of the will to do it, he will not know during his deliberations whether the power he does have is the power to x, or the power not to x; and at each swing from pro to con he will change his mind about which it is.

Still, we do have a use for the distinction between deliberating whether to do x or not-x, and deliberating on whether one has the power to do x. For before deciding which I shall do, I have to settle, as a *preliminary* question, which options are open, or, as we should ordinarily say, what is in my power to do. Having the notion of "open options" is prerequisite for the concept of voluntary action. It implies that in choice situations the outcome depends in part on the agent's preferences—or, as Hobbes would say, on his appetites. Hobbes is anxious to preserve the distinction between voluntary and involuntary action; so he has to make room for "open options," or the concept of "a power to do or not to do"—a power to do what is never done, coexisting with the power to do the act that is done, before the will exists to do either.

In a passage in *Leviathan*[36] corresponding to the ones cited above, Hobbes carefully avoids using the word "power," claiming instead that deliberation ends

> when that whereof they deliberate, is either done, or thought impossible; because till then we retain the liberty of doing, or omitting; according to our appetite, or aversion.

What concludes deliberation where an action is not done,

---

[36] *Leviathan*, Ch. 6, E.W., Vol. III, p. 48.

it now appears, is not that it *becomes* impossible, but that it is *thought to be* impossible; for on a strict view, if it is never done, it always was impossible, though that could not furnish the deliberating agent with grounds enough for thinking it impossible. By shifting from "power" to "liberty," however, Hobbes does not necessarily clear up the difficulty; for earlier in *Leviathan*,[37] he has roundly declared that "if a man should talk to me of . . . any *free*, but free from being hindered by opposition, I should not say he were in an error, but that his words were without meaning, that is to say, absurd." Elsewhere, Hobbes insists repeatedly that to lack freedom is to be subject to some external impediment. Can reaching a decision and acting be properly said to hinder a man "by *opposition*" from doing something else, that he was formerly free to do?

Having the power of willing is not at all the same thing, of course, as having the power to do as one wills. An appetite once stimulated may remain a mere endeavour, or may become a cause of action. Endeavours may be frustrated either by intrinsic impotence or extrinsic impediment—and in this, animate agents are no different from inanimate. Hobbes's most general statement of the difference between liberty and power applies indiscriminately to both:

> *Liberty is the absence of all the impediments to action that are not contained in the nature and intrinsical quality of the agent;*

so that water is free to

> descend by the channel of the river, because there is no impediment that way, but not across, because the banks are impediments;

we do not say it lacks

> the *liberty* to ascend, but the *faculty* or *power*, be-

---

[37] Ibid., Ch. 5, pp. 32–33.

cause the impediment is in the nature of the water, and intrinsical. So also we say, he that is tied, wants the *liberty* to go, because the impediment is not in him, but in his bands; whereas we say not so of him that is sick or lame, because the impediment is in himself.[38]

The causal efficacy of appetite—which is the power of willing—makes no difference, then, to the *general* distinction between power and freedom, or rather, between powerlessness and unfreedom.

It is one thing to say a man hath liberty to do what he will, and another thing to say he hath power to do what he will. A man that is bound, would say readily he hath not the liberty to walk; but he will not say he wants the power. But the sick man will say he wants the power to walk, but not the liberty.[39]

David Gauthier claims, in a recent study of Hobbes's moral and political theory,[40] that external impediments surely do take away a man's power; that both the man who is bound and the man who is sick must want the power to walk. And since a man who cannot walk, for whatever reason, *will* not walk, it is clear that Hobbes is obliged to this conclusion. Gauthier argues, therefore, that "To make Hobbes's account of liberty and power consistent, we must suppose that power is considered in three different ways," viz., as "potential power," or "capacity," "actual power," and "present power." A man has the *potential power* or capacity to walk, he says, if and only if he could walk under physically possible external conditions. Thus man has the capacity to walk, but not to fly; and the well man, the sick man, and the bound man all have potential power to walk. A man has the *actual power*, according to Gauthier, if and only if he

---

[38] *Of Liberty and Necessity*, E.W., Vol. IV, pp. 273–74.
[39] *Liberty, Necessity and Chance*, E.W., Vol. V, p. 265.
[40] *The Logic of Leviathan* (London: 1969).

can now walk under physically possible conditions; so the well man and the bound man, but not the sick man, have the actual power to walk. Lastly, a man has the *present power* to walk if and only if he can now walk under actual external conditions; so neither the bound nor the sick man, but only the well man, has such power.

Now, I see no ground in anything that Hobbes actually says for such an interpretation; moreover, only the third will satisfy the actualist conditions for power laid down in *De Corpore*, and then only on the conditions that the man wants to walk and eventually does so. It is arguable that Hobbes ought to have recognised Gauthier's distinctions; but it is not necessary to suppose he did in order to make sense of anything he actually says. Gauthier's case rests on the assumption that because a man that is sick will not *say* that he lacks the liberty, but rather the power, and he that is bound will not *say* he wants the power but the liberty, that therefore, in Hobbes's view, the first has the liberty, and the second the power. But Hobbes nowhere expressly says this; on the contrary, because his purpose is rather to specify the conditions for freedom and unfreedom, denying that freedom implies unmotivated or unnecessitated action, he contents himself with explaining that the man whose powerlessness is not due to conditions making for unfreedom—namely, external impediments—will not say that he is unfree, but rather that he is lacking in power. But it is consistent with this that one who *is* unfree, also, and on that account, lacks the power. Being subject to external impediments is one way of lacking power; but anyone deprived of power in *this* way might prefer a specific rather than a generic description of his plight, viz., that he is unfree. I am less clear about whether Hobbes would want to say that the sick man is free but powerless to walk. One might argue—though I am not aware that Hobbes does so—that a man intrinsically incapacitated, without intrinsic endeavour, cannot properly be said to be either impeded or unimpeded; where there is no motion there can be no resistance or lack of resistance to it. Hobbes's actualism hardly leaves room for the freedom of the powerless.

IV—Power as Means, and Political Power

Chapter 10 of *Leviathan* begins, rather baldly, and with no obvious connection with what has gone before:

> The power *of a man*, to take it universally, is his present means; to obtain some future apparent good; and is either *original* or *instrumental*.
> *Natural power*, is eminence of the faculties of body, or mind: as extraordinary strength, form, prudence, arts, eloquence, liberality, nobility. *Instrumental* are those powers, which acquired by these, or by fortune, are means and instruments to acquire more. . . .[41]

Then follows a list of resources, whereby some men may exercise control over others. In this section I shall discuss the adequacy of an account of power as means and its special application to social power—to power compounded of the powers of other men "united by consent" in one person.

I shall consider, first, the *object* of power, "some future apparent good." On the face of it, this is an unsatisfactory characterization, since there is nothing incoherent in deploring a man's power knowingly to do evil. Hobbes is committed to it, however, in part by his actualist account of powers, in part by his account of human motivation. "Good," he wrote in the *Little Treatise*[42] "is to every thing, that which hath active power to attract it locally." Since (1) human action is voluntary, (2) voluntary action is appetitive, (3) the appetite is the response to the attraction of a Bonum, and (4) what a man has power to do depends on what he has a will to do, it follows that he *can* do only what appears to him

---

[41] *Leviathan*, Ch. 10, E.W., Vol. III, p. 74.
[42] Loc. cit., p. 165.

as a good, since the alternative would require that a man
be attracted to what he believed evil—for Hobbes, a contradiction in terms.

The common functions of "power" in explanations and
predictions of human behaviour might seem to lend a
certain persuasive force to Hobbes's argument; but these
functions really argue against it. We do discuss what a
man has the power to do, *if he wants to*. Even if we do
not follow Hobbes in treating the intention as a true
conditional, nevertheless, it is generally under the aspect
of an interest or possible goal that our attention is drawn
to things men have a power to do. If Jones tells us that
Smith has the power to carry ten pounds weight of
stones in his pockets to and from work each day, our
reaction is an incredulous "But why should he want to?"
But that is not to say, with Hobbes, that power is conditional upon will; rather, that the only interesting powers are ones that someone might conceivably exercise,
and that we are puzzled to know the point of attributing
any others.

A characteristic problem for the student of behaviour
is to predict what a man will do, given that he has the
power to do a, b, or c. Statements of powers define the
range of decision, the options open; interests suggest
the choice that will be made. The argument frequently
takes the form: "Since Smith has a greater interest in r
than in s, and could do a, b, or c, he would be wise to
do a." In such a case, it would be odd to include among
a, b, and c something that would not conduce to *any*
conceivable interest of Smith's; but the propriety outraged by doing so would not be logical; for Smith does
have the power to do things that he would never dream
of doing.

More interesting, perhaps, is the identification of
power and means. A central objection to this move is
that the means/ends model of action presupposes an
agent *using* a means, to realise a goal. An agent is not
a propertyless nullity: he possesses intrinsic properties,
skills, courage, cleverness perhaps, and these are dis-

tinct from the means at his disposal. They are, more-over, properties characteristically referred to as powers or capacities. A man who owns, but cannot drive, a bulldozer has the means, but not the capacity, to shift a roadblock. Conversely, we might say of a painter that he has the power (skill, competence) to paint a prize-winning portrait: he simply lacks the means (brushes, canvas). ("He can do it all right; just give him the chance!" One would not say, "He can do it all right; he has the brushes, just give him the skill!")

There is one sense of "power," it is true, in which possessing the means may be a necessary condition for possessing the power. That is the sense corresponding to what J. L. Austin[43] called the "all-in" sense of "can," the sense in which to say "A can do P" means "there is absolutely nothing to prevent his doing it." It is clearly "power" in this sense—the outright possibility that a thing will happen—that is the subject of the analysis in *De Corpore*. But if that is the "power" that is in question here, it cannot be identified with "means"—for one can have the means but lack the power to achieve an end, for lack of opportunity or want of skill.

We frequently explain a failure by distinguishing, say, the power, which the agent had, from the opportunity, which never arrived; or his skill, which was insufficient; or (in the painter's case) the means, which were un-available. It seems that, on some occasions at least, we use "power" in a context-relative way, distinguishing the "power" intrinsic to the man or the situation from some other condition, considered variable, and therefore ex-plaining how it was that a thing that a man had the power to do he nevertheless did not do. Such a usage, however, would clearly be inconsistent with the analysis of "power" in *De Corpore*.

Hobbes is led to identify "the power of a man" with present means to some future apparent good, by the account he wants to give of the objects of desire.

---

[43] Op. cit.

Felicity [he says] is a continual progress of the desire, from one object to another. . . . [T]he object of man's desire is not to enjoy once only . . . but to assure for ever, the way of his future desire. And therefore the voluntary actions, and inclinations of all men, tend, not only to the procuring, but also to the assuring of a contented life. . . .

But this commits a man to

. . . a perpetual and restless desire for power after power, that ceaseth only in death, . . . not . . . that he cannot be content with a moderate power: but because he cannot assure the power and means to live well, which he hath present, without the acquisition of more. . . .[44]

Felicity lies in the satisfying, not in the satisfaction of desire; and there is no felicity without security of future satisfactions; our efforts bend, therefore, toward acquiring resources or power bases now, for

Whosoever . . . expecteth pleasure to come, must conceive withal some power in himself by which the same may be attained.[45]

For how else can I conceive a power in myself to future satisfaction, except by pursuing the means now? And the means that Hobbes instances are very *general*—a resource that can be employed for any of a *variety* of future goals. Power is now firmly distinguished from will—resources that can serve the will at a future date.

"The restless pursuit of power after power" does not logically entail "a power struggle"; Robinson Crusoe would be as much committed to it as anyone else, for it is the pursuit of means, not necessarily the struggle for power over men. Yet men are the chief obstacles to our felicity, because means are scarce, and competition

---

[41] *Leviathan*, Ch. 11, E.W., Vol. III, pp. 85–86.
[45] *Human Nature*, VIII.3, E.W., Vol. IV, p. 37.

fierce; "[T]he way of one competitor, to the attaining of his desire, is to kill, subdue, supplant, or repel the other".[46] Accordingly,

> because the power of one man resisteth and hindereth the effects of the power of another: *power* simply is no more, but the *excess* of the power of one above that of another: for equal powers opposed, destroy one another; and such their opposition is called contention.[47]

This is, on the face of it, a curiously paradoxical conclusion. For if power is the excess of power, what is it an excess of? Yet one can well see how Hobbes gets into the paradox. If A's power inhibits B's power from producing any effect, B's power has caused nothing, and is therefore a null cause, and no power at all. If the converse is also true, if there is mutual frustration, neither has exercised power. So on Hobbes's account, neither *has* power. Still, if A had had *less* power, B would have prevailed over him. Can one not say that A's power was exercised in frustrating B? It is possible that Hobbes could have resorted to some device like "endeavour" to put this right. In fact, however, he does not, and rests on the paradox. We have now come a long way, in any case, from the initial identification of power and cause; for Hobbes is now happily using riches, reputation, friends, and so on, as *kinds* of generalized power, with no apparent need to say what they are powers to do, or when they can be expected to be exercised. But though it seems to make perfectly good sense to conceive of riches as a generalized *power*, what kind of sense can be made of a "generalized cause"?

Hobbes seems to oscillate between two conceptions of confrontations of powers. In the first place, there is the simple competition for a common objective, the success of one contender implying simply failure for the

[46] *Leviathan*, loc. cit., p. 86.
[47] *Human Nature*, VIII.4, E.W., Vol. IV, p. 38.

rest. The winner's *excess* of power is manifest in success; it lies in a greater skill, strength, or other capacity, that ensures that he arrives first, or gets the job, or wins the girl; others might as well have been powerless, for all the good their powers have done them. Nevertheless, they are no worse off than before. By contrast, there is a contention that arises from the effort of one man to control another, to win power over *his* power. The more powerful will be able to deploy the power of the less powerful for his own purposes; his "excess of power" will then be his own, *plus* that of the loser, who will be able to exercise what power he has only at the behest or with the forbearance of the victor. In the first case, the powers that are matched are the powers to gain primary objectives, like desired objects, jobs, or sweethearts; in the second, they are powers *against* each other, the power to inflict harm or confer benefits, used to induce compliance. Among these must be included not only coercive relations, but also, for instance, dependence on the judgment of leaders, or of men believed wise. The excess of power that one man has *against* another yields power *over* him to control his actions, to use *his* power as a means for one's own apparent goods. This power, therefore, is a resource—a means capable, if used with skill, knowledge, and judgment, of yielding primary desired objectives. (It can, of course, be a primary objective, too, but it is a mistake to think that Hobbes regards power over other men for its own sake as in any way characteristic of human motivation.)

The paradox that equal powers are no powers lies close to the heart of Hobbes's theory of the state. The rough equality of powers that men possess in the state of nature make stable power relations impossible; it is a state, therefore, of chronic mutual frustration; the "restless pursuit of power after power" that is the condition for felicity issues only in a universal powerlessness. More strictly, since no one has present grounds for believing his future resources will exceed those of his competitors, no one can have confidence in his own power to secure any future satisfaction. The only way "to assure for ever the way to his future desire" is to submit to a common sovereign power, that will confirm every man in the enjoyment of at least some powers, by lending its own power to his, on condition that he forbear in respect of the exercise of similar powers by others. And this can be done by the creation of "the greatest of human powers, . . . that which is compounded of the powers of most men, united by consent, in one person, natural or civil, that has the use of all their powers depending on his will, such as is the power of a commonwealth."[48] By consent is created a *summa potestas*, a sovereign authority, that is also a *summa potentia*; for unless it is the latter, there would be no point in its being the former. It can deploy an overwhelming power against any contender, and therefore power *over* every individual—a power that, beyond a certain point, is self-reinforcing, since the power it has over some is a power against recalcitrants, to ensure, not merely submission, but their collaboration in the enforcement of its will. The existence of a supreme power is a necessary condition, then, for the assured exercise of any human powers whatsoever.

---

[48] *Leviathan*, Ch. 10, E.W., Vol. III, p. 74.

LIBERTY

J. W. N. WATKINS

According to Hobbes, what a man primarily demands from civil society is protection; and he is willing to pay for this by forgoing whatever liberty it costs. But, of course, he would like to buy protection as cheaply as possible. Liberty is not his chief political desideratum, but it is *a* desideratum. So we must now consider what idea of liberty Hobbes could, and did, accommodate within his determinist and mechanist theory of human nature. Then, punishment being an infringement of liberty, we will consider what idea of punishment he could accommodate.

1 Liberty in a causal setting

One negative point is obvious: whatever liberty may be, it cannot, for Hobbes, involve any interruption of causal processes, any genuine spontaneity; a man's will cannot be self-determining:

> Nothing taketh beginning from itself, but from the action of some other immediate agent without itself.

Reprinted from J. W. N. Watkins, *Hobbes' System of Ideas* (London: Hutchinson, 1965), with the permission of the author & the publisher. References to *Leviathan* are to the first edition (whose pagination is also given in the Oxford edition). In a run of references to the same work, the work's title is dropped after the first reference. References to Hobbes's writings are, where convenient, twofold: first to the individual book and second to the *English Works*. Thus "*De Corp.* I, i, 1 & *EW* i, p. 1" means that the passage is in *De Corpore*, Part I, chapter 1, section 1, and in *English Works*, volume 1, page 1. For Leibniz's references the following abbreviations are used: *G* = C. I. Gerhardt, *Die philosophischen Schriften von Gottfried Wilhelm Leibniz*, 7 vols., 1875–90; and *PPL* = *Philosophical Papers and Letters*, translated and edited by L. E. Loemker, 2 vols., 1956.

. . . Therefore, when first a man hath an appetite or
will to something, to which immediately before he
had no appetite nor will, the cause of his will, is not
the will itself, but something else not in his own dis-
posing.[1]

Liberty must be so conceived as to be consistent with
causal necessity.[2]

If Hobbes were to tie his concept of liberty down to
his fundamental ideas, he had to tie it to his ideas of
motion. As a first approximation he suggested a very
simple connection:

> LIBERTY, or FREEDOM, signifieth, properly, the absence
> of opposition; (by opposition, I mean external im-
> pediments of motion;) and may be applied no less to
> irrational, and inanimate creatures, than to rational.[3]

But this needed qualifying before it applied to human
liberty. It says that a stone is free while rolling down a
mountain; and as it stands, it also says that a mountain-
eer is free who is rolling (involuntarily) down a mountain. Absence of external impediments to *voluntary* motion is what Hobbes took human liberty to be:

> A FREEMAN, *is he, that in those things, which by his
> strength and wit he is able to do, is not hindered to
> do what he has a will to do.*[4]

So far, so good: a man whose voluntary movement is
unimpeded is free; a man whose movement is involuntary is not free. But what physical justification could
Hobbes give for this crucial distinction between voluntary and involuntary movement? A man who is moving
voluntarily is a physical system whose movements have
been predetermined by causal lines stretching away in-

---

[1] *E.W.*, vol. IV, p. 274.
[2] See e.g., *Lev.*, p. 108 & *E.W.*, vol. III, pp. 197–8.
[3] *Lev.*, p. 107 & *E.W.*, vol. III, p. 196.
[4] p. 108 & pp. 196–7.

definitely, backwards and outwards, from his present behaviour. And so is a man who is moving involuntarily. We ordinarily tend to regard voluntary movement as in some sense guided by something non-physical—by an aim, policy, or intention. We regard the kick of a footballer scoring a penalty goal, unlike a patient's involuntary knee-jerk, as voluntary because controlled. How can such a distinction be drawn by a materialist who regards all kinds of muscular movement as determined by nothing but physical causes? Indeed, can a materialist even admit the existence of anything so intangible as aims, intentions, etc.?

Hobbes's theory of voluntary movement is a most interesting and original answer to such questions. Yet no part of his system has been so undervalued. This may be partly because a really sharp statement of the theory was difficult without the concepts of the differential calculus, of which Hobbes had only certain anticipatory glimmerings. But the main reason for the relative neglect of his theory is that Hobbes signally failed to advertise its importance. He developed it at a time when a major concern of European philosophers was to find some solution for the formidable problems raised by Descartes' mind/body dualism. Had Hobbes presented it, as he could justifiably have done, as a solution of Descartes' problems, it would surely have been eagerly examined then, and historians of philosophy would have attended to it subsequently. Unfortunately, after Descartes' cold reception of the 'Objections' which Hobbes wrote in 1640 to the *Meditations*, Hobbes ignored Descartes, in his published writings, almost completely for the next twenty years.[5] Hobbes seems to have considered Des-

---

[5] I have found only one reference to Descartes during this period: an approving mention of the latter's explanation of the rainbow (*De Corp.* IV, xxvii, 14 & *E.W.*, vol. I, p. 463). The causes of the hostility between the two men are unravelled in F. Brandt's *Thomas Hobbes' Mechanical Conception of Nature*, ch. iv. In his last years Hobbes's attitude softened: there are friendly references

cartes' idea that the soul is an immaterial thinking substance which inhabits the body as so absurd that it
scarcely needed answering. One result of his scornful dis-
missal of Descartes' immaterialist account of mind was
that Hobbes's materialist account was, usually, scorn-
fully dismissed in turn, on the mistaken supposition that
he had merely evaded the problem by crassly rejecting
one side of Descartes' mind/body dichotomy. In fact,
Hobbes *overcame* that dichotomy in a very interesting
way.

There was one young man who did perceive the importance of Hobbes's theory. Leibniz, as I shall show,
took it up and subsequently developed it into his mona-
dological theory of matter—which is, at bottom, an inverted version of Hobbes's materialist theory of mind.
Leibniz's theory was not neglected; Leibniz did, of
course, have the benefit of the calculus (in his case, it
was the *integral* calculus which was of most assistance);
and Leibniz did explicitly relate his theory to Descartes'
ideas and problems. I shall, therefore, use Leibniz to
illuminate Hobbes. My programme will be this. The key
concept with which Hobbes overcame the body/mind
dichotomy was his concept of *endeavour* (or *conatus*).
I shall first consider only the physical significance of this
Hobbesian concept. Then (in § 2) I shall examine Leibniz's development of it, and the use he made of it in his
attack on Descartes' problems. In the light of this I shall
(in § 3) examine the psychological significance of
Hobbes's endeavour-concept, showing how it enabled
him to distinguish between voluntary and involuntary
motion, and to provide a psycho-physical basis for his
concept of liberty.

I begin with this definition of Hobbes's:

I define ENDEAVOUR *to be . . . motion made through*

---

to 'Monsieur Des Cartes, a very ingenious man' in the *Decameron
Physiologicum*, published when Hobbes was ninety (see e.g.,
E.W., vol. VII, p. 136).

the length of a point, and in an instant or point of time.[6]

This appears to equate 'endeavour' with instantaneous speed. Suppose we want an expression for the speed, at any given instant, of a body whose speed is changing. Let it, at that instant, have travelled a distance *s* during a time *t*. During the next small time-interval Δt it will travel Δs at an average speed of $\frac{\Delta s}{\Delta t}$. As Δt and Δs diminish, the value of $\frac{\Delta s}{\Delta t}$ will tend to a definite limit, which may be designated by $\frac{'ds'}{dt}$. This expression represents the speed of the body at an instant. Nowadays, we are careful not to regard this as a fraction. But it often was regarded as a fraction, as a vanishingly small distance ('the length of a point', to use Hobbes's phrase) divided by a vanishingly small time ('an instant or point of time').

However, Hobbes's definition of 'endeavour' does not do full justice to his idea. He defined 'velocity' as the *power* by which a body moves at its present speed.[7] And it becomes clear that by 'endeavour' he meant, not instantaneous speed, but instantaneous velocity in his sense —the pressure or motive force behind the movement, rather than the movement itself.[8]

There is another complication. So far, we have considered a moving body as having, at any instant, *one* endeavour, corresponding to its motion. But Hobbes saw

---

[6] *De Corp.* III, xv, 2 & *E.W.*, vol. I, p. 206. For an illuminating discussion of Hobbes's endeavour-concept, see F. Brandt, *op. cit.*, pp. 294–316. Yet Brandt did not appreciate its significance for the body-mind problem. He asked wonderingly how Hobbes could 'quite calmly identify the psychical with matter and motion' (p. 355). My answer is: by means of his endeavour-concept—which Brandt overlooked at the very place where its philosophical interest is greatest.

[7] *De Corp.* III, xv, 1 & *E.W.*, vol. I, pp. 204–5.

[8] See e.g. III, xxii, 1 & p. 333.

that its motion might be regarded as the resultant of several endeavours. He speaks of a 'concourse' of 'movents',
ånd indicates that a single endeavour corresponds, not
necessarily with the body's actual motion, but with the
motion it would have if it had no other endeavours: a
stone twirled round in a sling has, among others, a tangential endeavour, but it will fly off at a tangent only if
its centripetal endeavour ceases.[9] This complication is
important: it opens up a metaphysical theory of matter.
Had Hobbes postulated just one endeavour corresponding to a body's actual motion, he would merely have introduced an *ad hoc* duplication. But the idea that its
motion may be the resultant of various endeavours prepared the way for a 'haunted-universe' doctrine whereby
the physical world is filled by an invisible system of endeavours, powers, pressures, or forces. Even the most
dead-seeming chunk of inert matter is, one might almost say, brought to life by this idea, transformed into
something humming silently with incipient motion.

Now let us see what Leibniz did with Hobbes's
endeavour-concept.

2 Endeavours and monads

It is well known that the young Leibniz greatly admired
Hobbes (as is clear from a long letter which Leibniz,
then twenty-five, wrote in 1670 to Hobbes, then eighty-
three).[10] And the possibility that Leibniz's mature philosophy was significantly indebted to Hobbes's has naturally been investigated. Tönnies, the great Hobbes
scholar, claimed that the fundamental idea of Leibniz's
De Arte Combinatoria, and indeed the general plan of
the Universal Characteristic, were due to Hobbes.[11]

---

[9] See III, xv, 6 & pp. 215–16.

[10] *PPL* i, pp. 162–6 & G vii, pp. 572–4.

[11] F. Tönnies, 'Leibniz und Hobbes', *Philosophische Monatshefte,*
xxiii, 1887, pp. 557–73; and see G. C. Robertson, 'Leibniz and
Hobbes', *Mind,* 1888, pp. 312–14.

Couturat, the great Leibniz scholar, opposed these claims.[12] Tönnies also claimed that Hobbes's mechanism and nominalism greatly influenced Leibniz. I shall now contend that Leibniz's fundamental idea, the idea that the world is a concourse of *monads,* was derived from Hobbes. In what follows it should be remembered that in the English translation of *De Corpore* the word 'endeavour' corresponds to the word 'conatus' in the Latin original.

A year after his letter to Hobbes (in which Leibniz uses the term 'conatus' in Hobbes's sense), Leibniz wrote a paper entitled 'Theory of Abstract Motion',[13] in which Hobbes's influence is manifest, and which already contains, in a rudimentary form, some of the key ideas of Leibniz's monadology. Here, Leibniz affirms the real existence of indivisibles or *unextended beings,* considered as the 'rudiments' or 'beginnings' of continuous or extended things; thus a line, or a stretch of time, is an infinite aggregate of points or instants; and a finite physical movement is an infinite aggregate of conatuses. Leibniz follows Hobbes closely in his account of conatus. For instance, he says that 'conatus is to motion as a point to space' and that it is the 'beginning' of motion. He also shares Hobbes's idea that conatus is not just a measure of instantaneous speed, but is rather a pressure or force causing movement, and that the overall movement of a body may be the resultant of a plurality of conatuses: there can, Leibniz says, 'be many contrary conatuses in the same body at the same time'.

Hobbes held that any motion (however small) propagates a disturbance throughout the universe, and he carried this idea over into his account of endeavour: the

---

[12] L. Couturat, *La Logique de Leibniz,* 1901, app. ii, 'Leibniz et Hobbes', pp. 457–72.

[13] *PPL* i, pp. 217–22 & *G* iv, pp. 221–40. This paper contains what I believe to be his first mention of the principle of sufficient reason (pp. 222 & 232).

pressures behind motion are likewise propagated through the universe:

> All endeavour, whether strong or weak, is propagated to infinite distance.[14]

Leibniz writes in a similar vein:

> *Whatever moves*, no matter how feeble, and no matter how large may be the obstacle it meets, *will propagate its conatus in full against all obstructions* into infinity, and furthermore it will impress its conatus on all the rest.[15]

Hobbes had written:

> As a point may be compared with a point, so one endeavour may be compared with another endeavour, and one may be found to be greater or less than another.[16]

And Leibniz wrote:

> *One point is greater than another point, one conatus is greater than another conatus*, but *every instant is equal to every other one.*[17]

Leibniz's justification for this was as follows: in a given time-interval the distance traversed by a faster body will be greater than that traversed by a slower body, however

---

[14] *De Corp.* III, xv, 7 & *E.W.*, vol. I, p. 216.

[15] *PPL* i, p. 218 & *G* iv, p. 229, his italics. This eventually evolved into his idea that each monad mirrors the whole universe from its point of view. The intermediate step was the idea that to every change, however small, in a person's body there corresponds a certain perception, however faint: '. . . So our body must be affected in some way by the changes of all the rest. Now to all the motions of our body there correspond certain perceptions or thoughts of our soul, more or less confused; *thus the soul will also have some thought of all the motions of the universe.* . . .' (*PPL* i, pp. 521–2 & *G* ii, pp. 112–13, my italics).

[16] *De Corp.* III, xv, 2 & *E.W.*, vol. I, p. 206.

[17] *PPL* i, p. 220 & *G* iv, p. 230, his italics.

small the time-interval: so, if the time-interval becomes vanishingly small—an instant—the *point* traversed by the faster one will still be greater than the point traversed by the slower one.[18]

Now I come to what is, for my present purpose, the most interesting statement in this early paper by Leibniz. He says that the idea of conatus 'opens the door to *the true distinction between body and mind*, which no one has explained heretofore'.[19] Later in the same year (1671) Leibniz, in a letter to Arnauld, after summarizing the conclusions of his 'Theory of Abstract Motion', continued:

> From these propositions I reaped a great harvest, not merely in proving the laws of motion, *but also in the doctrine of mind*. For I demonstrated that the true locus of our mind is a certain point or centre. . . . *Thought consists in conation*, as body consists in motion.[20]

So far as I know, it was with these statements in 1671 that Leibniz first broached the idea that mind and matter are not two separate substances, but that the relation between them is analogous to that between an infinitesimal and the finite whole composed by an infinite sum of infinitesimals.

An awkward-looking implication of the idea that a conatus is something psychical, as well as the 'beginning' of something physical, is that there is something psychical in all moving bodies and, indeed, in all stationary bodies too, since their zero-movement is the result of

---

[18] Thirty years later, Leibniz, equipped now with his law of continuity, gave a more elegant argument for the idea that one point may have a greater magnitude than another in his 'Justification of the Infinitesimal Calculus by that of Ordinary Algebra' (*PPL* ii, pp. 885–7). (Incidentally, he assumed that if $x = y$, then $\frac{x}{y} = 1$ even if $x = y = 0$.)

[19] *PPL* i, p. 220 & *G* iv, p. 230, my italics.

[20] *PPL* i, p. 231 & *G* i, pp. 72–3, my italics.

mutually opposed conatuses. Leibniz accepted this implication, and he handled it in the same way that Hobbes
had handled it. Hobbes had conceded that inanimate
bodies may possibly have momentary phantasms; but,
he added, they have no memory, and memory is indispensable for sense-experience as we understand it.[21] And
Leibniz, in that letter to Arnauld, went on to say: 'Every
body can be understood as a momentaneous mind, or
mind without recollection.'[22]

When Leibniz wrote this he had not yet invented his
differential and integral calculus: that came some four
years later. I now turn from his youthful affair with
Hobbes's endeavour-concept to his mature criticism of
Descartes.[23]

According to Descartes, mind is utterly unlike body:
'there is nothing included in the concept of body that
belongs to the mind; and nothing in that of mind that
belongs to the body'.[24] A body is an extended (or three-
dimensional) thing which does not think; a mind is a
thinking thing which is not extended. Nevertheless, Descartes claimed that there is interaction between mind
and body: he rejected as false the supposition 'that if the
soul and the body are two substances of diverse nature,
that prevents them from being capable of acting on one
another'.[25] But it seemed clear to his contemporaries
that Descartes had deceived himself, here. If, as Descartes insisted, a body's state can be altered only by con-

---

[21] *De Corp.* IV, xxv, 5 & *E.W.*, vol. I, p. 393.
[22] Leibniz, *loc. cit.* (This foreshadows his idea of unconscious perception.) Tönnies drew attention to this parallel.
[23] For many years Popper has lectured on the development of theories of matter from Parmenides, via Descartes, Leibniz, Kant, and
Boscovic, to Faraday, Maxwell, Einstein, and Schroedinger. Leibniz's criticisms of Descartes are a turning-point in the story, as Popper tells it. (See K. R. Popper, 'Philosophy and Physics', *Proc.
XIIth Int. Cong. of Philosophy* (1958) [Firenze, 1960], vol. ii, pp.
367–74.) Although my account will be given largely in Leibniz's
words, it is essentially indebted to Popper.
[24] *PW* ii, p. 101.
[25] *PW* ii, p. 132.

tact with other bodies,[26] how can a person's body be affected by his mind? 'So far as we can know from his writings,' Leibniz commented, 'Descartes gave up the struggle over this problem.'[27] Moreover, not only body-mind interaction but interaction between *bodies* was, according to Leibniz, rendered inexplicable by Descartes' system:

> Important philosophers having attributed the essence of matter only to extension, there has resulted a notion of bodies, previously unheard of, which fails to do justice to . . . the phenomena of nature. . . . For it can be demonstrated that extension without the addition of other qualities is not capable of either action or its passive reception; that everything becomes fluid in the most extreme way, that is, becomes vacuous; that then the cohesion of bodies and what is felt as solid in them cannot be explained. . . .[28]

That the parts of a thing tend to cohere, so that it resists penetration by other bodies, was not at all explained by Descartes' merely geometrical account of matter as essentially extended in three dimensions.

Nor was it explained by atomism, which Descartes rejected. As early as 1669, when he was twenty-three, Leibniz argued that the atomists' explanation of the cohesion of bodies involved a hopeless regress. The atomists

> asserted that the whole cause of cohesion in bodies may be explained naturally through the interweaving of certain shapes such as hooks. . . . But these interlocking instruments themselves must be hard and tenacious in order to do their work of holding together the parts of bodies. Whence this tenacity? Must we assume hooks on hooks to infinity? Yet whatever reason there

---

[26] *Principes* II, 37.
[27] *PPL* ii, p. 746 & *G* iv, p. 483.
[28] *Leibniz: Selections*, ed. P. P. Wiener (1951), pp. 62–3; and see pp. 102 f.

is for questioning this in the first case will exist also in the second and third, and so without end.[29]

Seven years later, in 1676, soon after he had worked out his notation for the integral and differential calculus, Leibniz suggested, in an unpublished note, 'that perfectly fluid matter is nothing but a multitude of infinitely small points or of bodies less than any assignable ones', and that, since solid matter is liquefiable, all matter 'is composed of points'.[30] To someone searching, as Leibniz was, for the indestructible substance(s) which persist(s) through all physical changes, the idea that the physical world is composed out of *points* of some kind has this important advantage over the atomic hypothesis: as we saw, the atomists could give no reason for the alleged physical indivisibility of their atoms; but points are necessarily indivisible.

But what character was Leibniz to attribute to these points? One negative answer is clear: he could not conceive them merely as vanishingly small areas or volumes, for an infinite aggregate of geometrical points would merely yield, once more, 'vacuous' Cartesian matter.

As a way of introducing the positive answer, let us proceed to Leibniz's refutation, in 1686, of Descartes' fundamental principle of the conservation of momentum (*mv* or mass times velocity). Leibniz argued, with the help of Galileo's law of falling bodies, that this principle of Descartes has the absurd implication that more work can be got out of a machine than is put into it, so that a perpetual motion machine could easily be constructed.[31]

---

[29] *PPL* i, pp. 172–3 & *G* iv, p. 108. Popper has re-stated Leibniz's argument very clearly: 'Leibniz rejected atoms (which he had believed in when young). For atoms, at the time, were nothing but very small bodies, . . . very small *extensions*. The problem of their extension and impenetrability was precisely the same for atoms as for larger bodies: extended atoms could not help to explain extension, the most fundamental of all the properties of matter' (*op. cit.*, pp. 368–9).

[30] *PPL* i, pp. 244–5.

[31] *PPL* i, pp. 455–63; and see *PPL* ii, pp. 648–51 and 725–7.

He concluded that what is conserved is *force* $\left(\dfrac{mv^2}{2}\right)$; and that which is conserved through all changes is, precisely, the stuff or substance of which the world is made: 'the substance of things itself consists in the force of acting and being acted upon'.[32]

> There is something prior to extension, namely, a natural *force* . . . a conatus or effort which has its full effect unless impeded by a contrary conatus. . . . This force . . . must constitute the inmost nature of bodies. . . .[33]

The points out of which bodies are composed are the loci of forces.

> *Material atoms* are contrary to reason. . . . There are only *substantial atoms*, that is to say, real unities absolutely destitute of parts, which are the sources of action and the absolute first principles out of which things are compounded. . . . One could call them *metaphysical points*.[34]

Later, Leibniz said that such a conatus or 'primitive motive force' is 'what I call a monad'.[35]

As we saw, from the time of his Hobbesian paper on abstract motion in 1671, Leibniz believed that the idea of conatus would yield a solution of the Cartesian body-mind problem; for it suggested a way of overcoming Descartes' absolute dichotomy between matter and mind. A conatus is a physical magnitude, but it is not extended. It is an intensity,[36] and it has a direction. Now feelings

---

[32] *PPL* ii, p. 815 & *G* iv, p. 508.

[33] *PPL* ii, p. 712.

[34] *PPL* ii, p. 745 & *G* iv, p. 482.

[35] p. 818 & p. 511.

[36] Popper has often emphasized the importance of this for the body-mind problem. 'Being an intensity attached to a point, a force may be compared to, say, the steepness of a curve at a point, that is, to a "differential" . . . ; and being unextended intensities, forces cannot be "material", in the Cartesian sense' (*Proc. XIIth Int. Cong. Phil.*, ii, p. 369).

and appetites are intensities, and they usually have an orientation. In Leibniz's concept of force, the physical and the psychical merge:

> Matter . . . is but a collection or aggregate of parts to infinity. Now a multitude can derive its reality only from *true unities*. . . . To find these *real unities*, I was obliged to have recourse to a *point real and animated*, so to speak, or to a substantial atom . . . I found that their nature consists of force, which involves something analogous to feeling (*sentiment*) and appetite; and that therefore it was necessary to conceive them in imitation of the notion we have of *souls*.[37]

One might say that Leibniz integrated matter from psycho-physical intensities, whereas Hobbes differentiated motion into psycho-physical intensities. To Hobbes we must now return.

3 Liberty as unimpeded endeavour

When Hobbes first introduced his endeavour-concept, in *The Elements of Law*, it was in a psycho-physiological context. Previously, in the *Tract*, he had said that desire or appetite 'is a motion of the animal spirits towards the object that moveth them'. Now he refined this: appetite consists, not necessarily of an actual movement towards the object, but of a *tendency* to move towards it.

> This solicitation is the endeavour or internal beginning of animal motion, which when the object delighteth, is called APPETITE.[38]

In *Leviathan* he spoke of appetites or desires as the 'beginnings of motion' within the human body.

---

[37] *PPL* ii, p. 741 & *G* iv, pp. 478–9. (I have considerably modified Loemker's translation, which is rather misleading here.)
[38] *El. of L.*, I, vii, 2 & *E.W.*, vol. IV, p. 31; and see F. Brandt, *Thomas Hobbes' Mechanical Conception of Nature*, p. 301.

Although unstudied men do not conceive any motion at all to be there, where the thing moved is invisible; or the space it is moved in is, for the shortness of it, insensible; yet that doth not hinder, but that such motions are . . . these small beginnings of motion, within the body of man, before they appear in walking, speaking, striking, and other visible actions, are commonly called ENDEAVOUR.

This endeavour, when it is toward something which causes it, is called APPETITE, or DESIRE.[39]

Hobbes could have argued along the following lines that his endeavour-theory of desire has the great merit of providing a solution for the Cartesian body-mind problem: 'Descartes was right to insist that thoughts, desires, etc., are not extended. He was also right to insist that material objects are extended. And it does indeed follow that thoughts and desires are not material objects. But it does *not* follow that thoughts and desires are essentially immaterial, or non-physical. By no means all the properties of an extended body have an extensional character. For example, a moving body has, at each instant, a certain speed. Its instantaneous speed is as much a physical property of it as its volume or its weight. But instantaneous speed is not an extensional property: it is a point divided by an instant. And those instantaneous forces which I call 'endeavours' are likewise non-extensional physical magnitudes.

'Descartes got into a hopeless difficulty by erroneously concluding that, since thoughts and desires are not extended, they must be modifications of some immaterial thinking substance. We can form no conception of such a substance; and if, *per impossible*, we could, we still could not conceive how such a substance could move the body it is supposed to inhabit. But the fact that a

---

[39] *Lev.* p. 23 & *E.W.*, vol. III, p. 39. The idea that fear is incipient flight, anger incipient attack, etc., has often been revived since. See, for example, Stuart Hampshire's inaugural lecture, *Feeling and Expression* (1961).

man's desires often result in bodily movement ceases to
be unintelligible if we understand a desire to be a special
kind of endeavour. An endeavour is a tendency to move
in a certain direction; and so is a desire. An endeavour
results in movement unless it is checked by contrary endeavours; and desire for an object results in movement
towards the object unless checked by contrary desires
or external impediments. A desire is unextended; and so
is an endeavour. A desire may be strong or weak; and so
may an endeavour. A man is not a machine inside which
an angel is trapped.[40] He is a unitary system which, like
other physical systems, has extensional and also non-
extensional properties.'

We can now answer the question posed at the beginning of this chapter about what physical justification
Hobbes could provide for the distinction between voluntary and involuntary movement. An object in a man's
environment may cause a heightening, or lowering, of
his vital motion, resulting in an endeavour in him towards, or away from, the object. An endeavour may be
smothered by countervailing endeavours; but there will
be a predominant, or resultant, endeavour which, environment permitting, will be amplified into large-scale
bodily motion. Such motion, and only such motion, is
voluntary; and a man is free while his voluntary motion
is not hindered by external impediments.

'External impediment' is to be understood quite literally as an impediment outside the man's body. Impediments to voluntary motion within his body reduce his
power but not his liberty. A man 'fastened to his bed by
sickness' is not thereby deprived of his liberty;[41] and a
lame man is not unfree 'because the impediment is in
himself'.[42]

A politically significant implication of this concept of

---

[40] See C. D. Broad, *Ethics and the History of Philosophy* (1952),
pp. ix–x and 167.
[41] *Lev.* p. 107 & *E.W.*, vol. III, p. 196.
[42] *E.W.*, vol. IV, p. 274.

liberty is that there is no loss of liberty in obeying a command from *fear* of the consequences of disobeying it. A man's liberty is reduced if something external opposes his endeavour-initiated behaviour, but not if something external *alters the endeavour itself* without opposing the behaviour initiated by his new endeavour.

> For impediment or hinderance signifieth an opposition to endeavour. And therefore if a man be necessitated by extrinsical causes not to endeavour an action, those causes do not oppose his endeavour to do it, because he has no such endeavour to be opposed; and consequently extrinsical causes that take away endeavour, are not to be called impediments.[43]

This means that 'subjects are free, who are not fettered and imprisoned'.[44] Even someone who is voluntarily obeying a gunman is free, for he is not being hindered from doing what he (now) has a will to do, which is to avoid being shot. On this view, laws do not take away liberty, provided they are simple enough and few enough to be easily known and remembered, so that we do not land in gaol through inadvertent transgressions of them.[45] (It should be added that Hobbes sometimes uses the term 'liberty' in a different sense, associated with 'natural right' and contrasted with 'obligation'. In this sense, a man in the state of nature has entire liberty, however constrained his movements may be.)

4 Punishment

If all our acts are causally determined, a man who breaks the law is causally necessitated to do so. Then is it just to punish him for something which, given Hobbes's determinist account of human behaviour, he could not help

---

[43] *E.W.*, vol. V, p. 352.
[44] *De Cive* ix, 9 & *E.W.*, vol. II, p. 120.
[45] xiii, 15 & p. 179.

doing? Bishop Bramhall supposed not.[46] Hobbes replied:

> The intention of the law is not to grieve the delin-
> quent, for that which is past and not to be undone; but
> to make him and others just, that else would not be so,
> and respecteth not the evil act *past*, but the good to
> *come*.[47]

But if the magistrate, in questions of punishment, must
'look not at the greatness of the evil past, but the greatness of the good to follow',[48] might it not sometimes be
right to 'punish' an innocent person? If the perpetrator of
a particularly noxious crime cannot be discovered, may
it not be right, on this purely forward-looking view of
punishment, to frame someone and to inflict, with much
publicity, severe 'punishment' on him in order to deter
others from committing similar crimes?

To this Hobbes's answer is that, while the question of
punishment should be answered in a utilitarian spirit
when it arises, it arises only in connection with men
guilty of breaking the law: 'for punishment is only for
transgression of the law, and therefore there can be no
punishment of the innocent'.[49]

But where does the sovereign's right to punish law-
breakers come from? More especially, from where does
he get the right (which Hobbes allows him) to inflict
the death-penalty in the case of serious crimes? His authority comes from the people below; and their primary
aim, in giving him supreme authority, was to be *protected* from being killed. In the previous century Luther's
friend Melanchthon had argued that, since the sovereign
obviously does have the right to punish with death—for

---

[46] *Works* (1842–5), iv, pp. 90–1.
[47] *E.W.*, vol. IV, p. 253.
[48] *Lev.* p. 76 & *E.W.*, vol. III, p. 140.
[49] p. 165 & p. 304. Warrender draws attention to this passage
(*The Political Philosophy of Hobbes*, p. 184). Hobbes's point has
been developed independently by A. M. Quinton ('On Punishment' in *Philosophy, Politics and Society*, ed. P. Laslett [1956]).

this is the essential feature of political authority—and since subjects can hardly be supposed to have given him any right to kill them, he must have received it from God.[50] Afterwards, Clarendon used the same argument against Hobbes's quasi-democratic account of the sovereign's authorization: God, by

> putting the sword into the hand of the supreme magistrate, hath qualified and enabled him to execute that justice which is necessary for the peace and preservation of his people. . . . And this sole proposition [accepted by Hobbes], that men cannot dispose of their own lives, hath bin always held as a manifest and undeniable argument, that sovereigns never had, nor can have their power from the people.[51]

Is Hobbes's civil philosophy vulnerable at this point? When he considers 'by what door the right or authority of punishing . . . came in', the first point he makes is that it 'is not grounded on any concession, or gift of the subjects'.[52] Then was Hobbes obliged to concede that, since the sovereign did not receive it from below, he must have received it from above? No; according to Hobbes, he did not *receive* it from anywhere: in the state of nature he, like other men, had the right to kill others; and he, unlike other men, retains this right intact.

When men make a commonwealth, the man who becomes sovereign gives up no part of this right. Each subject renounces the right to defend other subjects against the sovereign and, moreover, agrees to assist the sovereign in exercising his natural right against other subjects who break the law. No man renounces his right to defend himself. Thus

the right, which the *commonwealth* hath to put a man

---

[50] See J. W. Allen, *A History of Political Thought in the Sixteenth Century* (3rd ed., 1951), p. 32.
[51] *Brief View* . . . pp. 40–1.
[52] *Lev.* p. 161 & *E.W.*, vol. III, p. 297.

to death for crimes . . . remains from the first right of *nature*, which every man hath to preserve himself.[53]

And a subject's right to resist the death-penalty likewise remains from the first right of nature: 'a man cannot lay down the right of resisting them, that assault him by force, to take away his life'.[54]

---

[53] *E.W.*, vol. IV, p. 254.
[54] *Lev.* p. 66 & *E.W.*, vol. III, p. 120.

MAN AND SOCIETY IN HOBBES
AND ROUSSEAU

Both Hobbes and Rousseau believed that a life suitable
to human needs is possible—given the world as we find
it—only in the context of the state, and that the state can
exist only where there is sovereign authority of a sort
which is as absolute as it is possible to conceive. What is
more, they agree that a society in which such absolute
sovereign authority is exercised will not be maintained in
the natural course of events: human effort and artifice are
necessary. In particular, men must be *taught* to understand those conditions of human life which necessitate its
acceptance. Thus the whole of Hobbes's *Behemoth* is an
exposure, illustrated by the follies of the men of the Long
Parliament, the Presbyterians, the Sectarians, the King's
advisers, etc., of what Hobbes claims inevitably happens
if men are ignorant of the principles of the true science
of politics (as expounded in *Leviathan*).

> You may perhaps think a man has need of nothing else
> to know the duty he owes his governor, and what right
> he has to order him, but a good natural wit; but it is
> otherwise. For it is a science, and built upon sure and
> clear principles, and to be learned by deep and careful
> study, or from masters that have deeply studied it.
> And who was there in the Parliament or in the nation,
> that could find out those evident principles, and derive
> from them the necessary rules of justice, and the nec-
> essary connexion of justice and peace?[1]

This essay was especially written for this volume by Peter Winch,
Professor of Philosophy, King's College, University of London.
[1] *Behemoth*, Dialogue IV.

Compare this with Rousseau in *A Discourse on Political Economy*:

> I conclude this part of public economy where I ought to have begun it. There can be no patriotism without liberty, no liberty without virtue, no virtue without citizens; create citizens, and you have everything you need; without them, you will have nothing but debased slaves, from the rulers of the State downwards. To form citizens is not the work of a day; and in order to have men it is necessary to educate them when they are children.

Of course Rousseau differs from Hobbes more strikingly than he resembles him in what he says about the relation between education and politics. For one thing, the content and general tendency of the education Rousseau recommends is the very reverse of what Hobbes would have approved. But there is another, equally important, difference. Whereas Hobbes thinks in terms of inculcating his citizens with a theory, a "science," Rousseau is concerned with a whole course of training, from childhood up. The theory of *The Social Contract* is indeed taught to Emile at the culmination of his education; but it is clear that Rousseau would have thought this futile if the ground had not been carefully prepared first.

This difference in understanding of the sense in which education is related to politics is a manifestation of a very deep division between the philosophies of Hobbes and Rousseau. The "science" which Hobbes would have his citizens taught is based on a theory about what human nature *is*. This theory in its turn is based on an elaborate monistic, materialist metaphysics, which claims to show that everything that can intelligibly be said must be reducible to a statement about the motion of a material substance. This metaphysical underpinning serves to emphasize that men must be just accepted for what they necessarily are and that any account of the possible social relations between men must take this basic human nature as a datum. The science of politics in fact consists of a demonstration of the possible relations between beings of this sort: either a *bellum omnium contra omnes* or a commonwealth consisting of subjects owing allegiance to an absolute sovereign.

In his *New Science,* Giambattista Vico's most serious criticism of Hobbes is that the men who could conclude Hobbes's covenant and thereby set up a sovereign would have already to be philosophers: and my quotation from *Behemoth* does indeed suggest that this must be so. What Vico in effect urges is that men who could understand the reasons for covenanting away their freedom to a sovereign are conceivable only as the products of a very considerable and extremely sophisticated social development.

In his brief, but very interesting, discussion of the origin of language in *A Discourse on the Origin of Inequality* Rousseau makes a closely related point. He emphasizes there what is lacking from Hobbes's account of language, the enormous complexities of grammar which have to be presupposed if we are to understand the apparently simple relation between name and object (which forms the basis of Hobbes's account). Rousseau concludes that "if men need speech to learn to think, they must have stood in much greater need of the art of thinking, to be able to invent that of speaking."[2] Hobbes of course had tried to credit his individual man with the power of thought prior to the power of speech; but this is not Rousseau's point. "Man hardly thinks at all by nature. Thinking is an art which, like any other, has to be learnt, and with even greater difficulty."[3] And he objects to Condillac, as he might to Hobbes, "that he assumes what I question, *viz.* that a kind of society must already have existed among the first inventors of language."[4] On Rousseau's view, questions about the development of language and of human society go together.

---

[2] *A Discourse on the Origin of Inequality.*
[3] *Emile,* Bk. V.
[4] *A Discourse on the Origin of Inequality.*

If thinking has to be learnt, *how* a man comes to think will depend on the conditions under which this learning has taken place, i.e., on the nature of his education. The concept of human nature plays as large a role in Rousseau's account of politics and its relation to education as it does in Hobbes's but it is a quite different role. Where Hobbes thinks that the citizen must be taught what man's nature unchangeably *is*, Rousseau's view is that a man's nature is *created* by his education. This does not mean, however, that there are no principles on which such an education can be based. A man must be taught what his true needs are and the conditions under which they can be fulfilled. It is true that men's needs are not immutable, but are modified by their changing social environment,[5] but still, children are born into a specific social environment and we can understand their needs by reference to that environment. But social life does not merely create perfectly genuine needs, it also generates forces tending to obscure from men what their needs really are and to deceive them into thinking they have other needs which are not in fact genuine. It is for this very reason that education is necessary.

A large part of Rousseau's *Emile* analyses these obscurantist forces in social life, summed up under the general heading of "opinion." The analysis is closely bound up with epistemological ideas adumbrated in the "Profession de Foi du Vicaire Savoyard" and elsewhere in *Emile*, about which something must now be said. Rousseau distinguishes between sensation and judgment. In sensation a man is passively affected by things outside himself; for this reason it involves no explicit self-consciousness, as Rousseau argues in a way reminiscent of Hume:

> For, being affected continuously by sensations, how can I know if the sentiment of *myself* is something

---

[5] Cf. *Emile*, Bk. III. "Now, men's needs change according to their environment. There is a big difference between natural men living in the state of nature and natural man living in the social state."

beyond these same sensations and if it can exist independently of them?[6]

Judgment, on the other hand, is an activity consisting in the comparison of sensations and the perception of relations between them. It is by way of such perception of relations that a child forms ideas of objects and becomes capable of entertaining thoughts which he can recognize as true or false. "On my view the distinctive faculty of an active or intelligent being is the ability to give a sense to the word *is*."[7] Rousseau argues that it is an essential concomitant of the capacity to judge that its possessor should come to make a distinction between himself, who judges, and the world concerning which he judges.

> Give what name you like to that power of my mind which brings my sensations together and compares them: call it attention, meditation, reflection, or what you will; it remains true that it is in me and not in things, that I alone exercise it, although I do so only on the occasion of the impression which objects make on me. I cannot control whether I sense or do not sense, but I can control whether I examine more or less attentively what I sense.[8]

Truth is to be found in the relations which actually do subsist between objects and is to be arrived at by attention to those independently existing relations; error, on the other hand, is the product of the judger's own activity. Hence "the less I put of myself into the judgments I make, the surer I am of approaching the truth." But this elimination of the self from judgment is difficult; for judgment consists in the perception of relations and one possible *relatum* which is *always* present—one moreover in which I have a very special interest—is myself. So the very structure of judgment provides me with the tempta-

---

[6] *Emile*, Bk. IV.
[7] Ibid.
[8] Ibid.

tion to evaluate and understand things according to their relations to *me* rather than according to their relations to *each other*. Moreover, I do not live alone in the world but am surrounded by other men who are equally attached to those judgments of which they themselves are the source. My consciousness of myself involves the consciousness that I am an object for the consciousness of other men and from this arises the possibility, indeed the probability, of vanity or *amour-propre*. Hence the tyranny of *opinion*: in its extreme form this consists in judging according to the relations between myself and other men rather than according to the relations between the ostensible objects of my judgment. I say what gratifies other men's expectations of me rather than what I have good reason to believe true. This tyranny is increased by the mechanism of social development analysed in the *Discourse on Inequality*, by which the increasing division of labour increases inequalities in wealth and prestige. The power of the wealthy and prestigious to harm me is added to my natural desire to be thought well of and I come to say, and perhaps even to believe, what the powerful want me to say and believe.

My judgment concerning my own needs and interests is just as susceptible to clouding by these forces as is my judgment concerning anything else, perhaps more so. Rousseau distinguishes between *amour-propre*, which involves a necessary relation to others in the sense just adumbrated, and self-love, consisting in a concern for my own true interests, which he regards as perfectly natural and unexceptionable. Self-love favours a clear judgment concerning what my true interests are and such a judgment requires a clear understanding of my place in the world and of my position vis-à-vis other men. But this understanding can only be achieved as long as I am interested in what is truly the case rather than in the figure which I shall cut in men's eyes—my own included—in professing certain beliefs.

If a man's presence in the world is for Rousseau fundamentally that of an intelligence who judges the relations

between things, what is it for Hobbes? The answer is
that, like everything else in the world, a man is a body
that moves in certain ways, distinguished from other
bodies only by the characteristic mode of his motion. Sensations are internal bodily motions produced by the impact of external bodies. These internal motions linger and
reverberate in the form of images which come to be
strung together into a "*consequence*, or train of
thoughts."[9] Thus there is no fundamental distinction of
kind to be made, as in Rousseau, between sensation and
judgment. And it is worth remarking that, at this early
stage, Hobbes has failed to see the importance of grammar in making the distinction between senseless strings
of images and structured thoughts, a distinction which
Rousseau is enabled to make by his insistence that sensations become ideas, capable of forming part of a judgment, only insofar as they are seen as having a determi-
nate relation to each other.

In addition to this capacity to be affected in characteristic ways by the impact of external bodies, a man's body
itself moves spontaneously toward, or away from, certain
external bodies: motions which Hobbes labels "desire"
and "aversion." These desires and aversions tend to affect
the trains of thoughts which the impact of external bodies
has set up in us.

> For the impression made by such things as we desire
> or fear, is strong, and permanent, or, if it ceases for a
> time, of quick return: so strong it is sometimes, as to
> hinder and break our sleep. From desire, ariseth the
> thought of some means we have seen produce the like
> of that which we aim at; and from the thought of that,
> the thought of means to that mean; and so continually,
> till we come to some beginning within our own
> power.[10]

Practical reason—deliberation—consists in the succession,

---

[9] *Leviathan*, Pt. I, Ch. 3.
[10] Ibid.

to and fro, of such desires and aversions, along with their accompanying trains of thoughts; and the will is nothing more than the last member of such a series.

It is a consequence of Hobbes's general metaphysico-epistemological position that men's actions, i.e., the movements of their bodies, cannot be said to be "guided" by judgments of good and evil. On the contrary, the concepts of good and evil are epiphenomenally related to those movements. "But whatsoever is the object of any man's appetite or desire, that is it which he for his part calleth *good*: and the object of his hate and aversion; *evil*; and of his contempt, *vile* and *inconsiderable*. For these words of good, evil, and contemptible, are ever used with relation to the person that useth them: there being nothing simply and absolutely so; nor any common rule of good and evil, to be taken from the nature of the objects themselves. . . ."[11] Indeed, it is misleading to speak of "judgment" in this connexion at all: good and evil are simply "sensed." "*Pleasure* therefore, or *delight*, is the appearence, or sense of good; and *molestation* or *displeasure*, the appearence, or sense of evil."[12]

In all this, then, there is no question of any sort of "grammar," springing from the nature of the life a man leads with other men, according to which he can formulate the difficulties which arise in the course of such a life and attempt to overcome those difficulties. In saying this I want to point out a contrast with Rousseau's procedure in *Emile* of developing his pupil's capacity to judge of good and evil by bringing him into relations with other men in a way which brings certain practical moral problems into focus. I have in mind, for instance, the instruction in the notion of property embodied in the clash between Emile and the gardener in Book II; and the lesson in the evils of vanity conveyed by the fairground incident in Book III. The point of these lessons, in terms of Rousseau's account of judgment, is to place

---

[11] Ibid., Pt. I, Ch. 4.
[12] Ibid.

Emile in a position from which he can see his actions for what they are, in their relation to the impact they have on other people's lives, and so encourage him not merely to respond immediately to his own desires and aversions.

Because Hobbes does not recognise the possibility of such a point of view he must hold that the world simply confronts an individual as something which acts upon him and is acted upon by him; not as an intelligible realm, immersion in which can stimulate the growth of the understanding. For Hobbes all practical questions arising from my relation to the world—including the world of other men—have the form: what are the obstacles to my desires and how can I remove the obstacles and avail myself of instruments to my advantage?

> The power *of a man*, to take it universally, is his present means, to obtain some future apparent good. . . .[13]

So one of the most important aspects of a man's ability to satisfy his wants will be his understanding of the causal processes in the world around him and the extent to which he can intervene in the operation of those processes and divert them toward the satisfaction of his wants. Correspondingly, since one of the most important features of a man's environment is the existence of other men, the principles on which these other men will tend to act are among the most important causal processes which he will do well to understand. He will try to achieve this understanding both by careful observation of the ways in which other men behave and attention to the motives which seem to make them behave thus; and also by attention to the principles on which he himself acts, which he will then extrapolate to explain the actions of others. Like everything else in the world, other men are, for this Hobbist individual, obstacles or instruments in relation to his desires and aversions; he will understand that he himself is equally such an instrument or obstacle in the eyes of other men; so he will realise that

---

[13] Ibid., Pt. I, Ch. 10.

an important means of influencing their actions in his own interest will be the use of his own instrumental or counter-instrumental status for them as a bargaining counter.

> Also, what quality soever maketh a man beloved, or feared of many; or the reputation of such quality, is power; because it is a means to have the assistance, and service of many.[14]

It is this feature of human relationships which makes the covenant possible.

Here the fundamental difference in Rousseau's account of a man's relation to other men, as compared with that of Hobbes, is most apparent. Whereas for Hobbes it is important to know what other men's beliefs are, simply because we can thereby predict how they are likely to behave, Rousseau says roundly: "To know what they think is an evil, if one does not know whether what they think is true or false."[15] The evil against which Rousseau warns here is precisely that of acting so as to flatter the beliefs and expectations of other men without considering whether those beliefs and expectations are justified. He insists that any power which depends, by way of what is in fact a Hobbist mechanism, on the support of other men is illusory.

> Domination is itself servile when it depends on opinion; for it depends on the prejudices of those whom you govern by prejudice. In order to make them behave according to your wishes, you have to behave according to their wishes. . . .
>
> As soon as you have to see with others' eyes, you have to will with their wills.[16]

His point is that such a posture is incompatible with a

---

14 Ibid.
15 *Emile*, Bk. III.
16 Ibid., Bk. I.

genuinely independent and critical point of view in that it smothers any possible consideration of what is really the best way to live under consideration of what one can get away with in a world full of watchful eyes.

Now, of course the whole purpose of Hobbes's argument is to remove the possibility of such an independent critical standpoint. For Hobbes, Rousseau's enquiry into the truth or falsity of men's judgments—when these are judgments involving the concepts of good and evil—is an enquiry into a non-question. And Hobbes does in fact move straight from the contention that there is no "common rule of good and evil, to be taken from the nature of the objects themselves" to the conclusion that the only alternatives are an anarchy of conflicting individual judgments or a commonwealth under an "arbitrator or judge, whom men disagreeing shall by consent set up, and make his sentence the rule thereof." If there is to be any sort of coherent social life, that is, all claims to independent criticism of policy proposals affecting the life of that society must be given up to an all-powerful sovereign. Rousseau could hardly have found a better advocate for his own views about the true nature of power; though he would have added that the so-called "power" of Hobbes's sovereign is really a form of servility.

The disagreement between Hobbes and Rousseau turns on whether it does indeed make sense to raise the kind of question Rousseau wants to raise. Hobbes's way of attacking the political point of view upheld by Rousseau is to argue that it rests on the attempt to raise questions which are only pseudo-questions. That is why the issue is a philosophical one. It depends on what account we can give of judgment and, more particularly, what account we can give of judgments concerning good and evil. Obviously I cannot consider that question further here. What I shall do instead is to pursue the development of Hobbes's and Rousseau's arguments further, into the realm of the more strictly political, and indicate, with the help of Rousseau, how Hobbes's philosophy of human nature leads to incoherencies in his political philosophy.

The central question of political philosophy concerns the nature of the authority of the state. The concept of such authority generates characteristically philosophical puzzlement because it seems to involve a paradox: on the one hand it seems to involve a power to override the will of the individual citizen, while on the other hand its existence seems in a certain sense to depend on the wills of the individuals who are subject to it, in that they can decide whether or not to acknowledge it as *legitimate*. Where there is not (at least some measure of) such acknowledgement, such recognition of legitimacy, one feels hesitant in saying that one is dealing with an instance of "political" authority at all. This paradox concerns both Hobbes and Rousseau, though they cope with it very differently. To understand what they say, therefore, we must be clear about the accounts they give of the relation between power and will in a political context.

Rousseau expresses the paradox thus in Book I, Chapter 3 of *The Social Contract*:

> The strongest is never strong enough to be always the master, unless he transforms strength into right, and obedience into duty. Hence the right of the strongest, which, though seemingly meant ironically, is really established in principle. But will no one ever explain this expression for us? Strength is physical power; I do not see what morality can ever result from its effects. To yield to force is an act of necessity, not of will; at the most it is an act of prudence. In what sense can this be a duty?

No doubt questions of quite different sorts are raised in this passage. There is, for instance, a "sociological" question about the conditions under which someone can maintain his power over a society. There is the question of what sort of state we ought to recognize as legitimate. But there is also—and this is what I want to concentrate on here—the question of *what it is* to recognize a state as legitimate. Concerning this question, Rousseau is saying that any acceptable answer to it must allow such recognition to be "an act of will," rather than an act of either necessity or of prudence. Let us now ask where Hobbes's account of the authority of the sovereign stands in relation to this requirement.

In Part II, Chapter 25 of *Leviathan*, Hobbes devotes some care to distinguishing clearly between what he calls "command" and "counsel" as a vital part of his attempt to explain what sovereignty is and to locate it unambiguously in one will. This is partly because he needs to distinguish between acts of the sovereign and acts of the sovereign's ministers, who both advise him and execute his will. But it is also important for his account of the relation between sovereign and subject. For the sovereign owes his position to the wills of his subjects and he will continue to remain in that position only for as long as he more or less fulfills the expectations (the maintenance of security) which his subjects had in placing him there.[17]

> COMMAND is, where a man saith, *do this*, or *do not this*, without expecting other reason than the will of him that says it. From this it followeth manifestly, that he that commandeth, pretendeth thereby his own benefit: for the reason of his command is his own will only, and the proper object of every man's will, is some good to himself.

> COUNSEL is, where a man saith, *do*, or *do not this*, and deduceth his reasons from the benefit that arriveth by it to him to whom he saith it. From this it is evident, that he that giveth counsel, pretendeth only, whatsoever he intendeth, the good of him, to whom he giveth it.

Now if "the proper object of every man's will is some

---

[17] As Rousseau says: "*Pour les conduire comme il te plaît, il faut te conduire comme il leur plaît*" (*Emile*, Bk. I).

good to himself," then the proper object of the will of one who obeys a command (as well as that of the one who issues it) must be some good to himself. But in that case, a man who gives a command "without expecting other reason" than his own will to be the reason why the one commanded does what he is told must surely be deluded. For the man commanded, like everyone else, will act only if he sees, or thinks he sees, some good for himself in so doing. So the reason why he does what X tells him to do is not simply that X has told him to do it, but rather that he expects some good (or the avoidance of some evil) to himself in doing what X tells him to do. "The bonds of words are too weak to bridle men's ambition, avarice, anger, and other passions." Well, if this is true of the expression of a man's will in a covenant, it is equally true of the expression of a man's will in a command: and in that case there is the added difficulty that the command expresses the will of *another* man. The expression of the commander's will is, for the one commanded, just words, words which have no reality sufficient to move *his* will unless he can find some ulterior reason why he should take notice of them. Rousseau's words seem to characterize the situation exactly: "at the most it is an act of prudence."

The general difficulty here is that of seeing what room there can be for the notion of the subject's *will* in the political relation, as is essential if we are to be able to talk about "legitimacy," "duty," and "right" in this connection. Hobbes wishes to be able to talk like this but makes it more than ordinarily difficult for himself to do so by espousing the doctrine (which is bound up, in its turn, with much else in his philosophy) that the object of a man's will must always be some good to himself. But it is a difficult enough notion to elucidate without this complication. How can obedience to the will of a political authority ever be more than an act of "prudence" or "necessity"? If it is necessity, my will does not come into the matter at all and there can be no question of my recognizing the authority's legitimacy. If it is prudence, then indeed my act can be said to spring from my will; but in this case the existence of the authority is for me no more than an external fact of my environment which I have to take account of, and I shall only continue to act according to its dictates as long as it seems worth my while to do so. This once again seems to leave out any recognition of legitimacy and duty. But how can I follow the will of someone else in any other sense than these? Only, it seems, if it is somehow possible for me to recognize that will as *my* will; and in fact, both Hobbes and Rousseau, in very different ways, try to establish this possibility.

Rousseau raises a closely related issue in his argument to establish that sovereignty cannot be delegated.

> I maintain, therefore, that sovereignty, being no more than the exercise of the general will, can never be alienated, and that the sovereign, who is a collective being only, can be represented by no one but himself. Power can be transmitted, but not will.

> If, therefore, the People undertake simply and solely to obey, they, by that very act, dissolve the social bond and so lose their character as a People. Once the Master appears upon the scene, the sovereign vanishes, and the body politic suffers destruction.[18]

This is worth comparing with the point Hobbes was making in his distinction between command and counsel. "Power can be transmitted, but not will." A ruler may delegate his power to a minister, in the sense that the operations necessary to carrying out a measure, even the actual decision to carry it out, are taken entirely by the minister. But insofar as the minister's actions and decisions are taken to be legitimate exercises of state authority, they are taken to be expressions not of his will, but of the will of the state (of the sovereign). If we try to think of *that* as delegated, we entirely lose the con-

---

[18] *The Social Contract*, Bk. II, Ch. I.

ception of measures as carrying the sovereign authority.

Hobbes had seen this point as a cornerstone of his doctrine of the relation between sovereign and subject. Yet Rousseau seems to advance the very same point in refutation of the Hobbist doctrine. Who is in the right here?

Rousseau's claim is that the notion of an undertaking "simply and solely to obey" is an incoherent one, anyway; but that even if we could make sense of it in general, it could only yield a relation antithetical to the political relation. For my acquiescence in an edict of the state must be on the grounds that it is the exercise of a power which I recognize as legitimate; that is, I accept what is decreed simply because it is the state (recognized by me as legitimate) which has decreed it. Now, the difficulty is to understand the force of the word "because" in that last sentence. Rousseau's objection to Hobbes is that an undertaking simply and solely to obey leaves no free space in which I can continue to exercise my judgment that a given decree really is the exercise of a legitimate state authority. Hobbes had wanted questions about legitimacy to be settled once and for all in the original covenant; the sovereign has to be sole judge of legitimacy —otherwise he is not sovereign. Rousseau, while agreeing with this last point, argues, in effect against Hobbes, that this is only intelligible as long as we think of the citizen himself as in some sense the *continuing* source of the state's legitimacy, i.e., as long as we think of sovereignty as vested in the citizen.

Let us look a little more closely at Hobbes's account of sovereignty in the light of Rousseau's remark that "power can be transmitted, but not will." Hobbes thinks of the covenant on which sovereignty is based in terms of a "renunciation of rights" on the part of those who are to be subjects. Now, we might expect that the renunciation of a right could be understood as something like a transmission of will; and Hobbes does seem to treat it like this in one context, viz., his discussion "Of Persons, Authors, and Things Personated."

A PERSON, is he *whose words or actions are considered, either as his own, or as representing the words or actions of another man, or of any other thing, to whom they are attributed, whether truly or by fiction.* When they are considered as his own, then is he called a *natural person*: and when they are considered as representing the words and actions of another, then is he a *feigned* or *artificial person.*[19]

The covenant plainly creates such an "artificial" or "feigned" person whose acts are "considered" to be the acts of the person represented. But it is of the highest importance that we should not forget that this is "*by fiction*": which is as much as to say that "will" cannot *really* be transmitted.

What Hobbes does think is really transmitted to the sovereign in the covenant is power. For the "right of nature" is "the liberty each man hath, to use his own power, as he will himself, for the preservation of his own nature"; and this liberty consists simply in "the absence of external impediments."[20] To "renounce" a right, of which transferring a right (e.g., to the sovereign) is a special case, is "to divest himself of the *liberty*, of hindering another of the benefit of his own right to the same. . . . So that the effect which redoundeth to one man, by another man's defect of right, is but so much diminution of impediments to his own right original."

On the other hand it is really essential to Hobbes that he should be able to speak of the relation of subject to sovereign in the legalistic way apparently provided by his account of "representation." It is essential, e.g., to his attempt to account for the sense in which a body politic forms a unity and thus to his attempt to provide criteria for determining over whom precisely sovereignty is being exercised. But it is important in a wider context too. All political philosophers have perceived that there

---

[19] *Leviathan*, Pt. I, Ch. 16.
[20] Ibid., Pt. I, Ch. 14.

is a sense in which the legitimacy of a regime depends on its relation to the special character of a particular society. Hobbes's account of this seems to be unequivocal:

> A multitude of men, are made *one* person, when they are by one man, or one person, represented; so that it be done with the consent of every one of that multitude in particular. For it is the *unity* of the representer, not the *unity* of the represented, that maketh the person *one*. And it is the representer, that beareth the person *one*, and but one person: and *unity* cannot otherwise be understood in multitude.[21]

Now, some of his most important contentions hang on this point, for instance, the impossibility of supposing there to be any covenant between sovereign and subject. In the first place, there can be no covenant between a sovereign and a society as a whole, because no unitary society exists in the absence of a sovereign. And a covenant between sovereign and each subject individually will not work: "sovereign and subject" are categories created by the covenant; a series of unrelated individual covenants between one individual and a multitude of other individuals would not make that one individual sovereign, since sovereignty is essentially exercised over a body politic and there is no body politic where there is no unitary will. In other words, the covenants which establish a sovereign must be mutually related. Of course the peculiar form which Hobbes gives his covenant (in Ch. 18) is part of an attempt to solve this difficulty:

> as if every man should say to every man, *I authorize and give up my right of governing myself, to this man, or this assembly of men, on this condition, that thou give up thy right to him, and authorize all his actions in like manner.*

The importance of this formulation is that it seems to provide, simultaneously, universal mutuality and also a fo-

---

[21] Ibid., Pt. I, Ch. 16.

cus. This is clear from the way Hobbes uses it to define a "commonwealth" as

> one person, of whose acts a great multitude, by mutual covenants one with another, have made themselves every one the author, to the end he may use the strength and means of them all, as he shall think expedient, for their peace and common defence.

But the difficulty is to see how there can be such mutuality as Hobbes conceives the "each one" in the state of nature. How then can there be a passage from "each one" to "them all"?

Here we are close to familiar difficulties concerning the compatibility of what Hobbes says about the state of nature with what he says about the covenant. I will resist the temptation to embark on a general discussion of these difficulties here and simply emphasize an aspect of Hobbes's argument which is particularly relevant to the main issues I have raised in this paper. What I have just been noticing is the split in Hobbes's argument between a legalistic way of speaking (in what he says about "authorization," "transference of rights," and "representation") and what we might call a "sociological" way of speaking. I mean by this latter expression a reference to his talk about the "sword," with which military metaphor he refers to social forces which *compel* people to act in a way which will maintain the cohesion of a political unit. What he does not sufficiently recognize is that the concepts of "feigning" and "fiction" (or, as we might say, "deeming") which are indispensable to his account of representation are at home only within the confines of a settled legal system, whereas it is essential to his purposes to be able to use them in his analysis of the conditions which make such a settled legal system possible.

The same fusion of two different types of question appears in Hobbes's refusal to recognize any distinction between questions of legality and questions of justice. Now, the central contention in what Rousseau says about the relation between citizen and sovereignty is that this relation is unintelligible except in terms of a notion of justice which cannot be reduced to concepts of legality. The distinction is made clearly by Simone Weil in a Rousseauesque essay on the legitimacy of the French Government in the period immediately preceding and during the 1939 war:

> After 1937, the government did not merely *de facto* abandon the forms of legality—that would not matter much, for the British government did the same, and yet there never was a British Prime Minister who was more legitimate than Winston Churchill—but the feeling for legitimacy was gradually extinguished. Practically no Frenchman approved of Daladier's usurpations. Practically no Frenchman became indignant about them. It is the feeling for legitimacy which makes one indignant about usurpations.[22]

This extralegal conception of justice is used by Rousseau in his account of the way in which he conceives the citizen to be the continuing source of a regime's legitimacy. Hobbes had contended that talk about legitimacy can only be made sense of within the framework provided by the dictates of the sovereign will. He regarded it as a corollary that, once the sovereign has been established, no further questions can be raised about his legitimacy. Here we have to ask how we can talk about the "establishment" of a sovereign unless the act of establishment is the establishment of a rule which commits people to a certain course of conduct in the future.[23] The notion of the sovereign's *power* is insufficient to allow us to talk in this way, since what is in question is precisely the warrant we have for talking of a continuing sovereign whom we can regard as *entitled* to exercise that power. Rousseau avoids this difficulty by adding to the Hobbist contention (which he accepts) that the notion of the sov-

---

[22] "La Légitimité du Gouvernement Provisoire," in *Écrits de Londres.*
[23] Cf. H. L. A. Hart, *The Concept of Law* (Oxford: 1961), Ch. 4.

ereign will is required if talk about legitimacy is to be intelligible, the further contention that talk about the sovereign will (the general will as distinct from the will of all) is only intelligible where the citizens have what Simone Weil calls "the feeling for legitimacy."

This is as much as to say that the relation between citizen and sovereign cannot be understood simply in *quantitative* terms (Hobbes's "strengths united") but requires a certain *quality* of life shared by the citizens. What it requires is a life in which the citizens can exercise judgment and in which they do apply that judgment to questions about the justice of social arrangements. It is at this point that the various strands in Rousseau's thought, which I tried to distinguish earlier in this essay, come together. As he emphasizes in both the *Discourse on Inequality* and *Emile,* men are born and grow up in societies which are all riddled with injustices of various sorts. This must be taken as a datum in any discussion of the possibility of political arrangements which will embody conceptions of justice, permit of liberty in the relations between citizen and state, and thereby allow us to think of the state as legitimate. That is to say, we cannot make sense of an immediate Hobbist transition from a state of nature in which considerations of justice make no sense at all to a civil society in which all justice is embodied in a concrete set of factual political arrangements. Conceptions of justice are only developed through discussions of injustices. Men capable of becoming citizens must then receive an education which enables them to understand what those injustices are, an education which consists not merely in inculcating a "science" of what human relationships necessarily are, but rather in creating human beings of a sort who will be capable of discerning qualitative distinctions between different types of human relationship and who will therefore be capable of entering into such relationships.

ON THE INTENTION OF ROUSSEAU

LEO STRAUSS

I

The antiquarian controversy about the intention of Rousseau conceals a political controversy about the nature of democracy. Modern democracy might seem to stand or fall by the claim that "the method of democracy" and "the method of intelligence" are identical. To understand the implications of this claim one naturally turns to Rousseau, for Rousseau, who considered himself the first theoretician of democracy,[1] regarded the compatibility of democracy, or of free government in general, with science not as a fact which is manifest to everyone but rather as a serious problem.

An adequate understanding of Rousseau's thesis presupposes a detailed interpretation of the *Contrat social* and *Émile*. For reasons of space alone, to say nothing of others, we must limit ourselves here to a discussion of Rousseau's "first discourse" which is now conveniently accessible, thanks to Mr. George Havens, in a beautiful and well annotated edition.[2] Rousseau himself said that all his writings express the same principles. There are

Reprinted, by permission of the author and the publishers, from *Social Research*, Vol. 14, 1947.

[1] "La constitution démocratique a jusqu'à présent été mal examinée. *Tous* ceux qui en ont parlé, ou ne la connaissaient pas, ou y prenaient trop peu d'intérêt, ou avaient intérêt de la présenter sous un faux jour . . . La constitution démocratique est certainement le chef-d'œuvre de l'art politique; mais plus l'artifice en est admirable, moins il appartient à tous les yeux de le pénétrer" (*Lettres écrites de la Montagne*, VIII, p. 252, Garnier ed.; the italics are mine).

[2] Jean-Jacques Rousseau. *Discours sur les sciences et les arts.* [Édition critique avec une introduction et un commentaire par George R. Havens.] New York: Modern Language Association of America, 1946. This work will be cited in the following notes as "Havens"; Rousseau's first discourse will be referred to as *Discours* and the pages and lines cited will be those of the first edition which are indicated in Havens' edition.

then no other Rousseauan principles than those underlying his short discourse on the sciences and arts, however imperfectly he may have expressed them in that
earliest of his important writings.[3]

The specific thesis of the *Discours* is slightly obscured
by the immediate purpose for which it was written. It
was composed as an answer to the question raised by the
Academy of Dijon whether the restoration of the sciences
and arts had contributed to moral betterment. Accordingly, what strikes the reader first is the fact that Rousseau had the courage, in the heyday of the Enlightenment, "to blame the sciences and to praise ignorance"
in the interest of morality. Yet the denial of the harmony
between civilization and morality is not the specific thesis
of Rousseau. It was anticipated by the very question of
the Academy of Dijon. It was anticipated above all by
a tradition whose most famous representatives would
seem to be Montaigne and Seneca and which can be
traced, with some degree of justice, to Socrates.[4] As a
matter of fact, what Rousseau calls Socrates' praise of
ignorance occupies an important place in the *Discours,*
which quotes *in extenso* a pertinent passage from Plato's
Apology of Socrates. But one has merely to restore the
quotation to its immediate context to realize the most
obvious difference between the *Discours* and the tradition to which it is related. Rousseau quotes Socrates' cen-

---

[3] "J'ai écrit sur divers sujets, mais toujours dans les mêmes principes" (*Lettre à Beaumont,* p. 437, Garnier ed.; compare *ibid.,*
p. 457). See also Rousseau's letter to Malesherbes of January 12,
1762 (Havens, p. 5). Havens rightly says: "Le premier *Discours*
[de Rousseau] est la pierre angulaire de toute son œuvre." As to
Rousseau's own judgment on the *Discours,* see *Discours,* "Avertissement," and Havens, p. 169 note 24.

[4] *Discours,* 1–2; 13, 8–14, 5; 30, 10–12; Havens, pp. 25, 64–71, and
167. Also compare *Discours,* 47, 9–15, with Xenophon's *Oeconomicus,* 4.2–3 and 6.5 ff., and *Discours,* 57, 16–19 (the idea of a comparison of agriculture and philosophy) with the subject of the
Oeconomicus as a whole. Regarding the general thesis of the *Discours,* compare Xenophon's *Cyropaedia,* 1 2.6, *Resp. Lac.,* 2, and
Memorabilia, IV 7.

sure of the poets and the "artists"; he fails to quote his censure of the politicians.[5] Far from being directed against the democratic or republican politicians or statesmen, as was Socrates' "praise of ignorance,' Rousseau's "praise of ignorance" is even inspired by a republican or democratic impulse: he attacks the Enlightenment as a pillar of despotism or of absolute monarchy.[6]

Rousseau's view is not unintelligible. That enlightenment is a pillar of absolute monarchy was admitted by the two men who are still popularly considered the greatest defenders of despotism in modern times, Machiavelli and Hobbes. To see this, one has to take into account the fact that Rousseau regards the Enlightenment, which he attacks in the *Discours*, as essentially hostile to religion[7] and thus by considering the Enlightenment a pillar of despotism he implies that despotism, as distinguished from free government, can dispense with religion. Now, Machiavelli had intimated that whereas free commonwealths absolutely require religion as perhaps their strongest bond, the fear of God can be replaced by the fear of an able prince, and he had described, in the same context, the age of the good Roman emperors, and not the republican period of Rome, as the golden age when everyone could hold and defend any opinion he pleased.[8] As for Hobbes, whose political demands find

---

[5] Compare *Discours*, 22, 12–24, 9, with *Apology of Socrates*, 21 b ff. Socrates speaks not of artists but of artisans. The change from "artisans" to "artists" may also be due to Rousseau's democratic intention; it is at any rate in agreement with that intention.

[6] *Discours*, 6, 6–27; 16, 21 ff.; 21, 1; 28; 54, 18–21 (compare with *Contrat social*, 1 6). See also some later statements by Rousseau on the purport of the *Discours* (Havens, pp. 5, 53, and 172) as well as Diderot's and d'Argenson's comments (Havens, pp. 31 and 33). That Rousseau's praise of Louis XIV in the *Discours* (55, 15–17) is of doubtful sincerity is apparent from a moment's consideration of an earlier passage (*ibid.*, 28, 11–22).

[7] *Discours*, 36, 8–37, 4; 59, 6–60, 3; 11, 3–16.

[8] *Discorsi*, 1 10–11 (compare 1 55). See also Spinoza, *Tractatus politicus*, VI 40 (separation of religion and state in monarchies) and VIII 46 (need for public religion in aristocracies and, by implication, in democracies).

their complete fulfilment only in absolute hereditary monarchy, he had taught that the civil order rests on fear of violent death as distinguished from fear of "Powers Invisible," that is, religion. Since the fear of invisible powers naturally endangers the effectiveness of the fear of violent death, the whole scheme suggested by Hobbes requires for its operation the weakening, if not the elimination, of the former kind of fear; it requires such a radical change of outlook as can be brought about only by the diffusion of scientific knowledge. The absolute monarchy favored by Hobbes beyond any other form of government is possible, strictly speaking, only as enlightened, and enlightening, monarchy.[9]

The ground for Rousseau's attack on despotism was laid by Montesquieu's *De l'esprit des lois,* which appeared about a year before the *Discours* was conceived. Montesquieu contrasted fear as the principle of despotism with virtue as the principle of democracy. The virtue in question he characterized as political virtue—that is, patriotism or love of equality—and he explicitly distinguished it from moral virtue; he was compelled, however, implicitly to identify political virtue with moral virtue.[10] Montesquieu found the natural home, as it were, of virtue in classical antiquity, and he contrasted the "small souls" of the subjects of the modern monarchies with the human greatness of the citizens of the classical

---

[9] *De cive,* x 18–19; *Leviathan,* chs. 12 (pp. 54–57, Everyman's Library ed.), 14 (p. 73), 29 (p. 175), 30 (pp. 180 and 183), and 31 (end). Compare Ferdinand Tönnies, *Thomas Hobbes,* 3rd ed. (Stuttgart 1925) pp. 53–54, 195, and 273–76. For a present-day discussion see Louis Marlo, "Le droit d'insurrection," in *Les doctrines politiques modernes,* ed. by Boris Mirkine-Guetzévitch (New York 1947) pp. 111–34. Marlo says: ". . . [le] progrès de la science . . . favorise le coup d'état et détruit matériellement et moralement les forces de résistance" (p. 124).

[10] Compare *Esprit,* Avertissement de l'auteur and v 2, with iii 3, iii 5, and iv 5. The same ambiguity characterizes the thesis of the *Discours* (compare, for example, 20, 3 ff., with 44, 7 ff.). See Havens, pp. 183 note 72, and 200 note 137.

commonwealths.[11] He stressed the opposition between
classical political science, which took its bearings by virtue, and modern political science, which was attempting
to find a substitute for virtue in economics.[12] He dwelled
on the inseparable connection between the principle of
democracy, on the one hand, and the prohibitions
against luxury and against the undue freedom and power
of women, on the other.[13] He indicated that the cultivation of superior talent is not a primary need, and perhaps
no need at all, for democracies.[14] He questioned "the
speculative sciences" and "the speculative life" with a
view to the demands of a healthy and vigorous republic.[15]

To arrive at the theses of the *Discours*, Rousseau
merely had to isolate Montesquieu's analysis of democracy, or of republics in general, and to make explicit
certain points that Montesquieu had left unstated. It is
true, he could not do this without deviating from Montesquieu's teaching as a whole, or without criticizing him.[16]

---

[11] Compare *Esprit*, III 3, III 5, IV 4, and XI 13, with the following
passages of the *Discours*: 6, 17–18; 20, 3 ff.; 26, 5 ff.; 29, 1 ff.; 47,
9–49, 3; 51 note.
[12] "Les politiques grecs, qui vivaient dans le gouvernement popu-
laire, ne reconnaissaient d'autre force qui pût les soutenir que celle
de la vertu. Ceux d'aujourd'hui ne nous parlent que de manufactures, de commerce, de finances, de richesses et de luxe même"
(*Esprit*, III 3). "Les anciens Politiques parloient sans cesse de
mœurs et de vertu; les nôtres ne parlent que de commerce et d'ar-
gent" (*Discours*, 38, 12–15).
[13] *Esprit*, VII. Compare *Discours*, 6 note, on the connection between
luxury and monarchy (for the example of Alexander and the Ich-
thyophagi, compare *Esprit*, XXI 8), and 37, 12–45, 12.
[14] Compare *Esprit*, V 3 (mediocrity of talents) with *Discours*, 53,
6 ff., and *Contrat social*, IV 3 (equality of talents).
[15] *Esprit*, IV 8, XIV 5 and 7, XXIII 21. Compare also the censure of
China in the *Discours* (16, 18–17, 18) with *Esprit*, VIII 21.
[16] "Le chevalier Petty a supposé, dans ses calculs, qu'un homme
en Angleterre vaut ce qu'on le vendrait à Alger. Cela ne peut être
bon que pour l'Angleterre: il y a des pays où un homme ne vaut
rien; il y a en a où il vaut moins que rien" (*Esprit*, XXIII 18). "L'un
vous dira qu'un homme vaut en telle contrée la somme qu'on le

For in spite of all his admiration for the spirit of classical antiquity, Montesquieu oscillated, at least apparently, between the classical republic and the modern (limited) monarchy, or, what is perhaps more precise, between the type of republic represented by classical Rome and that represented by eighteenth-century England.[17] The apparent oscillation was due to his awareness of the problem inherent in "virtue" as a political principle. The demands of virtue are not identical with those of political liberty; in fact, they may be opposed to them. To demand that virtue should rule is likely to be tantamount to demanding a large measure of interference with the private life of the citizens; the demand in question may easily conflict with that indulgence of human whims and weaknesses which Montesquieu seems to have regarded as an integral part of humanity. Observations such as these led him to stipulate that the requirements of virtue be limited by considerations of "prudence" and hence to identify the virtue of the legislator with moderation, which he regarded as a virtue of a lower order. From the point of view of liberty as distinguished from virtue he preferred the English order to that of the classical republics, and from the point of view of humanity as distinguished from virtue he preferred the commercial republics to the military republics. He was thus led, or led back, to the modern approach, which consisted in trying to find a substitute for virtue in the spirit fostered by trade or even in the feudal notion of honor.[18] Rousseau refused, at least at first, to follow Montesquieu in his return, or his adaptation, to the modern principle. While he thus remained faithful to the cause of virtue, he did

---

vendroit à Alger; un autre en suivant ce calcul trouvera des pays où un homme ne vaut rien, et d'autres où il vaut moins que rien" (*Discours*, 38, 15–26).

[17] *Esprit*, ii 4, v 19, xx 4 and 7; compare vi 3 with xi 6.

[18] *Esprit*, iii 5, xi 4, xix 5, 9–11, 16, xx 1, xxix 1 (compare iii 4). For a discussion of this problem, see, for example, Burke's letter to Rivarol of June 1, 1791, in *Letters of Edmund Burke, A Selection*, ed. by H. J. Laski (Oxford World Classics) pp. 303–04.

not prove to be completely impervious to the critique of virtue that motivated Montesquieu's return to modernity.

At any rate, it is not misleading to say that in the *Discours* Rousseau starts by drawing the most extreme conclusions that a republican could draw from Montesquieu's analysis of republics. He directs his explicit and passionate attack not merely against luxury and against the economic approach of modern politics but likewise against "the sciences and the arts," which, he contends, presuppose luxury and foster it. He attacks especially science or philosophy as incompatible in its origin, its exercise, and its effects with the health of society, patriotism, wisdom or virtue. He is consistent enough to praise the Spartans for not having tolerated in their midst arts and artists, as well as science and scholars, and he even praises the Caliph Omar for having ordered the burning of the books of the library of Alexandria.[19] While contending that science as such is immoral, he considers modern science even more dangerous than pagan science. He does not say whether the particular character of modern science is due to the particular character of its origin; he limits himself to indicating that whereas science is normally preceded by ignorance, modern science was preceded by something worse than ignorance— namely, medieval scholasticism—and to tracing the liberation from scholasticism not to the Reformation but to "the stupid Moslem" (the conquest of Constantinople).[20] Realizing the difference between, and the possible opposition of, virtue in the strict sense and political virtue, he occasionally praises, in the spirit of his later attacks on civil society as such, the life of the savages.[21] The theses of the *Discours* are explicitly based on nothing but historical inductions and philosophical reasoning,

---

[19] *Discours*, 13, 8–14, 5; 17, 2–7; 21, 3–5; 29, 6–11; 32, 7–21; 34, 12–35, 2; 37, 13 ff.; 49, 16–18; 51, 28; 54, 3–18; 60, 15 ff.

[20] *Discours*, 4, 7–21; 7, 6–14; 25, 1–5; 37, 18–38, 15; 59, 6 ff. Compare Havens, p. 219 note 196.

[21] *Discours*, 5, 14–6, 27; 19, 15–24; 44, 7 ff. Compare Havens, pp. 9, 49, 54, 181 note 62.

that is, on considerations fully accessible to the "natural light." Although Rousseau's attack on the Enlightenment partly agrees with the views of the Biblical tradition and though he occasionally defers to these views, his argument is certainly not based on specifically Biblical beliefs.[22] One cannot even say that it is based on natural theology. Rousseau introduces one of his most important authorities almost explicitly as a polytheist and he implies that the state of innocence is characterized by polytheism.[23] When he attacks science on the grounds of its detrimental effect on religion, he has in mind "civil religion," that is, religion considered merely as a social bond.

II

The contemporary critics of Rousseau's "praise of ignorance" were quite understandably under the impression that he had denied all value to science or philosophy and that he had suggested the abolition of all learning. In his rejoinders, however, he declared that they had not understood him and that he considered preposterous the views that were generally attributed to him. Yet, since he had said the things which he practically denied having said, one seems forced to conclude that he had not meant them. According to the editor of the *Discours*,

---

[22] *Discours*, 3, 4–5; 31, 2–4; 32, 1–4; 44, 2–4; Havens, pp. 85, 173 note 33, and 177 note 48. See also the passages indicated in note 7 of this article. Compare the end of note i of the *Discours sur l'origine de l'inégalité*. That Rousseau never changed his mind in this respect is apparent, not only from the general statement quoted before (note 3 of this article) but above all from what one may call his last word on the subject. In his *Rêveries d'un promeneur solitaire* he says: "Dans le petit nombres de livres que je lis quelquefois encore, Plutarque [that is, not the Bible] est celui qui m'attache et me profite le plus" (iv, at the beginning). Compare the statement with *Rêveries*, iii.

[23] Compare 44, 7 ff. with 26, 11 (the beginning of the prosopopoeia of Fabricius, that is, of the core of the whole *Discours*). Compare Archbishop Beaumont's *Mandement*, §7 beginning.

Rousseau had meant only that science must not be preferred to, or made independent of, morality. But, he adds, Rousseau was so carried away by his enthusiasm for virtue or by his rhetorical power as to exaggerate grossly, to maintain a "somewhat puerile thesis" and unconsciously to contradict himself.[24] This interpretation might seem to be borne out by the *Discours* itself. Especially toward its end, Rousseau explicitly admits the compatibility of science and virtue. He bestows high praise upon the learned societies whose members must combine learning and morality; he calls Bacon, Descartes, and Newton the teachers of the human race; he demands that scholars of the first rank should find honorable asylum at the courts of princes in order to enlighten the peoples from there and thus contribute to the peoples' happiness.[25]

The view of Rousseau's intention that Havens adopts—a view that led, and leads, directly to Kant's assertion of the primacy of practical reason—is exposed to a difficulty that I consider insuperable. It is a view suggested by one of the men who attacked the *Discours* shortly after its publication.[26] But Rousseau declared about ten years

---

[24] Havens, pp. 36, 38, 46, 52, 58, 59, 64, 80, 87, 88, 176 note 45, 179 note 54, 239 note 259, 248 note 298.

[25] *Discours*, 55, 4–56, 22; 62, 15–16; 64, 3–65, 6; 24, 10–25, 2. Compare especially 66, 3–12, with the parallels in the "profession de foi du vicaire Savoyard." Compare Havens' notes on these passages, as well as Havens, pp. 32–33 and 173 note 35 on the favorable reception of the *Discours* by the *philosophes*. The apparent concessions to the common view seem to be retracted, at least partly, in the final paragraphs (65, 8 ff.). Yet these very paragraphs seem destined to explain why Rousseau had stressed throughout the *Discours* the incompatibility of science and virtue, for by limiting his final suggestion to "the present state of things," he seems to indicate that the general thesis of the *Discours* is valid only so long as society is not radically reformed: only in a corrupt society are science and virtue incompatible. See, however, note 40 below.

[26] Havens, p. 239 note 259. See also Havens, pp. 40–41: Havens asserts, and Rousseau denies, that a certain critic of the *Discours* has "saisi l'état de la question."

later that none of those who had attacked him had ever succeeded in understanding his crucial thesis.

It cannot be denied that Rousseau contradicts himself. The contradiction confronts us, as it were, on the title page. The title is followed by a motto from Ovid, whose name is added to the motto, and who is condemned in the text of the *Discours* as one of those "obscene authors whose very names alarm chastity."[27] To solve the difficulty in a manner that does not do injustice to Rousseau's intelligence or literary ability, one is tempted to suggest that he entrusted the two contradictory theses —the thesis favorable to the sciences and the thesis unfavorable to them—to two different characters, or that he speaks in the *Discours* in two different characters. This suggestion is not so fanciful as it might appear at first sight. In the concluding paragraphs Rousseau describes himself as a "simple soul" or a "common man" (*homme vulgaire*) who as such is not concerned with the immortality of literary fame; but in the preface he gives us clearly to understand that he intends to live, as a writer, beyond his century.[28] He draws a distinction between himself who knows nothing and, being neither a true scholar nor a *bel esprit*, is only a common man, and those who teach mankind salutary truths; yet he knows that as the author of the *Discours* (which teaches the salutary truth that the sciences are dangerous) he cannot help also belonging to the second type, that is, to the philosophers or the scientists.[29] Just as the *Discours* may be said to have two different authors, it may be said to be addressed to two different audiences. In the concluding section Rousseau makes it clear that in his capacity as a common man he addresses common men. Yet in the preface he states that he writes only for

---

[27] *Discours*, 15, 13–15.

[28] *Discours*, II, 14–16 and 65, 8 ff. It is hardly an accident that that section of the *Discours* which Rousseau wrote immediately after the conception of the work was a prosopopoeia.

[29] *Discours*, I, 1–11; 1, 7–9; 56, 11–22; 64, 19; 65, 8 ff. Compare Havens, p. 201 note 142.

those who are not subjugated by the opinions of their century, of their country, or of their society, that is, only for true scholars; in other words, he states that the *Discours* is addressed not to "the people" or "the public" but only to "a few readers."[30] I suggest, then, that when Rousseau rejects science as superfluous or harmful, he speaks in the character of a common man addressing common men, and when speaking in that character he does not exaggerate at all by rejecting science absolutely. But far from being a common man, he is a philosopher who merely appears in the guise of a common man: as a philosopher addressing philosophers he naturally takes the side of science.

It can be proved that this is the correct interpretation of the *Discours* and therewith fundamentally of Rousseau's thought. In defending the *Discours* against the same critic who may have originated the accepted view of his intention, Rousseau explains the frontispiece of the *Discours* as follows: "The torch of Prometheus is the torch of the sciences which is made for the purpose of inspiring the great minds . . . the satyr who sees the fire for the first time, runs toward it and wishes to embrace it, represents the common men who, seduced by the lustre of the letters, give themselves indiscreetly to studies. The Prometheus who shouts and warns them of the danger is the citizen of Geneva. This allegory is just, beautiful and, I venture to believe, sublime. What shall one think of a writer who has pondered over it and has not succeeded in understanding it?"[31] Rousseau who warns the common men of the dangers of science is so far from considering himself a common man that he boldly compares himself to Prometheus who brings the light of science, or of the love of science, to the few for whom alone it is destined.

About ten years later Rousseau declares in his *Lettre à M. de Beaumont:* "the development of enlightenment

---

[30] Compare *Discours,* I, 14–II, 16, with 2, 1–5. See Havens, p. 56.
[31] Compare Havens, pp. 227 note 224 and 247 note 297.

and vice always takes place in the same ratio, not in the individuals, but in the peoples—a distinction which I have always carefully made and which none of those who have attacked me has ever been able to understand."[32] Science is not compatible with the virtue of "the peoples"; it is compatible with the virtue of certain individuals, that is, of "the great minds." Science is bad, not absolutely, but only for the people or for society; it is good, and even necessary, for the few among whom Rousseau counts himself. For, as he says in the *Discours*, the mind has its needs as well as the body; but whereas the needs of the body are the foundations of society, the needs of the mind lead to what is merely an ornament of society; the satisfaction of the needs of the mind is not the one thing needful for society and is for this very reason bad for society;[33] but what is not a necessity for, and hence a danger to, society is a necessity for certain individuals. Since the needs of the body are "the need" par excellence, Rousseau can also say that society is based on "need,"[34] whereas science is not, and he can therefore imply that science, being radically "free," is of higher dignity than society. As he put it when defending the *Discours* against its critics, "science is not made for man," "for us," "for man in general"; it is good only for certain individuals, for the small number of true scholars, for "heavenly intelligences." One cannot help being reminded of Aristotle's praise of the philosophic life which is the only free life and essentially transsocial and of

---

[32] ". . . Ces réflexions me conduisirent à de nouvelles recherches sur l'esprit humain considéré dans l'état civil; et je trouvai qu'alors le développement des lumières et des vices se faisait toujours en même raison, non dans les individus, mais dans les peuples: distinction que j'ai toujours soigneusement faite, et qu'aucun de ceux qui m'ont attaqué n'a jamais pu concevoir" (*Lettre à Beaumont*, p. 471, Garnier ed.).

[33] *Discours*, 5, 14–6, 6; 33, 3–9; 34, 15–35, 6. Compare *Lettre à d'Alembert*, p. 121, Fontaine ed.

[34] *Discours*, 6, 6–8.

which man is capable not qua mere man but qua partaking of the divine.[35] It is only to the few who are capable of a life devoted to science that Rousseau seriously wishes to address himself, not only in the *Discours*, but in all his writings with the possible exception of the merely apologetic ones.[36]

The view set forth in the preceding paragraph is confirmed by the *Discours*, although rather by seemingly incidental remarks than by the guiding theses.[37] In fact,

---

[35] *Discours*, 62, 12–14 and 63, 3–10. See Havens, pp. 36, 37, 45, 52, 53, and 60. Compare Aristotle, *Nicomachean Ethics*, 1177 a32 ff. and b26–31, and *Metaphysics*, 982 b25–983 a11.

[36] "Tout ceci est vrai, surtout des livres qui ne sont point écrits pour le peuple, tels qu'ont *toujours* été les miens . . . [Quant à *l'Émile*] il s'agit d'un nouveau système d'éducation, dont j'offre le plan à l'examen des sages, et non pas d'une méthode pour les pères et les mères, à laquelle je n'ai jamais songé. Si quelquefois, *par une figure assez commune,* je *parais* leur adresser la parole, c'est, ou pour me faire mieux entendre, ou *pour m'exprimer en moins de mots*" (*Lettres écrites de la Montagne,* v, p. 202, Garnier ed.). See on the other hand *ibid.,* ix, p. 283: "Si je parlais à vous seul, je pourrais user de cette méthode; mais le sujet de ces *Lettres* intéresse un peuple entier . . ." The *Letters* happen to be an apologetic work. See also *ibid.,* iii, pp. 152–53, the distinction between the "hommes sages qui sont instruits et qui savent raisonner" and who alone can have "une foi solide et sûre," on the one hand, with "les gens bons et droits qui voient la vérité partout où ils voient la justice" and who are apt to be deceived by their zeal, as well as "le peuple" "en toute chose esclave de ses sens," on the other.

In the preface to his *Lettre à d'Alembert,* Rousseau makes the following remark which is important for the understanding of the *Discours* in particular: "il ne s'agit *plus* ici d'un vain babil de philosophie, mais d'une vérité de pratique importante à tout un peuple. Il ne s'agit *plus* de parler au petit nombre, mais au public; *ni de faire penser les autres, mais d'expliquer nettement mes pensées. Il a donc fallu changer de style*: pour me faire mieux entendre à tout le monde, j'ai dit moins de choses en plus de mots . . ." (Italics in quoted passages are mine.)

[37] "The peoples" are explicitly addressed (29, 18); Rousseau expresses his respect for true scholars (2,5) or for the small minority to whom it is appropriate to erect monuments in honor of the human mind (63, 8–10); he indicates that ignorance is despicable (4, 12–13); he speaks of the populace as unworthy to approach the sanctuary of the sciences (62, 1–4). Above all, he quotes Mon-

one of these theses appears to contradict our interpretation, for Rousseau seems to contend in the last section of the *Discours* that science is compatible with society. Actually, however, he does not go beyond saying that the study of science by the very few who are by nature destined for it may be permissible from the point of view of society and even salutary, provided they use their natural gifts for enlightening the people about its duties; and what he manifestly does in the *Discours* is not more than precisely this, namely, enlightening the people about its duties. He does not endorse, he even rejects, the suggestion that the philosopher should make accessible to the people the philosophic or scientific knowledge itself; science is permissible or salutary only in so far as it is not, as such, a social factor. Its social effect is necessarily disastrous: enlightenment paves the way for despotism. Accordingly Rousseau repeatedly and most emphatically attacks popularized science or the diffusion of scientific knowledge.[38] There can be no doubt that in rejecting popularized science Rousseau did not exaggerate, but expressed directly and adequately what he seriously thought.

We must add an important qualification. When Rousseau asserts that there is a natural incompatibility between society and science, he understands "natural" in the Aristotelian sense,[39] and he means that genuine science is incompatible with a healthy society. In answering one of the critics of the *Discours* he warns the reader against the conclusion "that one should burn all libraries

---

taigne's "J'aime à contester et discourir, mais c'est avec peu d'hommes et pour moi" (12 note).

[38] *Discours*, II, 6–14; 24, 19–21; 36, 10–37, 11; 59 note; 61, 12–63, 7. "Ne verra-t-on jamais renaître ces temps heureux où les peuples ne se mêlaient point de philosopher, mais où les Platon, les Thalès et les Pythagore, épris d'un ardent désir de savoir, entreprenaient les plus grands voyages *uniquement* pour s'instruire. . ." (*Discours sur l'origine de l'inégalité*, note j; the italics are mine). Compare *Rêveries d'un promeneur solitaire*, III, p. 18, and VII, p. 72, Garnier ed.

[39] See the motto of the *Discours sur l'origine de l'inégalité*.

and destroy the universities and academies *today*" (italics mine). In a corrupt society, in a society ruled despotically, science is the only redeeming thing; in such a society, science and society *are* compatible; in such a society the diffusion of scientific knowledge, or, in other words, the open attack on all prejudices is legitimate because social morality cannot become worse than it already is. But Rousseau, who wished to live beyond his time and who foresaw a revolution, wrote with a view to the requirements of a healthy society which might be established after the revolution and which would have to take as its model Sparta rather than Athens. This prospect was bound to influence his own literary activity.[40]

Everyone will admit that in the *Discours* Rousseau attacks the Enlightenment in the interest of society. What is commonly overlooked is the fact that he attacks the Enlightenment in the interest of philosophy or science as well. In fact, since he considers science superior in dignity to society, one must say that he attacks the Enlightenment chiefly in the interest of philosophy. When

---

[40] "Il y a des préjugés qu'il faut respecter . . . Mais lorsque tel est l'état des choses que plus rien ne saurait changer qu'en mieux, les préjugés sont-ils si respectables qu'il faille leur sacrifier la raison, la vertu, la justice, et tout le bien que la vérité pourrait faire aux hommes?" (*Lettre à Beaumont*, pp. 471–72, Garnier ed.). For another application of the same principle, see *Lettre à d'Alembert*, pp. 188–90, Fontaine ed. Compare Havens, pp. 45, 46, 54, and 229 note 232. On Rousseau's anticipation of a revolution, see Havens, pp. 38, 46, and 50.

When Rousseau indicates toward the end of the *Discours* that "in the present state of things" he will not strive for literary fame or attempt to instruct the peoples in their duties he does not mean then that the incompatibility of science and society is due to "the present state of things," but rather that he considers the present situation so hopeless that he cannot perform the social duty of the philosopher beyond what he has been doing in the *Discours*. The statement in question may also reflect a crisis in his self-confidence (see Havens, p. 226 note 222). It was the success of the *Discours* that induced him to continue performing what he considered his social duty by writing the second *Discours*, the *Contrat social*, and *Émile*.

he attacks the belief that the diffusion of scientific knowledge has a salutary effect on society, he is chiefly concerned with the effect of that belief on science. He is shocked by the absurdity of philosophy having degenerated into a fashion or of the fight against prejudice having itself become a prejudice. If philosophy is identical with the liberation of one's mind from all prejudices, the degeneration of philosophy into a prejudice would destroy forever, humanly speaking, the possibility of intellectual freedom.[41]

III

Rousseau himself admitted that he did not reveal in the *Discours* the principles underlying that work.[42] Since the purpose of the work is to warn the people against any contact with the sciences, it would of course have been impossible to stress there the superior dignity of science; to do this would have been tantamount to inviting the people to learning. In other words, since philosophy can become known on the market place only as popularized philosophy, a public attack on popularized philosophy inevitably becomes an attack on philosophy *tout court*. Rousseau then exaggerates in the *Discours* by attacking science as simply bad; he does this, however, not because he is carried away by irresponsible zeal or rhetoric, but because he is fully alive to the responsibilities that his principles impose upon him. In a public utterance on the incompatibility of science and society he had, according to his principles, to side flatly with society against science. This is not in contradiction with the fact that the *Discours* is ultimately addressed only to "the few," for every book is accessible, not merely

---

[41] Compare the passages indicated in note 38 above, especially the beautiful passage in the preface: "Tel fait aujourd'hui l'esprit fort et le philosophe, qui, par la même raison n'eût été qu'un fanatique du temps de la ligue."

[42] Compare Havens, pp. 51 and 56. See also note 36 above.

to those to whom it is ultimately addressed, but to all who can read. Nor is our contention at variance with the circumstance that Rousseau revealed in his later writings certain points which he did not reveal in the *Discours;* for by failing to reveal in the later writings certain points which he had revealed in the *Discours,* he succeeded in never revealing his principles coherently and hence fully, or in speaking through his publications merely to those whom he wanted to reach. It is only by combining the information supplied by the *Discours* with that supplied by Rousseau's later writings that one can arrive at an understanding of the principles underlying each and all of his writings. Whereas the *Discours* does not state clearly the precise qualification of his attack on science, it states more clearly than the later writings the decisive reason why science and society are incompatible.

The foregoing remarks do not agree with the fairly common opinion according to which Rousseau was absolutely frank—an opinion that derives apparently strong support from his protestations of his unbounded sincerity.[43] We have therefore to explain as clearly and as briefly as possible Rousseau's views regarding the duty of truthfulness.

Rousseau discusses this subject in the fourth "promenade" of the *Rêveries d'un promeneur solitaire.* The importance of the discussion may easily escape the unwary reader. In the first place, his habits will be confirmed by the artful character of the whole book, which claims to be written in a situation and in a mood in which considerations of prudence have ceased to carry any weight; it claims to be more outspoken even than the *Confessions* since it is said to be written exclusively for the author, who has no longer any thought or hope of reaching his readers. Moreover, the matter to which Rousseau applies his rule of conscience by way of expounding it is of the

---

[43] For example, near the beginning of the *Rêveries* he describes himself as follows: "Sans adresse, sans art, sans dissimulation, sans prudence, franc, ouvert, impatient, emporté. . . ."

utmost triviality; he discusses at great length and in the spirit of unusual scrupulousness the question whether an author may pretend that his work is the translation of a Greek manuscript,[44] and also a number of minor falsehoods which it had been Rousseau's misfortune to utter. As for the rule itself, which he claims to have followed throughout his adult life, it can be reduced to the proposition that the obligation to speak the truth is founded exclusively on the utility of truth. From this it follows that one may not only suppress or disguise truths devoid of all possible utility, but may even be positively deceitful about them by asserting their contraries, without thus committing the sin of lying. Rousseau takes the trouble to add that the few lies he had uttered throughout his adult life were due to timidity or weakness.[45] It is perhaps more important to note that he limits himself to discussing only one kind of the truths that are devoid of all utility, namely, the merely useless truths: he does not say a word about the other kind which would have to be called dangerous truths. But we are entitled to infer

---

[44] This question is a substitute for the somewhat more relevant question whether Rousseau was entitled to ascribe a certain profession of faith to a Catholic priest. That profession happens to be the central subject of the preceding "promenade."

[45] ". . . Tant d'hommes et de philosophes, qui dans tous les temps ont médité sur ce sujet, ont tous unanimement rejeté la possibilité de la création [*sc.* de la matière], excepté peut-être un très petit nombre qui paraissent avoir sincèrement soumis leur raison à l'autorité; sincérité que les motifs de leur intérêt, de leur sûreté, de leur repos, rendent fort suspecte, et dont il sera toujours impossible de s'assurer tant que l'on risquera quelque chose à parler vrai" (*Lettre à Beaumont*, p. 461, Garnier ed.). In the same work Rousseau expresses the principle explained in the *Rêveries* as follows: "Pour moi, j'ai promis de dire [la vérité] en toute chose *utile*, autant qu'il serait en moi" (p. 472; italics mine), and "Parler au public avec franchise, avec fermeté, est un droit commun à tous les hommes, et même un devoir en toute chose *utile*" (p. 495 note; italics mine). Compare also the statement on the art of changing public opinion in the *Lettre à d'Alembert*, pp. 192 ff., Fontaine ed. Regarding the general question of Rousseau's "prudence," see Havens, pp. 165 note 8 and 177 note 48.

from his general rule that he would have considered himself obliged to conceal dangerous truths and even to assert their contraries—assuming that there are such truths.

In the light of this conclusion, we can understand the specific contribution of the *Discours* to the exposition of Rousseau's principles. In the introduction he declares that he takes the side of truth. He does this by teaching the truth that science and society are incompatible. But this is a useful truth. The *Discours* is so far from siding with truth as such that it attacks science precisely because it is concerned with truth as such, regardless of its utility, and hence is not, by its intention, protected against the danger of leading to useless or even harmful truths. And Rousseau contends that all the secrets that nature hides from the people are so many evils against which she protects them; science accessible to the people would be like a dangerous weapon in the hands of a child.[46] The practical consequence that this assertion entails cannot be evaded by reference to Rousseau's contention that in times of extreme corruption no truth is any longer dangerous, for he wrote for posterity rather than for his own time. To say nothing of the fact that persecution was not precisely extinct in Rousseau's age.[47]

In accordance with the general character of the *Discours* Rousseau maintains the thesis that the scientific or philosophic truth (the truth about the whole) is simply inaccessible rather than that it is inaccessible to the people. He asserts therefore the dangerous character of the quest for knowledge rather than that of knowledge acquired:[48] the quest for knowledge is dangerous because the truth is inaccessible and therefore the quest for truth

---

[46] *Discours*, 1, 9–11; 3, 2–5; 29, 11–30, 4; 33, 18–19; 34, 12–13; 36, 5–10; 55, 6–20; 56, 18–22. Compare *Lettre à d'Alembert*, p. 115 note, Fontaine ed.

[47] See p. 271 and note 45 above.

[48] The central thesis of the *Discours* is not affected by this incongruity since both contentions lead to the conclusion that quest for knowledge is dangerous to society.

leads to dangerous errors or to dangerous skepticism.[49] Science presupposes and fosters doubt; it forbids assent in all cases in which the truth is not evidently known, and it is at least possible that the truth about the most important subjects is not evidently known. But society requires that its members be sure regarding certain fundamentals. These certainties, "our dogmas," are not only not the acquisitions of science, but are essentially endangered by science: they become exposed to doubt because their lack of evidence is brought to light as soon as they are scientifically investigated. They are the objects not of knowledge but of faith. They, or the ends which they serve, are sacred.[50] It is the faith in the sacred foundations of society, or in that which makes them sacred, that Rousseau has in mind when praising ignorance: he praises ignorance accompanied by reverent assent. It is fundamentally distinguished from the ignorance, also praised by him, which is accompanied by suspense of assent and which may be the ultimate result of the scientific effort. Following a lead given by Rousseau, we may distinguish the two kinds of ignorance as popular ignorance and Socratic ignorance; both kinds are opposed by him to the dogmatism of pseudoscience or of popularized science.[51]

---

[49] *Discours,* 11, 14–16; 29, 6–15; 33, 8–34; 60, 1–2.

[50] If the foundations of society are identical with the civil religion, and if the civil religion is identical with the religion of the Gospels, it follows that the suppression of all books with the exception of the Gospels, or at any rate of all scientific books, might be legitimate. It is the problem implied in the second conditional clause of the preceding sentence that Rousseau indicates by praising the Caliph Omar for having ordered the burning of the books of the library of Alexandria: ". . . supposez Grégoire le Grand à la place d'Omar et l'Évangile à la place de l'Alcoran, la Bibliothèque auroit encore été brûlée, et ce seroit peut-être le plus beau trait de la vie de cet illustre Pontife" (*Discours,* 60, 23–27). Compare *Acts,* 19: 17–20, and Havens, p. 46.

[51] *Discours,* 36, 20–37, 4; 1, 8–9; 23, 18–24, 14; 34, 6–8; 34, 18–24; 55, 18–20. It should be noted that the true doctrine—namely, that science and society are incompatible—the exposition of which

Since Rousseau believed that genuine faith could only be the outcome of sound reasoning and would therefore be a privilege of the wise, it is preferable to say that according to him opinion rather than faith is the basis of society. In conformity with this position he indicates in the *Discours* that only genuine scholars are not subjugated by the opinions of their century, their country, or their society, whereas the majority of men necessarily are.[52] We may therefore express the thesis of the *Discours* as follows: since the element of society is opinion, science, being the attempt to replace opinion by knowledge, essentially endangers society because it dissolves opinion. It is fundamentally for this reason, it would seem, that Rousseau considered science and society incompatible. Now, the view that the element of society is opinion becomes dangerous only if quest for knowledge is a human possibility and especially if it is the highest human possibility. Rousseau asserts therefore in the *Discours* that science is bad as such rather than that it is merely bad for society. By expressing the useful truth that he wants to convey in an exaggerated manner, he expresses it in a most reserved manner.

It is advisable to illustrate the reasoning underlying the *Discours* by a few more specific considerations, which are at least intimated in the same work. According to Rousseau, civil society is essentially a particular, or more precisely a closed, society. A civil society, he holds, can be healthy only if it has a character of its own, and this requires that its individuality be produced or fostered by

---

is the purpose of the *Discours*, is based not on faith but on reasoning (see concluding paragraph of Section I of this article).

[52] *Lettres écrites de la Montagne*, III (see note 36 above). Compare note 30 above. See also the remark in the *Discours* (37, 6–7) that the popularizers of science are enemies of "l'opinion publique." While public opinion is the element and, in a sense, the standard of free society, it becomes questionable from a transpolitical point of view. Compare *Lettre à d'Alembert*, p. 192, Fontaine ed.: "opinion publique" is merely "opinion d'autrui." Compare *Discours*, 65, 18, and *Contrat social*, II 12 and IV 7.

national and exclusive institutions. Those institutions must be animated by a national "philosophy," by a way of thinking that is not transferable to other societies: "the philosophy of each people is little apt for another people." On the other hand, science or philosophy is essentially universal: it is common to all wise men. The diffusion of philosophy or science necessarily weakens the power of the national "philosophies" and therewith the attachment of the citizens to the particular way of life of their community. In other words, whereas science or philosophy is essentially cosmopolitan, society must be animated by the spirit of patriotism, a spirit which is by no means irreconcilable with national hatreds. Political society being essentially a society that has to defend itself against other states, it must foster the military virtues and it normally develops a warlike spirit. Philosophy, on the contrary, is destructive of the warlike spirit.[53]

Furthermore, free society presupposes that its members have abandoned their original or natural liberty in favor of conventional liberty, that is, in favor of the obedience to the laws of the community or to uniform rules of conduct to the making of which everyone can have contributed. Civil society requires conformance, or the transformation of man as a natural being into the citizen; compared with man's natural independence, all society is therefore a form of bondage. But philosophy demands that the philosopher follow his "own genius" with absolute sincerity, or without any regard to the general will or the communal way of thinking; in philosophizing,

---

[53] In the *Discours* Rousseau states the case chiefly from the point of view of society (11, 12–14; 27, 15–17; 45, 10–49, 15) and therefore accepts "the military ideal of the Romans" (Havens, p. 206). But one cannot say that he does this "without criticism" (*ibid.*, 206); in *Discours*, 33, 2–3, he condemns wars as unmistakably as he condemns tyranny. Compare *Discours sur l'origine de l'inégalité*, note j; *Gouvernement de Pologne*, chs. 2 and 3; *Lettres écrites de la Montagne*, I, pp. 131–33, Garnier ed.; *Contrat social*, II 8 (toward the end); and the first pages of *Émile*. See also Havens, p. 187 note 85.

man asserts his natural freedom. Philosophy and society therefore necessarily come into conflict as soon as philosophy becomes a social factor.[54]

Moreover, free society comes into being through the substitution of conventional equality for natural inequality. The pursuit of science, however, requires the cultivation of talents, that is, of natural inequality; its fostering of inequality is so characteristic that one may even wonder whether the concern with superiority, that is, desire for glory or pride, is not the root of science. Whatever might have to be said about political glory, it is less conspicuous than the glory attending on intellectual achievement—Sparta was less brilliant than Athens—and, above all, society, as such, having its roots in need cannot possibly have its roots in pride.[55]

IV

To say that science and society are incompatible is one thing; to say that science and virtue are incompatible is another thing. The second thesis could be reduced to the first, if virtue were essentially political or social. There can be no doubt that Rousseau frequently identifies virtue with political virtue. Yet, the mere fact that he sometimes attacks civil society, as such, in the name of virtue by praising the virtue of primitive man shows that he makes a distinction between political virtue and another kind of virtue.[56] This does not mean that his

---

[54] *Discours,* 5, 17–6, 2; 63, 3–11. Compare *Gouvernement de Pologne,* ch. 2; *Contrat social,* I 1, 6 and 8; and the first pages of *Émile.*

[55] *Discours,* 53, 6–12. Compare *ibid.,* II, 14–16; 19, 10–11; 21, 17–18; 29, 8; 30, 8–17; 32, 12–13; 41, 1–2; 41, 11–14; 65, 8–11; 66, 11–14; Havens, pp. 211 note 172, 223 note 215, 226 note 222; *Contrat social,* I 9 (end) and II 1.

[56] Compare notes 10 and 21 above. *Discours,* 14, 1–15; 21, 17–21; 26, 5–28, 10. Compare 49, 18, with 50, 2–3 and 51, 3 ff.; compare 8, 18–19 ("la vertu est la force et la vigueur de l'âme") with 47, 9–15 and *Gouvernement de Pologne,* ch. 4 ("à cette

attack on science in the name of virtue, as such, is simply an exaggeration, for it is at least possible that the distinction between two kinds of virtue is only provisional. In his later writings Rousseau explicitly distinguishes between "goodness" and "virtue": goodness belongs to man as a natural being, whereas virtue or morality belongs to man as a citizen, since it essentially presupposes the social contract or convention. The good man as distinguished from the virtuous man is only good for himself, because he is good only as long as he derives pleasure from being good or, more generally expressed, because he cannot do anything which he does not do with pleasure. A being is good to the extent to which he is self-sufficient, "solitary," or not in need of others and hence absolutely happy. A man who is good and not virtuous is therefore unfit for society or for action. In the most important case he will be a *contemplatif solitaire* who finds in the joys and raptures of pure and disinterested contemplation—for example, the study of plants in the spirit of Theophrastus—perfect happiness and a godlike self-sufficiency. A man of this kind, that is, the philosopher, in so far as he is exclusively concerned with learning as distinguished from teaching, is a useless member of society because he is exclusively concerned with his own pleasures, and "every useless citizen may be regarded as a pernicious man."[57]

---

vigueur d'âme, à ce zèle patriotique. . ."). What Rousseau says about the incompatibility of science and political virtue must not be mistaken for, indeed it belongs to an entirely different level from, what he says about the incompatibility of the teaching of the Gospels, or of humanity in the sense of the Gospels, and patriotism. For the teaching of the Gospels is as much a teaching of duties as is the teaching of political society. The conflict between Christianity and political society is an intramoral conflict, whereas that between science and society is not.

[57] *Discours*, 35, 4–6; *Rêveries*, v–vii; *Contrat social*, i 8 and iii 4; *Émile*, iv, vol. 1, p. 286, and v, vol. 2, pp. 274–75, Garnier ed. Compare note 38 above, as well as Havens, pp. 183 note 74 and 172 note 32. "Wer wollte nicht dem im höchsten Sinne verehrten Johann Jakob Rousseau auf seinen einsamen Wanderungen folgen,

We note in passing that it is somewhat misleading to say that according to Rousseau virtue is an active quality, whereas goodness is merely passive. This description fits only one type of goodness, the goodness of the presocial or primitive man who is "a stupid animal." It does not quite fit the goodness of the man who is good and at the same time wise. The latter's not being active or even his being "idle" means that he has withdrawn from the hustle of the active life and devotes himself to solitary contemplation. In other words, one misunderstands Rousseau's notion of natural goodness if one does not bear in mind the fact that it refers to two different types, who stand at the opposite poles of humanity (the primitive man and the wise) and who yet belong together as natural men, as self-sufficient beings, or "numerical units," in contradistinction to an intermediate type, the citizen or social man, that is, the man who is bound by duties or obligations and who is only a "fractionary unit."[58] It is the function of Rousseau's autobiographical statements to present to the reader an example of, and an apology for, the natural or good man who is, or is becoming, wise without being virtuous.

---

wo er, mit dem Menschengeschlecht verfeindet, seine Aufmerksamkeit der Pflanzen und Blumenwelt zuwendet und in echter gradsinniger Geisteskraft sich mit den stillreizenden Naturkindern vertraut macht" (Goethe, "Der Verfasser teilt die Geschichte seiner botanischen Studien mit," in *Goethes morphologische Schriften*, selections by Troll, Jena 1926, p. 195). It does not seem that the importance of Rousseau's *Rêveries* for Goethe's work as a whole, and in particular for the *Faust*, is sufficiently appreciated.

[58] *Rêveries*, VIII, p. 80, Garnier ed., and VII, pp. 64 and 71; *Émile*, I, vol. 1, p. 13, Garnier ed. Compare Havens, p. 184 note 74. The notion connecting "natural man" with "wise man" is "genius" (compare *Discours*, 10, 1; 61, 20; 62, 13–14 and 19; 63, 5–11; Havens, p. 227 note 224). Émile, who is called a natural man, is an "esprit commun" or "homme vulgaire" (see pp. 263–64 of this article) who as a child comes as near to a natural man as a future citizen could come; that is to say, he is only an approximation to a natural man. Compare *Émile*, I, vol. 1, pp. 16 and 32. Compare Montesquieu, *De l'esprit des lois*, IV 8: "les sciences de speculation . . . rendent [les hommes] sauvages."

To return to our argument, it is as a radically selfish pursuit of pleasure that Rousseau in his capacity as citizen of Geneva attacks philosophy or science at the beginning of his career, in the *Discours*.[59] At its end, in the *Rêveries*, he openly confesses that he himself has always been a useless member of society, that he has never been truly fit for civil society, and that he has found perfect happiness in the pleasure of solitary contemplation. In tacit reference to what he had indicated in the *Discours* about the connection between society and the needs of the body, he says in the *Rêveries* that nothing related to the interest of his body could ever truly occupy his soul. But even there, or rather precisely there, he feels obliged to excuse his life before the tribunal of society by explaining how the way of life which was really his own, and hence his happiness, had been forced upon him by his misfortunes: cut off from society by the malice of men, from pleasant dreams by the decline of his imagination, from thinking by the fear of thinking of his sufferings, he devoted himself to the sweet and simple pleasures of the study of botany.[60] Since he now admits that he himself, the citizen of Geneva, is, and always was, a useless citizen, he can no longer with propriety allow society to regard him as a pernicious man: whereas in the *Discours* he had said that "every useless citizen may be regarded as a pernicious man," he says in the *Rêveries* that his contemporaries have done

---

[59] A life devoted to science is irreconcilable with a life devoted to duty (33, 3–9); science as "agréable" is distinguished from what is "utile" or "salutaire" (54, 11–12; 56, 21–22; 53, 15–16; 5, 14–22; 36, 7–10); there is a necessary connection between science, on the one hand, idleness and luxury, on the other (37, 14–18; 34, 15–16; 36, 11–12). Compare *Lettre à d'Alembert*, pp. 120, 123, and 137, Fontaine ed.

[60] *Rêveries*, v–vii. Compare especially the remarks on the idleness of the *contemplatif solitaire* Rousseau (pp. 46, 64, and 71, Garnier ed.) with *Émile*, iii (vol. 1, p. 248, Garnier ed.) where we read: "tout citoyen oisif est un fripon." Compare *Rêveries*, vii, p. 68, with *Discours*, 5, 14 ff.

wrong, not in removing him from society as a useless member, but in proscribing him from society as a pernicious member. His last word on his central theme would then seem to be that science and citizenship are indeed irreconcilable, but that society can afford to tolerate a few good-for-nothings at its fringes, provided that they are really idle, that is, do not disturb society by subversive teachings—in other words, provided society does not take cognizance of them or does not take them seriously.[61]

V

Having reached this point we have still to face the greatest difficulty to which our attempt at a consistent understanding of Rousseau's intention is exposed. How can the conclusion at which we have arrived be reconciled with Rousseau's admission that science and virtue are compatible in superior minds or that they are incompatible only in "the peoples"? How can his admission that he was always a useless member of society, and in fact unfit for society or for a life of virtue and duty, be reconciled with his public spirit and sense of duty as evidenced by his political writings and by his conviction that the understanding reader of the "Profession de foi du vicaire Savoyard" would "bless a hundred times the virtuous and firm man who had dared to instruct mankind in this manner?"[62] One may answer, indeed one must answer, that the natural antagonism between science and society, or between science and virtue, does not preclude the possibility that science and society may be brought into some kind of agreement by violence, that is, the possibility that the philosopher can be forced by society, or by himself as a citizen, to put his talents

---

[61] This view is already indicated in the *Discours* (36, 11–16). Compare *ibid.*, 35, 2–6, with *Rêveries*, vi (end).
[62] *Lettres écrites de la Montagne*, i, p. 124, Garnier ed. Compare note 40 above.

to the service of society[63] by teaching the peoples their duties while refraining from teaching them philosophy or science. But this answer is clearly insufficient. Rousseau did not limit himself to teaching the peoples their duties; he rather taught them their rights. His political teaching is not a popular or civil teaching; it is indubitably a philosophic or scientific teaching. His political teaching is a part of the whole edifice of philosophy or science, presupposing natural science and crowning it.[64] If society and science are incompatible, if science must not in any circumstances become a social factor, social science, which is intended to be a practical teaching, would seem to be impossible. How then is Rousseau's own political philosophy possible on the basis of his view of the relation of science and society?

Rousseau admits that in a corrupt society (such as the one in which he lived) only science, and even general enlightenment, can provide man with a measure of relief. In a society where it is no longer necessary or desirable that any prejudices be respected, one may freely discuss the sacred foundations of society and freely seek not merely for remedies of the prevailing abuses, but for what would be simply the best solution to the political problem.[65] Under such conditions the direct and scientific presentation of that solution would at its worst be an innocent pastime; but assuming that there is a prospect of a revolution, the new political science might prepare public opinion not merely for the restoration of a

---

[63] Compare Plato's statement of the problem in the *Republic*, 519, c4–520 b4, with *Discours*, 56, 1–11 and 57, 1–6.

[64] Regarding Rousseau's view of the place and the character of political philosophy, see *Discours*, 3, 10–4, 3 (compare Havens' notes) and the beginning of the preface to the *Discours sur l'origine de l'inégalité.*

[65] Compare pp. 267–68 of this article. Rousseau's thesis is a modification of the more common view according to which private men are not allowed to dispute what would be the best political order for the society to which they belong. Compare Calvin, *Institutio*, IV 20 §8 (vol. 2, p. 521, Tholuck ed.), and Hobbes, *Leviathan*, ch. 42 (p. 299, Everyman's Library ed.).

healthy society, but for the establishment of a more perfect society than ever existed before.

From Rousseau's point of view the problem of society cannot be clearly seen and hence truly solved except on the basis of that radical criticism of society or of that fundamental reflection on the relation between society and science with which we have been hitherto concerned. The fundamental reflection reveals society as essentially a kind of bondage; the antagonism between science and society is the most important example of the antagonism between natural liberty and man-made bondage. The natural independence of man over against society determines the general character of the best solution to the political problem: the best solution is a society in which man remains as free as possible.

To discover the precise solution, Rousseau proceeds as follows. Like Hobbes and Locke, he finds the sufficient natural basis of society in everyone's natural desire for self-preservation. As soon as man's faculties have developed beyond a certain point he is unable to preserve himself without the aid of others. The foundations of society are then really not more than the needs of the body, the selfish and most pressing needs of each individual. It is these needs that immediately motivate the concern with freedom: no superior can be presumed to have the same interest in the individual's self-preservation as the individual himself. To enjoy the advantages of society everyone must accept its burdens; everyone must submit his own will, which is directed toward his own good, to the general will, which is directed toward the common good. Freedom in society is possible only within these limits. Man is free in the political sense if he is subject only to the impersonal will of society, and not to the personal or private will of any other individual or group of individuals. To avoid any kind of personal dependence or any kind of "private government," everyone and everything must be subjected to the social will, which expresses itself only in the form of general laws to the establishment of which everyone must have been

able to contribute by his vote. Rousseau knew very well
that "the total alienation of each associate with all his
rights to the whole community," or the complete submission of the private will to the general will, in order
to be reasonable or legitimate requires that a number of
conditions be fulfilled which rarely are fulfilled. The real
difficulty to which his doctrine of the general will is exposed, the difficulty to which it is exposed on the level
of the question it is meant to answer, is expressed by
these two questions: How can the general will which
is always well intentioned since it is always directed toward the good of society, be presumed to be always enlightened about the good of society? And how can the
transformation of natural man, who is guided exclusively
by his private will, into the citizen, who unhesitatingly
prefers the general will to his private will, be effected?[66]

Now, according to Rousseau, this problem can only
be stated by political philosophy; it cannot be solved by
it; or, more precisely, its solution is endangered by the
very political philosophy that leads up to it. For its solution is the action of the legislator or of the "father" of a
nation, that is, of a man of superior intelligence who by
ascribing divine origin to a code which he has devised,
or by honoring the gods with his own wisdom, induces
the citizen body to submit freely to his code. This action
of the legislator is necessarily endangered by philosophy,
since the arguments by which the legislator has to convince the citizens of his divine mission, or of the divine
sanction for his laws, are necessarily of doubtful solidity.[67] One might think that once the code were ratified,
a "social spirit" developed, and the wise legislation accepted on account of its proved wisdom rather than its

---

[66] "Les particuliers voient le bien [*sc.* public] qu'ils rejettent; le
public veut le bien qu'il ne voit pas. . . Voilà d'où naît la néces-
sité du législateur" (*Contrat social*, II 6).
[67] Compare in this connection Rousseau's discussion of the problem of miracles in the *Lettres écrites de la Montagne*, II–III.

pretended origin, the belief in the divine origin of the code would no longer be required; but this suggestion overlooks the fact that the living respect for old laws, "the prejudice of antiquity," which is indispensable for the health of society, can only with difficulty survive the public "debunking" of the accounts regarding their origin. In other words, the transformation of natural man into the citizen is a problem coeval with society itself, and therefore society has a continuous need for at least an equivalent for the mysterious and awe-inspiring action of the legislator. The legislator's action, as well as its later equivalents (traditions and sentiments), serve the purpose of "substituting a partial and moral existence for the physical and independent existence which we have received from nature." Only if the opinions or sentiments engendered by society overcome, and as it were annihilate, the natural sentiments, can there be a stable and healthy society.[68] That is to say: society has to do everything possible to make the citizens oblivious of the very facts that are brought to the center of their attention, as the foundations of society, by political philosophy. Society stands or falls by a specific obfuscation against which philosophy necessarily revolts. The problem posed by political philosophy must be forgotten, if the solution to which political philosophy leads shall work.

This intelligible, if uncomfortable, position could satisfy Rousseau who had the "well-contrived head for which doubt is a good cushion." The easiest way out of this predicament, the way that "the next generation"

---

[68] *Contrat social,* II 6 and 7; III 2 and 11. In the chapter on the legislator (II 7) Rousseau clearly refers only to Moses and Mohammed as examples of legislators; but he clarifies his position sufficiently by quoting in one footnote a passage from Machiavelli's *Discorsi* and by praising in another footnote the theologian Calvin (the legislator of Geneva) as a statesman of the first order. Compare Plato, *Laws,* 634 d7–e4 (757 d–e and 875 a1–d5), and Aristotle, *Politics,* 1269 a15 ff. (also *Metaphysics,* 995 a3–6 and 1074 b1–14).

could not help choosing, was to accept his final and practical solution (his "rediscovery of the community," his
notion of the general will, the primacy of conscience or
of sentiment and tradition) and to throw overboard, or
to forget, his theoretical premise ("the state of nature,"
the independent individual, the primacy of theoretical
reason). The simplest solution of Rousseau's problem is
the "romantic" solution. It may be said to be a genuine
solution since it consists precisely in doing what Rousseau himself demanded for the era following the establishment, or restoration, of a true society—namely, in
forgetting the "individualistic" premise and keeping all
one's thoughts and wishes within the compass of man's
social life. The price, which has to be paid for it, is, directly or indirectly, the subordination of philosophy to
society, or the integration of philosophy into "culture."

It is true of course that Rousseau's doctrine of the
legislator is meant to clarify the fundamental problem of
society rather than to suggest a practical solution for
modern Europe, except in so far as that doctrine adum-
brates Rousseau's own function. The precise reason why
he had to go beyond the classical notion of the legislator
was that that notion is apt to obscure the sovereignty of
the people, that is, to lead, for all practical purposes, to
the substitution of the supremacy of the law for the full
sovereignty of the people. The classical notion of the
legislator is irreconcilable with the demand, so strongly
made by Rousseau, for periodic appeals from the whole
legal and constitutional order to the sovereign will of the
people, or from the will of past generations to the will
of the living generation.[69] Rousseau had, therefore, to
find a substitute for the action of the legislator, a substitute that would be compatible with the highest possible

---

[69] *Contrat social,* iii 18. (For the interpretation consider Paine,
Rights of Man, pp. 12 ff., Everyman's Library ed.). Compare *The
Federalist,* ed. by E. M. Earle (Washington: National Home Library Foundation) no. 49, pp. 328–39: frequent appeals to the
people prevent opinion, or the prejudices of the community, from
acquiring the necessary strength.

degree of freedom of the people. According to his final suggestion, the most fundamental function originally entrusted to the legislator,[70] namely, the transformation of natural man into the citizen, has to be discharged by a civil religion of the kind described from somewhat different points of view in the *Contrat social,* on the one hand, and in *Émile,* on the other. We need not go into the question whether Rousseau himself believed in the religion he presented in the profession of faith of the Savoyard vicar, a question that cannot be answered by reference to what he said when he was persecuted on account of that profession. What is decisive is the fact that according to his explicit view of the relation of knowledge, faith and "the people," the citizen body. cannot have more than opinion regarding the truth of this or any other religion. One may even wonder whether any human being can have genuine knowledge in this respect since, according to Rousseau's last word on the subject, there are "insoluble objections" to the religion preached by the Savoyard vicar.[71] Therefore every civil religion would seem to have, in the last analysis, the same character as the legislator's account of the origin of his code, in so far as both are essentially endangered by the "dangerous pyrrhonism" fostered by the rigorous demands of

---

[70] Regarding the other problem that the legislator has to solve, namely, the enlightening of the general will about its objects, Rousseau seems to have believed that not its solution, but indeed a prerequisite for its solution in a complex society is supplied by a political system that favors the wealthy and the rural population over against *la canaille.* This political demand transforms the egalitarian implication of his doctrine of the general will into something comparable to the "sophisms" of classical politics. (Compare Aristotle, *Politics,* 1297 a14 ff., and Xenophon, *Cyropaedia,* I 2.15.) That Rousseau was aware of this can be seen from what he says in approving the constitutional changes effected by Servius Tullius (*Contrat social,* IV 4; compare *ibid.,* III 15).

[71] *Rêveries,* III, pp. 23 and 27, Garnier ed.; *Lettre à Beaumont,* p. 479, Garnier ed.; *Lettres écrites de la Montagne,* I, pp. 121–36, Garnier ed., and IV, p. 180. Compare notes 36 and 45 above. For the question of "insoluble objections," compare Leibniz, *Théodicée,* Discours préliminaire, §§24–27.

philosophy or science: the "insoluble objections," to which even the best of all religions is exposed, are dangerous truths. Rousseau's personal horror, and impatience, of intolerance is primarily responsible for the fact that he did not dwell in his writings subsequent to the *Discours* on the consequences that this view entails.

VI

Rousseau maintained then, to the last, the thesis that he had set forth most impressively at the beginning of his career. That thesis, to repeat, is to the effect that there is a fundamental disproportion between the requirements of society and those of philosophy or science. It is opposed to the thesis of the Enlightenment, according to which the diffusion of philosophic or scientific knowledge is unqualifiedly salutary to society, or more generally expressed, there is a natural harmony between the requirements of society and those of science. One can trace Rousseau's thesis directly to Descartes' distinction between the rules regarding the reform of one's own thoughts and those regarding the reform of society.[72] But considering the facts that Descartes' relation to the Enlightenment is ambiguous as well as that Rousseau attacks modern politics in the name of classical politics, it is preferable to understand Rousseau's thesis as a restatement of the view underlying classical political philosophy, and his attack on the thesis of the Enlightenment as a part, although the most important part, of his attack on modern politics in the name of classical politics.[73] It may therefore be permissible to

[72] *Discours de la méthode,* ii–iii. Descartes is mentioned in the *Discours* twice (34, 19 and 62, 15). Compare also *ibid.,* 63, 6 ("marcher seuls"), with *Discours de la méthode,* ii (Adam-Tannéry 16, 30).

[73] Regarding Rousseau's relation to classical politics, compare the passages indicated or quoted in notes 5, 11, 12, 20, 22, 35, 39, 63, and 68 above. Compare the explicit reference to Plato's *Republic* in *Discours,* 41 note, and to the *Laws, ibid.,* 19 note.

conclude our essay on Rousseau's intention with a cursory consideration of the relation of his political philosophy to classical political philosophy.

For the proper understanding of that relation, one must disregard the accidental difference, which is due to the difference in the social status of philosophy in the classical period, on the one hand, and in that of Rousseau, on the other. The classical statements about science and society, especially those of Plato, still had to serve the purpose of combating a common prejudice against philosophy, whereas Rousseau had to fight perhaps an even more dangerous prejudice in favor of philosophy: by his time, philosophy had become not merely a generally revered tradition, but a fashion. In order to grasp the essential difference, it is advisable to start as follows. The basic premise of classical political philosophy may be said to be the view that the natural inequality of intellectual powers is, or ought to be, of decisive political importance. Hence the unlimited rule of the wise, in no way answerable to the subjects, appears to be the absolutely best solution to the political problem. This demand is obviously irreconcilable for all practical purposes with the character of the political community. The disproportion between the requirements of science and those of society leads to the consequence that the true or natural order (the absolute rule of the wise over the unwise) must be replaced by its political counterpart or imitation, which is the rule, under law, of the gentlemen over those who are not gentlemen.

The difficulties to which this doctrine as a whole is exposed have tempted political thinkers from very early times to take the natural equality of all men as a starting point for their reflections. These attempts gained considerably in significance when the natural character of the inequality of intellectual capacities was explicitly questioned, and therewith the stronghold of the classical position was attacked as a consequence of the emergence of a heightened belief in the virtue of method as distinguished from natural gifts. It is this radical change that led to the Enlightenment attacked by Rousseau. In opposition to the Enlightenment he reasserts the crucial importance of the natural inequality of men with regard to intellectual gifts.[74] But he avoids the political consequences that the classics drew from this principle, by appealing to another classical principle, namely, the disproportion between the requirements of science and those of society: he denies that the conclusion from the fact of natural inequality to the demand for political inequality is valid. The disproportion between the requirements of science and those of society permits him to build a fundamentally egalitarian politics on the admission, and even the emphatic assertion, of the natural inequality of men in the most important respect. One is tempted to say that Rousseau was the first to meet Plato's and Aristotle's challenge to democracy on the level of Plato's and Aristotle's reflections, and that it is this fact that accounts for his unique position in the history of democratic doctrine.

It goes without saying that the relation between Rousseau and the classics is not exhausted by that part of the discussion which is carried on by Rousseau on the level of classical political philosophy. Rousseau makes a radical departure from classical political philosophy by accepting the principle of Machiavelli's criticism of classical political philosophy and by building his doctrine on modern natural science. He is thus led to replace the classical definition of man as the rational animal by the definition of man as a free agent, or the idea of human perfection by that of human perfectibility, to exaggerate the distinction between political virtue and genuine virtue into the opposition between virtue and goodness, and, last but not least, to initiate the fateful combination of the lowering of the moral standards with the moral pathos of "sincerity." All the serious difficulties

---

[74] Compare *Discours,* 61, 20; 62, 13–14 and 19; 63, 5–11; compare also the end of the *Discours sur l'origine de l'inégalité* as well as *Contrat social,* I 9 and II 1.

with which the understanding of Rousseau's teaching remains beset, even if the principle suggested in the present article is accepted, can be traced to the fact that he tried to preserve the classical idea of philosophy on the basis of modern science. Only in a few cases is there any need for recourse to his private idiosyncrasies to clear up apparent or real contradictions in his teaching. In particular, I do not wish to deny that on a few occasions his irritable *amour-propre* may have blurred his amazingly lucid vision.[75]

---

[75] Compare *Discours*, 29, 1–5.

THE SOCIAL CONTRACT AND
ROUSSEAU'S REVOLT AGAINST SOCIETY

J. MC MANNERS

We have a delightful engraving of Jean-Jacques Rousseau dating from the very time when he was engaged on
the final draft of the *Social Contract*. There he sits in the
corner beside his kitchen fire, arrayed in night-cap, long
dressing gown and buckled shoes; behind him are his
books and the pots and plates and frying pan; his cat
'Ninette' on his knee and his dog 'Duke' at his feet (now
renamed 'Turk,' to spare the susceptibilities of the Duc
de Luxembourg, a friendly neighbour). Rousseau had
forsaken the vanities of the world, had turned his back
on a corrupting civilization, had broken with the
philosophes, had discarded lace on his clothing, his
watch and his sword. He was ill, too, suffering from a
urinary constriction—that was why he affected dressing
gowns, to conceal the catheters which were the only
relief for his malady. And he was writing feverishly.

This was his volcanic period. He erupted into literary
immortality with *La Nouvelle Héloïse* (February 1761),
Le Contrat Social (April 1762) and *Emile* (May 1762).
Within little over a year, he published a novel, a treatise
on political theory, and another on education, each
prophetically attuned to the faintly stirring aspirations
of a new generation and, perhaps, inspiring them. They
were works springing directly from the heart of the
writer. Others wrote as an intellectual game, or to make
their reputation; but Rousseau wrote to know himself.
'I would have written all my books,' he says, 'if I'd been

"The Social Contract and Rousseau's Revolt Against Society" reprinted by permission of the author and the Leicester University
Press.

confined for life on a desert island.'[1] It is one aspect of this white-hot inner inspiration that I wish to consider, and to go on to make a reckless suggestion concerning the interpretation of the *Social Contract*.

Let me remind you how the problem of the *Social Contract* goes. It does not fit comfortably with the rest of Rousseau's writings.[2] In it, he binds his citizens together into a monolithic moral unity. Yet he began his career of authorship with an essay which proved that the arts and sciences had corrupted morals, and went on to an essay on inequality, which damned civilization altogether. *Emile* shows how to bring up a boy in isolation from the corruptions of society, and also contains the 'Profession of faith of the Savoyard *Vicaire*,' which implies that religion is the direct relationship of the individual to God—the antithesis of the social-cement religion of the *Social Contract*. How do we reconcile this back-to-nature individuality with the *Social Contract's* absorption of the individual in the community? Some contemporaries said the attack on civilization was a fraud: some later commentators, taking the opposite tack, have argued that the *Social Contract* must be an aberration. This sort of criticism, however, is rather old-fashioned now, since Hubert's researches[3] have shown how the central theme of the General Will had been formulated between 1744 and 1756, how it was taken up again at the beginning of 1760, shortly before the *Nouvelle Héloïse* was published, and was worked on simultaneously with *Emile*. The evidence supports Rous-

---

[1] *Les Rêveries du promeneur solitaire,* ed. J. S. Spink (1948), p. 40 (3e Promenade).

[2] One of the greatest historians of French literature held this view. Daniel Mornet considered the *Social Contract* as a work of pure dialectic—a sort of showing off on Rousseau's part ('Questions de méthode'—a review of A. Schinz, *La Pensée de Jean-Jacques Rousseau* [1929] in *Rev. hist. litt. de la France,* XXXVII [1930], pp. 236–7).

[3] R. Hubert, *Rousseau et l'Encyclopédie: essai sur la formation des idées politiques de Rousseau. 1742–1756* (n.d. 1928), pp. 24, 56, etc.

seau's claim that, as early as his sojourn at Venice in 1743–4, he had seen that 'tout tenait radicalement à la politique.'[4] In his own mind, at least, the *Social Contract* was part of his general system of ideas.

This being so, the problem of the detailed exegesis of the book becomes acute. What are we to make of 'forcing men to be free'?—of the fantastic unanimity, in which an individual who differs from the majority is expected to blame himself, of the institutions, more especially the Civil Religion, to mould the minds of men? These are scandals that have brought down on their inventor the wrath of right-wing commentators,[5] accusing him of fathering the doctrines of Jacobin and Bolshevik tyranny, with Bertrand Russell coming in from the other side to make him responsible for Hitler. These accusations have been given a more sophisticated form in Professor Talmon's study of 'totalitarian democracy,'[6] and a new argument for this side of the controversy has lately been produced by Lester G. Crocker, who detects a suspicious insistence upon indoctrination in *Emile* and the *Nouvelle Héloïse*, as well as in the *Social Contract*— 'the goal is to make the people think they want what some have decided they ought to want.'[7] In the end, even Starobinsky, so subtle and sympathetic in his psychological interpretation, abandons the master on the brink of his grim Civil Religion, with its menacing subconscious linkages of terror and adoration: 'is it detracting from Rousseau's greatness to say that he holds in his hands the keys of a terrible world?'[8]

---

[4] *Les Confessions*, ed. Jacques Voisine (1964), p. 480.

[5] e.g. E. Faguet, 'he does not know what liberty is . . . his liberty is equality' (*Rousseau penseur* [n.d.–1912], pp. 346–8).

[6] J. L. Talmon, *The Origins of Totalitarian Democracy* (1952).

[7] Lester G. Crocker, *Nature and Culture: Ethical Thought in the French Enlightenment* (1963), p. 476.

[8] J. Starobinski (reviewing), *Annales Jean-Jacques Rousseau*, XXXI (1946–9), p. 287. Of the contributors to the *Etudes sur le 'Contrat Social' de Jean-Jacques Rousseau: actes des journées d'étude organisées a Dijon, 1962* (Publ. de l'Univ. de Dijon, XXX, 1964;

On the other side, we have theorists of liberal democracy, saying that the General Will is a cosy sort of unanimity after all, just like the 'Quaker sense of the meeting.' Their case is drawn out by J. W. Chapman, who shows how Talmon failed to observe that the General Will was expressed in 'a process of dynamic interaction of individual wills' operating within the rule of law. Having said this, however, he admits that Rousseau 'is trying to achieve liberal ideas by totalitarian means,'[9] which puts Talmon back in business. Similarly, de Jouvenel's defence of the liberalism of the civic machinery ends up with the admission that our freedom is found only in the tiny city state, whose 'totemism'[10] flouts the interests of the human race in general. More effectively, R. L. Leigh,[11] the learned editor of Rousseau's correspondence, points out that natural law is meant to be in force in the contractual society, so that there is a private sector of life over which the General Will has no authority. True, but there is no gainsaying Grosclaude's reply,[12] that the sovereign alone decides where the limits of that private sector are drawn; the sovereign, indeed, decides when a man must be executed because 'he cannot be allowed to live without danger.'[13] This shocking phrase is typical of Rousseau's style, of course; he ad-

---

henceforward referred to as *Etudes: Dijon* [1964]), F. Gilliard, J. Dehaussy and S. Cotta regard the *Social Contract* as totalitarian in its implications (pp. 112, 135–6; 187, 189), while M. de Soto holds that the system appears totalitarian though Rousseau himself really thought it was liberal (p. 235).

[9] J. W. Chapman, *Rousseau, Totalitarian or Liberal?* (1956), p. 139.

[10] Bertrand de Jouvenel, 'Essai sur la politique de Rousseau' in his ed. of *Du Contrat Social* (1947), p. 120. Cf. P. Burgelin, *La Philosophie d'existence de Jean-Jacques Rousseau* (1952), pp. 521–2.

[11] R. L. Leigh, 'Liberté et autorité dans le *Contrat Social*,' *Jean-Jacques Rousseau et son oeuvre: problemes et recherches* (Comité National pour la Commémoration de J.J.R., Paris, 1964), pp. 255–6 (thereafter cited as *Commémoration*, 1964).

[12] ibid., pp. 263–4.

[13] *Contrat Social* II, 5; C. E. Vaughan, *The Political Writings of J-J. Rousseau* (2 vols, 1962), II, p. 47.

vances a shattering proposition, then explains it.[14] But he never explains it away. If we consider his thought as a tight intellectual unity, we are doomed, it seems, to live with these totalitarian oddities—setting alongside them, of course, the evidence to show how he hated violence, the oppression of minorities, and so on, and reflecting that, in the nature of the case, there must always be a tension between authority and freedom.[15]

I suppose that, as a political theorist, this is what Rousseau was implying. What I do not believe, however, is that he himself accepted arguments founded on 'the nature of the case' or what 'must necessarily be so' as satisfactory. His 'totalitarian' passages are so grim, and by contrast, his love of freedom was so intense, that I cannot be satisfied that the paradox has been explained. The debate so far has fitted the *Social Contract* into the pattern of Rousseau's thought at the expense of pushing it out of the pattern of his genius. The full explanation is to be found, I would maintain, in the context of his passionate, intensely personal revolt against society. This is my subject, and if, in the end, my theory seems to you frivolous, I must console myself with having enjoyed reflecting upon, and talking about, a strange, tragic and attractive personality.

For the first thirty-seven years of his life, Rousseau had led an uprooted wandering existence, but in the shoddy bohemian catalogue of his doings, there came two supreme moments. One, at the age of seventeen, was when he met Louise Eléanore de la Tour, Baronne de Warens. Fifty years later, that golden day was fresh in his memory: it was the moment that decided the whole course of his life. This ash-blonde adventuress, who was subsidized to maintain a sort of hostel for potential converts, did more for her *protégé* than maintaining him in

[14] 'A blow, followed by a caress' (M. Launay, 'L'art de l'écrivain dans le *Contrat Social*,' *Etudes: Dijon* [1964], p. 372).
[15] Roughly, the position reached by J. H. Broome, *Rousseau: a Study of his Thought* (1963), pp. 62 ff.

idleness while he read, and offering him a friendly, glacial initiation to sexual experience. With her, Jean-Jacques crossed the frontier into another world, the world of those who do not have to work for their living, whose status is assured, who can afford to refine and subtilize every emotion—a dream world to which he yearned to belong. From the start, in the *Confessions* we see the working of a social ambition which turned down ordinary girls in the hope of real young ladies to love.[16] 'A single *château* was all I wanted,' says Rousseau—to be the favourite of the *seigneur*, the suitor of his daughter and the protector of the neighbourhood.[17] In all his wanderings, he never slipped off into an ordinary trade: he is held by magnetic attraction on the parasitic fringe of high society. After his conversion to the simple life, we still see hints of the yearning for the aristocratic dream world he had abandoned. The great love of his life (by definition, unfulfilled) is to be for Sophie d'Houdetot, another aristocratic dream-woman, and the object of the *Nouvelle Héloïse*, said Voltaire, with wicked insight and over-simplification, is to prove that the baron of the pays de Vaud ought to allow Julie to marry 'Jean-Jacques.'[18]

From meeting Mme de Warens, Rousseau lived on the borderline between two worlds, and his moth-like flutterings towards the glittering sphere above him lasted until 1749, the year of the other supreme moment in his life. Then, under the tree in the park of Vincennes, he received the illumination which led to the pathway of renunciation—when he read the title of the Dijon essay competition. 'If I had ever been able to write down a quarter of what I saw and felt under that tree,' he wrote

---

[16] *Confessions*, pp. 148–9. On the theme see also F. Chadeville and C. Roussel, 'Le Vocabulaire de l'ascension sociale dans le livre II des *Confessions*': *Ann. J-J. Rousseau* xxxvi (1963–5), pp. 57–8.
[17] *Confessions*, p. 48.
[18] P. Van Tieghem, *La Nouvelle Héloïse de Jean-Jacques Rousseau* (1929), pp. 91–2.

to Malesherbes in 1762, 'with what clarity I would have revealed all the contradictions of the social system, with what force I'd have exposed all the abuses of our institutions, with what simplicity I would have demonstrated that man is naturally good and that it is by their institutions alone that men become wicked.'[19] Now this famous letter, it can be shown, exaggerated what really happened in 1749.[20] This need not concern us. It is a letter written in the year of the *Social Contract*, and it reveals what the illumination of Vincennes had come to mean to Rousseau as the basis of the faith by which he lived.

If the word 'faith' has a religious sound, in this case it is appropriate. Like the Christians, but unlike the *philosophes*, Rousseau saw man in desperate need of redemption. With all the thinkers of the Enlightenment, he rejected the doctrine of Original Sin, but he left their company completely when he rediscovered this terrible shadow over mankind, not in human nature, but in human institutions.[21] Somewhere at the beginning of human society, the Fall had taken place. This is the essence of the revelation of Vincennes—'that man is naturally good, and that it is by their institutions alone that men have become wicked.'

And so, from this complex of wickedness that is so-

---

[19] *Quelques Lettres à M. le Président de Malesherbes, Oeuvres Complètes* ed. B. Gagnebin & M. Raymond (3 vols, 1959–61), I, pp. 1135–6.
[20] F. C. Green, *Jean-Jacques Rousseau: a Critical Study of his Life and Writings* (1955), pp. 97–100.
[21] E. Cassirer, *The Question of Jean-Jacques Rousseau* (E.T. by Peter Gay, 1954) pp. 74–5. The original article in German was published in 1932. For the theological background, J. F. Thomas, *Le Pélagianisme de J-J. Rousseau* (1956). If we substitute Rousseau's view of Original Sin for the Christian view, the opening sentence of the *Social Contract* can be seen as an echo of the opening sentence of a pious work which greatly influenced Rousseau's early reading—'Nous sommes fait pour connôitre la vérité, mais le péché nous en a éloigné en nous éloignant de Dieu' (B. Lamy, *Entretiens sur les sciences*, 1684, 3rd ed. 1706); (ed. F. Girbal and P. Clair, 1966, p. 37).

ciety, Jean-Jacques henceforward strove for emancipation. How he did so—not all at once, but ultimately
as far as in him lay,[22]—how he abandoned the prizes
civilization offered him, how he sought the natural man
within himself, under the layers of false personality that
vanity creates, how he fought strange battles[23] within
his mind to establish the independence of his conscience
against the blandishments of the aristocratic dream
world which beckoned and tempted him, is a psychological study in itself. To become the simple and spontaneous
individual according to nature, he had to use every resource of his superbly subtle and introspective intellect.

There are obvious physical and temperamental explanations why Rousseau turned his back on society.[24] He
admits, 'I would have enjoyed social life as much as
anybody, if I had not been certain to show myself, not
only to my disadvantage, but entirely other than I really
am.'[25] Let those who have never been reduced to misery
by using the wrong knife and fork, and who can give
confident orders to railway porters and waiters, laugh at
this; and remember, with Rousseau, this was not just
the odd incident: his *gaucherie* had become a panic
obsession. He had risen into polite society too late to
build up a fund of automatic social responses, to grow
a carapace of unselfconscious poise within which the
sensitive interior man could manœuvre. Then, there was
his physical affliction, his uraemia.[26] Quite apart from
its toxic effects, Rousseau was haunted by its continual
embarrassments. How could he wander about a court,

---

[22] For the stages, through 'heroic virtue' to 'gentleness of soul,' R.
Grimsley, *J-J. Rousseau: a Study in Self Awareness* (1961), p. 81.
[23] A moving, pathetic example is the letter of 7 October 1760 to
Mme de Boufflers refusing the Prince de Conti's partridges, *Corresp.
générale* ed. Th. Dufour (Paris, 20 vols. 1924–34), V, pp. 210–11.
[24] On the whole subject, B. Munteano, 'La Solitude de Rousseau,'
Ann. J-J. Rousseau, xxx (1946–9), pp. 103–46.
[25] *Confessions*, p. 129.
[26] Latest state of the problem in J. Starobinski, 'The Illness of
Rousseau,' *Yale French Studies*, xxviii (1961–2), pp. 64–74.

he writes, with ladies and lackeys everywhere, obstructing the stairs and asking him where he was going?[27]

This *gaucherie*, and the uraemia (and, one might add, an addiction to onanism) were not so much causes of a state of mind, as symptoms—an admission of, and excuses for defeat in an interior aspiration. This search, and this failure, are at once Rousseau's tragedy and the precondition of his genius. At the heart of his doctrine and personality (as we see in the subtle psychological studies of Starobinski and Grimsley)[28] was a hopeless, unfulfilled yearning for an immediacy of relationship with God and man. Hence his preoccupation with ways of concealment and communication—with masks, veils, language, music—all part of his search for 'transparency'; in human terms, the search for the true self, and for the ideal 'other' to whom his soul could be open and his conscience clear. The shadow over the *Confessions* is the failure of that quest. 'Devoured by the need to love, without ever having been able to satisfy it, I saw myself on the threshold of old age, dying without having lived.'[29] In whatever social order his lot had been cast, inevitably, unless he had sacrificed his genius, Rousseau would have been alienated. Men in the mass live institutionally, by processes of approximation and compromise. They cannot live transparently, without intermediaries. I do not believe that the city of the *Social Contract* could have satisfied its author's inner yearnings.[30]

True, its supremely coherent social *milieu* offers to the

---

[27] To the Marquis de Mirabeau (Fragments), about 25 March, 1767, *Corresp. générale*, ed. Dufour, XVII (1932), pp. 3–4.

[28] Grimsley, op. cit.; J. Starobinski, *J-J. Rousseau: la transparence et l'obstacle* (1957). Baldensperger defined Rousseauism as the 'indifference or hostility to intermediaries.'

[29] *Confessions*, p. 504.

[30] 'He would have been as much a misfit, just as unhappy, even in the ideal society' (P. D. Jimack, 'Rousseau and the Primacy of Self', *Studies on Voltaire and the 18th Century*, ed. Th. Besterman, XXXII [1965], pp. 76–7.)

citizens the very thing that is missing in Rousseau's own consciousness—the feeling of 'belonging'; it is significant that this epic of patriotic unity was written by a stateless person. Like Bonaparte, Rousseau was not a Frenchman; he was a great *déraciné*. Unlike the Emperor, however, he did not use France to serve his ambitions, indeed throughout his life he carried on a hopeless love affair with the country which nourished his genius.[31] In his garret in Paris he composed a comedy in which the hero, a dashing French officer, Dorante, has a clumsy batman, a Swiss called Jacquard—a pathetic revelation of his own aspirations. And even when he had abandoned the attempt to transform Jacquard into Dorante, and had attacked the arts, civilization and everything France stands for, the love-hate relationship continued. As against the corruptions of his adopted country, the theorist of the *Social Contract* cites his native Geneva as an ideal, and boasts of being 'born a citizen of a free state and member of the Sovereign.'[32] Yet Geneva was an oligarchy, run by the twenty-five families of the Petit Conseil, and Rousseau knew it. His father and grandfather had been in the fight to try to get legislative power into the hands of the Grand Conseil, and through Toussaint-Pierre Lenieps he was in touch with the exiles of the Genevan popular party in Paris.[33] 'Born a citizen of a free state and member of the Sovereign' is a bland, deadly statement of a man insisting upon rights that have been filched from him. This is the measure of Rousseau's isolation and of the pessimism behind the *Social Contract*—he claims citizenship only in a free republic that has died, that has, perhaps, never existed.

Lonely and rootless, Rousseau had learned to hate

---

[31] G. May, 'Rousseau and France', *Yale French Studies*, xxviii (1961–2), pp. 122–39. See also F. Jost, *J-J. Rousseau Suisse* (2 vols, 1961), II, pp. 177 ff. ('Antagonismes et antinomies: Rousseau et la France').

[32] *Contrat Social*, i (Introd.); Vaughan, ii, p. 23.

[33] Jean Fabre, 'Réalité et utopie dans la pensée de Rousseau,' *Ann. J-J. Rousseau*, xxv (1959–62), pp. 188–99.

the social order he knew. It was sordid and unjust. For long, he had planned to write a *Morale sensitive*, to show how climate and physical surroundings could play a therapeutic role on the souls of men. It was never written, but he proved his point in a negative way by showing the degradation of man by the noise, dirt, huckstering and promiscuity of cities.[34] As for injustice, his indictment of the age was inventive and comprehensive: he lumps the rich with the aristocracy in the same condemnation, and with terrible insight, he detects the vast, unseen gravitational field of corrupt deference that riches and formal privilege build around them—the right to drive carriages dangerously, to seduce the daughters of ordinary people, to be immune from police investigations and the verdicts of ordinary courts of justice.[35]

The inspiration of this savage bitterness is a glowing hatred of injustice intensified by refraction through the manifold prisms of an introspective and anti-social temperament.[36] Yet there is more to his hatred of society than this. Society was responsible for his inexpiable crime, and the dark promptings which told him that this crime was really his own, made his hatred of the social order into a pathological obsession which he dared not question, lest the weight of his guilt sweep his sanity

---

[34] Rousseau's condemnations of Paris are well known. Notice that he has not a word of admiration for the beauty of Venice in the *Confessions* (H. Vianu, 'La Lumière et l'ombre dans l'œuvre de J-J. Rousseau,' *Rev. des sciences humaines* 1963, p. 209).

[35] See the article *Economie politique* (1755), Vaughan, op. cit., I, pp. 237–73, esp. pp. 267–8. Rousseau is a master at detecting the economic injustice intensified by the insult to the under-dog's self-respect (e.g. his comments on his own treatment in the Venice embassy, *Confessions*, pp. 185–6). He had been a lackey, and in his early poetry he cannot avoid the strong verb 'ramper' (L. Ducros, *J-J. Rousseau*, 2 vols. 1908, I, p. 156). Notice too how his hatred of social injustice is bound up with his religious beliefs—for the rich and successful would be glad if there was no future life.

[36] For the connexion between temperament and the desire for social justice, B. Baczki, 'Rousseau et l'aliénation social,' *Ann. J-J. Rousseau*, xxxv (1959–62), p. 229.

away. By Thérèse, he had five children, and all were sent to the *Enfants trouvés*.[37] In the ciphered letter of April 1751 to Mme de Franceuil, he gave explanations: Thérèse was ill, the children would be happier brought up to simple trades, Plato had recommended education by the State, he could not have done his writing amidst squalling brats (he has a point here); but the essential explanation lay in the wickedness of the social order. 'It is the class (*état*) of rich folk, it is your class that steals from mine the bread of my children.'[38]

Here is one of the indispensable texts for the most recent trend in Rousseau studies—the attempt to place Jean-Jacques and his revolt against society in the hierarchy of classes in eighteenth-century France. By his Genevan origins, by the kind of life he ultimately chose, and by some of his friendships, the writer of the *Social Contract* belonged to the lesser-bourgeois-artisan stratum, a connexion which M. Launay is skilfully interpreting.[39] Yet, in the end, I think, Rousseau must remain classless and *déraciné*. There was, indeed, one group in society to which he indisputably belonged, and it was against the conventions of this group that he revolted most decisively. The profession of man of letters gave Voltaire invested capital, a feudal seigneury complete with parish church, the freedom of the *salons*, the familiarity of kings. To Rousseau, it opened the gates of the aristocratic dream world for which he had yearned;

---

[37] For a bibliography of the discussions concerning his children, R. Lelièvre, 'Julie d'Etanges ou la maternité frustrée,' *Rev. d'hist. litt. de la France*, LXII (1962), pp. 369–70, note.

[38] *Corresp. complète de Jean-Jacques Rousseau*, ed. R. A. Leigh, II (1963), pp. 142–4.

[39] M. Launay, 'Les Problèmes politiques dans la correspondance de Rousseau,' *Commémoration* (1964), pp. 269–71; 'La Société française d'après la correspondance de J-J. Rousseau,' *J-J. Rousseau pour le 250e anniversaire de sa naissance* (Soc. des Etudes Robespierristes, 1963); J. Lecercle, 'Rousseau et ses publics,' *Commémoration* (1964), p. 289. Notice also O. Krafft's contention about the decline of Rousseau's family from the upper caste of Genevan society (*La Politique de J-J. Rousseau*, 1958, pp. 110–12).

even when he had gone back to nature, it gave him the alliance of the Prince de Conti,[40] the Prince de Ligne, and Malesherbes. He had meant to rise this way. In 1749, on the very eve of his 'conversion,' he was producing *Le Persifleur*,[41] the first number of a satirical periodical— this is how he was intending to prostitute his genius. But when he turned his back on society, Jean-Jacques adopted a new, altruistic doctrine of the integrity and independence of the writer. Unlike Montesquieu and Voltaire, he put his name to everything he wrote—quaking with terror as he did so—refusing to be one of those theoretically anonymous writers who evade the risks but take the kudos.[42] He would accept no patronage. In writing, as distinct from real life, no rank could overawe him. 'Whenever it is a question of reasoning,' he says, replying to a king, 'men fall back into the right of nature, and regain their original equality.'[43] So that he could write with absolute honesty, he even refused to live by his publications. The whole logic of the appalling letter explaining why he abandoned his children depends upon the proposition that he would not write for money. That was why he copied music, refusing the lucrative rewards of reviewing: 'They thought I could make a trade of my pen, like all the other men of letters, whereas I can only write out of passion.'[44]

By genius, Rousseau had fought his way to acceptance in the dream world of high society where he did not belong: by genius, he manœuvred himself out of it into a work-a-day world from which he had arisen and to which he belonged even less. Therefore, he above all

---

[40] Jean Fabre, 'Rousseau et le Prince de Conti,' *Ann. J-J. Rousseau* XXVI (1963–5), pp. 21 ff.

[41] *Oeuvres complètes*, ed. B. Gagnebin and M. Raymond (3 vols. 1959), I, pp. 1103–4. Notice the phrase 'Si j'étois un auteur connu' and the following ironical argument.

[42] J. Guéhenno, *Jean-Jacques* (4 vols. 1948–52), III, p. 96.

[43] Cit. Guéhenno, 'La réforme de Jean-Jacques,' *Ann. J-J. Rousseau*, XXXI (1946–9), p. 10.

[44] Guéhenno, *Jean-Jacques*, III, p. 24.

men was entitled to demand equality—true equality, not the Revolution's opening of careers to talent, which was only inequality made logical.[45] Yet this uncompromising leveller was, in practical affairs, a conformist.[46] This romantic dreamer, this sensitive lay confessor, had had to tighten his belt. He knew the compelling hardness of circumstances. So he would leave serfdom in Poland; he told the enthusiast who brought up his son on the lines of *Emile* that he was a fool; he advised a young man stranded in a seminary without a vocation to stay on and become 'an officer of public morality.'[47] Now this is the voice of the Rousseau of the lesser-bourgeois-artisan stratum, of those who are used to putting up with their lot, who grumble and conform. It is the genuine *grands seigneurs* of revolutionary speculation, those who inherit the world of culture like Marx, of money like Engels, of rank like Saint-Simon, who dare to follow the logic of their arguments into the subversion of existing institutions here and now, on the way to Utopia.

Yet, in his theoretical works, I would argue, Rousseau is not writing from the everyday level of his lesser-

---

[45] Rousseau's ideal is that all must be equal—not even distinctions arising from wisdom or virtue will be recognised (*Narcisse*, Preface, in *Oeuvres Completes*, ed. Gagnebin and Raymond, II, p. 956). On the other hand, he was prepared to recognize a limited property and other common-sense modifications; equality was not just an end in itself, but a pre-requisite of liberty (R. Polin, 'Le sens de l'égalité et de l'inégalité chez J-J. Rousseau,' *Etudes: Dijon* [1964] pp. 143–64).

[46] 'His thought is revolutionary, but he himself is not' (B. Groethuysen, *J-J. Rousseau*, 1949, p. 206). Revolutionary arguments lead to conservative practical conclusions (P. M. Masson, *La Religion de Rousseau*, 3 vols, 1916, II [*La Profession de Foi de Jean-Jacques*], pp. 116–7). Notice some temperamental characteristics that fit in—how he runs his own life on a contractual basis (C. W. Hendel, *J-J. Rousseau: Moralist*, 2 vols, 1934, II, pp. 165–6). Perhaps, too, the fact that he does not like wild scenery (M.-L. Buchner, *A Contribution to the Descriptive Technique of J-J. Rousseau*, 1937, p. 104).

[47] P. M. Masson, op. cit., II, p. 173.

bourgeois status. In a letter of April 1759,[48] he said that he was submissive to all the rules, because this was the price one had to pay for undertaking 'the dangerous employment of a defender of the truth.' To do justice to his courage, we ought to admit that his theoretical works are uncompromising. He was not (as he said in the preface to *Emile*) writing about 'possible things,' which can 'ally themselves to the existing evil.'[49] On the contrary, the sense of inferiority and lower-middle class compromise vanishes when he dons his prophetic mantle —he is the *grand seigneur*, the self-conscious genius who had fought his way into the aristocratic dream world, and had voluntarily abandoned it. In him speaks the uncompromising voice of one who has made the splendid renunciation, the voice of the anarchist that lurks within the soul of the aristocrat turned revolutionary. And so, in interpreting the *Social Contract*, we ought to put Rousseau's conformism and realism in practical affairs out of our minds. We should not make comparisons with the constitutions for Poland and Corsica, or try to explain awkward passages by the reflection that the system of the General Will is meant only for the small city state. The *Social Contract* is not a handbook on political theory proposing new ways of going about old business. It is the work of a revolutionary condemning all existing institutions, whose only camouflage is an insistence on keeping the discussion in the realm of things as they could be.

Consider Derathé's[50] comparison of the doctrine of the

---

[48] To Lenieps, 5 Apr. 1759, *Corresp. générale*, ed. Dufour, IV (1925), p. 220.

[49] *Emile: ou l'éducation*, ed. F. and P. Richard (n.d.), p. 3.

[50] R. Derathé, *Jean-Jacques Rousseau et la science politique de son temps* (1950). Cf. the insistence that the heart of the *Social Contract* is the ending of confusion between the 'Sovereign' and the 'government' and the subjecting of the latter to the former (J. J. Chevallier, 'Le mot et la notion du *gouvernement* chez Rousseau, *Etudes: Dijon* [1964], p. 294, and P. Bastid, 'Rousseau et la théorie des formes de gouvernement,' ibid., p. 316).

Social Contract with that of the theorists of the natural
law school. They begin with men equal, but by postulat-
ing sociability end up with submission. The *Social Contract* places sovereignty, undivided in the General Will.
When that Will speaks, the Government is suspended.
The people can make new arrangements as they wish.
They are never trapped by the past. The General Will is
not ultimately sovereign, or sovereign once upon a time,
or partly sovereign, or potentially sovereign—it is always, inalienably so. There may be problems about Rousseau's meaning, but there is none at all concerning his
meaning for the social order of eighteenth-century Europe. The whole glittering complex founded on inequality is condemned, totally condemned.

It is true that the people, to produce the General Will,
have to rise above themselves in a supreme effort of
moral regeneration, and that the machinery to ensure
this, more especially the Civil Religion, has the totalitarian bias that has caused so much controversy. Most of us,
liberal democrats with a realistic knowledge of political
theory and administrative techniques, would be prepared
to defend the position with 'in the nature of the case'
arguments—conceding that force is ultimately necessary
to maintain civilization. But for his part, Rousseau rejects the paraphernalia of *raison d'état* which we assume
is compatible with free government. Helvétius described
how starving men on a becalmed ship might properly
draw lots and resort to cannibalism: 'everything becomes
legitimate, even virtuous, for *le salut public*.' In the
margin Rousseau wrote, '*Le salut public* is nothing if
every individual is not enjoying security.'[51] One man
might perish for the safety of a people: only, says Rousseau, if a virtuous patriot willingly offers himself—the
argument is not allowed to governments.[52]

So the writer of the *Social Contract* himself is not a
totalitarian, though his book advocates totalitarian ma-

---

[51] Derathé, op. cit., p. 357.
[52] Ibid., pp. 357–8.

chinery. My suggestion is that we stop trying to explain away one or both of these facts, or to harmonize them, and that we simply assume that Rousseau himself had no illusions. He knew the *Social Contract* had its sinister side: he was telling us that this must be so. The city of the *Contract* is not *his* Utopia. It may be ours, if we strive to obtain it. The book was written for us, not for Rousseau, who had chosen to be the man according to nature. 'I was never really suited to civil society,' he wrote at the end of his life, 'with all its burdens, obligations and duties . . . My independent nature made me always incapable of the submissions necessary to whoever wishes to live among men.'[53]

We are accustomed to assuming that constitution-makers (Bismarck is a good example) invent systems in which they themselves will be indispensable. Rousseau was different: he devised a constitution with the strict understanding that he himself was excused from participation.[54] He had other dream worlds,[55] which were infinitely more attractive to him than the Spartan zeal of the city of the *Contract*. One was in the past, the primitive Golden Age described in the essay on the origin of language, the pastoral Arcadia at the point in history at which men formed groups, but were still not united in a permanent organization for the satisfaction of material needs.[56] Even today, some letters in the *Nouvelle Héloïse*

---

[53] *Les Rêveries du promeneur solitaire*, p. 122 (6e Promenade).

[54] In *Emile*, Rousseau is also proposing a scheme for *our* benefit, one which would not do for him. See M. Raymond's discussion of the question, 'Is Emile destined to become another Jean-Jacques?' in his *J-J. Rousseau: la quête de soi et la rêverie* (1962), p. 83.

[55] J. Shklar makes the point that Fénelon had two contrasting, equally valid alternative Utopias ('Rousseau's two models: Sparta and the Age of Gold,' *Political Science Quarterly*, LXXXI [1966], pp. 25 ff).

[56] 'The golden age is the period of equilibrium between unawareness of self and alienation, between solitude and "civilized society"' (L. Gossman, 'Time and History in Rousseau,' *Studies in Voltaire and the 18th century*, XXX [1964], p. 333). The precise point in the *economic* development of society is established by H. Grange,

suggest, echoes of this primeval happiness remain among simple mountain folk.[57] Or—another dream world—a pedagogue of genius might bring up a boy according to nature, marry him off under careful supervision, and direct him to live a sheltered life, with an occasional foray into the world to perform inescapable civic duties. Or, best of all, a small group of friends might form a happy, isolated community—Jean-Jacques was always haunted by the myth of the desert island.[58] Thus, in the *Nouvelle Héloïse*, Wolmar, Julie, Saint-Preux and Claire lived at Clarens, their souls transparent to one another's understanding, forgiving gaze. Yet, their inventor is aware that these worlds of his splendid imaginings can have no permanence. For the mass of men, the golden age is gone for ever; lost innocence cannot be regained; history is irreversible. Emile cannot hope to reform the social order, and we know that, in the sequel, *Les Solitaires*, Rousseau was going to show how Sophie betrayed him and a corrupt society claimed its victories. And, though innumerable readers and even the author himself, have been mesmerized by the idyll of Clarens, the grim truth is that this 'neo-feudal' paradise is a fraud, a contrivance of psychological and social engineering.[59] Wolmar manipulates the lives of his servants, manipulates Saint-Preux's reform, manipulates Julie's memories of love, manipulates everyone for their own good, until death comes to Julie as a release from her manipulated happiness. She dies, admitting she loves Saint-Preux, and Wolmar admits that she is glad to go. 'Haven't I lived enough for happiness and for virtue,' she asks,

---

'Rousseau et la division du travail,' *Rev. des sciences humaines*, 1957, pp. 143–54.

[57] *Nouvelle Héloïse*, I, xxiii (ed. D. Mornet, 4 vols. 1925, II, pp. 75–88).

[58] M. Eigeldinger, *J-J. Rousseau et la réalité de l'imaginaire* (1962), pp. 150–5.

[59] Phrases of L. Gossman, 'The Worlds of *La Nouvelle Héloïse*,' *Studies on Voltaire and the 18th century*, XII (1966), p. 260.

with shattering irony.[60] Only in God, only in the next world, is there real hope.

If the return to nature is not for the rest of us, if the primitive Arcadia is gone for ever, if Emile's conditioned impulses are in danger from the world, if Clarens is a paradise founded upon fraud—what then of the city of the *Social Contract?* It will abolish great evils, it will bring true equality, it will make every man feel he 'belongs,' it will give us a new kind of liberty, through community with our fellows. But it will cost us dearly. The natural man has a quiet, ineffectual *bonté:* social man must have the hardy, self-sacrificing *vertu*.[61] For himself, Rousseau claimed no more than *bonté*, but he has chosen to abandon society and all its compulsions. We too must make our choice.[62] And clearly, we have made it. We

---

[60] For all this discussion, see Lester G. Crocker's incisive article, 'Julie: on La Nouvelle Duplicité,' *Ann. J-J. Rousseau*, XXXVI (1963–5), pp. 105–52.

[61] This is a reversion to the view of Rousseau as an 'either—or' thinker whose thought is an unity in duality—well expressed by B. Groethuysen (*Jean-Jacques Rousseau*, 1949, p. 136) in the formula, 'an anarchist by nature, a socialist by love.' R. Mauzi (*L'Idée du bonheur dans la littérature et la pensée françaises au 18e siècle*, 1960) has emphasized that Rousseau was the only thinker to see that nature and virtue were not synonymous, and that the citizen differed from the man. The others all 'project into social reveries the great myths of individual happiness' (p. 656).

[62] Indeed, it is inevitable that we live in society; thus, 'un animal stupide et borné' is made into 'un être intelligent et un homme' (*Contrat Social*, I, 8; Vaughan, II, p. 36). By choosing to be the natural man himself, Rousseau is not, of course, making himself into an Hottentot. His concept of *l'homme sauvage* is double. There is the natural man according to the Second Discourse, and l'homme naturel vivant au sein de la société.' He specifically emphasizes the difference. 'Il y a bien de la différence entre l'homme naturel vivant dans l'état de nature et l'homme naturel vivant dans l'état de société. Emile n'est pas un sauvage à reléguer dans les déserts; c'est un sauvage fait pour habiter les villes' (*Emile III*, ed. Richard, pp. 239–40). By self-analysis and self-sacrifice, Rousseau had reconquered the immediacy and sincerity of l'homme sauvage'—he is 'un homme dans toute la vérité de la nature,' he tells us in the *Confessions.* (For all this see the masterly article by R. Derathé,

choose the arts and sciences, society and government. Very well then, we must pay the price. *Bonté* is no longer sufficient—we must have *vertu*. We must accept the austerities of community duty. In choosing civilization, we make true Christianity impossible as our guide: we must accept the social-cement religion of the *Social Contract*. In civil society, we acquire a different kind of freedom and the hard duties that go with it. Like a bishop drawing up a constitution for a colony of atheists, Rousseau, who has chosen another ideal from ours, writes in harsh terms to make us aware of the price we must pay.

This picture of Rousseau, challenging us as he reassures us, rescuing us from our degradation but ironizing still over our complacent insistence on the comforts of civilization, brings the *Social Contract* into line with his other masterpieces in method and inspiration.[63] He said that he could write only in a 'fever,' with 'passion.' His *Nouvelle Héloïse* was the product of a dream within a dream, Sophie d'Houdetot, unattainable but real, appearing in time to give intense poignancy to the burning imaginations which were already pouring out of his

---

'L'Homme selon Rousseau,' *Etudes: Dijon* [1964], pp. 203–17). A rather different interpretation of l'homme naturel vivant au sein de la société, in *Emile* is given by P. D. Jimack ('*Homme* and *Citoyen* in Rousseau's 'Emile', *Romanic Rev.*, LVI [1965], p. 187), but the suggestion is complementary to Derathé's analysis, not contradictory. One might reflect that it is not possible to adopt Rousseau's deceptively simple, but in reality highly sophisticated, stand as a 'natural man living in society,' without a social system of some kind to react against, a social system in any case being essential if reason and conscience are to develop. This helps to explain the inner compulsion driving Rousseau to help the rest of us who live in society, by telling us the revolutionary secret of the General Will and, in the end, by intervening as the Legislator.

[63] Rousseau himself said that he spent more time on his *Institutions politiques* than on his other works, and enjoyed it more (Dreyfus—Brissac, introd. *Contrat Social* [1896], p. 23). Launay points out that the *Social Contract* begins with 'Je' and ends with 'Moi' (L'art de l'écrivain . . .', *Etudes: Dijon* [1964], p. 371).

soul.[64] *Emile* began as a treatise, but its author progressively identified himself with the two main characters —and, as Jimack's work on the manuscripts has shown, only thus did Rousseau come to remorse for the abandonment of his children.[65] Notice too the method which is the vehicle for the inspiration. Rousseau's favourite device for presenting an argument is the 'dialogue'—[66] epistolatory dialogues between his fictional characters, dialogues between himself and imaginary interlocutors, dialogues between contrasting selves within his own personality, dialogues between reason and emotion, heart and mind. In this continual internal dialectic, his own passions, uncertainties and divisions are present everywhere. The *Social Contract* is no exception. Like his other great works it was written with passion, with himself and the contradictory selves within himself as the central point of reference. In the *Confessions*, Rousseau tells us how his imagination loved to work by contraries: to depict spring, he must be in winter, to describe a rustic scene, he must be indoors, 'if I were put in the Bastille, I should paint a picture of liberty.'[67] When he wrote the *Social Contract*, he was not in the Bastille; he was at the freest time of his life, emancipated from ambition, uncondemned by authority, courted by the great yet withdrawn from the world, his intellect not yet obscured by paranoia and suspicion. Free, living near to nature, he depicted the opposite—to be fair, this was not servitude, but a Spartan régime that would end injustice, that elevates, but has its constraints and obligations. It is the life that *we* have chosen but which he himself has rejected.

So Rousseau is in the *Social Contract* as he is in the

---

[64] F. C. Green, op. cit., p. 195.

[65] P. D. Jimack, *La Genèse et la rédaction de l'Emile* (1960), p. 256.

[66] B. Munteano, 'Les Contradictions de *J-J. Rousseau*,' *Commémoration* (1964), pp. 108–11, with comments of Spink and Osmond, p. 112.

[67] *Confessions*, p. 194.

Emile and the *Nouvelle Héloïse*. He is there in his interior duality, in dialogue with himself. His revolutionary hatred of the injustices of society inspires the theme of the General Will. But, haunted and lonely, unwilling and unable to accept the responsibilities and compulsions of his own ideal society, he continually looks at us through the web he is weaving, to remind us that our freedom is not his freedom, our choice is not his choice. Our way may be nobler than his, but it must be more costly. We are warned in the opening sentences: 'Chains' can be made 'legitimate.'[68]

There is hope in the *Social Contract* as Rousseau the revolutionary speaks of the new, egalitarian society of the General Will; but the shadows close in when Jean-Jacques, the lonely, passive, anarchistical dreamer reveals the full implications. No social order can last for ever. Like the Golden Age, like the household of Emile and Sophie, like the transparent mirage of Clarens, the city of the *Contract* will come to its days of disillusionment.[69] To stave off the end and, indeed, to establish the new order in the first place, there must be a moral regeneration, bringing men up from natural *bonté* to self-sacrificing *vertu*. Though Rousseau had transferred Original Sin from man to society, he knew that this dramatic switch was only a sharp, shorthand way of saying that there are evil tendencies in man which even the most rudimentary social relationships evoke.[70] *Amour de soi*

---

[68] *Contrat Social*, I, i. Another good example of the extra turn of the screw is the reference to slavery in Sparta, leading to the sombre generalization: 'Quoi! la liberté ne se maintient qu' à l'appui de la servitude? Peut-être. Les deux excès se touchent. Tout ce qui n'est point dans la nature a ses inconvénients, et la société civile plus que tout le reste.' (*Contrat Social*, III, 15; Vaughan, II, p. 97).
[69] Bertrand de Jouvenel describes the *Social Contract* as 'a clinical analysis of political deterioration' ('Rousseau the Pessimistic Evolutionist,' *Yale French Studies*, XXVII [1961–2], p. 85).
[70] A. O. Lovejoy, 'The Supposed Primitivism of Rousseau's Discourse on Inequality,' *Essays in the History of Ideas* (1948), pp. 27–8. Cf, 'Il y a un principe du mal . . . la source en est dans notre liberté' (Burgelin, op. cit., p. 572). Lester G. Crocker de-

(enlightened self interest)[71] is beginning to change into *amour propre* at the first stirring of human self-consciousness, as soon as man feels a thrill of pride at his superiority to the animals. From the start, we are on the slope towards finding our satisfaction in the submission, or the approval, of others. This is why our minds need psychological conditioning to be fitted to maintain freedom in the world of the General Will.

But how can this process of conditioning begin? The laws will not do it, for as we are told, laws can only be accepted when men are already what the laws seek to make them.[72] The revolutionary Rousseau has held out to us the ideal of the General Will: the lonely Jean-Jacques has revealed its totalitarian implications. Except to men of a regenerated mind, the new world will be a tyranny. The way out, the one hope of salvation, is offered to us by a third personality in Rousseau, one we might call the 'visionary,' the author of the Profession of faith of the Savoyard *vicaire* and of Julie's death scene. The Profession was meant to be an integral part of Emile's education (we now know that P. M. Masson was mistaken in regarding it as a separately contrived essay);[73] the insular Utopia of Clarens is possible only because Julie received the strength to be faithful to Wolmar and her duty by a sort of divine illumination on her marriage day.[74] Surely, in the *Social Contract* there must be some real religion, some authentic divine illumination? Surely, we are not left with nothing better than that contrived, tyrannical Civil Religion? True Christi-

---

tects Rousseau's 'semantic trick' in the description of man as 'naturally good.' What Rousseau should have said is that man is 'naturally evil,' though not 'originally so.' ('The Relation of Rousseau's Second Discourse and the *Contrat Social*,' *Romanic Rev.*, xxi [1960], p. 35).

[71] The translation is suggested by Broome, op. cit., p. 40.

[72] *Contrat Social*, II, 7; Vaughan, II, p. 53.

[73] A. Ravier, *L'Education de l'homme nouveau* (1941), pp. 255, 274.

[74] *La Nouvelle Héloïse*, ed. Mornet, III, pp. 62–8.

anity, Rousseau tells us, is destructive of the State. But what if God intervenes to start the regeneration of the citizens by purely rational means,[75] in the person of self-sacrificing, prophetic leaders?

This is where the Legislator[76] fits in: 'a superior intelligence, beholding all the passions of men but moved by none of them,' 'whose happiness is independent of ours, yet who is willing to concern himself with us,' 'who works in one century and looks forward only to recognition in the next.' Rousseau is too great an artist to be totally identified with any of his creations, but it seems to me that one aspect of his personality is as surely mirrored in the Legislator as others are reflected in the unhappy lover of the *Nouvelle Héloïse* or in the pedagogue of the *Emile*. In the *Social Contract*, we can detect three masks, aspects, personalities of the author. Formally, the writer is a revolutionary, devising a new society based upon the General Will, that instrument of equality, of civic, social liberty. The quintessential Jean-Jacques, the lonely man according to nature, has tamed his burning revolutionary fervour into practical political proposals for our benefit, though he cannot resist the mordant aside, the final over-emphatic turn of the screw of his argument, which reminds us of the austerities that we who have chosen the social life must face. But he does want to help us and, pessimistic about our human condition, he is willing to accept the grievous burden of the Legislator,

---

[75] That the God-given means should be 'rational' is important (R. Derathé, *Le Rationalisme de J-J. Rousseau*, 1948).
[76] Burgelin emphasizes the religious background of the concept (op. cit., pp. 561–2). P. Polin, 'La Fonction du Législateur chez Rousseau,' *Commémoration* (1964), would deny this. If the Legislator is simply the principle of reason, or something of the kind, L. Gossman's logical objections to the concept apply ('Rousseau's Idealism,' *Romanic Rev.*, LII [1961], pp. 174–7). Notice that the Legislator must be chosen from outside the community (B. Gagnebin, 'Le rôle du Législateur dans les conceptions politiques de Rousseau,' *Etudes: Dijon* [1964], p. 279).

lonely still, unsocial as ever, the Christ-like figure,[77] God's agent of regeneration.

In this triple rôle, the quintessential Jean-Jacques, the sensitive inner personality, is continually sacrificed. Rousseau, the inventor of the General Will, is haunted by his own inability to take part in the life of fellowship which he is organizing for us, but at least he can still remain consciously aloof in the world of his own private choice, which has its compensations. As the Legislator, however, he must commit himself, acknowledging that the disadvantages of the civil state can be overcome, that our world, in the last resort, will be superior to his, and that, in the end, he must remain lonely solely because of his own inadequacies. The Legislator is brought to the aid of the theorist of the General Will only by stripping the last remnants of pride, the last savour of contented singularity, the last pathetic claim to be happy in autarchy, from the lonely man according to nature. Is it fanciful to see in this process something of the working of the pattern of the *ménage à trois* which, for deep psychological reasons,[78] bedevilled Rousseau's emotional existence? He accepted sharing Mme de Warens with others, he played the hopeless lover to Sophie d'Houdetot while encouraging her to remain faithful to Saint-Lambert; the *gouverneur* brings up Emile, only to give him to Sophie; Saint-Preux loses Julie to Wolmar, yet must live with them and from them relearn how to live. In every case, Rousseau himself (or the figure with which he is principally identified) has to be the lonely one of the three, whose sacrifice and self-torturing make the amity of the triangle possible. I am not sure how far the parallel ought to be taken, but at least, I would think that the working of the process of sacrificial self-repression can be detected in the *Social Contract*, as in the life of its author, as in the *Emile* and in the *Nouvelle Héloïse*. Sometimes,

---

[77] For Rousseau's subconscious self-identification with Christ, P. M. Masson, *La Religion de Rousseau*, II, pp. 246–51.
[78] Grimsley, op. cit., esp. p. 129.

as is inevitable, the machinery of self-abnegation breaks down—he pleads passionately with Sophie d'Houdetot, just as Saint-Preux cannot conceal his desperate longing to win Julie back again. So too, in the *Social Contract*, the lonely Jean-Jacques forgets his sacrificial role, in the bitterness of the realization that he himself can never find the fulfilment and unification of the personality which he is designing for us—his sense of deprivation erupting in the notorious 'totalitarian' passages.

Yet it is in the *Social Contract* and through the process of self-humiliation that Rousseau finally breaks through the infinite webs of loneliness, fine as gossamer yet resilient as steel, that he weaves around himself. When the Legislator appears, it is as if Wolmar takes over the direction of Clarens—and of Julie. Just as Wolmar helps Julie (and others) to make the sacrifices upon which a Utopia is built, so the Legislator shows us the road of civic duty, the hard road of the General Will. Wolmar is a strange figure from a distant land, mysterious and lonely, an embodiment of reason.[79] He is a benevolent void, into which a real personality could one day be fitted. In the *Social Contract*, the empty shell of the Wolmar figure is filled; Rousseau himself, purged of desire and purified by suffering, at last achieves fulfilment. He is Saint-Preux *and* Wolmar now. He remains alone, the natural man who has abandoned society; but he has found a rôle to serve society, in which he could never find a home. As the natural man, he could not help reminding us of the totalitarian implications of the sort of life we have chosen under his guidance as a revolutionary; but as the Legislator, he himself will begin the regeneration which will enable us to transcend necessity, and be as free as we were before, truly free, in the service of our fellows.

In an internal dialectic of three personalities, the tragic, lonely central personality continually sacrificed to

---

[79] R. Mauzi, 'Le Problème religieux dans *La Nouvelle Héloïse*,' *Commémoration* (1964), pp. 161 ff.

the outgoing generosity of the other two, Rousseau wrote the *Social Contract*. In his nightcap and dressing gown, amid his pots and frying pan and broken china, with the agony in his reins, relinquishing the brilliant prizes of civilization which we cling to, he pours out his soul, to promote a revolution for a just social order, to convert us to the unselfishness which alone can make liberty compatible with equality, unmoved by our passions, dead to our happiness, working in one century and looking forward to recognition in a future, distant age.

"CE QUI NE SIGNIFIE AUTRE CHOSE
SINON QU'ON LE FORCERA D'ÊTRE LIBRE"

JOHN PLAMENATZ

These words have shocked and puzzled many readers of
the *Social Contract*. May I begin by saying that, though
they have often puzzled, they have never shocked me.
My purpose in commenting on them is certainly not to
defend Rousseau against critics who say of him that he
is a traitor to liberty, putting forward an account of it
which allows of its suppression in its own name. This has
always seemed to me an odd charge to bring against a
man who insists that there cannot be true liberty unless
all citizens are members of the assembly which makes
the laws, and unless each of them comes to his own opinions, *n'opine que d'après lui*. For, clearly, he cannot come
to them unless he is free to express them and to vote in
accordance with them. If we look carefully at the conditions which Rousseau says must be satisfied if the assembly is to be the bearer of the general will, we see
that the citizen has all the guarantees he can reasonably
expect. Rousseau tells us that the citizen who is not excluded from the sovereign assembly, nor exposed inside
it to pressures and intrigues which make his opinions and
his votes count for nothing, is bound to obey the laws
made by the assembly. Whatever the defects of this doctrine, it is not dangerous to liberty. And nothing that
Rousseau says about the general will detracts anything
from it. To say that whoever is constrained to obey the
law is forced to be free may be perverse, but it does not
contradict what Rousseau says about the right of all citizens to take part in the making of the laws.

Perverse or not, this phrase about being "forced to be

Reprinted, by permission of the author and publishers, from *Annales de Philosophie Politique*, Vol. 5, Paris, 1965.

free" is certainly obscure. How are we to interpret it? If we take it literally, it is impossible to make sense of it; but it may be that, if we do not insist on so taking it, we can find in it a clue to certain connections between law, duty and freedom, which Rousseau, if he was not the first to notice them, interpreted in new ways. It may be that Rousseau, when he speaks of freedom, has something important to say which is not to be found in Hobbes, Locke or Montesquieu, in the French Encyclopaedists or the Benthamites.

It has been claimed for Rousseau that he offers us a new idea of freedom. I would prefer to say that he offers us new ideas about freedom. I doubt whether we can find in his writings a definition of freedom which is both new and acceptable, but I believe that we can find in them new ideas about the social and psychological conditions of freedom.

I

On the face of it, the words, *on le forcera d'être libre*, are self-contradictory. As Rousseau himself admits, *il y a bien de la différence entre exécuter ce qu'on a promis, à cause qu'on l'a promis, et le vouloir encore*.[1] A man's having promised to do something in the past and so put himself under an obligation to do it does not ensure that he actually wishes to do it when the time comes to keep his promise. This is the common sense view of the matter, and, as we have seen, it is also Rousseau's. When, therefore, we find him saying that a man constrained to do what he has undertaken is being forced to be free, we must not conclude that he is abandoning a common opinion which he ordinarily shares; we must conclude rather that he is trying to say something more, something not included in that opinion but (so he believes) compatible with it.

---

[1] *Du Contrat social*, first draft, Bk. II, chap. II. VAUGHAN, *Political Writings of Rousseau*, vol. I, p. 480.

Rousseau is here resorting deliberately to paradox. Who resorts to paradox in this way is ordinarily not concerned to deny the received opinion which his paradox appears to challenge. His purpose is to jolt the reader or listener into recognizing something which he might otherwise overlook. Of course, there may be nothing there which has been overlooked; the maker of the paradox may be mistaken. He may be talking nonsense, but we do not prove that he is doing so by the simple expedient of appealing to the received opinion which his paradox seems to contradict.

I have suggested that we can find in Rousseau, not so much a new conception of freedom, as new ideas about the social and psychological conditions of freedom. These ideas are as much about the conditions of our conceiving of freedom and aspiring to it as of our achieving it. And they are not clearly put. As Rousseau himself tells us in his *Confessions*, he had great difficulty in putting his thoughts into words. Quite often, he thought he had succeeded when he had not; he was the dupe of his own eloquence. Yet today there are few who would impugn his originality, who would endorse Mme de Staël's judgement on him: *il n'a rien découvert, il a tout enflammé.* We are the more aware of his originality the better we understand society and its influence on our minds; and we are aware, also, of how much he helps us to interpret the metaphors which men have long used to express their deepest feelings about themselves, about morality and law, about the communities they belong to. And this is what might be expected, since men acquire the capacity to express these feelings in words long before they are able to explain them or to discover their social and psychological origins. No doubt, Rousseau's explanations are confused and inadequate. Original minds often only half possess the ideas on whose account posterity honours them.

In Europe ever since Greek times—and elsewhere perhaps even earlier—men have spoken of "slavery to the passions" and of freedom as a form of self-discipline.

They have also spoken of freedom as if it involved obedience to a higher law, a law of God or nature. The idea that freedom is obedience to a higher law, an obedience impeded by the passions, has long been familiar to the sophisticated and is not even specifically European. It appears as soon as morality ceases to be purely a matter of conforming to custom, as soon as custom is subjected to criticism, as soon as man becomes a moralist and not just a moral being; it appears with Socrates and the Buddha. And for those who do not aspire to systematic philosophy, it is implicit in the words of St. Paul to the Romans: *For the good which I would I do not; but the evil which I would not, that I do.* But Socrates and the Buddha, the Stoics and the theologians, do not speak, as Rousseau does, of a general will. What is the significance of his speaking in this way?

Rousseau did not reject the old conception of a higher law discoverable by reason, though he sometimes—as in the *Discourse on Inequality*—came close to doubting that there is one.[2] He was not as bold, lucid and consistent as, say, Hume was, in his doubts; and he lacked Hume's skill in the making of fine and precise distinctions. There is little sign in his writings that he ever saw clearly— whether to reject or accept them—the implications of the doctrine that there are *moral truths*. And so we often find him, in what was still (in spite of Hume) the fashion among philosophers in his day, speaking as if "moral truths" were statements about the world in the same sense as scientific laws are so. Indeed, he sometimes speaks even of the general will as if it were a kind of knowledge rather than of will. He does so, for example, in the first draft of *Du Contrat social*, when he says:

En effet, que la volonté générale soit dans chaque individu un acte pur de l'entendement qui raisonne dans le silence des passions sur ce que l'homme peut

---
[2] Vaughan, *op. cit.*, I, p. 137.

exiger de son semblable et sur ce que son semblable est en droit d'exiger de lui, nul n'en disconviendra.[3]

Yet he feels the need, even when he speaks of this *acte pur de l'entendement qui raisonne,* to call it *a will.* And in the *Discourse on Inequality,* in the passage to which I have just alluded as the one in which Rousseau expresses his doubts about the traditional account of a law of nature, he offers this explanation of how men have come to believe that there is such a law:

> On commence par rechercher les règles dont, pour l'utilité commune, il serait à propos que les hommes convinssent entre eux; et puis on donne le nom de loi naturelle à la collection de ces règles, sans autre preuve que le bien qu'on trouve qui résulterait de leur pratique universelle.[4]

Rousseau is here doing more than just deny that natural man could know the law of nature of which the philosophers speak; he is actually suggesting that there is no such law to be known—at least not in the sense understood by the philosophers. Nowhere else does he come as close to Hume's belief that fundamental moral rules are neither self-evident *truths* nor are logically implied by a true description of human nature and the human situation, but are solutions to practical problems. Since men's needs, capacities and situations are in some respects the same everywhere, there are problems common to all mankind, and therefore also common solutions. To arrive at these solutions men must, of course, use their reason; they must take stock of themselves and their situations, they must describe, predict and infer; they must make many judgements of which it can be asked whether they are true. But the rules which embody these solutions, taken barely as rules, though they are accepted only by creatures who describe, predict and infer, and though

---

[3] VAUGHAN, I, p. 452.
[4] VAUGHAN, I, p. 137.

whoever urges their acceptance must appeal to judgements, descriptive, predictive and inferential, are not themselves descriptions, predictions or inferences. They are neither true nor false but well or ill suited to the ends they serve; though the judgement that they are the one or the other may be true or false.

Rousseau only once came close to this belief, and even then did not understand its implications as Hume did. But it is important to notice that someone who accepted Hume's reasons for rejecting the traditional concept of a law of nature could also accept, in large part, Rousseau's account of freedom and the general will. For in that account there are important truths neglected both by Hume and by his contemporaries who clung to what he rejected. And to show what these truths are, there is no need whatever to resort to the metaphysics of the German Idealists.

II

Rousseau speaks of at least three kinds of liberty: *natural*, *civil*, and *moral*. By *natural liberty* he means merely men's not being dependent on one another. This kind of liberty can exist where rules, and therefore also rights and obligations, are unknown. It is the only liberty which men can have in the state of nature as Rousseau imagines it, for in that state man is not yet a moral being; he has no conception of rules, rights or obligations. *Civil liberty* exists only where there are rules; it is the right to do what the rules do not forbid. Rousseau, by calling it *civil* liberty, implies that the rules are laws; that they are rules enforced or applied within a community by persons recognized as having authority to do so. But, clearly, it is possible to conceive of rules not so enforced or applied, as (for example) in the state of nature as Locke described it. Rousseau, because he imagines the state of nature as an unsocial state and is not much concerned—except in the *Discourse on Inequality*—with communities which are without organized government, does not ordinarily trouble to distinguish social rules which are not laws (because they are not enforced by a recognized public authority) from laws in the proper sense of the word. But this distinction is not important when we are considering his ideas of freedom. In all communities, whether or not they are States, important rules are supported by sanctions; that is to say, whoever breaks such a rule risks being treated in ways which ordinarily discourage such breaches. *Civil liberty*, as Rousseau understands it, is at bottom the right to do what socially important rules do not forbid.

Moral liberty is defined as *l'obéissance à la loi qu'on s'est prescrite.*[5] Though it, too, can exist only where there are rules, it is not the same as *civil liberty*. Rousseau, having warned us that *il faut bien distinguer la liberté naturelle . . . de la liberté civile, qui est limitée par la volonté générale*, goes on to say: *on pourrait ajouter à l'acquis de l'état civil la liberté morale, qui seule rend l'homme maître de lui.*[6] Civil liberty is merely the right (or, in some contexts, the ability) to do what the laws, the rules imposed by the community on its members, do not forbid, whereas moral liberty is obedience to self-imposed rules. Of course, it is part of Rousseau's creed that the rules imposed by the community on its members are also, when certain conditions hold, imposed by each member on himself. Nevertheless, there are here distinguished two sorts of liberty: of which the first is a right or an ability which individuals enjoy in a community, and the second is a relation of the individual to himself.

Evidently, it is moral liberty that Rousseau has in mind when he utters his notorious paradox about a man's being forced to be free. But before going on to consider this moral liberty, let us look closer for a moment at natural liberty or, as Rousseau also calls it, *indépendance*. Natural man, though there are sometimes obstacles in his way, has needs that are modest and easily satisfied. He

[5] *Du Contrat social,* I, viii.
[6] *Ibid.,* I, viii.

is independent because, except on rare occasions and
almost by accident, he is not compelled to do what others
want him to do. Ordinarily, he satisfies his needs without
their assistance, as they satisfy theirs without his. He
comes as near as man ever can come to being in the situation in which (*il*) *ne veut que ce qu'il peut, et fait ce
qu'il lui plaît.*[7] This is the situation in which he must be
if he is to be free. In the state of nature, he is in it without
contriving that he should be, without knowing that he is.
This is the situation which must be reproduced in the
very different conditions of social life, if man, as a social
(and therefore also a moral) being is to be free when he
can no longer satisfy his needs without the assistance of
others.

Man in the state of nature does not conceive of freedom although he is free. And he is not a "slave" to his
passions. Not because he has no passions, but because
he is not yet a moral being, and is therefore without the
needs and aspirations with which the passions interfere.
Indeed, though he is not without passions, he does not
yet have the passions which "enslave" man; for these
passions spring from vanity, and "natural man" is not
vain. Thus, to be a slave of the passions, it is not enough
that a man should have passions and be ungoverned by
reason—or, in other words, should be without self-
discipline. The brutes are not slaves to their passions;
and men are not so either until they have acquired needs
and aspirations of which they alone are capable. They
acquire them in society as they become rational and
moral beings. It is such beings alone who can aspire to
freedom or be "slaves of the passions". It is precisely
because man is a moral being (and he becomes one in
society) that he feels the need to be on guard against
himself, to master himself.

When we, who are not in the state of nature, imagine
the situation of the man who is, we see that he has no
master. But he does not see it; he has no idea of mastery,

---

[7] *Emile*, ed. Classiques Garnier, p. 69.

either of one man over another or of a man over himself.
Only man in society, man subject to a social discipline,
can conceive of either mastery or freedom. But he, precisely because he is a social being, has acquired needs
which bind him to society; and therefore, if he is to find
freedom in society, must find it under discipline, under
law.

III

*L'homme vraiment libre ne veut que ce qu'il peut, et
fait ce qu'il lui plaît.* This sentence comes, not from Rousseau's description of natural man, but from *Émile*. And
the next two sentences read: *Voilà ma maxime fonda-
mentale. Il ne s'agit que de l'appliquer à l'enfrance, et
toutes les règles de l'éducation vont en découler.*[8] But
Émile's tutor is preparing his pupil to be a free man in
society.

Essentially, the problem for Émile's tutor is the same
as that of which the social contract is a solution. Émile
is to be a good neighbour, a good citizen, and also free;
just as the social contract is to create an association in
which *chacun, s'unissant à tous, n'obéisse pourtant qu'à
lui-même, et reste aussi libre qu'auparavant.*[9]

To be truly free, man must want only what he can get.
He must not have insatiable appetites nor incompatible
desires. His needs must not be greater than his ability
to satisfy them. But Rousseau does not take over unchanged this old doctrine of the Stoics. The insatiable
and incompatible desires are, he thinks, acquired in society; they spring above all from the passion, unknown to
"natural man", to be preferred to others. And this passion
is "unnatural", not only in the sense that savage and isolated man is without it, but in the much more important
sense that it prevents man achieving happiness after he
has become a social and rational being consciously as-

---

[8] *Emile*, p. 69.
[9] *Du Contrat social*, I, iv.

piring to happiness. Rousseau puts his mind to a problem which the Stoics ignored: What is the social and political order in which men do not acquire the needs and passions which prevent their being happy?

What is the order which would do for all what Émile's tutor does for his pupil; which would quicken their faculties without producing in them needs beyond their power to satisfy?

Rousseau quite often speaks of Émile—and also of man in general—as if he could be free only if he depended upon nobody else. For example, he says: *Le seul qui fait sa volonté est celui qui n'a pas besoin, pour la faire, de mettre les bras d'un autre au bout des siens.*[10] And elsewhere he says: *Quiconque dépend d'autrui, et n'a pas ses ressources en lui-même, ne saurait être libre.*[11] But these are not statements to be taken literally; for, as Rousseau himself reminds us again and again, every man formed by society has needs which cannot be satisfied without the help of others. In every society everyone *met les bras des autres au bout des siens.*

Only in the state of nature are men independent; in society they can aspire to no more than a mutual dependence. They cannot help but have needs which move them to make demands on one another. But if the demands are willingly met, then no man feels that he is required to give more than he is allowed to ask, that he is at a disadvantage.

Thus we have here two social conditions of freedom: that society should not produce in its members needs which they cannot satisfy, and that the needs which it does produce should not move them to make demands on one another which they are unwilling to meet. This second condition calls to mind Rousseau's assertion (already quoted) that the general will is *l'entendement qui raisonne. . . sur ce que l'homme peut exiger de son*

---

[10] *Emile,* p. 69.
[11] *Projet de constitution pour la Corse,* Vaughan I, p. 308.

*semblable, et sur ce que son semblable est en droit
d'exiger de lui.*

Rousseau speaks of what a man *can* require of his fellow, and of what his fellow *has the right* to require of
him. But there is no question here of a contrast between
power and *right*. By what a man *can* require is meant
what it is *reasonable* for him to require; and reasonable
has here (as in so many contexts) two meanings. When
we say that a demand is *reasonable* we may mean either
that it is likely to be satisfied or that the maker of it has
the right to make it; or we may mean both the one and
the other, without troubling to distinguish between them.
For a demand which is reasonable in the first sense will
ordinarily be thought reasonable in the second, *if the
maker of it lacks the power to compel compliance.*
Where one man has another in his power, it may be *reasonable* for him to demand of his victim what it would
be *unreasonable* of his victim to demand of him. And
his victim may admit that it is so; that the stronger should
profit from his strength. But then he will admit it only
in the first sense of the word. He will not admit that the
stronger has the right to make demands on him. The
demands which a man makes on others arise out of his
needs, while his willingness to meet their demands depends on their willingness to meet his. This is ordinarily
so except where the strong take it upon themselves to
provide for and to protect the weak, as parents do their
children. Thus, where grown men have need of one another and none is in another's power, there is a rule
which they all accept because it is clearly in the interest
of them all: *that none shall require of the others what
he is not willing to concede to them.*

This rule, if you like, is the maxim familiar to all peoples: *Do as you would be done by.* But it is a variation
which serves to throw light on what Rousseau calls the
general will. It is of the essence of that will that those
who share in it recognize one another as equals. And of
the right of equality Rousseau says that it derives *de la
préférence que chacun se donne et par conséquent de*

la nature de l'homme.[12] Because every man prefers himself to others and yet cannot do without them, no man will freely concede to another more than the other concedes to him. To be recognized as an equal is the most that one man can expect of another who is not weaker than he is.

But, as Rousseau knew, in all societies there is a tendency for power and wealth to be unequally distributed. *C'est précisément parce que la force des choses tend toujours à détruire l'égalité, que la force de la législation doit toujours tendre à la maintenir.*[13] And where inequalities arise, there arise prejudices, passions, and eventually even laws, which serve to perpetuate them. These are the prejudices and passions that generate the insatiable and incompatible desires which make men unhappy.

Thus man formed by society, who reasons and is a moraliser, is *equalitarian*: he prefers himself to others and yet is dependent on them, and it is therefore his interest to be recognized by them as an equal. No doubt, when he is more powerful or wealthier than another man, he may treat him as an inferior; but he is not more powerful or wealthier than all other men. No matter how strong or rich he is, it is often his interest to invoke the principle of equality, and the weaker and poorer he is, the more it is his interest.

Man in society is also inclined to liberty. He seeks to do much more than appease his appetites when they are upon him; he seeks a manner of life which will satisfy him, and resents whatever prevents his finding it. Since he has preferences and principles and is provident and self-critical, he cannot get what will satisfy him if he lacks self-discipline. And just as he can act against the principle of equality though it is his interest to assert it, so his passions stand in the way of self-discipline and of his getting what will satisfy him.

---

[12] *Du Contrat social*, II, IV.
[13] *Ibid.*, II, XI.

IV

How can men who depend on one another, whose needs impel them to make demands on one another, be free? They can be so only if they do willingly what is demanded of them, if their obligations are what they want them to be. But their obligations are determined by the rules which society imposes on its members, by the laws.

In two places, in almost identical terms, Rousseau asks: *Par quel art inconcevable a-t-on pu trouver le moyen d'assujettir les hommes pour les rendre libres? . . . Comment se peut-il faire qu'ils obéissent et que personne ne commande?* And he answers: *Ces prodiges sont l'ouvrage de la loi.*[14]

A man can be free in obeying the law only if the law expresses his will. But it must express more than his will, or he alone will be free. It must express the will of all who belong to his community, to the circle of mutual dependence which includes him. They must all take part in making the law.

But a man may not now want to do what he freely undertook to do in the past, or he may vote against a proposal which becomes law. Rousseau asks: *Comment les opposants sont-ils libres et soumis à des lois auxquelles ils n'ont pas consenti?* And he answers: *Je réponds que la question est mal posée. Le citoyen consent à toutes les lois, même à celles qu'on passe malgré lui, et même à celles qui le punissent quand il ose en violer quelqu'une. La volonté constante de tous les membres de l'État est la volonté générale: c'est par elle qu'ils sont citoyens et libres.*[15]

Part of what Rousseau is saying here is simple enough: whoever takes part, freely and on the same terms as

---

[14] *De l'Economie politique*, Vaughan, I, p. 245. See also First draft of *Du Contrat social*, Vaughan, I, p. 475.
[15] *Du Contrat social*, IV, II.

others, in deliberations which lead to a decision binds himself to accept the decision, even though he votes against it. But what more does he say than this? Especially when he speaks of *the constant will* of the members of the state? Why should a law which I now want to break, even though I voted for it in the past, be called my *constant will*?

Rousseau does not give a direct answer to this question, but there is one implicit in his idea of the general will. Even the law-breaker can be said to respect the law, if he wants what is not to be had without breaking a law and yet also wants the laws to be observed. He may want to be law-abiding, though he also wants what he cannot have unless he breaks the law. But his attitude to these two desires is different. If he keeps the law and foregoes what involves breaking it, he may feel regret; but if he breaks the law, he feels ashamed or tries to persuade himself that he has not broken it or that, for some reason or other, his action is excusable. He either condemns his action or seeks to escape his own judgement upon himself. But this, of course, is true only to the extent that he thinks it his duty to keep the law.

More perhaps than any writer before him, Rousseau draws our attention to something peculiar to the sense of duty: we feel both thwarted and liberated by it. Who has a sense of duty does not submit to the will of another (even of God) but feels bound by a rule even though there is no one to compel him to keep it. He also wants the rule kept by everyone in all cases to which it applies.

Hobbes and Hume (and others too) have argued that men come to adopt rules which experience teaches them it is to their advantage to adopt. This argument is also to be found in the writings of Rousseau. But he adds something more. He agrees that men would not submit to rules unless they had appetites and passions needing to be controlled for their better satisfaction, but insists that they feel about the rules as they do not feel about the appetites and passions. That is why, though men speak of the rules as *restraining* them, they speak of the appetites as *enslaving* them. As creatures of appetite they feel thwarted by the rules, but as moral beings they wish to keep them. Though their appetites are often stronger than their desire to keep the rules, they wish it were not so. They wish they were law-abiding even when in fact they are not. This is what Rousseau calls their *constant will*. But it is strong in them only when they feel that the law is not the will of others imposed upon them.

In *Du Contrat social* Rousseau describes what he takes to be the social and political conditions most likely to make men feel this way about the laws they are required to obey. And he gives us to understand that these same conditions, which ensure that the laws are what those who have to obey them want them to be, are unfavourable to the passions which cause men to break the law. In the society of equals, the dangerous passions born of vanity are at their weakest, and man outside the state of nature is as close as he can be to the condition where he wants only what is within his reach, and does what he pleases (*ne veut que ce qu'il peut, et fait ce qu'il lui plaît*). He is not subject to the will of any of his fellows but to a law which expresses his will as much as theirs; and he is also self-sufficient, in the sense that to get what he wants he depends, not on their favours, but on laws which they all desire should be obeyed.

Even if we accept all this, we still cannot take Rousseau literally when he says that a man constrained to obey the law is forced to be free. But we can perhaps agree that Rousseau explains to us, as no one before him, how it is that men can find in the discipline, imposed by what they feel to be a just society, a moral support, a force which helps them and saves them from themselves.

ROUSSEAU'S IMAGES OF AUTHORITY

JUDITH N. SHKLAR

By nature men are free, but left to their own devices
they will inevitably enslave each other. Of all the "bi-
polarities" in the thought of Jean-Jacques Rousseau none
is more striking than this tension between natural freedom and the spontaneous march to inequality and oppression in which all men participate.[1] None aroused
more conflicting reactions in his own mind. If men are
the sole authors of their ills, and not the mere victims of
some external force, be it original sin, a malevolent nature or a hostile environment, then there is always hope
for self-improvement.[2] On the other hand, if men were
alone responsible for inventing and maintaining their
own social misery, they could scarcely be expected to
overcome conditions they had themselves chosen to
create. One could hardly hope that those who had devised and imposed their own chains, would either wish,
or know how to liberate themselves. If there was no need
for cosmic fatalism, there was every reason to despair
of mankind's own social powers. And indeed it was perfectly clear to Rousseau that every man left free to follow his own inclinations and every society allowed to
pursue its inherent tendencies would repeat all the familiar errors of the past. It was this conflict between possibility and probability that inspired all of Rousseau's
works. All of them are attempts to show some way out of
the horrors of history. And if all are marked by a deep
note of hopelessness, each one is also an act of rebellion
against the weight of the actual. The suggestions, the

Reprinted, by permission of the author and publishers, from *The
American Political Science Review*, Vol. LVIII, 1964.
[1] I owe the felicitous term, bipolarity, to Jean Wahl's remarkable
article, "La Bipolarité de Rousseau," *Annales Jean-Jacques Rousseau*, Vol. 33 (1953–1955), pp. 49–55.
[2] "Lettre à Voltaire," 18 aout, 1756, *Correspondance Générale de
Jean-Jacques Rousseau* (ed. Théophile Dufour, Paris, 1924–1932),
II, 303–324. (Hereafter cited as *C. G.*)

paths he traced and held out, were numerous and various. Among them the hope of salvation through the personal authority of great men was one of the most important. In almost all his writings, whether philosophical or fictional, some such dominating figure appears. An account of the character and work of these authoritative individuals thus not only illuminates an important, though relatively obscure part of Rousseau's thought, it also reveals much that is morally and psychologically most subtle in it.

1. The Need for Authority

That man needs a master is evident once it is fully recognized that the conditions in which men find themselves are entirely the work of their own propensities. These, moreover, are not an incidental part of social life or a superficial affliction. The will to dominate, itself a form of dependency, is present in every human relationship. As soon as men enter into enduring association mutual need, dependence and domination arise and will flourish unless checked by some external agent. The first cry of the infant is a plea for help, the second an effort to tyrannize over his mother.[3] From this first consciousness of dependence spring all subsequent ideas of tyranny and competition. No sooner does a human being identify himself with his own kind than he develops a false self whose *amour propre* finds compensation in inequality and ambition for the loss of independence. This only reinforces the actuality of weakness, though it hides it as each person comes to think of himself only in competitive comparison with others. Feebleness leads us together, but association does not strengthen us. It is only an intricate system of mutual needs which reduces us and estranges us. The more we become enemies of our own kind the more we need them.[4] This being the case,

---

[3] *Émile*, tr. Barbara Foxley (London, 1948), p. 33; "Lettre à Usteri," 13 septembre, 1761, *C. G.*, V, 211–212.
[4] C. E. Vaughan, *The Political Writings of Jean-Jacques Rousseau* (Cambridge, 1915), I, 447 (*Première Version du Contrat Social*). Weakness is indeed the source of all evil, see *ibid.*, I, 167, 203

nothing can be expected from spontaneous self-direction. The interplay between weakness and aggression, the force of *amour propre*, cannot be overcome even by radical social change. In the perfect republic *amour propre* is channeled from personal to public ends. Patriotism reorients vanity, but it does not destroy it.[5] Only the nuclear family might, though it rarely does, provide a closed fellowship free from the taint of *amour propre* and all its expressions. In either case, however, whether *amour propre* is to be organized for collective goals or entirely avoided in the isolated family, a guide and master is needed. Self-regeneration is no longer possible for people obsessed by *amour propre*.[6] Only someone who stands outside the system of prevailing political and personal habits can deliver men from this burden.

The most obvious difficulty would seem to be the impossibility of finding such an external authority. This, however, troubled Rousseau relatively little. He firmly believed in his Plutarchian heroes and such figures as the legislator, Emile's tutor and M. de Wolmar in *La Nouvelle Heloïse* show how well he could imagine men capable of reordering the lives of others. What *did* trouble him was the worth of even the most beneficent and necessary authority. On the one hand he was completely convinced that a liberating form of authority was possible and the only means of helping men out of their present muddle. The good and wise know how to "prevent, cure and palliate" that mass of abuses and ills that overwhelms us.[7] The possibility of "forcing men to be

---

(*Discours sur l'Origine et les Fondements de l'Inégalité Parmi les Hommes.* Hereafter cited as *Inégalité*); *Discours sur Cette Question: Quelle est la Vertu la Plus Nécessaire au Héros, Oeuvres Complètes* (ed. Pléiade, Paris, 1959-. Hereafter cited as *O. C.*), II, 1274.

[5] Vaughan, II, 344–345 (*Projet de Constitution pour la Corse.* Hereafter cited as *Corsica*); *ibid.*, I, 251 (*Économie Politique*). I. Fetscher, *Rousseaus Politische Philosophie* (Neuwied/Rhein, 1960), pp. 62–65, 198–199.

[6] Vaughan, I, 256 (*Économie Politique*).

[7] Vaughan, I, 207. (*Inégalité*. My translation.)

free," through complex psychological devices (though
not through the punitive means implied in the actual
context of that famous phrase) was, for him, a real one.
Yet, on the other hand, Rousseau never forgot that authority meant submission. Even the most self-liquidating
forms of authority involve subordination, and no one
knew more about it and hated it more intensely than
did Rousseau. That is why his discussion of authority,
even the best sort, is often marked by vacillation and
contradiction.[8] To the end, moreover, he doubted
whether authority could, after all, accomplish its true
end. It might cure and palliate, but once men needed a
master, they would never be able to do without one.
Authority may keep them from evil, but it does not fully
liberate. It only perpetuates dependence. For all his belief in the creative powers of great men, Rousseau never
quite overcame his fear of them. Nevertheless these mis-
givings did not outweigh his acute sense of the self-
destructiveness of untutored men. Here, as always, a
negative impulsion, a critical rather than a reforming
zeal, was his ultimate inspiration.

2. Actual Authority

To a degree Rousseau's vacillating attitudes to authority reflect his own emotional conflicts. His correspondence bristles with declarations of personal independence.
"First of all I want my friends to be my friends, and not
my masters."[9] In the end he concluded that his need for
personal liberty was such that he was simply not made
for civil society.[10] "He has ideas of independence," wrote

---

[8] Thus Emile who is educated for freedom is nevertheless reduced
to docility. He does nothing without the consent of his master, and
even as a young adult is submissive and afraid of offending the
latter. *Émile*, pp. 297–299, 387. "Let him have his freedom if you
would make him docile." *Ibid.*, 196.

[9] "Lettre à Mme. d'Épinay," 26 mars, 1757, *C. G.*, III, 44; "Lettre
à Diderot," *ibid.*, 50.

[10] *Les Rêveries du Promeneur Solitaire, O. C.*, I, 1059; *Confessions, ibid.*, Bk. I, p. 38.

the ever-observant Boswell, "that are completely visionary and which are unsuitable for a man in his position."
Boswell did not refer merely to Rousseau's social station
here. "Behold the man he is, and tell me if such a man
does not need a great deal of affection from his fellows—
and consequently if he does not depend on them as we
all depend on one another."[11] That was, of course, the
trouble, and Rousseau knew it only too well.[12] He knew
just as well as Hume did that he was at the mercy of
those he loved, even of his little dog, but he feared and
resented those whom he suspected of exploiting this
softness.[13] Eventually he felt that everyone had conspired
to tyrannize over him.

He was, therefore, torn all his life between an urge
for perfect freedom and a longing for submission and
for a return to childhood under the parental care of a
Mme. de Warens or a Marischal Keith. If patronage was
always rebuffed at first and every offer of a royal pen-
sion produced a crisis, Rousseau also longed for a super-
vising father. As St. Preux, Rousseau's imaginary self-
portrait, had addressed Wolmar, so he later would call
Marischal Keith "mon bienfaiteur et mon père" and speak
of himself as the "fils cadet."[14] Patronage could be en-
dured only if it was transformed into pseudo-paternity.
It was Hume's failure to recognize this that led to their

---

[11] *Boswell on the Grand Tour: Italy, Corsica and France, 1765–
1766*, ed. Frank Brady and F. A. Pottle (New York, 1955), p. 300.
[12] He regarded these as the lasting effects of his childhood experience of authority as exercised by Mademoiselle de Lambercier
who, he felt, had crippled him morally and sexually. *Confessions*,
Bk. I, pp. 15–17; "Je m'affectionnois aux actes de soumission,"
Ébauches des Confessions, O. C., I, 1157.
[13] *E.g., Lettres à Malesherbes, O. C.*, I, 1141; Hume, "Lettre à la
Marquise de Barbantane," 16 février, 1766, *C. G.*, XV, 62–63.
[14] *Confessions*, Bk. I, p. 56, Bk. XII, pp. 596–599; "Lettre à Milord
Maréchal," 8 décembre, 1764, *C. G.*, XII, 122–124; "Lettre à
Mme. la Comtesse de Boufflers," 28 decembre, 1763, *C. G.*, X,
278–280; *Lettres Écrites de la Montagne, Oeuvres Complètes* (Li-
brairie Hachette, Paris, 1905. Hereafter referred to as Hachette),
III, 195.

painful quarrel in England.[15] Thus Rousseau's first response to the approaches of his future patron, M. de Luxembourg, was an outburst of plebeian resentment. "I hate the great, I hate their estate, their hardness, their prejudices, their pettiness and all their vices."[16] This, however, presently changed to "Ah M. le Maréchal, I hated the great before I knew you, and I hate them even more now that you have made me feel so well how easy it would be for them to make themselves adored."[17] He would have wanted to seek him out, Rousseau later wrote to his patron, even if they had been equals. How was he to treat him now, without forgetting himself?[18] For he did not wish to forget the inequality between them, little though it mattered to M. de Luxembourg. Rousseau only wanted to transform grandeur into paternity and to replace class distinctions with emotional subservience. Much as he hated inequality, he did not want equality either, and the positions of superior and inferior were to be maintained.

Deeply rooted as these psychological tendencies were, they were exacerbated by Rousseau's experiences with the powers that be. To be sure, his distaste for impersonal relationships of any kind, and especially for those involving subordination, would have made it difficult for him to accept regular employment of the usual sort. However, Rousseau was also a man of supreme gifts forced to endure every indignity that society could inflict. If in his case apprenticeship, vagrancy and domestic service did not lead to a rejection of all authority, they did fill him with a deep contempt for all the cruel and incompetent masters of this world, in fact, for all actual masters. Being themselves corrupt, they can only maim and hurt those doomed to serving them. Had M. de Montaigue been a decent man, Rousseau, his secre-

---

[15] Ronald Grimsley, *Jean-Jacques Rousseau* (Cardiff, 1961), pp. 200–201.
[16] *Lettres à Malesherbes*, p. 1145. (My translation.)
[17] *Confessions*, Bk. X, p. 527. (My translation.)
[18] "Lettre à M. de Luxembourg," 30 avril, 1759, *C. G.*, IV, 231.

tary, imagined that he might have made a passable career for himself in the diplomatic service.[19] Had M. de la Roque been a kind man, he would have given his valet, Rousseau, the courage to confess a theft, rather than to callously allow an innocent girl to be blamed.[20] The reason why servants cheat and steal is that the masters are usurpers, liars and fools.[21]

It was not difficult for Rousseau to draw the obvious conclusions from these experiences. Actual authority was exercised only to maintain a destructive and false order. "Wherever I look, I see only masters and slaves, not a people and its chief."[22] The result is that no communication and no genuinely binding relationships are possible at all. "Neither master nor slave belongs to a family, but only to a class."[23] His travels up and down the entire social ladder had shown him only too clearly that "the great know only the great and the small only the small."[24] Enforced class isolation means mutual hostility and ir-responsibility—pride and cruelty at the top, servility and dishonesty at the bottom. What is astonishing is that in spite of these experiences and perceptions Rousseau should still have looked for "chiefs" and longed for individuals who possessed qualities that justified submission to their authority. Moreover, to a certain degree he even expected such persons to come from those very upper classes whose vices he had so eloquently exposed. It is not the offended plebeian St. Preux, but his patron Lord Bomston, an English aristocrat of immense wealth and power, who delivers the most scathing of all Rousseau's denunciations of the hereditary nobility and proclaims the cause of equality.[25]

This ambivalence emerges even in Rousseau's view

---

[19] *Confessions*, Bk. VII, p. 327.
[20] *Ibid.*, Bk. II, p. 87.
[21] *La Nouvelle Heloïse*, *O. C.*, II, Part IV, Lettre X. (Hereafter cited as *N. H.*)
[22] Vaughan, II, 31 (*Contrat Social*).
[23] *Émile*, p. 369.
[24] *Ébauches des Confessions*, p. 1150.
[25] *N. H.*, Part I, Lettre LXII.

of royal authority. On the whole he thought it completely
vicious. Even elective kings tend to be tyrants.[26] Nothing amused him more than the Abbé de Saint-Pierre's
belief that reform was in the "true" self-interest of kings.
Far from it, replied Rousseau. Their interest lies precisely in exploiting and oppressing their subjects.[27] Masters never prefer any interest to their own, and some are
positively malevolent.[28] Rousseau was outraged by M.
de Mirabeau's notion of a "legal despotism" as a cure for
all political ills. What a contradiction in terms! There are
only two alternatives, Rousseau replied. One must have
the pure rule of law in which all personal authority is
entirely eliminated, or, if this should be impossible (as
he thought it was), then one should accept the most
perfectly arbitrary, unlimited personal rule. The trouble
with this was that it would bring on rulers like Tiberius
and Nero, who could only inspire despair. However,
there are only two options, democracy, which is for
angels, or the most perfect Hobbism.[29] This stark either/
or is very revealing. It is a genuine conflict between
ideals, not a choice between the possible and the impossible. Neither one of the ideals is likely to be realized,
but both are valid. The actuality of bad kings does not
invalidate the ideal of beneficial personal rule any more
than the actuality of illegality destroys the ideal of the
pure rule of law. Here, as on many other occasions, Rousseau was torn by bipolar ideals—both of which could be
used effectively to criticize actuality.

3. Legislative and Creative Authority

The conflict between the ideals of personal authority
and of impersonal law was resolved in Rousseau's mind

---

[26] Vaughan, II, 447, 461, 464. (*Considérations sur le Gouvernement
de Pologne.* Hereafter cited as *Poland.*)

[27] Vaughan, I, 244 (*Économie Politique*); 389–392 (*Jugement sur
la Polysynodie*), II, 77 (*Contrat Social*).

[28] Vaughan, I, 358 (*Fragments*).

[29] "Lettre à M. de Mirabeau," 26 juillet, 1767, *C. G.*, XVII, 155–
159.

by making law the subordinate one. For ultimately the rule of law also depends upon a single human voice and hand to give it life. Hymns to the rule of law, of course, abound in Rousseau's writings. Only law is compatible with freedom.[30] Only law is a "joug salutaire."[31] Only under law can the dependence of man on man be ended.[32] Only law can subject men without constraining the will. Law liberates.[33] The great problem of politics is to make governments the guardians, rather than the enemies of law.[34] That is only a small sample of a recurrent theme. However, there were qualifications. The first was that law is psychologically ineffective. It can condition only external behavior. Public opinion and mores alone can touch the heart.[35] To be truly effective public authority must penetrate to the very heart.[36] To do this requires more than law, it depends on continuing education.[37] Secondly, laws do not grow spontaneously in society. A great legislator must not only invent them, but create the moral climate that is needed for their acceptance. Lastly, and this is the greatest weakness, law is not self-perpetuating. Like all the works of men, even the best institutions decline under the inevitable impact of moral weakness. And once corruption has set in, there is no stopping it.[38] If Sparta and Rome fell, what can endure?[39] Once the decline is total, then a new creative legislator can arise to restore society. Law ultimately is what personal authority can give society for a while; it

---

[30] Vaughan, II, 37 (*Contrat Social*).

[31] Vaughan, I, 126 (*Inégalité*).

[32] *Émile*, p. 49.

[33] Vaughan, I, 248 (*Économie Politique*).

[34] *Confessions*, Book IX, pp. 404–405; Vaughan, I, 246 (*Économie Politique*).

[35] Vaughan, I, 322 (*Fragments*).

[36] Vaughan, I, 248 (*Économie Politique*).

[37] Vaughan, I, 330–331 (*Fragments*); Vaughan, II, 426–427 (*Poland*).

[38] "Lettre à Vernet," 29 novembre, 1760, *C. G.*, V, 270–272.

[39] Vaughan, II, 88, 91 (*Contrat Social*). "Le Corps politique, aussi bien que le corps de l'homme, commence a mourir dès sa naissance."

does not replace that force, which alone can touch the human heart. That was the way of those ancient political paragons Moses, Lycurgus, Numa and Solon.[40] Of such men, alas, modern history knows nothing.[41]

Perhaps because he had never known a great man, or because historical imagination was not among his strong points, Rousseau was never able to draw a very convincing portrait of the great legislator. It has been suggested that his entire Plutarchian stance was more a way of rejecting contemporary men and institutions, than a genuine effort to present a constructive model that he or anyone else might imitate.[42] That is why his Spartan and Roman heroes are more the sum of all the virtues that modern men so conspicuously lack than living beings, of the past or present.[43] Often the great legislator seems merely a mechanical device invented by Rousseau to answer the question, *"how* can a legitimate state be established, men being what they are?" Of all Rousseau's images of authority this is the least well-drawn and the least convincing figure. How could it be otherwise, since the legislator is a miracle, a superhuman genius, who, though he knows our nature thoroughly, does not share it? His tasks and his powers have nothing in common with the more usual forms of political authority.[44] He neither coerces, nor argues. Everything is done by the force of personality.[45] A magnetic personality transforms lesser men.

---

[40] Vaughan, II, 427–429 (*Poland*); *ibid.*, I, 314–320, 330–332 (*Fragments*).

[41] Vaughan, I, 338 (*Fragments*).

[42] Grimsley, *op. cit.*, pp. 67–68, 70–71, 80; Albert Schinz, *La Pensée de Jean-Jacques Rousseau* (Paris, 1929), pp. 136–157.

[43] Rousseau admitted his lack of genuine interest in history, "La comparaison de ce qui est à ce qui doit être m'a donné l'esprit romanesque et m'a toujours jeté loin de tout ce qui ce fait," "Lettre au Prince de Wurtemberg," 10 novembre, 1763, *C. G.*, X, 217.

[44] Vaughan, I, 477–483 (*Première Version*); *ibid.*, II, 51–54 (*Contrat Social*).

[45] Thus Rousseau was quite ready to leave the political future of Corsica to the "soul and heart" of General Paoli. "Lettre à M. Buttafoco," 26 mai, 1765, *C. G.*, XIII, 334–336.

Force is self-defeating and reason is wasted on a disoriented multitude. Only direct experience and the force of example can touch unregenerate men.[46] It is useless to say, "be good," to them; they must be made so, but how are they to be reconstructed?[47] The great legislator has only one means at his disposal: illusion and stage management. And indeed it is not everyone who can make himself appear an agent of God and speak for Him.[48] The altering of public opinion, the revolution in attitudes that impinges upon behavior can only be done by an example so impressive that it inspires the wish to imitate. To change public opinion, popular judgments of right and wrong, he must also engage in the most detailed stage-setting, as Rousseau showed in his own plan to deglamorize dueling.[49] In all this the guiding hand must remain hidden. To rule over public opinion one must not only be above it, but out of its sight.[50] It is suggestive power that gives people new ambitions, and social instead of private aspirations. That also is why festivals, ceremonies and all other simple and striking ways of structuring the environment to press new feelings upon the populace are so important. All are necessary to protect the public self against the alluring calls of the private self.

Creative legislative authority that "multilates the human constitution" and reduces each person to a particle of a greater whole cannot be effectively exercised at all times. It can only be attempted in the youth of peoples. That is why Brutus and Rienzi failed.[51] For legislation is foresight and prevention. Like Émile's tutor the legislator

---

[46] "Lettre à M. l'Abbé de Raynal," juin, 1753, *C. G.*, II, 49. The multitude, Rousseau wrote, are sheep; they need examples, not arguments.

[47] Vaughan, I, 250–251 (*Économie Politique*), 476 (*Première Version*).

[48] Vaughan, II, 54 (*Contrat Social*).

[49] *Politics and the Arts: Letter to M. d'Alembert on the Theater,* tr. and ed. Allan Bloom (Glencoe, Ill., 1960), pp. 68–74.

[50] *Émile,* p. 159; Vaughan, I, 246–247 (*Économie Politique*).

[51] Vaughan, I, 324 (*Fragments*), 478, 483–484, 489 (*Première Version*); II, 53–54 (*Contrat Social*); *Letter to d'Alembert,* p. 74.

designs laws and institutions to prevent the vices of
civilization from emerging. Corsica was destined to escape the well-known consequences of undirected social
development: it was not to become civilized.[52] Even here
Rousseau feared that there might be no inclination for
eternal simplicity, especially in the absence of a dynamic
legislator.[53] Moreover, prevention was not the only task
of the great legislator. In the *Social Contract* especially,
Rousseau suggested that more than merely preventive
authority was needed. The legislator, built on the model
of Lycurgus, was to reconstruct every member of the
community on the stern Spartan model. However, as in
the case of mere prevention, he seriously doubted
whether this ambitious project could be accomplished.

The conclusion that creative legislative authority
would fail was not fortuitous. It was all but inevitable,
given Rousseau's psychological assumptions. For it is not
merely the fatal attractions of false social values that
threaten the good republic. It is not only civilization that
is bound to creep in. Perpetual denaturalization cannot
be maintained except by perpetual tutorial vigilance.
The difficulties of full socialization were so great because
Rousseau was so deeply aware of the individuality of
each person. Each one of us has a God-given self which
forms the core of our character. This personal self is not
inherently hostile to other selves, nor does it thrive in
permanent solitude.[54] It is indeed only too vulnerable
to social pressures, and in constant danger from that
side. The history of mankind so far has been one of un-
relenting self-deformation, and thus of inner conflict,
insecurity, insincerity and disordered passions. Rousseau,

---

[52] I. Fetscher, "Rousseau's Concept of Freedom," *Nomos*, Vol. 6
(1962), p. 46.

[53] "Je crois que mes idées différent prodigieusement de celles de
votre nation," "Lettre à M. Buttafoco, 24 mars, 1765, *C. G.*, XIII,
150–153.

[54] "Notre plus douce existence est relative et collective et notre
vrai moi n'est pas tout entier en nous," *Rousseau Juge de Jean-
Jacques*, II, *O. C.*, I, 813.

unlike so many of his contemporaries, was not a radical
environmentalist in psychology. The environment can
deform or nurture the self, but it does not make it. Heavy
as their impact is, especially upon children, external
forces cannot create personality. They can only mould
a pre-existing self for better or worse. Education is thus
a matter of either conflict or harmony between the self
and the outer world. Freedom lies precisely in avoiding
injuries to this self. Independence and inner strength
mean the preservation of one's integral character. To
this end one must retain the ability to withdraw into
oneself and to live by oneself even in the midst of society. "Commençons par redevenir nous, par nous con-
centrer en nous, par conserver notre âme."[55] Only then
will we find in ourselves that *moi humain* which is the
essence both of our own selfhood and of our shared humanity.

A cohesive community cannot be built by those who
cherish the *moi humain*. That is why civic education and
the education of the individual have nothing in common.[56] However, having invested the natural self with
such deep roots and recognized its profound value,
Rousseau was in no position to argue that the legislator
could easily supply the citizens with new communal
selves. That is why his task is, in fact, superhuman. He
must destroy nature and then replace it with an artificial
psychological substitute.[57] Unlike later nationalists Rousseau did not believe that the national self had any basis
in nature. On the contrary, its creation does violence to

---

[55] "Lettres Morales," VI, *C. G.,* III, 9.
[56] *Émile,* p. 3; Vaughan, I, 255–257 (*Économie Politique*).
[57] "Celui qui se croit capable de former un peuple doit se sentir en
état de changer, pour ainsi dire, la nature des hommes. Il faut qu'il
transforme chaque individu, qui est par lui-même un tout parfait
et solitaire, en partie d'un plus grand tout, dont cet individu reçoive
en quelque sorte sa vie et son être; qu'il mutile, pour ainsi dire, la
constitution de l'homme." Vaughan, I, 248 (*Économie Politique*),
324 (*Fragments*), 478 (*Première Version*); II, 51–52 (*Contrat
Social*).

all our spontaneous tendencies. National character was, for him, no "soul" at all, and in no sense a free emanation arising from the disparate selves of individuals. It was not even an historical accretion. Moses *created* the Jews. He gave them their distinctive, national identity. Before him there was only an inchoate herd. This was the example the Poles were to follow in *giving* themselves "a national physiognomy."[58] This was just what Peter the Great had failed to do. By merely imitating others he had not been able to devise a collective personality suited to the human material in his hands. Not that he had destroyed the Russian soul; there were no national souls. He was merely an artist who had no talent.[59] Whatever national character a republic is to have, and it must have one, will be an artificial imposition from above.

Since national character and patriotism are no part of our natural selves there can be no easy transition from private to public life. The second, being alien, is always a frail structure. Because the legislator must do more than just integrate existing personalities into a more coherent whole, his work does not endure. Laws and mores cannot withstand the assaults of nature for long. For in the last resort the *moi humain* is indestructible.[60] Republics, even the best, perish. The wonder is that Rousseau could believe that legislators had ever been able to create them. How did they perform this psychological miracle? He never really explained it. One must conclude that the sheer hypnotic power of a great personality can achieve, even if only temporarily, what neither force nor reason can produce. That is certainly what Rousseau believed.

---

[58] Vaughan, I, 355–356 (*Fragments*); II, 319, 428, 432 (*Poland*).
[59] Vaughan, II, 56 (*Contrat Social*). To the Poles he said, "Ils doivent rechercher uniquement ce qui leur est convenable, et non pas ce que d'autres font." *Ibid.*, II, 487.
[60] "C'est donc en vain qu'on prétendroit refondre les divers ésprits sur un modele commun. On peut les contraindre et non les changer." *N. H.*, Part V, Lettre III.

It has occasionally been suggested that Rousseau in providing Corsica and Poland with constitutional plans imagined himself to be a real legislator.[61] In fact, he thought nothing of the sort. In a most revealing passage he explained that he could never fulfill that rôle, precisely because he lacked the necessary personal qualities.[62] He declined, for that very reason, to participate directly in Corsican affairs.[63] No one had a clearer view of the differences between the life of action and the life of observation, and he knew himself to be capable only of the latter. At most he might help to guide some future statesman.[64] At times he claimed that he did not even wish to lead his contemporaries, but only to warn them against false prophets.[65] Not that he was modest. He alone among authors had revealed the nature and history of the human heart.[66] Now, knowing the human heart was certainly one of the main prerequisites of legislative authority, but it was not the only one. Rousseau therefore could dream of being a leader, but he knew that it was a mere fantasy. If he had the ring of Gyges he would certainly use it to make mankind happy. It would lift him above all partiality and weakness, but not even in a dream could it make him into a man of action. His force was bound to remain "negative." He would remain human, the equal, in spite of himself, of those over whom he should rule.[67] The personality that radiates authority eluded him. It was with St. Preux, not with M. de Wolmar, that Rousseau identified himself.[68]

[61] Jean Starobinski, "La Pensée Politique de Jean-Jacques Rousseau," in Samuel Baud-Bovy *et al.*, *Jean-Jacques Rousseau* (Neuchâtel, 1962), pp. 83, 99.

[62] *Les Rêveries*, VI, 1057–1059.

[63] *Confessions*, Bk. XII, p. 650.

[64] Vaughan, I, 350–351 (*Fragments*).

[65] *Ibid.*, I, 342 (*Fragments*).

[66] *Rousseau Juge de Jean-Jacques*, I, 728.

[67] *Les Rêveries*, VI, 1057–1059.

[68] *Confessions*, Bk. VIII, pp. 355, 438; *Rousseau Juge de Jean-Jacques*, II, 778.

4. Therapeutic Authority

If Rousseau thought himself too human to lead his
fellow men, few other men were fit. In his own lifetime
Rousseau seems to have known only one—Claude Anet,
Mme. de Warens' factotum, and Rousseau's immediate
predecessor as her lover. This, Rousseau noted several
times, was an extraordinary man, the only one of his kind
that he had ever seen. Slow, composed, thoughtful, circumspect and cold, he treated those around him like
children, and so made them happy. He managed to do
what Rousseau could never do: to keep order in Mme.
de Warens' affairs. He did this because she, like Rousseau and everyone else, esteemed and feared him, and
did so because they could not bear his disapproval.
Rousseau knew exactly where Anet's power came from
and why he could never emulate him. It was force of
personality alone. He had neither the *sangfroid* nor the
firmness of Anet. Though he was brighter and better
educated, he lacked that quality that made people in-
stinctively seek Anet's approval.[69]

Claude Anet might well have served as a model for
M. de Wolmar, Rousseau's most perfect portrait of the
man of authority. Wolmar, the elderly husband of the
heroine of the novel, Julie, is everything that St. Preux-
Rousseau, her former lover, is not. Born somewhere in
Eastern Europe, he is rich and a member of the highest
nobility.[70] After an active and adventurous life of travel
and soldiering he settles down in his later years to marriage and to running a model estate, Clarens. We are
told nothing of his appearance in the novel, but in a letter to his illustrator Rousseau insisted that Wolmar's
gaze must be "fin et froid."[71] Along with his vast experi-

---

[69] *Confessions*, Bk. V, pp. 177–178, 201–206, 264–265. That is why
Rousseau resented Anet so deeply: in the *Nouvelle Heloïse* he gave
the worthless valet Claude Anet's name.

[70] *N. H.*, Part III, Lettre XVIII.

[71] "Lettre à M. Coindet," décembre, 1760, *C. G.*, V, 295, and
other notes on the illustrations, *O. C.*, II, 762. The coldness of the

ence among all sorts of men, Wolmar is distinguished by
a total absence of any passion. He needs no one, not
even God. His only active love is for order; his one aversion, to see men suffer. His only interest in life is to read
the hearts of men.[72] That his penetrating eye has supernatural powers of looking into the hearts of others is
frequently noted by all who know him.[73] This talent is
the source of his unfailing judgment.[74] In Wolmar, alone
among men, action and observation are not distinct. He
acts to learn, and observes in order to act.[75] He not only
knows men completely, but he identifies entirely with
his plans for them, with the creation of order. In him
subject and object are one. In this he is indeed like God.
The reason Wolmar does not believe in God is that he
is God to all intents and purposes.[76] Certainly he has
all the attributes that Rousseau ascribed to God, self-
sufficiency, justice, love of order. If he is not God, he
certainly does God's work.[77] Not only does he create

---

true sage was often noted, *e.g., Rousseau Juge de Jean-Jacques,*
II, 861–862.

[72] *N. H.,* Part IV, Lettre XII.

[73] *Ibid.,* Part IV, Lettres XI, XII.

[74] "Au lieu de juger des autres par soi il faudroit peut être juger
de soi par les autres, mais sans s'arreter à l'apparence, il faudroit
pour cela lire dans leur coeur comme on croit lire dans le sien."
Ébauches des Confessions, p. 1158.

"What then is required for the proper study of men? A great
wish to know men, a great impartiality of judgment, a heart sufficiently sensitive to understand every human passion, and calm
enough to be free from passion." *Émile,* p. 206. Just so Wolmar.

[75] *N. H.,* Part V, Lettre XII.

[76] Vaughan, I, 211 (*Inégalité*); Jean Starobinski, *Jean-Jacques
Rousseau: la Transparence et l'Obstacle* (Paris, 1957), pp. 139–
140. It may be that Wolmar and Julie are meant to represent a
perfect whole, as is suggested by J. H. Broome, *Rousseau* (London,
1963), pp. 131, 140. However, it is quite plausible that Julie is
meant to play Christ to Wolmar's God. She is the very spirit of
mercy and charity at Clarens—and at the end there is even a false
impression of resurrection, all pointing to Rousseau's decidedly
moralistic, nonmystical view of the Christian message.

[77] "La véritable Grandeur consiste dans l'exercice des vertus bien-
faisantes, à l'example de celle de Dieu *qui ne se manifeste que par
les biens qu'il repand sur nous." Oraison Funèbre du Duc d'Or-
leans, O. C.,* II, 1277. (My italics.)

peace through justice on his estate, he returns corrupt or ill men to that natural moral condition in which God wants them to remain.[78] Because he *is* his end he has an immediate impact on others, moreover. To know Wolmar is to desire his approbation.[79] In this too he is god-like.

As a soul-surgeon Wolmar's task is to cure the heart-sick St. Preux by making him "himself" again. Above all, St. Preux's self-confidence, and so his freedom, must be restored.[80] St. Preux's sickness, according to Wolmar, is not that he is still in love with Julie de Wolmar, but that he is obsessed by his former love for her as a young girl—a young girl who no longer exists in fact. The hardest slavery, Rousseau noted, is that imposed by a passion from which one would like to deliver oneself, but cannot.[81] In this case the passion is a form of nostalgia. Wolmar's method is therefore to "cover the past with the present," so that St. Preux may recognize Julie as she is now, a wife and mother, and himself as an independent being. St. Preux must be released from his memories.[82]

The burden of the past was, indeed, a constant theme in Rousseau's writings.[83] If imagination leads men astray by giving them insatiable desires for unattainable and

---

[78] "Dieu veut que nous soyons tels qu'il nous à fait," *Lettre à Christophe Beaumont, Archevêque de Paris, Oeuvres Complètes* (Hachette), III, 88–89. God says to man, "Je t'ai fait trop faible pour sortir du gouffre, parce que je t'ai fait assez fort pour n'y pas tomber." *Confessions*, Bk. II, p. 64. In a sense the Wolmars of this world do better than God. They retrieve men from the abyss, rather than leaving them to suffer the consequences of weakness.

[79] As soon as St. Preux has met Wolmar he says, "Je commençait de connoitre alors quel homme j'avois à faire, et je résolus bien de tenir mon coeur en état d'être vu de lui," *N. H.*, Part IV, Lettre VI.

[80] Much as M. Gaime once returned Rousseau's self-confidence to him—*Confessions*, Bk. III, pp. 90–91; *Émile*, pp. 226–227.

[81] *Pensées d'un Ésprit Droit*, LXXI, *O. C.*, II, 1313.

[82] *N. H.*, Part IV, Lettre XIV.

[83] For a discussion linking Rousseau's and Proust's psychology of time, see M. J. Temmer, *Time in Rousseau and Kant* (Geneva, 1958), pp. 22–24; 27–33, 44–49.

harmful objects, memory chains them to the past and fills them with regret. We are thus always either ahead of, or behind ourselves.[84] Happiness and health, however, are to be found only in the ability to live in the present, to take each day as if there were neither yesterday nor tomorrow.[85] Memory makes us reflective. It is crippling, inhibiting and destructive. It prevents us from accepting the present, as we linger in the past.[86] It is not just a pleasant past, moreover, that chains us down. Rousseau was perhaps the first novelist to isolate nostalgia as a distinct psychological malady. That is what makes *La Nouvelle Heloïse* such a modern novel. Everything is seen nostalgically, filtered through regret. And it is the past as such that draws the lovers back. Bad conscience does not trouble them, for they are not regarded as guilty. Neither do they long for a lost happiness: they did not enjoy their love affair. It was, in fact, a time of acute misery and anxiety for both. It is pure nostalgia that obsesses St. Preux. He is the captive of daydreams projected into the past, rather than into the future. And there was nothing Rousseau did not know about the enervating effects of fantasies. If they turn toward the future they make men restless, if they linger on the past they lead to inactivity and inability to take charge of one's own life. That is why St. Preux is so helplessly dependent on other people. His friend, Lord Bomston, treats him like a child for years, until Wolmar gets to work on him. Emile, in contrast, is free and his judgment is sound, because he is a slave to neither routine nor memory.[87]

What is true of individuals is also true of nations. A young people has no memories. Old nations may be reborn only if they suffer experiences so intensely shock-

---

[84] Vaughan, I, 150, 178 (*Inégalité*); *Préface à "Narcisse,"* O. C., II, 970; *Émile*, pp. 44–45, 95, 245; *Les Rêveries*, V, 1046.
[85] *Émile*, pp. 46, 317.
[86] *Pensées*, XLVI, O. C., II, 1309.
[87] *Émile*, p. 124; Vaughan, I, 215–216 (*Inégalité*).

ing that they obliterate their past from memory. That is what happened to Sparta at the time of Lycurgus, to Rome after the Tarquins, and to Holland and Switzerland in the course of their liberation. That, too, was his hope for Poland.[88] To be sure, not all memories are bad; accumulated experience is wisdom in individuals and sound tradition in nations, but in its pathological forms it becomes nostalgia and, collectively, prejudice. Rousseau could on occasion speak of political cures, of destroying prejudices and even of "washing away" the past.[89] In the main, however, he thought old nations incurable. Some individuals, who were not yet totally corrupt, on the other hand, could be liberated: if there was a Wolmar to cure them.

How does Wolmar proceed? He never preaches, never reproaches, never punishes. What he does is to arrange situations which force St. Preux to face reality: first the reality of Mme. de Wolmar as a woman whom he no longer loves, then himself as a man capable of making decisions for himself. These situations are created with infinite care, the environment being structured in advance.[90] Often it is done against the wishes of Julie and St. Preux, as when Wolmar departs, leaving them alone for several days.[91] Sometimes it involves deception, as when Wolmar's collaborator, Lord Bomston, puts St. Preux in a contrived situation where he seems obliged to help his patron, and to take charge of the latter's life and future.[92] In both cases St. Preux is forced into self-recognition and so into freedom. He is cured of nostalgia and of insecurity. As Julie says of herself, Wolmar

---

[88] Vaughan, II, 55 (*Contrat Social*), 441 (*Poland*).

[89] Vaughan, I, 183 (*Inégalité*); II, 307 (*Corsica*).

[90] For the best account of this see Étienne Gilson, "La Méthode de M. de Wolmar," in *Les Idées et les Lettres* (Paris, 1932), pp. 275–298.

[91] *N. H.*, Part V, Lettre XII.

[92] *Ibid.*, Part II, Lettre XII; Part VI, Lettre III.

"returned her to herself," and now St. Preux is again sane; Wolmar, she notes, has been his "liberator."[93]

It is a slow process. At first St. Preux becomes completely dependent on Wolmar and feels unsure as soon as the latter's watchful eye is removed.[94] After passing all the contrived tests arranged for him, he is, however, not only prepared to accept Wolmar's offer to bring up his children, but he no longer fears Wolmar's "oeil éclairé" when it reads his heart.[95] He does not become a second Wolmar, to be sure; such is not his bent nor his station in life. Even when he is restored to himself he remains in need of Wolmar's guidance. His first response to a difficult situation is to lament Wolmar's absence: "where are your paternal cares, your lessons, your insight? What shall I do without you?"[96] When he finally does recognize that he is now a free and competent person, he is still aware that this has been Wolmar's work, not his own. It is then that he calls the former his benefactor and his father, and notes that "in giving myself to you entirely, I can give to you, as to God himself, gifts that I have received from you."[97] St. Preux's freedom will always depend on Wolmar's continued presence, not so much as a therapist, but as the guarantor of the order of Clarens in which St. Preux is to share. Wolmar himself accepts responsibility in advance. "Live in the present," he tells St. Preux, "and I will answer for the future." That too is Julie's cousin's advice: let Wolmar manage.[98] In short, St. Preux is now a full and useful man, but he

---

[93] *Ibid.*, Part III, Lettre XVIII; Part IV, Lettre VII; Part VI, Lettre XII.

[94] *Ibid.*, Part IV, Lettre XV.

[95] *Ibid.*, Part V, Lettre VII.

[96] *Ibid.*, Part V, Lettre XII. (All translations are mine.)

[97] *Ibid.*, Part VI, Lettre XII.

[98] *Ibid.*, Part IV, Lettres IX, XII. It is clear that both in his methods and ends Wolmar cannot be compared to a modern psychoanalyst. Indeed, there is no effort made here to represent Rousseau as a precursor of psychoanalytic theory, in spite of surface similarities.

is not, he never could be, Wolmar's equal. He will always depend on Wolmar's care.[99] Psychological dependence is here the condition of freedom and order. For even a small order, such as Clarens, is possible only through the constant authority of Wolmar.

5. Palliative Authority

Palliative authority alleviates the symptoms of social illness, even though it cannot remove their basic causes. This also is Wolmar's work at Clarens. Here again his guiding hand is felt but never seen. It is invisible, yet omnipresent. This social aspect of his authority exceeds what is needed for curing St. Preux. Wolmar sets the moral standards and tone at Clarens, and his mere presence ensures that they are observed. He needs to *do* very little, but he must *be* there. Without him this society would fall apart, because left to itself it would fall prey to the encroachments of the civilized world and its disrupting temptations. Without Wolmar, moreover, there would be no justice in the relationships among the individuals who live and work at Clarens. His authority is thus partly preventive: it keeps the "great world" away from Clarens and protects its rural simplicity. More significantly, however, it is also palliative. For even Clarens is "unnatural," as are all organized societies, since the division of labor, social inequality and constraint prevail in all. What "legitimizes" these fundamental evils is justice. That is the message of the *Social Contract*, and Wolmar's benevolent rule at Clarens illustrates it in a more informal setting.

The immense power that Wolmar exercises over his dependents and neighbors is justified by his method of ruling, which can be summed up in one word: justice. A rigorous system of rewards and penalties is adminis-

---

[99] Thus St. Preux notes, "si je n'y prends pas tout à fait l'autorité d'un maitre; je sens plus de plaisir encore à me regarder comme l'enfant de la maison." *Ibid.*, Part V, Lettre II.

tered by a man who is always "equitable without anger" to his servants. The neighboring peasants are helped to recognize that their estate, for all its hardships, is the best one open to mankind.[100] No one is encouraged to change his social position, but justice renders social inferiority bearable and gives it a degree of moral validity.[101] Each man gets his deserts and respects those of others. However, at no time does Wolmar, or anyone else, claim that inequality and domestic service are natural or agreeable conditions. Wolmar's justice can only render them tolerable. He lessens the force of resentment and his people endure their burdens without complaint.[102] Certainly none of Wolmar's servants want to leave his estate. Life at Clarens, autarchical, isolated from the "great world," without any disorder or luxury, and with some sense of common unity and justice, is not perfect, but at least there is less cause for dissatisfaction and hostility than in other societies. More than that even the semi-divine Wolmar cannot do. For political authority is at best a form of surgery, once the diseases of inequality have set in, and the social function of justice is to render subordination bearable, even when it involves serfdom, as in Poland.[103] That does not in any way lessen the value of justice as a virtue in Wolmar, who creates it, or in the citizens who abide by it and whose general will expresses nothing else.[104]

Order, regularity, security of expectations and fairness: everything in this stable, harmonious society reflects the soul of the master. And although everyone seems to be doing what pleases himself, it is Wolmar who directs each one, for all are united in their attachment

---

[100] *N. H.*, Part V, Lettre II.

[101] Vaughan, II, 497 (*Poland*).

[102] *N. H.*, Part IV, Lettre X.

[103] Vaughan, I, 181 (*Inégalité*); II, 497 (*Poland*).

[104] For the place of justice and fairness in the *Social Contract* see G. Kateb, "Aspects of Rousseau's Political Thought," *Political Science Quarterly*, Vol. 76 (1961), pp. 519–543.

to him. That is because Wolmar not only wants to be
well served, but because he is concerned with the moral
welfare of his servants and with the order of his estate
as a whole.[105] It is his responsibility and he attends to
it directly, never acting through, and thus depending on,
intermediaries.[106] This personal involvement also marks
the other efforts that Wolmar and Julie make to soften
the anguish of inequality. From time to time they practice "togetherness" with their servants and neighbors.
Festivities and celebrations in which all join are frequently held at Clarens in order that servants and masters might at least share some of the pleasures of life in
a spontaneous way, and occasionally recognize their common humanity. However, this too is palliative, a way of
reducing the coldness imposed by inequality. The differences in rank are not forgotten.[107] The brute reality
remains, and Rousseau was not disposed to forget it.
Even when he was looking for ways of transcending its
worst emotional and moral effects, he remained acutely
aware of inequality: the heaviest of all the chains that
society imposes upon us.

6. Domestic and Preventive Authority

Infrangible inequality is not the only limitation on
Wolmar's powers. He himself recognizes from the first
that he cannot do for his wife all that he can do for St.
Preux. He does not even try.[108] Her regeneration is not
his work, but an act of divine grace. It is, however, only
a partial cure, which is completed only when she all but
commits a sacrificial suicide. Neither Wolmar nor St.

---

[105] N. H., Part III, Lettre XX, Part IV, Lettres IV, X.
[106] See also Émile, pp. 48, 198, 202.
[107] Thus the tutor in Émile says of servants, "be their brother and
they will be your children," p. 59. Not equals, it should be noted,
but dependents. That too is the state of affairs at Clarens. N. H.,
Part V, Lettre VII. The importance of festivals and ceremonies is
also urged upon the Poles, Vaughan, II (Poland), 434–435.
[108] N. H., Part IV, Lettre XIV.

Preux can influence her in the slightest, simply because she has greater strength of character and a rare capacity to inspire servile love and devotion.[109] This all-attracting, but also subtly hateful portrait was entirely in keeping with Rousseau's general view of women. Women rule men and make of them whatever they please.[110] "Do you want to know men? Study women."[111] Clearly Rousseau did not like this monstrous regiment of women. Paris, the very epitome of modern corruption, was entirely ruled by women.[112] Indeed women were responsible for most of the moral evils of this world, but Rousseau could not help admiring authority, even in this case. The result was a considerable uneasiness. He composed two brief essays to show that women had been important in the great events of history and that in civic virtue and military heroism women were really the equals of men.[113] This did not deter him from claiming that "the law of nature bids women obey men," because men are active and strong, while women are passive and feeble.[114] To be sure, husbands ought to treat their wives well, but just or unjust, women must submit to the commands of their spouses.[115] However, in the end Rousseau decided that this submission was itself only superficial. Julie rules Clarens and when Emile's tutor resigns his authority over his pupil, he says, "My weighty task is now ended and another undertakes this duty. To-day I abdicate the authority which you gave me; henceforth

---

[109] *Ibid.*, Part V, Lettres III, X; for a religious interpretation of the relationship, see Pierre Burgelin, *La Philosophie de l'Existence de Jean-Jacques Rousseau* (Paris, 1952), pp. 447–455.

[110] "Lettre à Lenieps," 8 novembre, 1758, *C. G.*, IV, 115–116.

[111] *Letter to d'Alembert*, p. 82.

[112] *N. H.*, Part I, Lettre XXI.

[113] "*Essai sur les Evénements Importants Dont les Femmes Ont Été la Cause Secrète*," *O. C.*, II, pp. 1257–1259; *Sur les Femmes*, *ibid.*, pp. 1254–1255.

[114] *Émile*, pp. 322, 370–371; *Pensées*, VII, *O. C.*, II, 1300; *Letter to d'Alembert*, pp. 87–88.

[115] *Émile*, pp. 333, 359.

Sophie is your guardian."[116] If anything, her authority is greater even than that of the man who ruled Emile so completely, for she rules over an adult, not a child.

If the authority of women over men is no blessing, women's influence over their children is rarely wise. Though they desire the happiness of their young, most are too stupid to bring them up properly.[117] The ignorance of women is, however, not the only flaw in parental authority, a subject to which Rousseau gave much thought. Of all the actual and inevitable forms of authority it is the most important, and in all corrupt—that is, in all contemporary—societies, parents are the agents who transmit false traditions and habits from one generation to the next. Children are sacrificed to social vanity, cast too early into the conventional mould and, thanks to the ambitions of their fathers, forced into unhappy marriages.[118] Rousseau was, moreover, anxious to minimize the legitimate scope of paternal authority in order to prove, as Locke had, that it could not serve as a model or justification for absolute monarchy.[119] If, at times, he regretted the passing of paternal chiefs and familial society, he was just as deeply drawn to the republican ideal. Here again there was a conflict of ideals. Occasionally he would sing the praises of the virtuous family-man devoted to raising his children.[120] Just as often, however, he would dream of the true republic in which public education replaces not only the father, but the entire family.[121]

---

[116] *Ibid.*, p. 444.

[117] *Ibid.*, pp. 5, 87. He regretted that the law gave them too little power over their children mainly because he thought maternal affection less harmful than paternal harshness.

[118] Vaughan, I, 205 (*Inégalité*); *N. H.*, "Seconde Préface," p. 24; *Émile*, pp. 48, 149, 163.

[119] Vaughan, I, 185 (*Inégalité*), 237–240 (*Économie Politique*); *Émile*, p. 423; Vaughan, II, 80 (*Contrat Social*).

[120] *Émile*, pp. 16–17.

[121] Vaughan, I, 256–258 (*Économie Politique*), 278–279 (*Fragments*). Geneva, he thought, was an acceptable compromise between domestic and public education, "Lettre à Tronchin," 26 novembre, 1758, *C. G.*, IV, 143.

It is not just the socializing and political functions of the family that make it a suspect institution under present circumstances. It is also inherently inefficient as a way of educating the young. If a child is to be brought up for his own sake, to become a good and happy man, he needs constant attention. To be the perfect tutor of a single child is a lifetime's work.[122] It is a sobering thought. Nothing less than a full-time tutor for each child can bring about the regeneration of civilized men through education. And where are tutors to be found? Rousseau doubted whether any man was really fit for it.[123] The tutor, to be sure, need not have the magnetic personality, the immense social experience, nor the wealth and rank of a Wolmar. Indeed, a tutor should be no more than a man and should show his pupil that he was only human, a person with weaknesses and needs.[124] Nevertheless his talents like his responsibilities must be immense. Rousseau himself had been a wretched failure as a tutor. His inability to exercise authority had been his undoing, as he recognized perfectly clearly.[125] His *ideas* on education, however, were fully developed very early, and he adhered to them with unusual consistency. From his first to his last letter on the subject one point was, moreover, always emphasized: the tutor must have complete and absolute authority over his charge.[126] No one, not even the parents, may interfere.

Why does the tutor need such an extensive authority?

---

[122] *Émile*, p. 19.

[123] *Ibid.*, p. 17; according to Wolmar, "Il n'y a qu'un homme de génie en qui l'on puisse espérer de trouver les lumieres d'un maitre." *N. H.*, Part IV, Lettre XIV.

[124] *Émile*, pp. 208, 299–300. That is why a St. Preux would do.

[125] *Confessions*, Bk. VII, pp. 267–269; *Émile*, p. 18.

[126] Rousseau made this point in his first essay on private education written in 1740, "Mémoire Presenté à M. de Ste. Maire Pour l'Education de son Fils," *C. G.*, I, 367–379, and he repeated it many years later in advising a nobleman on the rules to be followed by the governess of the latter's daughter, "Lettre au Prince de Wurtemberg," 10 novembre, 1763, *C. G.*, X, 205–217; *Émile*, p. 20. The tutor, not the father, Rousseau insisted, chooses a wife for Émile, *ibid.*, p. 369.

He needs it in order to fulfill his task of prevention. The
child is to be educated *against* society and he must be
protected against parents, neighbors and servants who
would press their false values upon him. The tutor's direct authority over the child must be complete, because
the child is always so defenseless, so exposed to external
influences. The question is not, to rule or not to rule over
the child, but who is to create his environment for him
and to what end? Is convention or virtue to create the
man? If the tutor is to replace society, he must have more
than equivalent means to arrange the child's life, to structure his experiences and to replace all other human examples and influences. "Negative education," which is the
tutor's method, is far from being effortless or unplanned.

What then is "negative education?"[127] It differs from
conventional education not only in its ends, but also, of
necessity, in its entire method. Its aim is to make a self-
sufficient adult who lives at peace with himself.[128] To
achieve this one must at all costs avoid trying to impose
a foreign, social character upon the child. His natural
self must not be inhibited in any way. On the contrary,
everything must be arranged so that the child may learn
everything that he has to know, without losing his
God-given characteristics. "Fit a man's education to his
real self, not to what is no part of him."[129] "Negative
education" is negative in that it prevents the imposition
of an artificial, socially devised and socially oriented self
upon the child. It prepares him for knowledge by protecting him against error.[130] If Emile is docile to a degree and if his will is at the mercy of his tutor, it is because the latter has made himself loved and has made
himself the child's only model. He rules over the child's
will by pre-arranging experiences and situations, not

---

[127] *Rousseau Juge de Jean-Jacques*, I, 687; *Émile*, pp. 16, 57.
[128] *Ibid.*, p. 6.
[129] *Ibid.*, pp. 157, 216–217; *N. H.*, Part V, Lettre III. "Give nature
time to work before you take over her business." *Émile*, p. 71.
[130] *Lettre à Christophe Beaumont*, p. 71.

by any sort of direct imposition.[131] He never bullies and rarely, if ever, punishes.[132] He demonstrates and manipulates. Like Wolmar he does not hesitate to employ stratagems and deceits. His whole art lies in "controlling events."[133] He does not give orders, and again like Wolmar, is everywhere without being seen.[134] If Emile is in this way buffeted and protected at every point, he is compelled to *do* only one thing: to learn for himself.[135] In this sense he is forced to be free by being negatively educated. That is, he is prevented from becoming weak, and dependent, as he most certainly would have come to be without his tutor's care.

7. Conclusion: The Limits of Regeneration

Since Emile is a child, one would not expect him to enjoy full freedom under any circumstances. However, he remains in need of the tutor's protective guidance even in adulthood. For Rousseau did not think that even Emile could manage to remain free for long. If he would flounder, certainly corrupt, civilized men were entirely incapable of freedom. Without the directing intelligence, and an order maintained by it, most men would inevitably destroy the conditions of freedom.

At the end of *Émile*, the pupil, now fully grown and about to become a father, still feels in need of the protective presence of his tutor. "Advise and control us," he begs, "as long as I live I shall need you. I need you more than ever now that I am taking up the duties of manhood."[136] As he had said a few years earlier, "Resume the authority. I place it in your hands of my own freewill."[137] Even more revealing is the story of what happens

---

[131] *Émile*, pp. 84–85.
[132] *Ibid.*, p. 55.
[133] *Ibid.*, p. 209.
[134] *Ibid.*, pp. 84–85, 88–89, 107, 177.
[135] *Ibid.*, p. 169.
[136] *Ibid.*, p. 444.
[137] *Ibid.*, p. 290.

to Emile and Sophie once the tutor does leave. The sketch
for a sequel to _Émile_ that Rousseau left unfinished begins with Emile's lament, "If you had not left us, I should
still be happy!"[138] As soon as the tutor departs Emile and
Sophie cease to be able to cope with the difficulties that
beset them and commit one mistake after another until
their marriage and their happiness are destroyed. Emile's
education continues to stand him in good stead. He bears
adversity admirably. But he does not know how to avert
or end the troubles that afflict him and his wife. He cannot control his own future. What is impossible for the perfectly reared Emile, who possesses every virtue except
the quality that directs men and events, is certainly not
possible for lesser men. On the social level that meant,
for example, that although the Polish peasants and burgh-
ers who are to be freed and raised to the ranks of the
nobility are chosen for their merits, it is just when they
reach civic maturity that they need guidance most. They
are to be watched, protected and helped, not because
they are poor subjects, but because they are free.[139] It
is they who must have an orderly environment and a directing hand. After all, even that part of the public that
really desires the common good needs guides.[140] How
much more so the more feeble mass!

To Rousseau it did not appear that genuine authority
limits freedom. The real tension was between authority
and equality. Personal authority is not merely compatible
with freedom, it creates it. In its healing form, in ordering
the disrupted passions, it is psychologically liberating.
In ordering the environment it allows men to retain an
integrated self and to preserve their independence. Wolmar and Emile's tutor are nothing if not tolerant, especially in matters of faith and opinion.[141] Freedom, in any

---

[138] _Émile et Sophie,_ Hachette, III, p. 3. (My translation.)
[139] Vaughan, II, 501 (_Poland_).
[140] _Ibid.,_ II, 51 (_Contrat Social_).
[141] _N. H.,_ Part VI, Lettre XI. "No man is free from man's first
duty, no one has the right to depend on another's judgment,"

case, was for Rousseau not a matter of doing as one pleases, but of *not* being compelled, either from within or from without, to do what one does *not* wish to do.[142] Inner compulsion is thus a most severe form of enslavement. That is why an ordered existence is needed to support us in a free condition. That also is why moderate desires, a capacity to live in the present and dependence only on things are the prerequisites of the very possibility of a free life.[143] All of them, however, depend on an educative, preventive, curative and ordering authority. Authentic authority liberates.[144] It gives liberty to those who are incapable of creating it for themselves.

The strong then liberate the weak, but the distance between them remains. Nothing can alter the fact that St. Preux will never be Wolmar's equal, nor Emile his tutor's. However, though its extent is no less than the difference between God and man, this inequality is a natural one, and, as such, relatively unproblematic. It is only the addition of social inequalities to those of nature that creates our great miseries. If Rousseau's images of authority show any one thing it is the intensity and consistency of his hatred for all forms of personal dependence and social inequality, and for their psychological roots, weakness and *amour-propre*. It is these that cause even loving parents to destroy the happiness of innocent young people like Julie and St. Preux. It is these

---

Émile, p. 270. That men should be free is the will of Providence, *ibid.*, pp. 243–244.

[142] *Les Rêveries*, VI, 1059; *Lettres à Malesherbes*, p. 1132; *Lettres Écrites de la Montagne*, pp. 227–228; *Émile et Sophie*, p. 28.

[143] *Émile*, pp. 48–59, 125, 436; *Pensées*, XXXI, p. 1305.

[144] Vaughan, I, 184 (*Inégalité*). If most actual authority is merely a necessary response to the wickedness of the subjects, it is still true that even in good republics the glory of the citizen rests in obedience to legitimate masters. *Ibid.*, I, 127, 190–191 (*Inégalité*); "Lettre à M. d'Ivernois," 24 mars, 1768, *C. G.*, XVIII, 175–178. That the element of subjection remains is not to be forgotten. "There is no subjection so complete as that which preserves the forms of freedom; it is thus that the will itself is taken captive." *Émile*, pp. 88, 196.

that make even the best constructed republic a fleeting
palliative. It is these that render even the serene life at
Clarens galling to most of its inhabitants. *Amour-propre*
and its social expressions are, moreover, inseparable from
social life as such. In society their worst consequences
may be cured, palliated and, in the case of a chosen few,
prevented from arising. The evil itself remains ineradi-
cable. In his last years Rousseau felt that under prevailing conditions peace was worth more even than freedom.
For freedom existed now only in the heart of the just
man.[145] In short, things being what they are, peace, order
and quiet were the best anyone could hope for.

This resignation was not merely a matter of old age
and exhaustion. It had been implicit in Rousseau's work
all along. Indeed, it is less Burke's traditionalist rhetoric
than Rousseau's psychological insight that has set the
most severe limits on all hopes of easy reform. *Émile* is
anything but a manual for those eupeptic schoolmasters
who imagine that it is possible to reconstruct society by
fiddling with the curriculum and altering the atmosphere
of the classroom. A regenerative education *against* society and apart from its strains and prejudices would
require one perfect tutor for each newborn child. Apart
from a few Swiss peasants, each child would need the
constant attention of a man who was himself above society. Where are such teachers to be found? Yet this is
the only way to cure denatured men through educative
means. To be sure, it is neither morally nor psychologically impossible, but it is historically very unlikely. Society being what men have made it, and expressing, as
it does, the most deep-seated psychological deformities,
is not readily altered. The great men, whose personalities
can impinge upon the consciousness of those whom they
wish to improve, can effect some real, though never complete, alleviation. Such men, always rare, have now,
however, ceased to exist altogether. In their absence noth-

---

[145] "Lettre à M. Moultou fils," 7 mars, 1768, *C. G.*, XVIII, 147–
150, "ce n'est pas la peine de se battailler pour le reste."

ing can be done to morally reconstruct the European world.

To be sure, Rousseau's concerns were not limited to this single grand design. He was often deeply immersed in schemes for partial political reform, especially in Geneva. Moreover, the very act of devising standards for improvement, even excessively high ones, was an act of affirmation on his part. If disgust and distress were his immediate inspiration, the vision of equality was not a chimera. He was certain that he had known egalitarian societies in rural Switzerland and he believed that such communities had existed in the remote past. If criticism, indeed denunciation of the most devastating sort, were all that his contemporaries received from him, he was not the prophet of withdrawal either. However, at no time did he allow himself the illusion of painless reform or of the possibility of effortless social regeneration. His images of men of authority are so interesting because they are his answer to the question "how do we begin?" That his reply should have been cast in psychological, rather than in social terms, is scarcely surprising. Indeed it was inevitable, since for Rousseau politics was but a part of that study of the human heart which he had made his province. That also is the chief reason for his enduring relevance.

THE NOTION OF TIME IN ROUSSEAU'S
POLITICAL THOUGHT

WILLIAM PICKLES

Because of his often repeated assertions on that subject, the importance attached by Rousseau to *space* (along with size of population) in relation to the government of political societies is among the best known of his views. He believed that the only kind of society in which freedom of the individual could be reconciled with the degree of social organization that individual freedom demands was a small one. He also required it to be what he saw as voluntary. And for obvious reasons, few of his critics have challenged those views. Most of those of us who have thought about the subject must have recognised occasions in which a Rousseau-type general will could be seen to function in voluntary societies, small enough for their members never to lose sight of the community of interest between them. In some cases, indeed, that type of voluntary society can attain quite sizeable dimensions and still function by virtue of a general will, provided only that the subject of their common interest is of sufficient importance to its members to override all or most other considerations. The Society of Friends is perhaps the best known example of any real size, but a little thought can always reveal other, smaller ones. What nobody can imagine is finding the same degree of conscious community of interest, and therefore a search for and acceptance of a general will, in any non-voluntary society, even if it be no greater in area or population than Corsica in 1762. On that point, in other words, Rousseau's error was that he did not stress the limiting

This essay was written for this volume by William Pickles, University of London.

factor in his thesis heavily enough for all his readers to appreciate its vital importance.

Less attention has been paid to Rousseau's ideas on *time*, perhaps because Rousseau himself never presented them as such, even when the whole context shows that what was being considered was indeed the importance, the effects, the advantages and disadvantages, in politics and political institutions, of time, growth, change, and other related factors. The problem of his attitude to time is nevertheless closely related to many other problems that have troubled those who have tried, either to discover a coherent system in Rousseau's political and autobiographical writings, or even simply to understand parts of his system. It affects judgements of his position in relation to notions like tradition, evolution, and revolution, and it offers valuable clues in any attempt to decide whether—or to what extent—major works like the *Second Discourse* and still more the *Social Contract* are intended to be descriptive or prescriptive, utopian or realist, moral treatises, or attempts at factually based historical analysis. In all these contexts, other aspects of Rousseau's thought are probably more important, but the time factor is important enough to merit more attention than has hitherto been paid to it.

There are, in fact, three attitudes to time in Rousseau's political writings. He affirms both the testing and stabilizing effect of time on institutions and the corrupting effects of time on men. Or, in more polysyllabic terms, he combines traditionalism as regards institutions with a fatalistic and pessimistic belief in evolution as regards men. His third use of the notion of time is perhaps best described as stylistic. The three are now discussed in the order just given.

Rousseau's belief in the value of tradition is well known to specialists, but many of his contemporaries and some later commentators have found passages in the *Social Contract* which they read as incitements to revolution. Thus, in Chapter 12 of Book II of the *Social Con-*

tract,[1] Rousseau asks: "If the established order is bad, why should the laws that prevent it from being good be regarded as fundamental?" And he adds; "Besides, whatever the circumstances, a people is always entitled to change even the best of its laws." Again in Chapter 18 of Book III[2] he explains that "when it happens that a people sets up a hereditary Government, either monarchical in one family or hereditary in one class of citizens, it is in no sense entering into a binding undertaking, but only giving a provisional form to the administration, until it decides to order things differently."

Each of these much quoted passages is in fact immediately qualified within its own context. After the first one, Rousseau goes on—in the same sentence—"for if it wants to do harm to itself, who has the right to prevent it?" That rhetorical question turns the whole phrase into a philosophical defence of the right to self-government, in the limited way in which Rousseau defines self-government in the rest of the *Social Contract*. It is an earlier version of Gladstone's view that "good government is no substitute for self-government." The second of the passages quoted above is even more heavily qualified in the sentence immediately following. "It is also true," Rousseau goes on, "that in these cases it is essential to observe with all care the necessary formalities, in order to make clear the necessary distinction between a legal and legitimate act and a rebellious uprising." What Rousseau was clearly referring to here was not a change of a regime, but a change of government, that is, of the body chosen by the sovereign to administer the laws, as he had defined it in the first chapter of Book III.[3] The caution he advises before changing even what he saw as a purely administrative institution serves only to un-

---

[1] III, 393–94. The reference is to the Pléiade edition of the complete works, from which this and all other quotations not otherwise attributed are taken.

[2] III, 434–35.

[3] III, 395 sqq.

derline his objections to changes of the regime, of which the administration or "government," was only a subordinate element. Another much quoted passage in the same chapter,[4] claiming that "the act by which a people submits to its leaders is not a contract" is clearly shown by its context to be only another version of Rousseau's familiar assertion of the sovereignty of the people. All the way through the *Social Contract,* he maintained the distinction between what is justifiable in terms of *le droit,* especially of *le droit politique,* which clearly he is discussing here, and what is inadvisable in practice.[5]

These passages were widely read—and widely misunderstood—in 1788 and the following years. Professor Mornet's belief that the *Social Contract* remained largely unread until the coming of the Convention[6] was in fact wrong. The *Social Contract* remained largely unread up to about August 1788, after the end of the period of which Mornet examined the available catalogues of sales of private libraries. Mornet wrote before the appearance of a different examination of the same question, in the Tübingen doctorate thesis of F. Eppensteiner[7] in which the author had considered the same questions as Mornet, but by a different method—the examination of pamphlets and letters for the period January 1787–May 1789. The beginning of the revolt of the *Parlements* in May 1788, followed by the decision to summon the States General, the quarrel about the status and functions of the latter body, and the decision to treat the meeting as an opportunity for a fundamental transformation of the constitution changed the whole climate of political thinking. That much we already knew from André Lichtenberger.[8]

---

[4] III, 396.

[5] For a further explanation of this point, see below, pp. 389–95.

[6] Daniel Mornet, "Les Enseignements des bibliothèques privées (1750–1780)," in *Revue d'Histoire Littéraire de la France,* 1910.

[7] *Rousseau's Einfluss auf die Vorrevolutionären Flugschriften und den Ausbruck der Revolution* (Tübingen: 1914).

[8] *Le Socialisme au XVIIIᵉ siècle* showed, for instance, how the events of 1788 changed the thinking of a writer like Rétif de la

Dr. Eppensteiner shows Pétion, Cérutti, and others quoting Rousseau from August onwards, and showing great familiarity with concepts like that of a single, inalienable and indivisible sovereignty. Before the end of 1788, on his voluminous evidence,[9] these ideas had become the common property of all the pamphleteers, and by early 1789 were familiar to anti-reformers as well, while Rousseau himself had been deified as the "divine Jean-Jacques."

At that stage there were many better reasons than the passages quoted above for seeing Rousseau as a revolutionary.[10] The *Second Discourse,* which had been widely read, was indeed an egalitarian tract, and in many other of his attitudes Rousseau classed himself with what would now be called the Left. He believed in the formative power of institutions: "A people's opinions are born of its constitution. Although the Law[11] does not regulate morals, it is legislation that creates them."[12] In the Constitution for Corsica, distinctions were to be awarded only for "merit, virtue or services to the country" and they should then not be hereditary.[13] There was to be no currency; this had been seen in Switzerland as the source of poverty.[14] There were to be public food stores, as advocated by many pre-socialist writers of the seven-

---

Bretonne, who abandoned the pure Utopianism of his *Andrographe* ("a beautiful dream," in his own later words) for the moderate but possible reformism of the *Thesmographe.*

[9] See especially Ch. 3, pp. 27–66.

[10] Rousseau has also been seen by some writers, (e.g., Alfred Cobban, *Rousseau and the Modern State* [second edition], p. 57, as *prophesying* revolution. But the significance of the passages quoted by Cobban is uncertain, and the point is in any case irrelevant here.

[11] This is a literal translation of *la Loi,* but in Rousseau (as in Montesquieu) *la loi* and *les lois* are often most accurately translated as "institutions."

[12] *Social Contract,* Bk. IV, Ch. 7 (III, 459). See also similar sentiments in *Fragments on the Constitution for Corsica,* III, 948; *Second Letter to Malesherbes,* I, 1136; *Political Economy,* III, 538; *Confessions,* I, 404–5.

[13] III, 910, 919.

[14] III, 916.

teenth and eighteenth centuries.[15] Private property was to be confined within the narrowest limits,[16] and public affluence—to borrow and invert a modern phrase—was to be achieved even at the cost of private squalor.[17] The *geschlossene Handelsstaat*, which Fichte later borrowed from Babeuf, is there in the Constitution for Corsica.[18] There were to be sumptuary laws, and future holdings of land were to be equally distributed.[19] All this puts Rousseau so firmly on the Left in the long eighteenth-century debate on private property that illusions about his attitude to immediate and violent change can easily be forgiven.

In the long self-defence of the *Dialogues*, Rousseau nevertheless protested violently about that error of judgement. Speaking of himself (as he does in that work) in the third person, he said, "he always insisted . . . on the preservation of existing institutions, maintaining that their destruction would only get rid of the palliatives, while leaving the defects, and substitute brigandage for corruption. . . . If his doctrine could be of any use to others, it was by changing the objects of their esteem and thus perhaps delaying their decadence. . . . But in spite of his frequent and emphatic repetition of these distinctions, the bad faith of men of letters and the stupidity of that self-esteem that leads every one to think people are thinking of him when in fact they are not, led the big nations to think that what was intended only for small republics applied to them, so that men persisted in seeing a fomenter of riot and disorder in the man who, more than any other, has a true respect for laws and national constitutions and the greatest aversion to revolutions and agitators of all kinds, who indeed reciprocate his feelings for them. . . ."[20]

---

[15] III, 923.
[16] III, 931.
[17] III, 930.
[18] III, 908.
[19] III, 936, 942.
[20] I, 935.

Whatever views one may hold on Rousseau's state of mind when he wrote the *Dialogues,* there can be no doubt that in that particular passage he told the truth. Over and over again, from his earliest political writings, he shows himself to be a traditionalist, with all the typical traditionalist's belief in the value of habits and institutions tested by time, and indeed in the value of mere age, the accumulation of years, in manners and institutions, as a good in itself. The earliest avowal of this respect for tradition—indeed, of an explicit preference for tradition as compared with change—comes in the Dedication to the *Discourse on the Origin and Foundations of Inequality among Men,* better known as the *Second Discourse.* There, after describing some of the characteristics he would look for if he were allowed to choose his birthplace, he goes on to say, in a well known passage, "I should have had no desire to live in a newly created Republic, however good its laws, lest its regime, being out of accord with the needs of the time and therefore unsuited to the new Citizens, or the Citizens being unsuited to the new regime, the State be liable to be shaken and destroyed almost at birth. For liberty is like those solid and succulent foods or full-bodied wines that are well suited to feed and fortify such robust temperaments as are accustomed to them, but overburden, ruin and intoxicate the weak and delicate who are not made for them. Peoples that have become accustomed to overlords are no longer capable of doing without them. If they try to throw off the yoke, they confuse liberty with the unchecked license that is really its antithesis, and so become even less free, for their revolutions nearly always deliver them into the hands of seducers who only add to their chains."[21]

In that passage there are, as will have been noted, two complementary but separate ideas: that settled government is best because it is most likely to be "in accord with the needs of its time"; and that revolutions against

---

[21] III, 112–13.

tyranny must always fail, or nearly always—the qualification comes late in the passage, as if it were an afterthought. It will be necessary to return to the second of these ideas, but for the moment the first concerns us most. Rousseau's preference for order and stability is too often reaffirmed for the passage in his early work to be considered as an aberration, out of harmony with the many attitudes that he shared with revolutionaries. In the first chapter of the *Social Contract* he lays down that "social order is a sacred right, the basis of all others,"[22] and puts the meaning of that phrase beyond all doubt by presenting it as a refutation of the justification of revolution which he might have offered if he had considered only "force and the effects of force." In Chapter 8 of Book II he returns to the theme. "When once customs have been established and prejudices have taken root," he writes, "any attempt to reform them is both dangerous and useless."[23] Beneficent revolutions do happen, just as illnesses sometimes derange the mind and lead it to forget the past. "But events of that kind are rare; they are exceptions, explained by something special in the constitution of an exceptional State. They could not even happen twice to the same people, for a people can become free when it is merely barbarian, but it can no longer do so when the impulse to sociability is worn out. Then disturbances can destroy it with no possibility of its being restored by revolution, and as soon as its chains are broken, it falls to bits and no longer exists; from then on, it needs a master, not a liberator." In the eighth *Letter from the Mountains* he goes even further. "Amid the miseries of human affairs, is there any good that is worth buying at the cost of the blood of our brothers? Liberty itself is too dear at that price."[24]

When Rousseau turns from theory to more practical politics, his preference for time-tested institutions shows

---

[22] III, 352.
[23] III, 385.
[24] III, 836.

itself even more clearly. His only prolonged and intended incursion into that field of politics is the *Considerations of the Government of Poland*. (The title of that work, like that of its predecessor on Corsica, was ill chosen. Their contents would have been more clearly indicated if they had been entitled, respectively, "Considerations on the Government of Corsica" and "Draft of a Constitution for Poland." One wonders if Rousseau might not have found a more accurate title for his book on Poland if he had not already somewhat pretentiously applied to Corsica a term that would have been appropriate to what he had to say on Poland.) At various points in the *Social Contract*, and in particular in Chapter 8 of Book III, Rousseau had emphasised (with due acknowledgement of his debt to Montesquieu) the politically limiting effects of climate and material conditions. When he turned to study the notes prepared for him by Count Wielhorski[25] in order to undertake for the second time the task of giving practical advice about the government of a country, he discovered what was for him, if not a new dimension in politics, at least a new aspect of an old dimension. In 1754, when he wrote the *Inégalité*, the effects of time on institutions had been seen as a reassuring and stabilizing factor. Seventeen years later, in reading Wielhorski's notes and the works that Wielhorski recommended, he came to see them as a determining and limiting factor. His traditionalism was now no longer only an intuition or a philosophic conviction. It was a recognition of practical necessity.

In Poland he discovers "a nation with settled institutions, a nation whose tastes, morals, customs, prejudices and views are too deeply rooted to be easily killed by others newly sown."[26] It refuses to conform to any of the principles of law and politics discovered by the political science of the seventeenth and eighteenth centuries. "Monarchies, Republics, all those nations that have the

---

[25] See the note on this in III, 1735–41.
[26] III, 933.

best institutions, all those magnificent and carefully
thought-out systems, [have] fallen into decrepitude and
are threatened by imminent death, while Poland, depop-
ulated, devastated, oppressed, at the mercy of aggres-
sors, shows in the worst hours of its misfortunes and its
anarchy all the fire of youth, and dares to ask for laws
and a system of government, as if it had only just been
born."[27] And Rousseau's immediate reply is that of a traditionalist: "Be careful, good Poles; be careful lest in
seeking to make your position too good you make it
worse. When you think of what you can get, do not forget what you can lose. Remedy the abuses in your constitution, if it can be done,[28] but do not despise the constitution that has made you what you are. . . . I do not
say that things must be left as they are, but I do say that
what is done must be done with the greatest care. Today,
the abuses are more evident than the advantages. The
time, I fear, will come, when the advantages will be more
clearly seen, and by then, unfortunately, they will have
been lost."[29]

The second section of the *Considerations* is entitled:
"Esprit des anciennes institutions." M. Fabre, its editor,
points out in a footnote[30] that the word *institution* must
be understood here as having the sense given to it by
Montesquieu in the phrase, *"Rome fut sauvée par la
force de son institution,"* which means something like
"Rome was saved by the strength of the foundations on
which it was built"—those foundations being, of course,
moral and political. In this portion of the *Considerations,*
in other words, Rousseau is going a long way back in
history, to salute the spirit on which the Polish State was

---

[27] III, 934.
[28] Compare Rousseau's description in the *Dialogues* of his own intentions. "Thus his purpose [was] . . . only to check, *if it were
possible,* [my italics] the movement of those States whose smallness
and general circumstances have saved them from so rapid a movement towards the perfecting of society and the ruin of the race."
[29] III, 934–35.
[30] III, 1745.

founded and to attribute to that spirit the durability of
its institutions (in the modern English sense of that
term). At first sight, these looked like "a great body made
up of a great number of dead limbs and a small number
of disunited limbs, whose every movement—each almost
totally independent of the others—is so far from having
a common purpose with the others that all are mutually
destructive; a body that is always doing something and
never achieves anything, is incapable of resistance
against any destructive force, falls into dissolution half
a dozen times every hundred years and is paralysed by
every effort it makes and by every need it tries to
meet."[31]

Nevertheless, unlike other States more rationally conceived and managed, Poland "survived and kept its
strength."[31] How is she able to go on surmounting the
obstacles just enumerated and those of which Rousseau
adds a new list on his p. 959? By cultivating the national
virtues and the national feeling that have grown up with
time. Since "it is the institutions of a people that form its
genius, character, tastes and morals, that make it what
it is, instead of something else,"[32] then any new institutions must cultivate the virtues produced by the old ones
and teach the people above all to love their country.
"With that feeling alone, any legislation, even if it were
bad, would make good Citizens."[33] Rousseau's detailed
proposals, therefore, "scarcely touching the basis of your
(existing) laws,"[34] will seek only to strengthen patriotism in a nation already "unique in history"[35] because
it has survived for so long despite its too great size and
the other defects already mentioned. Its first rule, therefore, which Rousseau "cannot too often repeat,"[35] is,
"think well before you touch any of your laws, especially
those that have made you what you are."[35]

---

[31] III, 953-54.
[32] III, 960.
[33] III, 961.
[34] III, 962.
[35] III, 971.

In the detailed reforms that Rousseau goes on to propose, he tries "to move by steps" and to adapt his proposals "as far as possible to the existing form of government."[36] And when his proposals have all been presented, though they do not appear to him to be "fundamental or profound,"[37] he warns again: "whatever plan may be adopted, do not forget what I said in the *Social Contract* about the state of weakness and anarchy to which a nation is reduced when it is establishing or reforming its constitution. . . . It is important, therefore, so to arrange things that changes are made during a period of tranquility, such that the nation runs no risk in acting on itself and rejuvenating its constitution."[38] At the end as at the beginning, caution in tampering with the work of time is the watchword. The evidence for Rousseau's profound traditionalism, sometimes in his discussions of ethics and always when he turned to practical politics, is overwhelming, and is now generally accepted by scholars.

Along with Rousseau's belief in both the creative and the stabilizing values of time, however, there goes an acceptance of the inevitability of change through time, and a recognition, in both earlier and later works, that change is sometimes desirable. Like the recognition of the value of accumulated time and the traditions that it creates, this concomitant view finds its first expression in the *Second Discourse*. There, too, we find a conflict that Rousseau never satisfactorily resolves, between acceptance of change on the one hand, and on the other what might be called Platonic pessimism about its consequences in political life. The facts about this part of Rousseau's beliefs are well known and need be only briefly recalled before they are discussed.

The idea of a prolonged evolution occurs in the *Second*

---

[36] III, 1020.
[37] III, 1037.
[38] III, 1036.

Discourse in two forms. On the one hand, we are told in various places of the "successive developments" of man,[39] of the "vast distance" that separates the state of nature from the time when the development of language began,[40] and later from that of the state of society,[41] of the "complete changes" (*révolutions*)[42] that time of necessity brings, the "successive inventions"[43] of the various elements of human knowledge, and so on. In addition to these passing references, Rousseau lays down in much greater detail the order of events in his "hypothetical history" of the process of change from solitary natural man to civilized social man. His own summary sees only three stages.[44] Jean Starobinski, in his illuminating introduction to the Pléiade edition, divides the process much more accurately into what are, in effect, six stages, of which the first three all belong to the state of nature.[45]

Here there arise two problems about Rousseau's attitude to time and evolution. First, was evolution, and was this evolution in particular, avoidable or not? At first glance, it may seem that the first part, which, as we shall see, is in Rousseau's view the desirable part, was not inevitable. Physically, man in his most primitive stage had everything he needed, and was superior to modern

---

[39] III, 134.

[40] III, 147.

[41] III, 192.

[42] On the meaning of this word in the mid-eighteenth century, see F. Brunot, *Histoire de la langue française*, Tome 9, 2e Partie, p. 617. On its use specifically by Rousseau, see A. Hatto, "Revolution, An Enquiry into the Usefulness of an Historical Term," in *Mind*, LVIII, N.S., No. 232 (October 1949), pp. 506–7. What emerges is that the word was still often used to mean "complete change," but was also beginning to acquire its modern meaning.

[43] III, 174.

[44] III, 187.

[45] III, lxii to lxiv. The stages are: (1) primitive isolation; (2) sporadic association; (3) patriarchal society with little private property; (4) division of labour, primitive industry, agriculture and hence private property; (5) Hobbesian "war of all against all"; (6) civil society.

man.[46] Morally, he was more intelligent than the animals, and in addition had the gift of free will. While animals were compelled to obey the instinct that nature had implanted in them,[47] man could choose whether to obey or resist the commands of nature, and that faculty, indeed, was the source of his spirituality.[48] His only virtues and vices, if such they can be called, were tendencies that, respectively, helped or hindered his self-preservation.[49] What took him out of this most primitive state was as much a series of external accidents as anything in his own nature.[50] Since, however, he enjoyed freedom of will, he could—presumably—have resisted the temptation to adapt himself to the harsher environment produced by drought or earthquakes or whatever it was. Instead, he acquired new skills such as fishing and hunting, and learned the use of fire. From that part of his evolution, he gained a good deal, including enough of a limited sense of the value of mutual obligation to enable him to cope more efficiently with his individual short-term needs, without going so far as to sacrifice present—even momentary—satisfactions to the needs of any group of which he may from time to time have formed a part.[51]

So far, therefore, no part of his evolution was undesirable and most of it was only in part inevitable. Then came "the first revolution, which led to the establishment of separate and distinct families and introduced a kind of property."[52] With more settled society, sexual love appeared, along with notions of superiority and inferiority. This state of affairs—unlike the two previous ones —had disadvantages. There were quarrels over property and bloodshed about women. But each man was still

---

[46] III, 134–41.
[47] III, 141.
[48] III, 142.
[49] III, 152.
[50] III, 165.
[51] III, 165–67.
[52] III, 167.

judge and avenger in his own affairs, and *pitié*[53] was already developing into morality. Man's physical endurance was less, but all in all, this was the happiest stage in the evolution of mankind.[54]

The disappearance of this golden age, however, is presented to us as being, beyond all doubt, inevitable. Primitive property and primitive skills led to division of labour, metalworking and agriculture, and "from the cultivation of the earth, there followed *necessarily* [my italics] its division."[55] From then on man was subject to the "necessity of movement"[56] toward civil society. "This primitive state can no longer continue to exist, and the human race would perish if it did not change its manner of life."[57] Indeed, when Rousseau considers this stage of evolution, he half revises the opinions just quoted, and wonders if the whole process, instead of only its later stages, may not have been inevitable. "There is much to suggest that then [i.e., with the institution of private property] things had reached a stage at which they could no longer remain as before, for this idea of property, depending on many earlier ideas that can only have come into being one after the other, did not come suddenly into the human mind. Men had to progress in many ways, acquire knowledge and the habit of work, pass this on and increase it from age to age, before reaching this final stage in the state of nature."[58] Let us say, then, that the earlier stages of evolution as Rousseau saw it may have been inevitable, and the later stages certainly were.

From that, the second problem follows. The first stages of evolution were perhaps necessary, certainly desirable,

---

[53] This is usually translated as "symapthy." Littré says: "The feeling that takes hold of one on seeing suffering, and leads one to wish to relieve it." "Sympathy" therefore probably describes too sophisticated a feeling. "Pity" might be better.
[54] III, 170–71.
[55] III, 173.
[56] III, 187.
[57] *Social Contract*, Bk. I, Ch. 6, III, 360.
[58] III, 164.

and in accordance with nature. From Rousseau's "final stage of the state of nature"—Starobinski's "second state of nature"—onward, the remaining evolution was inevitable. God or nature had given to man the faculty of perfectibility and the capacity to develop the instinct of *pitié* into the full range of social virtues.[59] Man was "either sociable by nature, or at least made to become sociable."[60] Moreover, it is impossible to explain the discovery of all the techniques of agriculture without assuming divine assistance,[61] and Rousseau finds the full development of language through human capacity alone so totally inexplicable[62] that one is presumably entitled to assume in him some belief in divine intervention there too. Elsewhere he was more explicit. "It was Providence that made them [men] sociable, almost in spite of themselves."[63] The total picture is therefore the contradictory one of a prolonged evolution that is at one and the same time inevitable, a product of man's own naturally implanted instinct, divinely assisted, and yet wrong in the later stages.

Rousseau had been called upon to answer a charge of inconsistency on a very similar point—treating the natural evolution of natural instincts as unnatural—apropos of a passage in the *First Discourse*, in which he attributes the development of man's knowledge of physics to "empty curiosity."[64] To this—along with many other points— Stanislas of Poland replied in an article that appears to have been sent to Rousseau and later published anonymously in the *Mercure*.[65] "It is the *natural* curiosity of man that stimulates his desire to learn," wrote Stanislas, and this Rousseau dismissed with the simple observation that "he [i.e., man] ought then to try to restrain his curi-

[59] III, 162.
[60] "Profession of Faith of the Savoyard Curate" (in *Emile*).
[61] III, 144.
[62] III, 150.
[63] III, 17.
[64] *Essay on the Origin of Languages*, Ch. 9.
[65] See Note 1, III, 1257–58.

osity, along with all his natural inclinations."[66] That can only mean that nature gave man gifts that he was never intended to use, and that view, too, is in contradiction with the evolutionary belief in a natural man, endowed with gifts that can take him to a second state of nature. There is a possible resolution of this—real or apparent— contradiction. In the *Inégalité*,[67] Rousseau says that the latest stage of the evolution of man (Rousseau's third stage, Starobinski's sixth) is "the ultimate degree of inequality, the final point reached in the end by all the others, until the whole system of government is entirely dissolved by new transformations [*révolutions*] or *brought nearer to legitimacy*" (my italics). This last phrase implies that it may never be too late for man to mend, or in other words, given even more time, to reconcile himself with his true nature, or with divine intention, or with both.

It would be unreasonable, however, to try to resolve one of Rousseau's contradictions on the basis of a single sentence that stands alone in his work as an expression of contingent optimism. The real answer to the accusation of contradiction—and we shall see that it is only a partial answer—is a double one. First, Rousseau made a distinction between "man" and "men." "We have to show," he says in his letter to Christophe de Beaumont, "how, while man is good, men become wicked." The present tense is to be taken seriously, because the "man" of that phrase is "man in general"[68] or "man in the abstract."[69] Rousseau's *l'homme*, indeed, is probably best translated as "mankind," though even that is probably a more concrete concept than what Rousseau had in mind, which was some eternal and unchangeable essence, continuing to exist within changing beings.[70]

---

[66] III, 41.
[67] III, 187.
[68] III, 133.
[69] *Emile*, I, 1.
[70] On the goodness of "man," see also *Last Reply* (to Charles Bordes) (III, 80); "Although man is by nature good, as I believe

The distinction between good "man" and bad men appears to have arisen from the application of faulty logic to a doubtful eighteenth-century transmutation of a theological concept. Early Christian theology transferred the temporal (in both senses) notion of "this age" or "this century" to the spatial notion of "this world," first opposing eternity to time and spiritual to material things, and then substituting "the world" or more literally "the century" for the whole notion of material as opposed to spiritual values. Thus St. James's κόσμος is rendered by St. Jerome in the Vulgate as *saeculum* and by the Authorized Version as "the world."[71] Lewis and Short give several examples of the same usage in the third, fourth, and fifth centuries A.D.[72] This theological figure of speech went into old French as *le siècle*, and was still common in and after Rousseau's day, though its use today would seem a little precious.[73] What it all amounts to is that, by long-standing tradition, "eternity" and

---

and am fortunate enough to feel"; and on the concomitant wickedness of men, see also *Inégalité*, Note 1 (III, 202): "Men are wicked: a sad and uninterrupted experience makes proof of this unnecessary. Yet man is good by nature." There are many other examples of both views.

[71] St. James: ". . . ἀπὸ τοῦ κόσμου"; Vulgate: *"Visitare pupillos et viduas in tribulatione eorum et immaculatum se custodire ab hoc saeculo"*; Authorized Version (James 1: 27): "To visit the fatherless and the widows in their affliction and keep himself unspoiled from the world." It should perhaps be added that for St. Jerome this rendering is exceptional, his normal translation of κόσμος being *mundus*.

[72] The eighth of the Lewis and Short meanings of *saeculum*, with examples from Prudentius (ob. ca. A.D. 410), Pontius Paulinus Nolanus (i.e., St. Paulinus of Nola, ob. A.D. 431) and Tertullian (ob. ca. A.D. 220). For *saecularis* (second meaning), the same dictionary gives "temporal, worldly, profane, heathen," with an example from St. Jerome; for *saecularia*, "worldly matters" (Commodianus, A.D. 245); and for *saeculariter*, "in a worldly manner" (St. Cyprian, A.D. 257). I am indebted for valuable help on this point to a number of people, and in particular to Mr. David Graham of the BBC and Mr. Keith Louis of Reigate Grammar School.

[73] Littré lists it as the ninth of his ten meanings, and gives no example later than Chateaubriand.

"time" are equated, respectively, with "good" and "bad" (or at least with "sometimes bad"). And since it was beyond dispute in the creed of the eighteenth-century philosophers that "man" was good, then it followed that "man" had the characteristics of the eternal or divine, and was unaffected by the category of time. But "men" live within time, with their minds on *le siècle*, and are sinful. So the man–men distinction is a necessary concomitant of the eternity–time distinction. Men evolve under the influence of time into interdependent, and therefore envious and jealous beings, and so become wicked, but "man" is always the same, "naturally good, loving justice and order. . . . The first impulses of human nature are always right."[74] The distinction has a close parallel in the one so often made by General de Gaulle between "France," an immortal goddess in whom past, present, and future coexist, "made for a high and exceptional destiny,"[75] and today's Frenchmen, living within the bounds of time, for whom de Gaulle had scant respect. For the many to whom these ancient distinctions are real, part, at least, of the Rousseau contradiction under discussion here disappears.

So much for the first answer to the accusation of contradiction. The second answer is that for Rousseau, as for most of his contemporaries, time and history were philosophic concepts, in which facts are either unimportant or carefully selected in order to sustain a moral thesis. Paul Hazard has shown[76] that at the time of Rousseau's birth "history was a school of morals," which

---

[74] In the original, the last word of this quotation is *droit,* for which, as an adjective, there is no adequate English translation. It means "upright," "righteous," "virtuous," but without the overtone of smugness that accompanies these English words. On this, see, for instance, Marcel Prélot's discussion (*Histoire des Idées Politiques,* p. 279) of Bodin's well known reference to *un droit gouvernment,* in which Prélot equates *droitment* and *moralement.* On the problem of *droit* as a noun, see below, pp. 388–92. The quotation is from the letter to Christophe de Beaumont.

[75] Charles de Gaulle, *Mémoires de Guerre,* Vol. I, p. 1.

[76] *La Crise de la conscience européenne, 1670–1715,* pp. 31–37.

"teaches the understanding of character"; above all, it is "a spiritual anatomy of human character," in which facts are to be mistrusted. And despite the controversy between pragmatic and dogmatic historians, which had already begun in the period described by Hazard, Rousseau remained in the dogmatic school. That is why he begins the *Inégalité* by "setting aside all facts,"[77] rejecting "the uncertain testimony of history,"[78] and preferring to "examine fact in the light of what is right."[79] But he is not for that reason ignoring truth; he is merely recognising that "truth" and "the facts" are different things in the eyes of the moralist. He is presenting history "as I believe myself to have read it . . . in Nature, which never lies."[80] He "tried to set out the origins and progress of inequality, the establishment and abuse of political societies, as well as can be done by deduction from the nature of man, in the light of reason."[81] Although "the state of nature may never have existed,"[82] the whole story told in the *Second Discourse* is, in Rousseau's mind, the *kind* of thing that *must* have happened. "Such was, *or must have been* [my italics] the origin of society and of laws."[83] There must have been an evolution from non-sociability (or undeveloped socialibility) to socialibility, and that evolution must have coincided with the evolution of bad men out of and alongside good "man." The basis of that conviction was a belief in the goodness of man, which the philosophers of the middle and late eighteenth century adopted as a consequence of their rejection of the Catholic Church with its doctrine of original sin, and which was confirmed in Rousseau's mind by a combination of intuition and introspection.[84] And

---

[77] III, 132.
[78] III, 144.
[79] III, 182.
[80] III, 133.
[81] III, 193.
[82] III, 123.
[83] III, 178.
[84] On this, see the quotation from *Last Reply* in Note 70.

although the purpose of the essay was to explain that view of human nature, both the view itself and its explanation involved an acceptance of the importance of time—the historian's real time as well as the moralist's imaginary time.

That effort at historical and moral explanation, however, is itself divided into two parts. In the later stages of the *Second Discourse*, Rousseau abandons his examination of the evolution of mankind from solitude to a loose form of social organization, and moves on to consider the evolution of society. That second theme is taken up again in the *Social Contract*. In parts of that work (some of which, as we know, was written at about the time of or soon after the publication of the *Second Discourse*), Rousseau, in the words of M. Derathé,[85] "speaks of the social contract as if it had really existed." At the points at which he falls into that error, which, as we shall see, is an error of presentation rather than of reasoning, he departs still farther from his proclaimed purpose;[86] he lays down prescriptions about actual institutions and forms of government. In those passages, he returns to the consideration of the evolution of society and shows himself to be, in a very real sense, even more pessimistic than he had been in the *Second Discourse*.

For although, in that work, he had been presenting only "hypothetical and conditional arguments, better suited to make clear the nature of things than to show their true origin,"[87] it was, as we have just seen, the kind of history that was "real"—the only real history for the moralist, the history of what must have happened to man's *moral* self, even if there were no records of it, or even if what records there were contradicted him, and it was in looking at that "real" past that he saw change as both inevitable and regrettable. In the *Contract*, on the other hand, his prescriptions applied only to an

---

[85] Introduction to the *Social Contract*, III, lxxxvi.
[86] See below, p. 392.
[87] III, 133.

imaginary society, as perfect as any human society could be, and even there, as he looked into the future, he saw only disaster in the end.

That point needs no labouring. The argument of Chapters 10 to 14 of Book III of the *Social Contract* is well known. The body politic has within it an "inherent vice" which leaves it with the choice only between two methods of self-destruction: it can degenerate via aristocracy into monarchy, or it can collapse altogether through the usurpation of the authority of the sovereign people, either by the prince or by individual members of the government. That is the "natural and inevitable tendency even of the best constituted Governments." For "the body politic, like the human body, bears within itself the seeds of its own destruction." A "more robust" body politic can preserve the State from the alternative evils of tyranny and anarchy for a little longer than a weaker one, by having frequent meetings of the sovereign assembly of the whole people, since in their presence all other authority becomes null and void. But precisely for that reason, all Governments will do their best to prevent these meetings, and sooner or later all will succeed.

Not even the persuasiveness of M. Derathé[88] can wholly reconcile that persistent pessimism about past, present, and future with Rousseau's optimism about the goodness of eternal "man." Again the parallel with de Gaulle's France comes to mind. If at no point in recorded history has the behaviour of Frenchmen corresponded with de Gaulle's "France"; if at no point in the known past, the visible present and the hoped-for future, are "man" and men the same, then what can de Gaulle's "France" and Rousseau's "man" be but products of their own imaginations? In Rousseau's case, indeed, one suspects a defect in his intellectual equipment of which he was—or became—aware. "He confesses," says Cobban[89]

---

[88] III, xcii–xciii.
[89] *Rousseau and the Modern State*, second ed. p. 18. The allusion is probably to the fragment (I, 1129) in which Rousseau says: "I

"that though he can apprehend individual truths clearly, he cannot compare them or arrange them with method." He was, as Cobban points out,[90] "not a system-maker," and indeed he explains in the first *Letter from the Mountains*[91] how "illogicalities of detail can escape the eye of an author with too much to say, overwhelmed by the many ideas his subject suggests to him, distracted from some by others, and only just able to put together in his mind all the elements of an immense plan."

Pessimism about evolution, on the other hand, is not inconsistent with the other aspect of Rousseau's attitude to time, discussed in the first part of this essay, his traditionalism. Both of his pictures of human evolution represent decline, as he sees it, over very long periods of time. His traditionalism applies to the lifetime of individuals and of their more immediate ancestors. The pessimism is a part of his philosophy, the traditionalism an attitude to one of the immediate problems of current politics. Traditionalism probably also belongs only to civil society in its latest stage, for there had been a point in the course of the evolution of civil society itself, at which, instead of perpetually patching up an unplanned and empirically arising political order, "men ought to have begun by clearing the whole area and throwing out all the old materials . . . in order then to build a good Edifice."[92] In other words, revolution was once right, but when it missed its moment, prudence in the immediate became desirable, and ultimate decay inevitable.

Rousseau's third attitude to time is to be found in the *Social Contract,* where consideration of it helps to throw light on the problem of the main purpose of that book. Before it can be discussed, therefore, it is necessary to

---

find pleasure in meditating, seeking ideas, inventing; what I dislike is putting things in order, and the proof that I have less logic than wit is that it is always the transitions that cost me the biggest effort."
[90] Ibid., p. 20.
[91] III, 708.
[92] III, 180.

remind readers of the nature of that problem. We know from Rousseau himself that the chapters which became the *Social Contract* originally formed part of an unfinished book on political institutions which Rousseau abandoned because, as he says in the preliminary note, it had been "undertaken without proper consideration of my own ability" or, as he said in a letter to Moultou,[93] because it was "beyond my capacity." We know also, from Derathé,[94] that when he decided to publish part of the work, he changed the title twice and the sub-title three times, so that the sub-title finally chosen may be regarded as representing Rousseau's considered and definitive summary of his subject. It was a treatise on "les principes du droit politique," an expression inevitably but inadequately translated into English as "principles of political right."

Professors Cobban and Burns have corrected the translations of "le droit" and other terms in two of the English language versions of the *Social Contract*,[95] but in a note in which they did not attempt to discuss all the relevant meanings of that word. Its real meaning is, however, important in the present context, and something more must be said about it. Littré gives nine meanings of "droit" as a substantive, and of these it can fairly be said that no fewer than six concern us here. In their shortest versions they are as follows:

1. What is right; what is founded on uprightness of heart and mind.
2. What is in conformity with law.
3. The recognised ability, *natural or legal* [my italics], to perform or to avoid performing a particular act.
4. What confers influence or moral authority.
5. The totality of rules governing the conduct of man in society.

---

[93] Quoted in Note 2, III, 1431.
[94] *Jean Jacques Rousseau et la science politique de son temps*, p. 382.
[95] "Rousseau's *Du Contrat Social*: Some Problems of Translation," in *Political Studies* X, ii (1962), pp. 203–7.

6. The science or knowledge of laws.

German writers or translators dealing with this word
and its related ideas face a problem no more difficult
than that faced by their French counterparts, because
"le droit" is accurately translated by "das Recht," but
English and American writers who have not become accustomed to thinking in French do face a real problem
here. French meanings, as the Littré definitions show,
range from the subjective and imprecise notion of "what
is right" to the much more precise juridical notion of
"what the law allows," with jurisprudential and socio-
political notions intermingled as well. Like every French
writer in these fields who does not from time to time
turn aside to become conscious of these different meanings and separate one from another, Rousseau uses the
word with the whole range of the Littré meanings, sometimes separately, sometimes in varying combinations,
and sometimes, as we shall see in a moment, with added
refinements or extensions of his own. He also complicates
the problem still further by adding two additional limiting qualifications to his sub-title. He is discussing the
principles of the *political* aspects of his legal-cum-moral
concept. It is evident, therefore, that any consideration of
the book that can throw further light on the nature of
his intentions is worth undertaking.

Professor Derathé has provided his compatriots with
an authoritative version of the meaning of "*le droit politique.*" It is, he says, what modern lawyers call "the general principles of public law," or "general public law,"
and he adds that its subject matter is precisely the questions covered in the *Social Contract*: origin of the State;
nature, extent, and basis of civil power; forms of government, and relations between Church and State.[96] That
explanation, no doubt, is of help to all those who are
familiar with the concepts and methods used in the teaching of public law in French universities, but it leaves the

---

[96] *Rousseau et la science politique,* pp. 393–97.

rest of us only a little wiser. What is surely clear, however, is that Rousseau intended to tell his readers that what he was discussing was not a juridical concept, but the *moral* principles of "general public law." Other passages confirm that view of his intentions. In Book V of *Emile*, in which he summarizes the *Social Contract*, he speaks of "the true principles of *le droit politique*,"[97]—"true," undoubtedly, as opposed to what was normally taught. At the beginning of that Book he had said that "*le droit politique* is still to be born, and we may presume that it never will be born." It is "what ought to be"[98] and to make the point even clearer, he says of Montesquieu, the founder of the study of *le droit politique* as Derathé defines it, that "he was careful not to treat of *le droit politique;* he was content to consider the positive law of established governments; and nothing in the world is more different than these two studies."[98] This was written in or just before 1761, when Rousseau must have been preparing the *Contract* for the press. Six years later, in his Letter to the Marquis de Mirabeau, in which he acknowledged the copy of Mercier de la Rivière's *Ordre naturel et essentiel des sociétés politiques* that the Marquis had sent to him, he is still of the same opinion: "It seems to me that the evidence can be found in natural and political laws only if they are considered *in the abstract* [my italics]. . . . For the science of government is a science only of assemblage, applications and exceptions."[99] All that suggests that, if Rousseau's subject headings were the same as those of French teachers of "the general principles of public law," as Derathé believes, then his notion of their content was very different from theirs.

If at the points quoted Rousseau made this clear, at others his method of presentation helped to conceal his intention. For he did discuss political institutions in the

<hr>

[97] Extract reproduced in Vaughan, *Political Writings of Rousseau*, II, p. 158.
[98] Ibid., p. 147.
[99] Ibid., p. 159.

Social Contract, especially in Books III and IV, perhaps
because of his belief that "institutions make customs and
patterns of social behaviour,"[100] or perhaps simply because his pruning of that part of his cast-off work was
inadequate. He tends also to wander along sidetracks
and then return, without adequate signposting, to his
main themes. It may be, indeed, that these weaknesses
were in his mind when he wrote in the preliminary note
that the parts chosen for publication were "the least unworthy of being offered to the public." The expression
"the least unworthy" is striking and probably significant,
because it is so untypical of Rousseau. Modesty was not
one of his vices, and litotes was so far from being his
favourite figure of speech that it is difficult to remember
a single self-evident instance of it in the whole of his
works. So we may presume that he meant what he said.
What, then, dissatisfied him? The mixture of principles
and institutions? His own pessimism? The often discussed "contradictions"? Some lack of clarity in his presentation of the principles he was trying to elucidate?
We do not know, and it is unlikely that we ever shall,
but it is foolish to embark on any consideration of the
Social Contract without remembering that there were
doubts about it in Rousseau's normally over-confident
mind.

It is not surprising, in view of all the above, that specialists have held conflicting views as to what Rousseau
was trying to say. Some have thought that the *Social
Contract* described the society that Rousseau saw as resulting from a literal social contract that had actually
been made. Others, of whom Wright is perhaps the most
distinguished, have seen it as a kind of Utopia, an ideal
society which men ought to try to create. "It seeks," says
Wright, "to build a perfect state out of the very nature of
the men composing it."[101] And again, "The natural man

---

[100] See above, p. 370.
[101] *The Meaning of Rousseau*, p. 32. Rousseau had in fact himself denied, in the sixth *Letter from the Mountains*, (III, 810), that

is still his [i.e., Rousseau's] ideal, but in the full development which can come only in the right society. The *Social Contract* is the picture of such a society. In its way it is therefore a Utopia."[102]

There are many ways of showing that both these ways of looking at the *Social Contract* are mistaken, and there is no need to rehearse them here. The most convincing is probably that of Bertrand de Jouvenel, in his closely reasoned and fully documented argument about Rousseau's purpose in the *Social Contract*, in the "Essay on the Politics of Rousseau," which prefaces his own edition of that book.[103] "Rousseau," says M. de Jouvenel, "poured his *moral* conceptions of the general will into a mould strongly built by Hobbes to contain a *juridical* notion." And he goes on: "If it has been so agreed, the 'will of all' can create obligations for everybody. That is one thing. But to say that such a decision is *good* makes it a quite different thing. If men have made a contract of society, if they have promised to obey one man or several, or the majority, then obey they must. But the fact that a decision so made must be obeyed in no way implies that it is 'always right.'"[104] The morality of a decision is no part of a lawyer's business; when he has made obedience legitimate, his task is finished. Not that of Rousseau, who is a moralist. He knows and says emphatically that the "will of all" is not necessarily good. . . . In opposition to that will of all, which is of no more than juridical value, he sets the general will, which "is always upright and tends always to the public good. . . .

---

the *Contract* was a Utopia. "If I had merely constructed a System [of government] . . . they [his critics] would have been content to class *The Social Contract* along with Plato's *Republic*, the *Utopia*, and the *Sevarambians* in the category of chimeras." "System-making" in its French form is a very common eighteenth- and nineteenth-century synonym for Utopianism. Denis Vairasse's *Histoire des Sévarambes* (1675–77) was the earliest and best known French-language Utopia, owing a great deal to Sir Thomas More.
[102] Op. cit., p. 70.
[103] Geneva, 1947. The quotations are from pp. 106, 109, 110, 112.
[104] See Note 74 above.

To ask by what constitutional rules the general will is discovered is to ask the wrong question. If the will of all is a political fact, the general will is a moral phenomenon. . . . It is when men listen to that same voice of reason that teaches them all the same natural law that, inevitably, they desire together and that their desire is general."[105]

That explanation of the nature of the general will is deduced from and confirmed by many passages in Rousseau's works, of which the most significant is the introductory sentence to Book IV, which runs as follows: "*To the extent that*[106] a number of men gathered together see themselves *as a single body,* they have only one desire [will],[107] which concerns their self-preservation *as a body,* and their *general* well-being." The italics are mine (though almost every word requires emphasis on its full meaning), and the limiting words or expressions, so often repeated in the *Social Contract* and so often overlooked by commentators, are so clear that one writer has described the whole argument as tauto-

---

[105] "Desire" here translates "*volonté*." Much Anglo-Saxon misunderstanding of Rousseau arises from the habit of all translators of rendering *volonté* as "will," which in modern English almost invariably has the sense of "determination" or "resolve." It probably does at some points have that sense in Rousseau (though Littré does not include it among the six meanings he gives for *volonté*), but in most of the passages in which Rousseau uses the term, *la volonté générale* means no more than "what everybody wants." Rousseau's own glosses, however, make it clear, as we shall see in a moment, that the expression has that meaning only when the member of a society as Rousseau sees it is engaged in the strictly defined processes of lawmaking, and only if he has learned to ask himself in the midst of those processes what he wants, not for himself as a solitary individual, but for himself as a member of society. It is, in other words, "what everybody wants, when everybody is asking himself only what is ethically right for the whole society."
[106] "*Tant que*" is literally "so long as" and is often so translated. But it has long been used to mean also "in so far as," "up to the point that," and even "in such a way that" (Littré, 15, 16, 17), as well as, more loosely, simply "if." Its meaning here can only be quantitative, not temporal.
[107] See Note 105.

logical. It can indeed be rephrased as "if all men are thinking and feeling as one man, they will decide and act as one man." But that is not a tautology, because the protasis is a moral precondition and the apodosis a political deduction. A generalized moral attitude, it says, produces determinable political consequences. Professor Cranston puts the same idea in a different way. He says, "Rousseau is not offering a plan for reform, nor is he writing the kind of history and sociology that he provides in the *Discours sur l'Inégalité.* . . . In the *Social Contract* Rousseau is dealing, in the hypothetical mood, with abstract problems which seem to him to emerge from philosophical reflections on the actual nature of man and the possible nature of laws and government."[108] That is true, but it does not suffice to explain the whole of the *form* of the *Social Contract,* which is an attempt to present an abstract thesis in a manner comprehensible to minds accustomed only to image and narrative.

Professor Oakeshott has pointed out how Hobbes—one of Rousseau's mentors—did exactly that. "The *Leviathan,*" he says, "is a myth, the transposition of an abstract argument into the world of imagination."[109] Professor Derathé has shown that Rousseau was condemned to the image-and-narrative technique of exposition by his absorption of the doctrines and techniques of presentation of the whole natural-law school of juridico-political philosophers, including their addiction to going back to a fictitious "state of nature" and inventing a subsequent development of society as a method of explaining what in fact was a wholly abstract approach to a theory of society with its obligations and rights.

Perhaps because Rousseau came at the tail end of the natural-law epoch, his choice of the natural-law method of exposition led him into a wholly misleading use of the notion of time. The *Social Contract* has many allu-

---

[108] *The Social Contract,* Introduction, p. 27 of the Penguin Classics edition, 1968.
[109] Introduction to *Leviathan,* (Blackwell, 1957), p. xviii.

sions to what at first sight looks like a time sequence. "In
the evolution of man," he says, "there comes a point of
time when the obstacles to man's self-preservation in the
state of nature are greater than the strength that any
individual can bring to bear to maintain himself in that
state."[110] "At that stage, scattered individuals decide to
form themselves into a people."[111] What they then decide to make is the first and only social contract, and
their decision must be unanimous. Moreover, the terms
of the contract are, in the modern jargon, not negotiable:
"the clauses of the contract are to such an extent determined by the nature of the act that the smallest modification would make them null and void."[112] When the contract has been made, "we have given existence and life
to the social body."[113] "But that fact decides nothing as
to what the body shall do in order to preserve itself."[114]
So there have to be laws, and "the people subject to
laws must also be their author; only those who have
formed a society have the right to determine the conditions in which it shall function."[115]

It is important to note that, despite some similarities
of language, the time schedule of this part of the *Social
Contract* is vitally different from that of the *Inégalité*,
in that stages two to four[116] of the evolutionary sequence
of the earlier work are now omitted. In the *Inégalité*, the
pressure of natural forces had begun to be felt by man,
just as it is in the *Social Contract*, but while man was still
in the stage of primitive solitude, and he had then
moved by insensible stages through many centuries towards civil society. What in the *Inégalité* had been an
imagined but credible reconstruction of an evolutionary
process becomes in the *Social Contract* a conscious de-

---

[110] III, 360.
[111] III, 359.
[112] III, 360.
[113] III, 378.
[114] III, 378.
[115] III, 380.
[116] See above, Note 45.

cision by an organized gathering of unorganized individuals. It is "a mutual agreement between private citizens and the public. . . ."[117] But in the real world of time this is nonsense, because the purpose of the agreement is precisely to create something that could be called "the public." Moreover, these "private citizens" accept a unanimity rule at a stage when one of their principal characteristics is that they have no rules, and arrive by some unexplained process at the precise terms of the only contract that can prove legitimate and survive.

Nor do the paradoxes stop there. Rousseau continues to present his argument in terms of a time sequence, but the further he develops it, the more the paradoxes accumulate and the less credible the temporal structure of the whole argument becomes. In the same paragraph in which he has laid down that a people must be the author of its own laws, he also explains that the judgement of a people is not always enlightened enough to undertake that task. "Hence the necessity of a lawgiver."[118] And the lawgiver has to be the kind of paragon of disinterested wisdom and foresight that appears only at rare intervals in history, if indeed he ever appears at all, for "Gods would be needed to give laws to men."[119] So the newly constituted people, urgently in need of laws, has to wait for the appearance of a Moses, a Numa, a Lycurgus, or a Calvin, and while it waits, this people that is still without law or organization and is too lacking in judgement to be able to make any must nevertheless show enough judgement to detect impostors, of whom many will present themselves, and who can be seen to be impostors only when the test of time has revealed the impermanence of the institutions they create. It must also use its untrustworthy judgement to avoid waiting too long, because "people, like men, are teachable only in their youth and become incorrigible as they get

---

[117] *Political Writings*, (ed. Vaughan), II, 150.
[118] III, 380.
[119] III, 381.

older."[120] Neither, however, must it start too soon, for "with Nations as with men, there is an age of maturity that must be awaited before they can be given laws."[121] It must wait, too, for a period of peace,[122] and when the right moment comes, must aim at the optimum sizes of population and territory.[123] These ideas are presented in the sequence given above, though the reader has to trim away some of the surrounding material to make that clear. The mere impossibility of such a sequence makes clearer what we have already discovered by looking at some of Rousseau's positive assertions—namely, that what we are faced with is neither real history nor hypothetical history, but a pseudo-historical narrative in which time has no more reality than in a dream or a Virginia Woolf novel.

There are two possible explanations of Rousseau's use of the pseudo-historical type of narrative that was already becoming old-fashioned, in an argument in which the notion of time had no place and has indeed led to much confusion of thought. The first concerns the circumstances in which the *Social Contract* was written. We know that there was an earlier version, now called the Geneva manuscript, written, in part at least, soon after the *Second Discourse*, and into which something of the evolutionary notions of the *Discourse* were transposed. It also seems that in the first version, Rousseau was drawing normative conclusions from the historical presentation of his arguments. In Chapter 5 (the earliest part of the work, according to M. Derathé),[124] he says that, although all societies have probably been formed in different ways, "I am giving in this work only one method for the formation of political societies."[125] And in Chapter 2 he says, "Let us, if it can be done, find new

---

[120] III, 385.
[121] III, 386.
[122] III, 390.
[123] III, 386–88.
[124] III, 1416.
[125] III, 297.

associations to correct the error of general association."[126]
Both of these phrases, indicative of a prescriptive intention, were dropped from the final version, but much
of the rest was copied, modified, transposed, and in various other ways incorporated in the final version, and it
may be that the revision was not extensive enough to
convey Rousseau's new and more limited intention.

More limited, but not wholly unchanged. In the first
version he had given his readers the categoric assurance
that he was "seeking morality [*le droit*] and reason and
not arguing about facts."[127] So he was also in the second
version, and his treatment of the time factor shows that
time and history were among the facts he was excluding
with much greater determination than before. Equally,
if one looks again at Chapters 3 to 10 of Book II of the
second version, from which the quotations on pages 391–
94 are taken, it is clear that he was not presenting a
formula for the creation of a Utopia, because, again, the
conditions he lays down are contradictory and unrealisa-
ble. The account given in these chapters could much
more accurately be called a parable, in which, whatever
he may have attempted in the later chapters, Rousseau
has tried to teach his readers a manner of looking at society which, if it were accepted by all the members of a
society, would completely reconcile social order and individual liberty. Or to put it slightly differently, he is
saying that if one could imagine a society that had been
developed by some such stages as those he describes, one
would be better able to understand the individual attitudes required in every member of any society to reconcile order and freedom.

Getting rid of the confusions introduced by Rousseau
into the *Social Contract* by his use of the time factor does
more, however, than sustain what is by now a widely
accepted view of his primarily moral purpose in that
book. It also helps to get rid of two false views of Rous-

---

[126] III, 288.
[127] III, 297.

seau, namely, that he was an unpractical reformer of constitutions and political systems, and that he was an exponent of despotism—though it does not, of course, imply a denial of his influence on the many would-be disciples who have seen him in one or the other of those roles. To state, as a contribution to political philosophy, that every individual has a personal share of a limited number of collective interests, that that share is just as much a part of his individual interest as are those interests that he does not share with others, and that we should all be wiser if we took cognisance of those facts, is not to preach totalitarianism or any other political doctrine or to propose the creation of any particular set of political institutions. One hopes that this somewhat new approach to the problem may have contributed something to that necessary clarification.

THE STRUCTURE OF ROUSSEAU'S
POLITICAL THOUGHT

ROGER D. MASTERS

Rousseau's *Social Contract* is one of the most frequently read works in the tradition of Western political thought. It is also probably one of the most frequently misunderstood. Because it is tempting to seek contemporary applications of Rousseau's theory, one is often told that the *Social Contract* either establishes the principles of modern liberal democracy or justifies a totalitarian state.[1] How can such diametrically opposed meanings be found in a single book?

These conflicting interpretations, which have given rise to the charge that Rousseau was inconsistent (if not mentally unbalanced), must be placed in proper perspective. Why is it that Rousseau's eighteenth-century teaching is so often applied to the political experiences of the twentieth? Such an approach to a political philosopher is not, after all, either inevitable or even typical. Who tries to apply the thought of Montesquieu, Aristotle, or Kant to contemporary politics?

It is hardly an accident, as we shall see, that Rousseau's theory is interpreted in terms of its relevance to concrete political issues. But to understand the reasons for this, the *Social Contract* must be situated in the con-

---

An earlier French version of this article appeared under the title "'Principes' et 'Maximes' dans la Pensée Politique de Rousseau," in *The Australian Journal of French Studies,* II (September–December 1965), pp. 313–34. © Roger Masters and *The Australian Journal of French Studies.* Permission to translate and republish is gratefully acknowledged.
[1] E.g., J. L. Talmon, *The Origins of Totalitarian Democracy* (New York: 1960), Ch. 3; Carl J. Friedrich, "Law and Dictatorship in the *Contrat Social,*" *Rousseau et la Philosophie Politique* (Paris: 1965), pp. 77–97; Lester G. Crocker, "Rousseau et la Voie du Totalitarisme," *ibid.,* pp. 99–136.

text of Rousseau's other writings and read with extraordinary care. Without an analysis of the structure of Rousseau's thought, his substantive position is bound to be misinterpreted.

1. The Dual Objectives of Rousseau's Political Theory

The first paradox of the *Social Contract* is that to analyze it carefully one must have read the *Discourse on the Origin and Foundations of Inequality among Men* (the so-called *Second Discourse*). This necessity is implied in the *Social Contract* itself:

> I assume that men have reached the point where obstacles to their self-preservation in the state of nature prevail by their resistance over the forces each individual can use to maintain himself in that state.[2]

This presumed evolution of the human species, leading to the formation of political society, is described in detail in the *Second Discourse,* whereas it is taken for granted in the *Social Contract;* hence study of Rousseau's political principles in the latter work presupposes knowledge of the former one.[3]

In the *Second Discourse,* Rousseau analyzes human nature in a way that could be called scientific, for he compares his "reasonings" to those used by "physicists" in order to discover "the nature of things."[4] He assumes

---

[2] *Social Contract,* I, vi (*Oeuvres Complètes,* Edition de la Pléiade, III, 360). All translations of the *First Version of the Social Contract* and the *Social Contract* itself are from a forthcoming critical edition, translated by Judith R. Masters and edited by Hilail Gilden. Permission to reproduce is gratefully acknowledged.

[3] This procedure is all the more fitting because Rousseau himself claimed that his principles were "developed completely" for the first time in his *Second Discourse,* a work he elsewhere called one of his three "principal writings." *Confessions,* VIII (Pléiade, I, 388); Letter to Malesherbes, 12 January 1762 (Pléiade, I, 1135–36). Cf. *Rousseau Juge de Jean Jacques,* Dialogue III (Pléiade, I, 933–35).

[4] *Second Discourse,* Introduction, in Rousseau, *The First and Second Discourses,* trans. Judith R. and Roger D. Masters (New York:

that human nature can only be understood in terms of
its animal origins; since it is physically possible for man
to be an isolated animal, society is not natural for the
individual. As a result, Rousseau can speak of the "state
of nature" as an historical condition or "fact given as
real," antecedent to the civil state.[5]

On this basis, Rousseau can criticize all previous political theories:

> The philosophers who have examined the foundations
> of society have all felt the necessity of going back to
> the state of nature, but none of them has reached it.[6]

This famous sentence is an exaggeration, since Rousseau
knew perfectly well that some philosophers rejected the
concept of a state of nature.[7] But it emphasizes the importance he attached to placing the human species in
the "animal system." Indeed, in Rousseau's notes to the
Second Discourse, he raises the question of man's physi-

1964), p. 103. All translations of *The First and Second Discourses*
are from this edition.

[5] Ibid., Part I (p. 141); Letter to Philopolis (Pléiade, III, 232).
Cf. Note 12 below.

[6] *Second Discourse*, Introduction (p. 102).

[7] For example, the epigraph of the *Second Discourse* is taken from
Aristotle's proof that slavery is natural (*Politics* I. 1254a), perhaps
as a means of indicating that Rousseau will indirectly criticize Aristotle for having *failed* to go back to the state of nature. Rousseau
imagines that he is presenting his *Discourse* at the Lyceum in
Athens—i.e., at Aristotle's school—but with Plato and Xenocrates
(a head of Plato's Academy) as judges (*Second Discourse*, Introduction [p. 103]). Plato, unlike Aristotle, had described a sort of
state of nature (without giving it this title)—namely, the primitive
society that Glaucon calls the "city of pigs" (*Republic* II. 372d).
In contrast, Aristotle begins from the proposition that man is by
nature a "political animal," not merely a social one (*Politics* I.
1253a). The presumption that Plato will be the judge in Aristotle's
Lyceum implies that a philosophy that does not begin by considering man as a sort of uncivilized animal should not receive serious
attention. Cf. the explicit criticism of Aristotle's conception of natural slavery in the *Social Contract*, I, ii (Pléiade, III, 353) with
Second Discourse, Part II (p. 168).

cal evolution as a scientific problem to be studied by
comparisons with other species.[8]

If natural man was originally an animal who lived in
isolation according to mechanical impulsions, if not instincts, the very existence of society must be explained.
And if the power of one man over another does not have
a natural source, it is no longer possible to find the origins
of human justice in a natural law. All the traditions concerning a natural law discovered by reason are therefore
useless and without foundation, for man is distinguished
from beasts not by his capacity to reason, but by his perfectibility or his freedom.[9]

In seeking those physical or material causes that forced
men to leave the state of nature and form civil society,
Rousseau accepts what has been called the "modern
natural right" doctrine. According to this position, developed principally by Hobbes, Spinoza, and Locke,
"political right" is derived from each man's natural right
to self-preservation. Since the individual is the only judge
of this right to self-preservation before the founding of
civil society, the source of justice is found in a condition
in which there is neither justice nor established law, but
only force.[10]

---

[8] See *Second Discourse*, above all, Notes *c, d, e, g, h, j,* and *l*
(pp. 183–88, 191–92, 203–20). On the importance of these notes,
compare the "Notice on the Notes"—in which Rousseau says that
they need only be considered during the second reading of his
Discourse (ibid., p. 98)—with *Rousseau Juge de Jean Jacques*, Dialogue III (Pléiade, I, 932): it is impossible to understand Rousseau's theoretical "system" without this "second reading."

[9] *Second Discourse*, Preface (pp. 94–96); Part I (pp. 113–15). Although in Part I of the *Discourse* Rousseau replaces freedom by
perfectibility as the "specific quality" that distinguishes man from
other animals, he does so only because of the possible objections to
"freedom" as a "metaphysical" idea; speaking in his own name in
Part II, Rousseau asserts that freedom is one of the "essential gifts
of nature," which humans "receive from nature by being men."
(Ibid., p. 168; cf. *Social Contract*, I, iv [Pléiade, III, 356].) On the
rejection of natural law as the foundation of human justice, see
Contrat Social, Première Version, I, ii (Pléiade, III, 283–88).

[10] On the natural right teaching of Hobbes, Locke, and Rousseau,
see Leo Strauss, *Natural Right and History* (Chicago: 1953), Ch.
5, and Robert Derathé's extensive study of the relationship between

But while adopting Hobbes' criticism of natural law doctrines that would establish binding duties of sociability outside of civil society, Rousseau goes beyond Hobbes. According to the *Second Discourse*, Hobbes made two mistakes. First, he imagines that man in the state of nature had faculties (reason and foresight) and passions (*amour-propre* or egoism and fear of violent death) that are neither physically nor naturally necessary; second, Hobbes denies that natural man is good, because he fails to recognize that pity is a natural sentiment.[11] In short, Hobbes was not sufficiently scientific because he did not attempt to discover the historical epoch in which the human species lived among other animals in a true state of nature.[12]

Rousseau and the "school of natural right and the *droit des gens*" in *J.-J. Rousseau et la Science Politique de Son Temps* (Paris: 1950). Derathé fails to stress adequately Rousseau's own distinction between "our jurists" and moralists—who are criticized because they think that natural law is fully operative in the state of nature —and Hobbes or the other philosophers who denied that natural laws discovered by reason effectively bind individuals in the absence of society. Cf. *Second Discourse*, Preface (pp. 94–96), with Part I (p. 129): "Hobbes saw very clearly the defect of all modern definitions of natural right." On the difference between Hobbes' view of natural right and law, and that of other jurists in the seventeenth and eighteenth centuries, see also A. P. d'Entrèves, *Natural Law* (London: 1951), p. 60.

[11] *Second Discourse*, Preface (pp. 95–96); Part I (pp. 128–32); Note O (pp. 221–22).

[12] It is often not recognized that Hobbes' state of nature is different from Rousseau's. For Hobbes, this state was never the condition of the entire species ("I believe it was never generally so over all the world"); the true model of the Hobbesian state of nature is the moment when a civil war destroys the bonds of a previously existing political society. *Leviathan*, I, xiii, ed. Oakeshott (Oxford: 1960), p. 83. Cf. Sheldon Wolin, *Politics and Vision* (Boston: 1960), pp. 262–65. Although it was not original for Rousseau to have considered the state of nature as having existed, to my knowledge he was the first philosopher to treat it as an historical epoch that must be studied by means of comparative anatomy, biology, and modern anthropology. In this sense, Rousseau's criticism of Hobbes is based more on historical and scientific grounds than on the juristic and psychological considerations emphasized by Derathé (op. cit., pp. 131–41).

Rousseau's analysis of the basic animal impulsions in primitive man adds pity to the love of oneself or desire for self-preservation, which alone had been the basis of the natural right theories of Hobbes, Spinoza, and Locke. This addition is important because pity, viewed as an animal impulsion that "puts us in the position of him who suffers," is a non-rational substitute for the traditional concept of man's natural sociability as a rational being. At the same time, however, pity serves as a foundation of the conscience and those natural sentiments that Rousseau never ceased to defend against materialist philosophies.

In the name of nature, Rousseau is simultaneously opposed to traditional natural law doctrines (according to which all men can know and fulfill their duties to God and men, even outside of civil society) and to the theories of philosophers like Hobbes, who attacked this tradition on materialistic or atheistic grounds. Rousseau's thought thus has a double objective that is implicit in the duality of man's primitive impulsions in the state of nature. On one hand, his thesis of man's "natural goodness" is a critique of seventeenth- and eighteenth-century theories that substituted private self-interest for virtue as the foundation of society and morality; on the other hand, Rousseau's acceptance of this same modern philosophy, while limited, permits him to reject the traditional idea of rational virtues and moral obligations. In the state of nature, desires are limited and pity is not stifled by artificial passions; since "goodness" merely requires the absence of an intention to harm others, man is naturally good. In contrast, virtue is not natural; virtue requires the mastery of natural impulsions and the intention to act well toward others, and hence presupposes that men have learned to think within society.[13] Nature and society are radically opposed. The best civil society does not rest on natural impulsions, but requires a hu-

---

[13] On the distinction between "natural goodness" and "virtue" acquired "through reason," see *Second Discourse*, Part I (p. 133); *Emile*, II (Paris: Garnier, 1961, p. 99); V (pp. 567–69, 605).

man creation that "denatures" these animal impulses.[14]

Although incomplete, this summary suggests why Rousseau called himself a "man of paradoxes."[15] He rejects *both* the tradition of a rational morality founded on natural sociability, *and* the Hobbesian alternative of a materialist philosophy based on the calculation of private interest (in a civil society devoted to the satisfaction of individual desires). On the basis of modern conceptions of man as an animal who is neither social nor political, Rousseau arrives at a political solution like that of classical philosophers, who assumed that man is a political and social animal. While substituting the modern principle of freedom for the classical principle of order, Rousseau attempts to return to the concept of the classical *polis* by means of a modern natural science.

2. The Definition of "Political Right"

The above considerations permit a better understanding of Rousseau's most famous political work. He chose the title *On the Social Contract* because it shows the conventional or unnatural character of all civil society.[16]

---

[14] Ibid., I (pp. 9–10). It is not possible here to consider what could be called Rousseau's "romantic" solution for some individuals—i.e., the life of the *"promeneur solitaire"* or solitary dreamer who is good (because he merely follows his natural impulses) without being virtuous (because he has withdrawn from society). But it is important to note that Rousseau insists that there will be men who can legitimately reject the duties of any society, even the best, in the name of natural freedom. *Second Discourse*, Note *i* (pp. 201–2); *Emile*, II (Garnier ed., p. 99n); V (pp. 604–5); *Rêveries d'un Promeneur Solitaire*, I (Pléiade, I, 999–1001); II (1002–4); VII (1061–63); VIII (1075, 1081–84); and especially V (1040–49).

[15] *Emile*, II (Garnier ed., p. 82).

[16] I say "chose" because Rousseau at first considered the title "De la Société Civile" ("On Civil Society"), but then rejected this Lockean formula, which does not directly reflect the conventional status of society. See C. E. Vaughan, *The Political Writings of Rousseau*, 2 vols. (Cambridge: 1915), I, 22, n. 3. Note that the exact title of Rousseau's work is *Du Contrat Social*—i.e., technically "On" or "Concerning" the Social Contract, not merely *The Social Contract*.

The social order is a sacred right which serves as a basis for all the others. However, this right does not come from nature; it is therefore based on conventions. The problem is to know what these conventions are.[17]

Thus Rousseau insists, from the very outset, on the fact that society can only be understood on the basis of a philosophy, like that of Hobbes, according to which justice is not natural.

But speaking of a *Social Contract,* Rousseau is seeking a rational rule of right, not an historic agreement like the Mayflower Compact; the subtitle of the work, "Principles of Political Right," is a formula that recalls the traditional writings of jurists for whom the foundation of justice is a natural law discovered by reason.[18] Hence the dual orientation of Rousseau's political thought, stressed above, can even be found in the title of his book.

Since there is no law of justice that man is obliged to obey in the state of nature, the foundation of civil society precedes justice; the establishment of the laws was not itself a legal act.[19] In order to indicate that a just society can originate in an action lacking right and justice, Rousseau adds an epigraph from Virgil's *Aeneid:*

> *Foederis aequas*
> *Dicamus leges.*[20]

---

[17] *Social Contract,* I, i (Pléiade, III, 352).

[18] See, for example, Jean-Jacques Burlamaqui, *Principes du Droit Naturel* (Geneva: 1748) and *Principes du Droit Politique* (Geneva: 1751). See, incidentally, the ironic reference to Burlamaqui as one of those natural law theorists whose work is later contrasted to Hobbes; *Second Discourse,* Preface (p. 93) and Note 10 above. On the use of the term "Political Right" in the eighteenth century, see Derathé, op. cit., esp. pp. 393–95.

[19] *Second Discourse,* Part II (pp. 158–60); *Contrat Social, Première Version,* I, ii (Pléiade, III, 286–87); I, vii (p. 310); and above all II, iv (p. 329): "for law comes before justice and not justice before law."

[20] "In an equitable federation / we will make laws." Virgil, *Aeneid,* xi. 321. On the importance that Rousseau attaches to the epigraph of a work, see *Emile,* V (Garnier ed., p. 600), where he

Although this phrase seems to refer to an example of a social contract, it reveals the entire problem of political right to the careful reader.

In Virgil's poem, Rousseau's epigraph is part of a speech by the aged King of Latium, who proposes that the war between his people and the Trojans be ended by a federation; this discourse has no effect whatever on the assembly of the Latins, who are defeated by Aeneas in the battle that permits the foundation of Rome. And for those who might object that the epigraph comes from a poetic tale, Rousseau later adds another indication that Rome was founded by "the right of the strongest" and not by a social contract.[21] Historically, force creates law.

But although it is possible, if not probable, that the factual origin of political right is found in acts of force, force itself is not political right.

> For as soon as force makes right, the effect changes along with the cause. . . . If it is necessary to obey by force, one need not obey by duty, and if one is no longer forced to obey, one is no longer obligated to do so. It is apparent, then, that this word right adds nothing to force.[22]

The problem for Rousseau is not to describe the histori-

---

considers his epigraph as the summary of his thesis, and *Rousseau Juge de Jean Jacques,* Dialogue III (Pléiade, I, 941), where Rousseau compares two books on the basis of their epigraphs.

[21] "The name *Rome,* which supposedly comes from Romulus, is Greek, and means *force.* The name *Numa* is Greek too, and means *law.* How likely is it that the first two kings of that city had in advance names so highly relevant to what they did?" *Social Contract,* IV, iv, n (Pléiade, III, 444). This interpretation is restated more explicitly in *Considerations on the Government of Poland,* II, in Frederick Watkins, trans. and ed., *Rousseau: Political Writings* (London: 1953), p. 165. Although political origins are only known through fables, these fables reflect what actually happened. Cf. *Social Contract,* I, iii (Pléiade, III, 354): the "right of the strongest," although apparently ironic, is *"réellement établi en principe"* —i.e., "actually established at the beginnings" (in fact) as well as "actually laid down as a principle" (by many theorists).

[22] Ibid.

cal establishment of political society, but to find the reasons that could make obedience legitimate; Rousseau needs to discover—one can almost say, to create—political right.[23]

The first words of the *Social Contract* show that a double necessity must be satisfied if valid reasons to obey are to be established on the basis of factual injustice.

> I want to inquire whether there can be a legitimate and reliable rule of administration in the civil order, taking men as they are and laws as they can be. I shall try always to reconcile in this research what right permits with what interest prescribes, so that justice and utility are not at variance.[24]

Rousseau wants to find a rule that is simultaneously "legitimate and sure": without a *legitimate* reason for obedience, human society only reveals "the violence of powerful men and the oppression of the weak"; and without a *sure* or solid reason for obedience, "the laws of justice are ineffectual among men, for want of a natural sanction."[25]

In order to be "sure" or certain, the rules of political justice must begin with a natural necessity—namely, the certitude that men, "as they are," are primarily concerned with their own self-interest. Since right merely "permits," whereas "interest prescribes," laws should conform to the nature of man, a being who is not naturally just. Political right is a human creation that can replace

---

[23] Thus, according to *Emile*, V: "political right is as yet unborn" (Garnier ed., p. 584). The well-known words that open Book I, Chapter i of the *Social Contract* (Pléiade, III, 351) show that Rousseau believes he "can answer" the question of how obedience can become "legitimate"; he does not stop to discuss the factual origins of the "chains" that form civil society. On the difference between "fact" and "right" at the origin of political society, see *Contrat Social, Première Version*, I, v (Pléiade, III, 297).

[24] *Social Contract*, I, Introduction (Pléiade, III, 351).

[25] *Second Discourse*, Preface (p. 97); *Social Contract*, II, vi (Pléiade, III, 378). Note again the duality previously emphasized.

the ineffective traditional natural law, but only if utility is combined with justice.

Rousseau therefore does not seek justice in its ideal form. Instead of creating the best regime in words (like Plato's *Republic* and other works of classical political philosophers), Rousseau aims lower, and tries to define principles of government that would be "legitimate" in the variable conditions of each specific society.

> Therefore when the question is asked which is absolutely the best government, one poses a question that is insoluble because it is indeterminate. Or, if you prefer, it has as many correct answers as there are possible combinations in the absolute and relative situations of peoples.[26]

For justice to be useful, attention must be paid to the human and natural necessities that establish the limits of what is possible. Indeed, Rousseau's formulation of "principles of political right" has, as a logical consequence, the application of his principles to the particular conditions of each society.

The principles of political right are founded on an analysis of the "nature of the body politic" or the "nature of laws": as soon as civil society and laws come into existence, logic shows that the rational source of political obligation is the "general will"—a conception so well known that it is unnecessary to restate it here.[27] On the basis of this logic, Rousseau criticizes Montesquieu's proposition that virtue is the "principle of a republic":

> Because he failed to make the necessary distinctions, this noble genius often lacked precision, sometimes clarity; and he did not see that since the sovereign

---

[26] Ibid., III, ix (p. 419). Cf. ii, xii (p. 393).

[27] See *Contrat Social, Première Version*, I, i (Pléiade, III, 281); I, iii (pp. 290–92); I, iv (pp. 294–96); II, iv (pp. 326–28); *Social Contract*, I, vi–vii (pp. 360–64); II, i–vi (pp. 368–80). For a detailed exposition, see Roger D. Masters, *The Political Philosophy of Rousseau* (Princeton: 1968), Ch. 7, esp. pp. 323–34.

authority is everywhere the same, the same principle ought to apply in every well-constituted state, albeit to a greater or lesser degree according to the form of government.[28]

The principles of political right establish a fundamental distinction between the government and the sovereign, and the nature of the sovereign is everywhere the same, since it is directly derived from the nature of the body politic.[29]

There is no single form of government that is the best in itself; in order to find the best laws, the general principles of political legitimacy must be combined with a calculation of the particular characteristics of each society.[30] In the *First Version of the Social Contract*, Rousseau made this point emphatically by insisting that the perfect realization of his principles of political right is simply impossible:

The works of men—always less perfect than nature's—never move so directly toward their goal. In politics as in mechanics one cannot avoid acting more weakly or more slowly, and losing force or time. The general will is rarely the will of all, and the public force is always less than the sum of the private forces, so that in the mechanism of the State there is an equivalent of friction in machines, which one must know how to reduce to the least possible amount and which must at least be calculated and subtracted in advance

---

[28] *Social Contract*, III, iv (Pléiade, III, 405).

[29] Ibid., II, vi (pp. 377–80); III, i (pp. 395–96). "The continuous proportion between sovereign, prince and people is no arbitrary idea, but rather a necessary consequence of the nature of the body politic." Ibid. (p. 398). Note that Rousseau defends himself against the objection that his principles are unrealistic by pointing to circumstances in which they have been realized: "the inference from the existent to the possible seems solid to me." Ibid., III, xii (p. 426).

[30] Ibid., III, i (pp. 397, 400); III, iii (p. 403); III, vii (p. 413); III, viii (pp. 414–19); III, ix (p. 419).

from the total force, so that the means used will be exactly proportionate to the effect desired.[31]

The analogy between the general will and a frictionless surface, indicating the necessary shortcomings of every existing regime, was apparently in Rousseau's mind when he was first working out his political thought, for he also refers to it explicitly in the fragmentary *Etat de Guerre*.[32]

The principles of political right, like the idea of a frictionless surface in mechanics, are merely a rigorous abstraction that explains the "nature of things" and cannot be applied to the "machine" of state without a supplementary science. In the *First Version of the Social Contract*, this "science of the legislator" was very clearly distinguished from the "principles of political right" or "the idea of the civil state"; indeed, in that manuscript "the science of the legislator" was the explicit subject of Book II.[33]

The requirements of "strict right" would seem to be a limit, approximated more or less by the institutions of various actual societies. Or, as Rousseau put it before presenting a summary of his political teaching in the *Emile*:

It is necessary to know what should be in order to

---

[31] *Contrat Social, Première Version*, I, iv (Pléiade, II, 296–97). Cf. *Emile*, IV (Garnier ed., p. 299).

[32] "One should consider how much less, in the aggregation of the body politic, the public force is than the sum of the private forces, and how much friction there is, so to speak, in the play of the whole machine." *Etat de Guerre*, (Pléiade, III, 606). In addition to the references to levers, springs, and equilibria that were retained in the definitive text of the *Social Contract*, consider also such phrases in the first version as "I put the machine in running order" (*Contrat Social, Première Version*, I, i [Pléiade, III, 281]), and the legislator "is the mechanic who invents the machine" (ibid., II, ii [p. 313]).

[33] Ibid., I, iv (p. 297); II, i (p. 312). See also the reference to the "legislator's science" in the *Letter to d'Alembert*, translated by Allan Bloom in *Rousseau: Politics and the Arts* (Glencoe, Ill.: 1960), p. 66.

judge well concerning what is. . . . Before observing, it is necessary to establish rules for one's observations; it is necessary to establish a scale to which the measures that one takes can be compared. Our principles of political right are that scale. Our measures are the political laws of each country.[34]

Hence Rousseau's political principles are intended to be applied to practical judgments, albeit with the expectation that existing regimes always fall short of a perfect realization of the general will.

Unfortunately, most commentators on the *Social Contract* have not seen the importance of this distinction between the rigorous principles of political right and the prudence necessary to realize them in practice. While a few have referred to this problem in Rousseau's

---

[34] *Emile,* V (Garnier ed., p. 585). Schematically, the general will, as a "frictionless surface" or "scale," could be represented as the abscissa on a graph used to plot political observations; actual societies approach this co-ordinate, but would never fall directly on it:

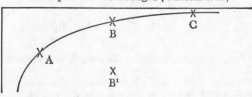

Principles of Political Right (General Will)

Empirical Conditions of Society

Assuming that A, B, and C on the diagram are different regimes, Rousseau's principles would therefore permit one to "judge well concerning what is"—C, being closer to a complete realization of the principles of political right, would be in some sense "better" than B or A. Following this schematic presentation, moreover, the other co-ordinate would represent those historical, geographic, and social conditions establishing the minimum of "friction" in each society. Hence a society whose laws are the equivalent of those of B' could be reformed to those of B; in contrast, society B would already have achieved the minimum "friction" possible under the circumstances.

thought,[35] only Bertrand de Jouvenel has given the "science of the legislator" the importance it deserves.[36] Yet the "Table of Books and Chapters," in the *Social Contract* as published in 1762, shows clearly that the work is not limited to abstract principles of political right: Books III and IV "discuss political laws; that is, the form of the government."[37] Although this part of the work is often hastily dismissed or ignored altogether, it is above all in his analysis of the various forms of government that Rousseau deals with the practical application of his principles of right.

3. "Principles of Right" and "Maxims of Politics"

One of Rousseau's fundamental propositions is that the establishment of government is not a contract, and that the people as sovereign can change its government at will.[38] Speaking of the effect of this principle, Rousseau says:

It is true that these changes are always dangerous, and that the established government must never be touched until it becomes incompatible with the public good. But this circumspection is a maxim of politics

---

[35] Vaughan, *Political Writings of Rousseau*, I, 1–4, 61, 69, 72, 74, 77–81; Alfred Cobban, *Rousseau and the Modern State* (London: 1934), pp. 80–90; Ernst Cassirer, *The Question of Jean-Jacques Rousseau* (New York: 1954), pp. 65, 123; Jean Fabre, "Réalité et Utopie dans la Pensée Politique de Rousseau," *Présence de Jean-Jacques Rousseau* (Paris: 1963), pp. 181–216.

[36] "Théorie des Formes de Gouvernement chez Rousseau," *Contrat Social*, VI (November–December 1962), 343–51. Cf. Roger D. Masters, *Political Right and the Art of Politics in Rousseau's Thought* (Unpublished Doctoral Dissertation; University of Chicago, 1961), esp. Ch. 5.

[37] Vaughan, *Political Writings of Rousseau*, II, 21–22. This original table of contents is unfortunately not reproduced in most translations, nor is it found in the Pléiade edition of Rousseau's *Oeuvres Complètes*.

[38] *Social Contract*, III, xiv (Pléiade, III, 427–28); III, xiv (pp. 432–33); III, xviii (pp. 434–36).

[*une maxime de politique*] and not a rule of right [*une règle de droit*], and the State is no more compelled to leave civil authority to its leaders than military authority to its generals.[39]

The "rules of right"—i.e., the principles of political right, including the "general will," popular sovereignty, and the like—are not the same thing as "maxims of politics" (which concern matters of "circumspection" or prudence in political action).

In the Introduction to the *First Version of the Social Contract*, Rousseau indicated more explicitly this difference between "principles" or "rules" of right in the strict sense (i.e., standards of justice) and prudential "maxims" or precepts concerning political action (i.e., guides to what the prudent citizen or statesman should do under given circumstances).

So many famous authors have dealt with the maxims of government and the rules of civil right that there is nothing useful to say on this subject that has not already been said. But perhaps there would be greater agreement, perhaps the best relationships of the social body would have been more clearly established if its nature had been determined at the outset.[40]

The first task of political theory is to discover the "nature" of the "social body." After this has been done, however, it will be possible to find "the best relationships within the

---

[39] Ibid. (p. 435). Rousseau's often discussed civil religion is intended to reinforce this "maxim" of prudence: cf. ibid., IV, viii (pp. 467–69) and *Second Discourse*, Part II (pp. 170–71). On the distinction between convenience or prudence and political right, see also *Contrat Social, Première Version*, I, vi (Pléiade, III, 306): "But what is convenient should not be confused with what is necessary, simple duty with strict right, and what can be required of us with what we should do voluntarily."

[40] *Contrat Social, Première Version*, I, i (Pléiade, III, 281). Note, however, that "the rules of *civil* right" are technically more restricted than and subordinate to the "principles" or "rules of *political* right." See *Social Contract*, II, xii (Pléiade, III, 393–94).

social body," and such "relationships" presuppose a balancing between "maxims of government" and "rules of right."

As we have seen, Rousseau's discovery of the "nature of the social body," in the form of his conceptions of the social contract and general will, leads him to speak in his manuscript of a supplementary "science of the legislator" guiding practical political action. When revising the *Social Contract* for publication, however, Rousseau seems to have blurred this distinction between "principles of political right" and "maxims of politics." In addition to deleting the analogy between the former and a frictionless surface, Rousseau removed the Introduction just cited as well as all references to the "science of the legislator"; in the final version, there remains only one mention of the *"art* of the legislator."[41]

A plausible reason for these changes is not hard to find. By weakening the distinction between "principles of right" and "maxims of politics," Rousseau could well have been attempting to reduce the danger that his "science of the legislator" would be misused by an ambitious politician (who might thereby perpetuate his own power at the expense of the sovereign people). While this is merely an inference, it must not be forgotten that Rousseau attached overwhelming importance to the social corruption that results from the public teaching of scientific truths.[42]

Be that as it may, Rousseau himself did not abandon the distinction between "principles of political right" and "maxims of politics," as is shown by the explicit passage in Book III, Chapter xviii of the *Social Contract* (cited above). Indeed, in the definitive version Rousseau speaks repeatedly of "maxims" of politics as general relationships that should guide the legislator or statesman. Only by

---

41 Ibid., III, ii (p. 402). Cf. Note 33 above.
42 See esp. *First Discourse,* Part II (pp. 49–50, 58–64). Note, for example, how the publication of the *Social Contract* necessarily undermines the prudential maxim cited at Note 39.

considering some of these maxims in detail can we gain a clearer understanding of the overall structure of Rousseau's political theory.

4. Rousseau's "Maxims of Politics"

According to Rousseau, one of the most important maxims of the "art" or "science" of legislation concerns the size of a political community.

> The more the social bond stretches, the looser it becomes, and in general a small State is proportionately stronger than a large one. A thousand reasons confirm this maxim [*maxime*].[43]

Similarly, in speaking of the various forms of government, he says:

> Therefore, the more numerous the magistrates, the weaker the government. Since this maxim [*maxime*] is fundamental, let us try to explain it more clearly.[44]

Or again:

> When the functions of the government are divided among several tribunals, those with the fewest members sooner or later acquire the greatest authority, if only because of the facility in expediting business that brings this about naturally.[45]

---

[43] *Social Contract*, II, ix (Pléiade, III, 386–87).

[44] Ibid., III, ii (p. 400).

[45] Ibid., III, iv (pp. 404–5). Cf. Max Nicholson, *The System* (New York: 1969), p. 178: "It is a rule in politics that the faster the business must move and the more there is of it, the more fully a large assembly must renounce any pretense of detailed consideration and decision in favor of some more businesslike smaller group." Although Rousseau describes this proposition as a "principle" (*principe*), his inconsistent word usage does not contradict the broad distinction between "principles of political right" and "maxims of politics." According to the classical dictionary of eighteenth-century French, "*principe* is also used for *maxime, motif,* etc." *Dictionnaire de l'Académie Française* (Paris: 1694), II, 325. In

These maxims are not formulas for what is just, but regularities that can be observed in the politics of all societies, whether legitimate or tyrannical. They are often presented as relationships or proportions between variables, on the assumption that "all other things are equal." The analogy between such propositions and the hypotheses of modern empirical political science is evident, though it is important to add that Rousseau did not consider his maxims to be "value-free" or unrelated to principles of right.

Although it would be illuminating to draw up a list of all the maxims of politics stated by Rousseau, it is only possible to suggest some of the more important ones. In his *First Discourse*, Rousseau had asserted:

> The daily ebb and flow of the ocean's waters have not been more steadily subject to the course of the star which gives us light during the night than has the fate of morals and integrity been subject to the advancement of the sciences and arts. Virtue has fled as their light dawned on our horizon, and the same phe-

---

general, the word *principe* had a theoretical meaning, as "first cause, . . . that of which things are composed, . . . all the natural causes by which things act and are moved" (ibid.). In contrast, *maxime* usually referred to a precept or rule of action; although defined as a "general proposition that serves as a principle, foundation, or rules [sic] in some art or science," the examples in the *Dictionnaire* are essentially practical: "the *maximes* of morality, the *maximes* of politics, *maxime* of State . . . follow certain *maximes*, each has his *maximes*, that is his *maxime*" (ibid., III, 34–35). Cf. *Dictionnaire de Trévoux* (Paris: 1771), V, 893; VI, 1001; Pierre Richelet, *Dictionnaire de la Langue Françoise* (Paris: 1769), II, 407; III, 284. Littré quotes Condillac's *Art d'Ecrire*, II, 9: "*Principe* and *maxime* are two synonymous words: they both mean a truth that is the summary of several others; but the former is more specifically applied to theoretical knowledge, and the latter to practical knowledge." As will be shown, Rousseau tries to provide a theoretical basis for his practical "maxims," which perhaps explains why on a few occasions he uses the word "principe" to describe what he elsewhere calls "maxims of politics." In any event, Rousseau explicitly denied that it was possible "to give the same words always the same meaning." *Emile*, II (Garnier ed., p. 104).

nomenon has been observed in all times and in all places.[46]

The moral corruption that necessarily results from popular enlightenment has political implications:

> [A people] can liberate itself as long as it is merely barbarous, but can no longer do so when the civil machinery is worn out. . . . Free peoples, remember this maxim: Freedom can be acquired, but it can never be recovered.[47]

A series of supplementary maxims, as Jouvenel has shown, explain the logic of this historical pattern; governments have a "natural tendency" to pass from "a large to a small number, that is from democracy to aristocracy and from aristocracy to royalty."[48]

There is little need to repeat Jouvenel's excellent analysis of these maxims, which indicates that even the best regime will necessarily decay due to the "nature of things." Instead, it will be more useful to consider two other aspects of Rousseau's "science of the legislator": first, maxims concerning the possibility of establishing

---

[46] *First Discourse,* Part I (pp. 39–40). Note that behind the somewhat extravagant rhetoric that characterized Rousseau's *First Discourse* lies a comparison between the effects of enlightenment on moral standards, and the then recently discovered effects of the moon's gravitational pull on the tides; i.e., Rousseau attempts to pattern the discovery of historical regularities upon modern astronomy.

[47] *Social Contract,* II, viii (Pléiade, III, 385). This maxim is reinforced by another: "censorship may be useful in preserving morals, but never in restoring them" (ibid., IV, vii [p. 459]). Note that while Rousseau is sometimes said to have altered his political teaching between the *First Discourse* and the *Social Contract,* the essential thesis of the former is explicitly restated in the latter (esp. III, ix, n [p. 420]). Cf. C. E. Vaughan, "Introduction," *Du Contrat Social* (Manchester: 1918), pp. xxxiv–xxxvii; Harry J. Benda, "Rousseau's Early Discourses (II)," *Political Science,* VI (March 1954), pp. 18, 25.

[48] *Social Contract,* III, x (Pléiade, III, 421). For an analysis, see Jouvenel, "Théorie des Formes du Gouvernement," translated and reprinted in this volume, Ch. 19.

a legitimate regime, and second those that determine the form of government suited to any given country. On both topics, Rousseau develops what would today be called empirical political analysis and relates it to questions of political right.

Rousseau adopts several conceptions from Montesquieu, such as the proposition that "freedom, not being a fruit of all climates, is not accessible to all peoples."[49] But it seems hardly sufficient to say that Rousseau did so merely to show himself as an equal of "that noble genius" or as a means of adding a little variety in a book that was "austere."[50] On the contrary, since the application of his principles of right follows necessarily from their logic, Rousseau is trying to show the conditions in which a legitimate regime is possible.

In order to show the kinds of society in which good laws can be established, Rousseau sets forth a number of general maxims. Some are historical (like the one just cited from Book II, Chapter viii, or those analyzed by Jouvenel). Others, however, are geographical, focusing on variations in climate, soil, and general physical or natural characteristics in different countries.

Consider some of the latter propositions:

The closer one is to the equator, the less peoples live on.[51]

Since the soil's fertility is greater near the equator, the needs of men are inversely related to natural abundance;

---

[49] *Social Contract*, III, viii (Pléiade, III, 414).

[50] Remarking on the passage in question, Derathé says: "Besides the desire not to be shown inferior to Montesquieu, Rousseau clearly had not only the intention of filling out his book, but also that of using concrete considerations to make less austere 'the difficult subject-matter of the *Social Contract*, fit for few readers.'" Pléiade, III, 1484, citing Rousseau's letter to Rey of 4 April 1762. But in this letter, Rousseau speaks of the book *as a whole*, not merely of the exposition of his principles of political right; see *Correspondance Générale de Jean-Jacques Rousseau* (Paris: 1934), VII, 173.

[51] *Social Contract*, III, viii (Pléiade, III, 417).

hence the agricultural surplus always tends to be greater in warmer climates.[52] This factor of an agricultural surplus is particularly crucial, according to Rousseau, because "it is the excess of private individuals that produces what is necessary for the public."[53]

But "what is necessary for the public"—i.e., the cost of government—is different in the various forms of government:

> The greater the distance between the people and the government, the more burdensome taxes become. Thus the people is least burdened in a democracy; more so in an aristocracy; and in a monarchy it bears the greatest weight.[54]

These maxims can all be resumed by a very simple formula:

> The effect of climate makes despotism suited to hot countries, barbarism to cold countries, and good polity to intermediate regions.[55]

Although climate in itself is not the only efficient cause of legislation, it establishes natural constraints on politics; a given form of government is not likely to be successful everywhere, and a truly legitimate regime is improbable except in a temperate climate.

It could be objected that such maxims are ridiculous, because modern experience shows that the most extreme despotisms can exist in the "temperate" or "intermediate" regions. But it is one thing to assert that climate is merely a necessary precondition, and another to claim that it is in itself a necessary and sufficient cause; Rousseau suggests only the former, granting in advance that "particu-

---

[52] Ibid. (pp. 416–18).
[53] Ibid. (p. 414).
[54] Ibid. (p. 415). By "distance" here, Rousseau means not only geographical distance, but the time required for the taxpayers to receive the benefits of their tax payments.
[55] Ibid. (p. 416).

lar causes can modify" the effect of the general tendencies he outlines.[56]

Actually, this maxim relating regimes and climate has a long history in political theory, since Aristotle formulated it in his *Politics* (VII. 1327b). Moreover, it is far from certain that the substantive proposition is absurd. Although Rousseau's political maxims are not being treated here as hypotheses of a modern political science, empirical evidence could easily be used to test the role of a temperate climate as a precondition for liberal democratic regimes.

In general, the constitutional democracies of the West profited from a temperate climate, making possible an agricultural surplus. And such a surplus, because it facilitated the transfer of capital from the agrarian to industrial sectors of the economy during the period of industrialization, doubtless made it much easier for Western societies to industrialize within liberal democratic institutions. In the underdeveloped nations where these preconditions do not exist, the effort to create an industrialized society seems to require either a regime that mobilizes resources coercively or a massive importation of capital (if not both together).

Be that as it may, it could be argued that this geographical or climactic part of Rousseau's "science of the legislator" no longer has the importance he accorded to it in the eighteenth century. Whereas Rousseau thought that certain natural conditions were, at least in the long run, "invincible,"[57] modern science and the Industrial Revolution have had as their aim the conquest of nature.

---

[56] Rousseau introduces this proposition by remarking: "Let us always distinguish between general laws and the particular causes that can modify their effect" (ibid.). Hence Rousseau's maxims about the effect of climate, like "general laws" in the natural sciences, only hold when all other variables are held constant; as soon as other variables also differ, as in most actual situations, any single "general law" or maxim cannot alone account for all observed phenomena.

[57] Ibid., II, xi (p. 393); III, viii (p. 416).

Hence, it could be argued, Rousseau may have fundamentally underestimated man's increasing control over his environment by means of an ever progressing technology.

Without attempting to answer this objection, let us turn to another series of maxims to which it does not apply—namely, the relationship between any political community and its government. In Book III, Chapter i, the only chapter of the *Social Contract* beginning with a warning that it is difficult and important, Rousseau distinguishes between the sovereign people, as the legislative power, and the government, which should merely execute the laws.

This distinction between the sovereign and the government, which is perhaps the most original aspect of Rousseau's thought, can be represented by a mathematical relationship:

> It is in the government that are found the intermediate forces whose relationships compose the relationship of the whole to the whole or of the sovereign to the State. The latter relationship can be represented by the extremes of a continuous proportion, of which the proportional mean is the government.[58]

Writing this proportion in its algebraic form:

$$\frac{S}{G} = \frac{G}{E}$$ where: S = Sovereign (the people as source of laws)

G = Government (executive force)

E = *Etat* or State (the people as subject to the laws)

Rousseau continues:

> The government receives from the sovereign the orders that it gives to the people; and in order for the

---

[58] Ibid., III, i (p. 396). On Rousseau's use of mathematical terms, see the editor's notes in the Pléiade edition (esp. pp. 1472–76).

State to be in good equilibrium, all things considered, the product or power of the government, taken by itself, must be equal to the product or power of the citizens, who are sovereign on the one hand and subjects on the other.[59]

Or, to summarize by a simple equation, a state is "well balanced" if:

$$G^2 = S \times E \quad \text{or} \quad G = \sqrt{S \times E}$$

Since the proportion requires that the government be subordinate to the sovereign people, to this point we merely have an algebraic formulation of the "principles of political right." That is, it is by no means necessary that the terms of the continuous proportion be, in *fact*, "well balanced"; on the contrary, most regimes are illegitimate precisely because the people are not sovereign.[60]

But Rousseau does not stop there:

Since there is only one proportional mean for each relationship, there is no more than one good government possible in a State.[61]

Thus the variety of good forms of government, varying according to the specific conditions of each society, can apparently be mathematically demonstrated on the basis of the continuous proportion. Indeed, this proportion gives rise to a series of "maxims of politics" of general

[59] Ibid., III, i (p. 396).

[60] Ibid., II, x (p. 391). One can go farther; on close analysis, it appears to be simply impossible either to deduce the continuous proportion in the manner described by Rousseau or to achieve this relationship in practice; see Masters, *The Political Philosophy of Rousseau*, pp. 340–48. While it is thus clear that the continuous proportion, like the frictionless general will, is a principle of political right rather than a maxim of politics, it is significant that Rousseau attempts to formulate his standard of political legitimacy in algebraic or quasi-scientific form.

[61] *Social Contract*, III, i (Pléiade, III, 397).

applicability, deduced from but not identical to the principle of popular sovereignty.

First of all, Rousseau's preference for a small political community—above all, the city-state[62]—can be derived from the continuous proportion:

> Thus since the subject always remains one, the ratio of the sovereign to the subject increases in proportion to the number of citizens. From which it follows that the larger the State grows, the less freedom there is.[63]

Other prudential considerations can also be deduced from the continuous proportion:

> Now the less relationship there is between private wills and the general will, that is between the mores and the laws, the more repressive force should increase. Thus in order for the government to be good, it ought to be relatively stronger in proportion as the people is more numerous.[64]

To which Rousseau adds the maxim:

> The more force the government should have to restrain the people, the more the sovereign should have in turn to restrain the government.[65]

Although the last two maxims cited specify relationships that "should" take place in order that the government and sovereign be "in good equilibrium," some of Rous-

---

[62] Ibid., III, xiii (p. 427); III, xv (p. 431).

[63] Ibid., III, i (p. 397). Cf. Jouvenel, "Théorie des Formes de Gouvernement," translated and reprinted in this volume, Ch. 19. Note that liberal regimes among industrialized societies have usually been either in relatively small societies (Great Britain) or those with a federal structure (the United States).

[64] *Social Contract*, III, i (Pléiade, III, 397). Note that this maxim restates quite directly one of the sources of "friction" in the machine of state.

[65] Ibid.

seau's propositions concern regularities that can be observed in all regimes, whether legitimate or not.

For example, Rousseau suggests a maxim whose operation is inevitable:

> The total force of the government, being always that of the State, does not vary; from which it follows that the more of this force the government uses on its own members, the less is left for acting upon the entire people.[66]

Deducing from this that there is an inverse ratio between the number of magistrates and the relative force of a government,[67] Rousseau adds:

> I have just proved that the government *becomes* slack in proportion as the magistrates multiply, and I have proved earlier that the more numerous the people, the greater the increase in repressive force *should be*. From which it follows that the ratio of magistrates to government *should be* the inverse of the ratio of subjects to sovereign, which means that the more the State grows, the more the government *should* shrink, so that the number of leaders diminishes in proportion to the increase of people.[68]

There is an important difference between the two maxims that Rousseau combines here. The first, the ratio between the number of magistrates and the force of a government, is a natural and invincible tendency; the

---

[66] Ibid., III, ii (p. 400). In an unpublished study of changes in the Secretariat of the Soviet Communist Party under Stalin, I found that this maxim explains cyclical changes in its structure. In fact, when political priorities required pressure on the populace in general, control within the CPSU diminished; and when questions of control over the party itself had priority, pressure on the population at large tended to be relatively lessened.

[67] *Social Contract*, III, ii (Pléiade, III, 400), cited above at Note 44.

[68] Ibid. (p. 402, italics added). Note that the final proposition in this passage contradicts the continuous proportion, and compare Note 60 above.

maxim is presented as a fact. The second, the relationship between the force of the government and population size, seems in part to be what would be called
"normative" in contemporary political science; the government "should" be restricted in order to maintain the
equilibrium defined by the continuous proportion.[69]

Hence the relationship between the forms of government and population size can be summarized as follows:

> If the number of supreme magistrates in different
> States ought to be in inverse proportion to the num-
> ber of citizens, it follows that in general democratic
> government is suited to small States, aristocratic to
> medium sized ones, and monarchical to large ones.[70]

As with the maxims concerning the effect of climate,
Rousseau is here speaking of the laws that *suit* a given
society. And although the regime that suits each society
must be determined in terms of maxims describing naturally inevitable relationships, "the science of the legislator" is not limited to phenomena that occur necessarily;

---

[69] Jouvenel interprets this passage differently, describing it as
"what we would currently call a 'positive law of political science.'"
"Rousseau's Theory of the Forms of Government," pp. 484–97
in this volume. Jouvenel is surely correct when he says, with reference to other maxims, that Rousseau sometimes uses the word
"must" to indicate a natural tendency; as Jouvenel puts it, Rousseau uses both "an 'ethical' must" and "a 'scientific' must." But
it is likely that the proposition in question combines the two elements; if there is a factual tendency for governments to become
smaller as a state gets larger, this tendency does not have the
same empirical probability as the "natural inclination" of every
government to escape the sovereign's control. *Social Contract*,
III, x (Pléiade, III, 521–23). Cf. ibid., III, ii (pp. 400–1), where
Rousseau shows the difference between the artificial ordering of a
perfect legislation and the "natural order." Besides, if Rousseau
proposes a ratio between population size and number of governmental magistrates as a "positive law of political science," this
law is not confirmed either by contemporary evidence (e.g., the
United States has more magistrates than Spain) or by the evidence
cited by Rousseau himself (e.g., Rome had more magistrates toward the end of the Republic than under the Tarquins—ibid., III,
x, n. (pp. 421–22), and IV, v (p. 455).

[70] Ibid., III, iii (pp. 403–4).

on the contrary, this science is directed to the selection of the institutions that would be the *best* for each country.[71]

Rousseau's "science" of politics is therefore not "value-free"; unlike modern political science, which is often viewed as an attempt to discover recurring patterns in political phenomena without reference to so-called "normative" preferences, Rousseau's maxims are means to implement his standards of justice insofar as possible. Paradoxically, he formulated propositions that today would be called scientific for a reason that now seems very unscientific—namely, as a guide for the statesman who seeks to put Rousseau's principles of right into practice.

Since the standards of the general will, like a frictionless surface, can never be totally achieved in practice, the political leader's attempts to approximate the ideal must take natural necessity into account:

> The constitution of a State is made truly solid and enduring when matters of expediency are so well satisfied that natural relationships and the laws always agree on the same points, and the latter only secure, accompany, and rectify, so to speak, the former. But if a legislator makes a mistake about his objective and adopts a different principle than the one arising from the nature of things—whether one tends toward servitude and the other toward freedom, one toward wealth and the other toward population growth, or one toward peace and the other toward conquest—the laws will imperceptibly weaken, the constitution be altered, and the State will not cease to be agitated until it is either destroyed or changed, and invincible nature has regained its dominion.[72]

---

[71] Ibid., II, vii (p. 381); III, i (p. 400); III, ii (p. 402). See also the maxims for determining voting procedures, IV, ii (pp. 440–41).
[72] Ibid., II, xi (p. 393). "For never do good laws change the nature of things; they only follow it; and only such laws are obeyed." *Letter to d'Alembert* (ed. Bloom), p. 79. Lest it be thought that this view of the relationship between laws and natural tendencies

One reason why the distinction between principles of political right and maxims of politics has rarely been noticed is that there is a very close relationship between the two. Rousseau's principles of legitimacy are intended to be realistic and realizable, and his maxims of politics —while often general propositions that one is tempted to call scientific—result from Rousseau's effort to create the closest possible approximation of a just regime in the varying conditions of each human society.

5. Conclusion

Rousseau's political thought shows that it is not necessary to abandon the concern for political right or justice in the process of creating a science of political phenomena. It can even be asked whether Rousseau's combination of maxims of politics and principles of right might be a model for modern political science. Since the alternative of a value-free science, based on the positivist distinction between facts and values, has been attacked as implicitly biased,[73] the theoretical issue of the relationship between principles of right and empirical propositions is far from settled.

On the critical level, Rousseau himself stated the grave defect of a purely objective science of politics, limited to a description of "facts."

> Montesquieu . . . did not bother to treat principles of political right; he contented himself with a treatment of the positive right of established governments —and nothing in the world is more different than these two fields of study. Nonetheless, anyone who wants to

is logically necessary, compare Machiavelli's argument that the laws should contradict the natural tendencies produced by the site of a good regime: *Discourses on Titus-Livy*, I, i.

[73] See, for example, Peter Bachrach, *The Theory of Democratic Elitism* (Boston: 1967); Charles A. McCoy and John Playford, eds., *Apolitical Politics* (New York: 1967); Herbert J. Storing, ed., *Essays on the Scientific Study of Politics* (New York: 1962).

judge soberly about governments as they exist is required to unite both of them: one must know what should be in order to judge well what is.[74]

If political right is rejected as a field that is neither scientific nor necessary to the understanding of politics, one has a tendency to accept the existing situation, even if it is unjust.

As Rousseau says of Grotius:

His most persistent mode of reasoning is always to establish right by fact. One could use a more rational method, but not one more favorable to tyrants.[75]

A political science that explicitly denies that it can directly analyze right or justice, always speaking of what exists and never of what should exist, runs the risk of equating existence with justice, and thereby of destroying the possibility of a rational distinction between the just and the unjust.

The appropriate objectives for modern political science are not our subject, and this question has been raised only in order to show the contemporary relevance of Rousseau's "science of the legislator." To go farther, it would be necessary to begin by judging the *truth* of Rousseau's philosophical system, whereas here we are merely trying to understand the structure of his political theory. It is therefore appropriate to conclude by summarizing the philosophical implications of Rousseau's distinction between principles of political right and maxims of politics.

Rousseau's point of departure is a radical distinction between nature and society. On the assumption that the human individual can, and naturally did, survive in isolation from other humans, society can be viewed as a result of the species' evolution (rather than as something natural to man). Since the state of nature is thereby

---

[74] *Emile*, V (Garnier ed., pp. 584–85).
[75] *Social Contract*, I, ii (Pléiade, III, 353).

presumed to have been an historical epoch, Rousseau can use freedom—the natural "quality of being a man" and principal characteristic of his primitive condition—as a standard for judging all subsequent human situations. But because the true state of nature has been destroyed forever, at least for most men, freedom is no longer a single or unitary principle.

In the *Social Contract,* Rousseau clearly distinguishes between three kinds of freedom, each of which roughly corresponds to a form of human excellence: "*natural freedom*" (corresponding to the *natural goodness* of the state of nature described in the *Second Discourse*); "*civil freedom*" (corresponding to the *civic virtue* of a legitimate regime described in the *Social Contract*); and "*moral freedom*" (corresponding to the *moral virtue* of an individual in a corrupt society, described in *Emile*).[76] A few individuals, like Rousseau himself in his later years, can achieve something like a return to natural freedom by retiring from society, abandoning themselves to their natural sentiments, and living the life of a "solitary dreamer." A few societies, like Republican Rome, can achieve civic freedom and virtue by establishing truly just laws, but such legitimate regimes are often impossible due to natural or historical contingencies (and in any event will ultimately decay). Finally, although the spread of enlightenment typically corrupts civil society, those few whose education protects them from the vicious customs of their times may, like Rousseau's imaginary pupil Emile, achieve moral virtue by freely conforming their actions to a self-imposed natural law or natural religion.

Rousseau thus thought it possible to use nature, and particularly man's natural attribute of freedom, as the guide for human happiness even in the unnatural condition of civil society. This apparent paradox was possible because Rousseau insisted that nature can never

---

[76] Ibid., I, viii (pp. 364–65). On the difference between goodness and virtue, see Note 13 above.

be completely stifled or conquered. Unlike those eighteenth-century optimists who saw in modern science and technology a means of conquering nature, Rousseau claimed that if human convention or art contradicts nature, "invincible nature" will always reconquer "its dominion."[77]

This conception of "the nature of things" lies behind the three versions of the good or virtuous man noted above. For the solitary dreamer who is willing to "go into the woods to lose sight and memory of the crimes of (his) contemporaries," a return to the natural goodness of the state of nature is always possible.[78] For the moral individual in a corrupt age, the conscience—an innate sentiment written "by nature in ineffaceable characters at the bottom of the human heart"—can serve as the basis of a natural religion and personal morality.[79] And even though a legitimate and virtuous civil society is a human creation that must "denature" man by "changing human nature," the standards of the just society are derived from nature in a double sense: first, a legitimate regime must conform to the "nature of law" if it is to be just; second, each society's positive laws must conform to the "nature of things" if it is to last.

Rousseau's political thought is thus founded on an understanding of nature. If his "maxims of politics" seem to be propositions that belong to a natural science of political phenomena, it is because Rousseau hoped that his principles of right would be consistent with natural science and applicable to the real world. Only in this way could he fulfill his promise that science, or rather, *his*

---

[77] *Social Contract*, II, xi (cited above at Note 72). Compare *Emile*, I (Garnier ed., pp. 7–8).

[78] *Second Discourse*, Note i (p. 202). Cf. the references cited in Note 14 above.

[79] *Emile*, IV, "Profession of Faith of the Savoyard Vicar" (Garnier ed., p. 348). Cf. ibid., II (p. 93 n); IV (p. 247); *First Discourse*, Part 2 (p. 64); *Etat de Guerre* (Pléiade, III, 602); *Rêveries*, Promenade III (Pléiade, I, 1021).

science, can ultimately be used to increase the "happiness of the human species."[80]

But at the same time that he tried to create a harmony between philosophy and natural science, Rousseau insisted on the fact that science itself is generally dangerous for society. From the first of his major writings to the last, he contended that the public teaching of science and philosophy, instead of establishing human happiness, corrupts social morals. In part, this danger arises because reason is neither natural nor capable of resolving the fundamental metaphysical problems—such as the status of nature itself—inevitably raised by philosophy and science.

To avoid this problem, Rousseau tried to present a political theory that would be free of the doubts that inevitably arise from all metaphysical explanations of nature and God.

> Philosophy, having on these matters neither basis nor limit, lacking primitive ideas and elementary principles, is only a sea of incertitude and doubt, from which the metaphysician never extricates himself.[81]

As a "metaphysical" or "moral" concept, for example, freedom is ultimately subject to "insoluble objections" or "insuperable obstacles"; hence, in the *Second Discourse*, Rousseau provisionally substitutes "perfectibility" for freedom as man's defining characteristic.[82]

But if man were merely *perfectible*, there would be no limit to the changes that society could impose on his nature, not to mention on physical nature more gen-

---

[80] *First Discourse*, Preface (p. 33); *Emile*, Preface (Garnier ed., p. 3); *Second Discourse*, Preface (pp. 91, 97); *Rousseau Juge de Jean-Jacques*, Dialogue III (Pléiade, I, 934–35).

[81] Letter to Jacob Vernes, 18 February 1758 (*Correspondance Générale*, III, 287). According to the *Second Discourse*, Part I (pp. 125–26), "metaphysical" ideas, such as "matter, spirit, substance, mode, figure, movement . . . have no model in nature."

[82] Ibid., Part I (pp. 114–15). On the problem raised by this passage, see Masters, *The Political Philosophy of Rousseau*, pp. 66–72.

erally. Why, then, does Rousseau claim that nature is "invincible" and that the works of men are "always less perfect than those of nature"? Modern natural science has not always led to this conclusion; on the contrary, much of the scientific and technological effort of the last two centuries has aimed at the mastery of nature, as if to deny Rousseau's assertion.

In the last analysis, it appears that Rousseau's conception of nature is not, properly speaking, either scientific or rational. Although nature is simultaneously the subject of an objective science and the standard of human happiness, Rousseau rejects the possibility of a philosophy that could provide a global understanding of nature itself. On the contrary, Rousseau's philosophical system —resting as it does on the assertion of man's "natural goodness"—ultimately presupposes a replacement of reason by sentiment as the ultimate criterion of human judgment.[83]

The underlying difficulty of Rousseau's position is nowhere more evident than in his concept of freedom. Although the natural freedom of the savage, or the civil freedom of the just regime are intended to be observable phenomena that do not depend on metaphysical presuppositions, the form of freedom that is relevant to civilized man as an individual and a thinker is moral freedom. Yet Rousseau admits that moral freedom can only be theoretically established by means of a dualist metaphysics or a natural religion, such as the one Rousseau presented indirectly in the "Profession of Faith of the Savoyard Vicar."[84] Rousseau's works try to teach man how he can be either good or virtuous, but this teaching rests on a personal belief or sentiment; according to Rousseau

---

[83] *First Discourse*, Part 2 (p. 64); *Second Discourse*, Preface (pp. 95–96); Part 2 (p. 133); *Émile*, I (Garnier ed., p. 48); IV, "Profession of Faith" (pp. 348–56). On the relationship of reason and sentiment, see Masters, op. cit., Chs. 1–2.
[84] *Émile*, IV (Garnier ed., pp. 322–60). Cf. *La Nouvelle Héloïse*, VI, xi (Pléiade, II, 714–16).

himself, a reasoning man who denies God's existence without becoming wicked "is either a liar or a fool."[85]

Despite his efforts, Rousseau failed to create a theory without metaphysical implications, and this is precisely why the *Social Contract* is rarely understood as an attempt to establish a science that is both practical and theoretical. Although he tried to formulate principles of political right that could be realized in practice, and outlined "maxims of politics" that could guide the statesman to this end, for most readers Rousseau, like Plato, merely imagined an ideal regime. Indeed, the main difference in modern times would seem to be that it is Rousseau (rather than Plato) whose ideals were transformed into a political ideology. But perhaps this only means that on a philosophical level, it was Plato (rather than Rousseau) who best understood the nature of the human condition.

---

[85] *Emile,* IV (p. 390). On the "Profession of Faith of the Savoyard Vicar" as generally similar if not identical to Rousseau's own view, see *Rêveries d'un Promeneur Solitaire,* Promenade III (Pléiade, I, 1018); Letter to M. de Franquières, 15 January 1769 (*Correspondance Générale,* XIX, 48–63); *Confessions,* IX (Pléiade, I, 407); *Lettres Écrites de la Montagne,* I (Pléiade, III, 694).

ROUSSEAU AND THE PROBLEM OF HAPPINESS

RONALD GRIMSLEY

Rousseau's insistence that the true goal of human existence was happiness—"we must be happy, dear Emile: that is the aim of every sensitive being: it is the first desire imprinted in us by nature and the only one which never leaves us" (IV, 814)[1]—merely echoed an idea that dominated most of the thinking of his age. Philosophers who had abandoned traditional religious and moral values eagerly sought to develop a view of life that would give man happiness on this earth instead of making him wait for it in the world to come; they believed that the betterment of the human condition would be achieved only when people had learned to free themselves from age-old prejudices and, in particular, from the oppressive influence of religious doctrines based on "revelation." Happiness would be possible when men became more rational, more tolerant, and more truly human.

Yet if most thinkers seemed to accept the same goal, few were agreed about the means of attaining it. Rousseau affirmed that the variety and multiplicity of contemporary viewpoints merely made simple people lose themselves in the "labyrinth of human opinions." Happiness, he agreed, was the true object of life, but where was it to be found? "But where is happiness? who knows? People spend their lives chasing it, but die without finding it." Those who put their trust in reason discover it to be without solidity, whilst the passions are equally untrustworthy, for they too remain at the mercy of the fickle human heart. Philosophers are for ever discoursing

This essay was especially written for this volume by Ronald Grimsley, Professor of French, University of Bristol.

1 All references, indicated by volume and page number, are to the Pléiade edition of the *Oeuvres Complètes*, edited by B. Gagnebin and M. Raymond, Paris, Vols. I–IV, 1959–69.

about knowledge; "each sect" claims to have found the truth, but "nobody is made happy. We merely pursue shadows which escape us" (IV, 1087–91).

Rousseau believed that the main cause of this uncertainty and confusion was the nefarious influence of "society" upon contemporary thought; since philosophy itself had originated in vanity and luxury, it could not throw adequate light on the ultimate principles of human nature. Philosophers were more concerned with satisfying the demands of their own pride than with showing their fellow-men the way to happiness. In any case, they would be unlikely to find the truth, even if they wished to do so, for they had lost all genuine contact with man's essential nature. In this respect they were simply suffering from a disability which affected all aspects of contemporary life: modern man had become a divided unhappy creature, forced constantly to live "outside himself" and to base his life on the "opinion" of others instead of his own true "nature." Consequently, "the whole order of natural feelings" had been either inverted or destroyed. A fatal split had occurred between what men "were" and what they "appeared" to be; appearance and reality were absolutely antithetical. Man had acquired an artificial being which he accepted as his own. "Men become other than what they are and society gives them, so to speak, a being different from their own" (II, 273). Man's true personality is concealed behind a mask. "The man of the world is completely identified with his mask. Being hardly ever in himself, he is always a stranger to himself and ill at ease when he is forced to go into himself. What he is, is nothing, what he appears is all that matters to him" (IV, 515).

Man cannot be happy, says Rousseau, unless he is himself; true happiness involves a mode of personal being with which the individual can be fully identified. "It is necessary to be oneself," Rousseau told Bernardin de Saint-Pierre in his last years. Instead of going constantly outside himself, the happy man accepts the immediate reality of his own "constitution" and "so to speak, compresses happiness around his heart." That is why silence rather than boisterous gaiety is the mark of true happiness: "Supreme enjoyment is in contentment with oneself" (IV, 587). There is no higher fulfilment than the "pure pleasure [*volupté*] which comes from contentment with oneself" and from "existing according to one's own nature." In other words, in order to be happy man has first of all to "withdraw into himself" and find his own true being.

In the *Discours sur l'Origine de l'Inégalité* Rousseau suggested that a useful lesson might be learned from comparing modern man with his primitive ancestors. Although he did not advocate, or even believe in, the desirability of a return to the "state of nature," he called attention to one particularly important difference between primitive and modern modes of existence: primitive man was happy, modern man is unhappy. The essential reason for this was the former's ability to give spontaneous expression to the inherent possibilities of his nature; accepting the "impulse of nature" and the "temperament he had received from nature," he was content to be what he immediately was. "His soul, which is disturbed by nothing, abandons itself to the feeling of its present existence." Admittedly, this existence which, with its lack of both "curiosity" and "forethought," allowed little or no room for reflection and imagination, fell far short of a genuinely human quality; primitive man was an instinctive animal-like creature, devoid of any sense of good or evil, and owing his happiness to the advantages of his condition rather than to his own deliberate effort. Nevertheless, Rousseau believed that when it was applied to a higher mode of being, this idea of fidelity to the "original" possibilities of "natural" existence could provide a valuable starting point to the search for a more genuinely human and mature form of happiness.

Unlike his forbears, modern man has to achieve happiness by an effort of will. For him "nature" involves more than the spontaneous "goodness" of an unreflective be-

ing, for it must result from the deliberate choice of a
certain mode of existence—a choice made all the more
urgent and necessary by the need to cast off the false
social values of his age. Already at the primitive level,
man's most characteristic attribute lay dormant within
him; the early savage was endowed with the potentiality
of "freedom," even though his independent and self-
sufficient mode of existence made it unnecessary for him
to develop it. He also possessed another possibility which
he did not need to develop because of his contented
situation: the "faculty of perfecting himself." These innate capacities remained inactive, because primitive
man's freedom was largely of a physical kind; living an
isolated life which brought him into no permanent contact with other men, he was limited only by the "necessity" of physical nature; he had the "health, strength and
the wherewithal" to lead a "simple, uniform and un-
changing mode of life." As Rousseau insisted in *Emile*,
the freedom of a fully developed moral being is of another kind; it not only involves the active choice of a
new "nature" and the conscious pursuit of a specific ideal,
but also the fulfilment of this ideal in a situation which
brings him into relationship and perhaps conflict with
other human wills as powerful as his own. Man's freedom is a quality progressively emerging from within his
own nature, and yet expressing itself through his complex relationships with his social environment. The "natural" freedom of the savage thus has to give way to the
"moral" freedom of a human being who recognizes the
existence of higher demands than those of physical
nature.

Rousseau was optimistic about the possibility of
achieving this difficult ideal, for he believed that man
did not exist as an isolated individual, but formed part
of the universal "order" created by God. No doubt Jean-
Jacques himself, in his personal writings, often complained of his loneliness and unhappiness as a persecuted
man, but he attributed his own particular fate to the
aberrations of society rather than to any inherent defect

in the universal scheme of things. Indeed, in moments of greatest distress, he would turn for consolation to the "common mother," Nature, who was always ready "to protect her children against the assaults of their enemies." One of his greatest delights was to "plunge headlong" into "the vast ocean of nature" and to "identify himself with the universal system." He was convinced that there existed "a congruence between man's immortal nature and the constitution of this world and the physical order he saw reigning in it" (I, 1019). That was why Emile's and the Vicaire's main problem was to find the "rank" they occupied in the "order of things." If man could trust his own "goodness" and fundamental *amour de soi*, it was because of his conformity with "order." The fact that most men were unable to perceive that order in no way impugned its existence. To people whose eyes had been opened to the truth, supreme happiness was to be found in the acceptance of those indestructible principles which God had implanted in nature. The Vicaire declares: "I acquiesce in the order which He establishes, sure of enjoying this order one day and of finding my felicity in it; for what sweeter felicity is there than to feel oneself part of a system in which everything is good?" (IV, 603).

The harmony which the "good" man perceives in the external world is also to be found in his own internal nature. In Rousseau's opinion, the exercise of freedom does not create discord within man's being but helps him to fulfil himself in accordance with the fundamental principles of nature, principles "engraved in the heart with indelible characters." Freedom, in Rousseau's view, does not involve man's anguished isolation from an "absurd" world but leads to a satisfying realization of his highest possibilities within the framework of the "universal order." If, in his last years, Jean-Jacques looked back with pride upon his earlier efforts to elaborate a philosophy of religious truth, it was because of his belief that he had worked out a "solid body of doctrine" that was "appropriate to his reason, his heart and his whole being, and reinforced by inner feeling" (I, 1018). Freedom does not operate in isolation, but functions in conjunction with other essential human faculties such as reason and conscience. Indeed, freedom cannot function effectively if it does not acknowledge that "the eternal laws of nature and order exist" and that "they are written in the depths of man's heart by conscience and reason"; it is to them that "he must subject himself in order to be free" (IV, 857). "Has not God," asks the Vicaire, "given me conscience to love the good, reason to know it and freedom to choose it?" (IV, 605). Since man has been made in the divine image, he must find ultimate fulfilment in being as "free, good and happy" as God himself (IV, 587).

Nevertheless, if existing society is bad, the social ideal remains indispensable to a fully developed moral life and the need to approach the universal order through an active participation in social life means that man has to choose a mode of existence that enables him to become "virtuous," that is, gives him the strength to sacrifice, if necessary, his spontaneous "goodness" to the stern duties required of him by the well-being of the community. The new social order thus created involves a radical transformation and "denaturing" of the natural man, which will make him capable of the moral happiness and freedom of civil life. Although this new order is based on conventions which, to a large extent, repudiate the independence of the state of nature, it does not violate the deeper moral aspects of man's being but helps to bring them to fulfilment. The ideal society is a kind of microcosm which in its essentials reflects the spiritual order governing the universe as a whole. Through his active participation in this higher order man will attain a happiness far superior to the merely instinctive "goodness" of primitive man.

Rousseau's marked predilection for small states was largely due to his belief that this kind of political society still allowed man to retain something of the spirit of the truly joyous and happy community. It is significant that after insisting upon the necessity of virtue, Rousseau advised Emile and Sophie to live far from the noise and corruption of large cities in order to try to find a "golden age" in an idyllic country life. Amid rural beauty they would enjoy abundance, happiness, and love. "I believe that I can see the people increasing, the fields growing fertile, the earth assuming a new garb, plenteousness and abundance transforming work into merry-making, shouts of joy being uttered in the midst of rustic games around the lovable couple which has brought new life into them" (IV, 859). This description reminds us of the spirit of the grape harvest in *La Nouvelle Héloïse* (II, 602 f), which reveals "all the charms of the golden age," and the happy social activities proposed by Rousseau to his fellow Genevans in the *Lettre à d'Alembert*. "Happy peoples, . . . it is in the open air, beneath the sky that you must assemble and give yourselves up to the sweet feeling of your happiness. . . . Act so that everyone sees and loves himself in the others, so that all may be the better united." Joy, fertility, spontaneity, reciprocal affection, beauty, and innocence are all experienced through direct contact with the warmth and light of physical nature and provide the elements which will animate a society concerned with the happiness of its members. Although Rousseau sometimes seemed to be uncertain about the possibility of achieving this ideal, he never doubted its desirability.

In spite of the importance of this social factor, Rousseau recognized that to achieve complete happiness, the individual had to look beyond the political order to a vaster realm of being, the universal order. It is only when both the individual and society realise their ultimate dependence on this total scheme of things that true fulfilment becomes possible. Yet, as soon as human happiness is related to this wider context, it involves a religious element. No doubt this is why Rousseau's final emphasis appears to be a contemplative one. Perfect fulfilment will be achieved only in the bliss of the next

world, a bliss that can be dimly and fleetingly appre-
hended through the wise use of contemplation in this
earthly life. In the next life, says the Vicaire, "we shall
enjoy the contemplation of the Supreme Being and the
eternal truths of which he is the source, when the beauty
of order will strike all the powers of our soul" (IV, 591).
In anticipation of this perfect "state of happiness, freedom and truth" the Vicaire "exercises himself in sublime
contemplations." In this respect his attitude is not unlike
that of Julie, who believes that we have to "detach ourselves from the things of the senses and all that is mortal
in us, in order to retire within ourselves (*nous recueillir*)
and give ourselves up to divine contemplations" (II,
380). The limitations of the human condition make it
impossible for us to find complete felicity on this earth,
but God will grant us some foreknowledge of our ultimate destiny if we are willing to accept the spiritual
reality of the order of which we form a part. "I meditate
on the order of the universe, not in order to explain it
by vain systems, but to admire it unceasingly, to adore
the wise author who reveals himself in it" (IV, 605).
That, no doubt, is why, in Rousseau's view, we do not
need to ask God to change anything for us. "Thy will be
done" is the only prayer we need utter.

Rousseau's final intention, therefore, was to take men
beyond the uncertainties of reflection, the vagaries of
passion, and the ambiguities of language to the happiness of a fully personal experience enjoyed through the
contemplation of the universal order. No doubt a man
who had dedicated himself to the task of teaching people "those truths which appertain to the happiness of
the human race" (III, 3) was obliged to set down his
ideas in writing, but he realised that didactic teaching
was valid only if it led to the renewal of experience.
Already at the end of his very first *Discours* he had
stressed the distinction between those who "act well"
and those who merely "speak well." His whole polemic
against modern culture rested on the assumption that it

had interposed a confusing screen of subtle reflection and jargon between man and the active enjoyment of his original nature. It was only when he had been liberated from the sophistication and corruption of modern society that man would find happiness in the direct renewal of his personal experience.

Deeply convinced though he was of the truth of his teaching, Rousseau's growing sense of isolation from society and the advent of personal misfortune made him aware of some of the difficulties involved in the individual appropriation of universal principles, however fundamental and "ineffaceable" they might be. Already at the didactic level his insistence on the priority of experience over reflection led him to acknowledge the ultimately incomprehensible nature of those very truths which he accepted as absolutely certain—the existence of God, and the supremacy of human freedom and conscience. The apparently rapid increase in personal difficulties and the onset of persecution (both real and imaginary) caused him to lay increasing stress upon the achievement of his own happiness. No doubt the exceptional nature of his position and character made it impossible and even unnecessary to attempt a simple transposition of universal into particular truths, but his persistent need to examine the implications of his own existence led him to look anew at the essential aspects of all earthly happiness.

The growing conviction that his misfortunes were irremediable made him turn more and more to the memory of those brief moments in the past when happiness had seemed to be within his grasp. He admitted that he was struggling to recapture an experience that lay beyond the range of language and reflection. True happiness, he confessed, was indescribable. Verbal description presupposed the ability to stand outside an object or experience in order to analyse it in a detached way, whereas happiness was something directly felt, an experience with which the personality was immediately and completely identified. In the *Confessions* he acknowledged his inability to describe the real nature of his happiness with Mme de Warens:

> But how can I describe what was neither said nor done, nor even thought, but felt, without my evoking any other object of my happiness than this feeling itself? . . . Happiness followed me everywhere; it was not in any specific thing; it was completely in myself, it could not leave me for a single moment. [I, 225.]

In spite of the impossibility of describing such an experience, Rousseau was impelled by circumstances, and, in particular, by the psychological tensions to which they gave rise, to reflect upon the implications of his attempts to transform a philosophy of happiness into the basis of lived experience. Moreover, the vivid memory of his brief periods of perfect bliss made him want to ponder over the significance of feelings which had played such a privileged role in his life, even though he knew them to be ultimately beyond description.

Of one thing he felt quite sure: happiness was not to be equated with intense but fleeting moments of pleasure. "These brief moments of ecstasy and passion, however vivid they may be, are only, by their very vivacity, scattered points in the line of life." Happiness, on the other hand, is "a simple, permanent state" that outlives the passing pleasures of the senses. "The happiness which my heart regrets," he insisted in the last years of his life, "is not composed of fleeting moments, but is a simple, permanent state that is not vivid in itself, but the duration of which increases its charm to the point of finding ultimate felicity in it" (I, 1046).

As is already implicit in this remark, the chief obstacle to the achievement of perfect happiness is man's involvement with time. The very nature of the feelings by which most men live seems to deprive them of any temporal stability. Men are either "ahead" of or "behind" themselves as they look anxiously towards the future or regretfully towards the past.

Everything is in a continuous flow on the earth: nothing keeps a constant, settled form and our affections which attach themselves to external things necessarily pass and change like them. Always ahead of or behind us, they recall the past which is no more or anticipate the future which often is not to be; there is nothing solid to which the heart can attach itself. [I, 1046.]

To overcome this difficulty Rousseau does not propose to repudiate the ordinary conditions of existence; he has no desire to lose himself in some kind of otherworldly mysticism. Time will not be abolished, but its three "moments" will merge into a kind of eternal "present." The completely happy man is no longer torn between different temporal dimensions, but enjoys a sense of sheer "duration"; he feels the reality of time without being tormented by the thought of its evanescence. The usual psychological reactions of pleasure or pain, desire or fear, are no longer operative, for they have been superseded by a higher state of consciousness, which Rousseau in his well-known fifth Promenade equates with the state of reverie or, in his own favourite expression, "the feeling of existence." The self seems to have reached a supreme, unsurpassable experience of the ultimate possibility of its being. We here find transposed into a higher and more spiritual key the theme of primitive man's spontaneous feeling of existence, a theme that is now deepened and enriched by a more highly developed mode of human consciousness.

The supreme "feeling of existence" does not sever all attachment to the earth; senses and emotions still continue to pulsate gently to the basic rhythm of nature's movements, but in a way that allows man's higher consciousness to exist in all its purity. Through this experience Rousseau believes that it is possible to enjoy a "perfect, sufficient and full happiness." He insists particularly on the idea of happiness as a plenitude. The truly happy man is one who enjoys the fullness of his own undivided existence and, in these privileged moments, "gathers together his whole being." Rousseau himself was able to obtain occasional glimpses of this idyllic happiness and, in his very last page, he spoke of the "pure and full happiness" of his life with Mme de Warens. He often insisted on the idea of the perfect plenitude of a truly happy existence. Of his lonely country walks he said in the second Promenade of the *Rêveries:*

> These hours of solitude and meditation are the only ones of the day when I am fully myself, when I belong to myself without diversion, without obstacle and when I can truly say that I am what nature wanted. [I, 1002.]

When the pressure of immediate circumstances seemed unbearable, he would turn back to those moments of the past, and especially of his life with Mme de Warens, which had brought him a similar sense of complete fulfilment. In the last unfinished Promenade he spoke of "this unique and short time of my life when I was fully myself, without admixture and without obstacle, and when I can truly say that I lived" (I, 1098).

Rousseau's tenacious belief in immortality owed a great deal to his confident hope that in the next life he would enjoy the unalloyed sense of selfhood only fleetingly experienced in this. Rousseau's mouthpiece, the Vicaire Savoyard, certainly acknowledged, as we have seen, that the good man's reward in heaven would involve "the contemplation of the Supreme Being and the eternal truths of which he is the source," but he also admitted:

> I long for the moment when, delivered from the shackles of the body, I shall be *myself* without contradiction, without division, and shall need only myself in order to be happy. [IV, 604–5.]

Yet Rousseau refused to allow the apparently subjective aspects of happiness to stifle his equally strong conviction that happiness contains a genuinely expansive element. This conviction is in complete conformity with his acceptance of the universal order. Since the physical universe has been created by God, man feels a spontaneous affinity with its spiritual essence. In the *Rêveries* Rousseau explains how "meditation in seclusion, the study of nature, the contemplation of the universe force a lonely man to move forward constantly to the author of things and to seek with a sweet anxiety the end of all he sees and the cause of all he feels" (I, 1014). This is a natural reaction when we recall the "conformity" existing between our "immortal nature" and "the constitution of this world and the physical order prevailing in it" (I, 1018).

Admittedly, the strange state of consciousness into which Rousseau was plunged by his dramatic accident on 24 October 1776, when he was knocked down by a large dog, was an exceptional experience. Nevertheless, it revealed the presence of those expansive feelings by which he had always set so much store. "I was born to life at that moment, and it seemed to me that I was filling with my airy existence all the objects I perceived. Completely abandoned to the present moment, I remembered nothing: I had no distinct notion of my individuality, not the least idea of what had just happened to me; I did not know who or where I was; I felt neither pain, fear nor anxiety. . . . I felt in my whole being a ravishing calm to which, whenever I recall it, I find nothing comparable in all the activity of known pleasures" (I, 1005). This experience was in complete harmony with the desire, expressed elsewhere in the *Rêveries* (I, 1056), "to extend his existence on to the whole universe."

That this sense of expansive plenitude was not restricted to the lonely enjoyment of personal feelings or the beauties of physical nature is shown by Rousseau's persistent dream of shared intimacy. He constantly speaks of himself as a man "devoured by the need to love and be loved"; his dependence upon the activity of his imagination is due, he insists, to his overwhelming de-

sire to create a "society of beings after his own heart";
his withdrawal into himself has been caused by other
people's failure to respond to his own expansive and affectionate feelings. Even the contemplative ideal, in
which his search for happiness so often culminates, involves an awareness of other people; he remains fascinated by the dream of an existence that allows a kind
of reciprocal sharing of intimate personal feelings. Already in his first *Discours* he points out that the men of
early times "found their security in the facility of reciprocal interpenetration" (III, 8). As well as feeling a sense
of plenitude, the happy man enjoys a remarkable openness of heart which lays bare his innermost feelings to
the other's affectionate gaze. As Jean Starobinski has
brilliantly shown, Rousseau was always fascinated by the
ideal of transparency.[2] It is only when man has achieved
full maturity as a human being that he will be able to
understand the full implications of this experience. Nevertheless, the truly "primitive" being, whether a child
or a savage, who still retains the innocence and simplicity
of natural impulses, can find a deep contentment in feeling himself to be the object of the gods' benevolent gaze.
In the "simplicity of early times" happiness reigned on
earth because "innocent and virtuous men . . . loved to
have the gods as witnesses of their actions" (III, 22).
Likewise, the young Jean-Jacques and his cousin Bernard
treated their guardians at Bossey, the minister Lambercier and his sister, like "gods who read into their hearts"
(I, 21); they felt as though they were living in "the
earthly paradise." If in his last years Rousseau transferred the "earthly paradise" to the solitary enjoyment of
his own existence (I, 1083), it was only because men
had cut him off from all communication with those who
might be capable of understanding his real emotional
needs.

When he was not inhibited by the irksome presence

---

[2] Jean Starobinski, *Jean-Jacques Rousseau, la Transparence et l'Obstacle*, (Paris: 1957).

of potential enemies, Rousseau abandoned himself willingly to the idea of shared intimacy. In *La Nouvelle Héloïse*, where his imagination was not restricted by the obstacles of everyday life, he gave a particularly powerful expression to his dream of ideal happiness. It is especially in the curious episode of *"la matinée à l'anglaise"* that the essential aspects of the experience are most clearly revealed. The idyllic society of Clarens, based mainly on the existence of "great souls," enjoys a bliss unknown to lesser mortals. "We spent a morning together in silence, relishing both the pleasure of being together and the sweetness of self-communion (*recueillement*). How few people know the delights of this state!" (V, 3; II, 558). Those who have attained such felicity do not need words to express their feelings. "But friendship, vivid celestial feeling, what discourse is worthy of thee?" The absence of strangers makes the enjoyment of this silent intimacy all the more delectable. "The friends need to be without witnesses in order to say nothing to one another at their ease. They want to be collected [*recueillis*], so to speak, in one another: the slightest distraction is distressing, the slightest constraint unbearable" (II, 558). This "state of contemplation" is one of the "great charms of sensitive men." There is an ecstatic element in the very absence of action at such a time. "Two hours have been thus spent in this ecstatic immobility, a thousand times sweeter than the cold tranquillity of the gods of Epicurus."

As Saint-Preux indicates at the beginning of his letter, the essential basis of the friends' rapt contemplation of one another's souls was the openness of their feelings. "We are beginning over again a fellowship that is all the more charming because there remains nothing in the depth of our hearts which we want to hide from one another." Julie herself was to recall this indispensable condition of true happiness when, later on, she wrote to Saint-Preux:

Agree at least that all the charm of the fellowship

that prevailed amongst us is in this openness of
heart which shares every feeling, every thought, which
causes each one, feeling himself to be such as he ought
to be, to show himself to all as he is. [II, 689.]

That Julie herself shares Saint-Preux's view of happiness as a kind of expansive plenitude is evident from
her observations at the moment when her own happiness
appears to be at its height:

I am surrounded by everything that concerns me,
the whole universe is here for me; I enjoy both the
attachment I have for my friends and their attachment
to me and one another. . . . I see nothing which does
not extend my being and nothing which divides it:
it is in everything around me: there remains no part
of it which is far from me. My imagination has nothing
more to do, I have nothing more to desire: to feel and
to enjoy are for me the same thing: at the same time
I live in all that I love, and I am absolutely full of life's
happiness. [III, 689.]

All the elements of Rousseau's ideal are here: plenitude, absolute inner unity, shared intimacy, harmonious
and expansive relationship with the immediate environment, and the spontaneous realisation of all possible
desires in an experience that is vivid and immediate.

Yet this account of perfect fulfilment is followed by
an astonishing remark, for Julie goes on to evoke the very
phenomenon which will destroy the perfection of her
experience. "O death, come when you will! I fear you no
longer: I have lived, I have forestalled you, I have no
fresh feelings to know, you no longer have anything to
steal from me." At the very moment when her happiness
seems to be complete, Julie not only begins to think of
death, but makes the startling admission: "Happiness
bores me."

Into the midst of apparently complete happiness there
intrudes a secret aspiration which threatens to destroy
its perfect plenitude. It was as though Rousseau's per-

sonality could not remain content with the idyll of "*la matinée à l'anglaise.*" The purely contemplative mood was unable to withstand the pressure of a more dynamic, progressive impulse within the personality. It will be recalled that Rousseau's view of human nature, as expounded, for example, in the *Discours sur l'Origine de l'Inégalité* and in *Emile*, constantly stressed the idea of growth and development: in the former work, Rousseau called attention to freedom and perfectibility as distinctive human qualities, whilst in the latter he insisted that the educator's main concern should be to control those expansive elements in the child's character which make him want to "extend" his being from what he immediately is to what he can and ought to be. Emile must be offered objects which allow proper expression to the "expansive force of his heart" (IV, 506), for he possesses "a superabundance of life which seeks to extend itself outwards" (IV, 502). Although perfect happiness may seem to involve the idea of a self-sufficient solitude, this is in fact an ideal state of being known only to God. Man, on the other hand, is impelled by his existence as a finite being to "love" something outside himself.

Although man's persistent tendency to extend and develop the potentialities of his being will ultimately lead to a kind of personal equilibrium through which he enjoys the feeling of existence as an absolute end in itself, Rousseau is aware that as soon as the goal has been reached, its stability is threatened by the very impulse which first inspired it. The nature of desire, and of perfection itself, is to reach out beyond immediate reality towards an as yet unrealised mode of existence. At the same time this very lack acts as an incentive to further effort. As soon as a particular goal has been attained, it is replaced by another which seems equally remote from immediate experience. It is, as Julie points out, the constant but vain effort to satisfy this lack which constitutes the ultimate meaning of existence:

Woe to him who has nothing more to desire! he

loses, so to speak, all he possesses. One enjoys less what one obtains than what one hopes for, and one is happy only before being happy. Illusion ceases at the point where enjoyment begins. The land of fancy is in this world the only one worthy of being inhabited, and such is the nothingness of human things that apart from the Being who exists by himself, there is nothing beautiful save what is not. [II, 693.]

In *Emile* Rousseau stresses the dependence of love on the activity of the imagination and the influence of subjective feeling. Because perfection does not belong to objects themselves but to the feelings they inspire in us, we are carried beyond the world of finite beings to the domain of unfulfilled longing. From this point of view the perception of an ideal goal is apt to conflict with the unity and plenitude of a completely happy existence.

Even the contemplation of physical nature could make Rousseau experience a similar sense of infinite yearning. The third letter to Malesherbes describes an apparently ideal day in his existence—a day when, freed from worldly cares, he enjoyed a blissful solitude in the midst of nature. His greatest delight, he declares, was to be alone with "the whole of nature and its inconceivable author" (I, 1130). Yet, in spite of the happiness obtained from exploring nature in all her beauty, his imagination could not remain satisfied with her as she was: he felt an overwhelming need to "populate her with beings after his own heart." Nature was transformed into the abode of a "charming society of which he did not feel himself to be unworthy." "I formed a golden age according to my fancy." Memories of the happy past and dreams of perfect bliss formed the basis of this paradisiac existence by filling out the empty spaces of the real world. Nevertheless, Rousseau himself was aware of the inadequacy of his escapist feelings. "In the midst of all that, I admit, the nothingness of my dreams would sometimes come and suddenly make my soul sad." He goes on: "Even though all my dreams had been turned into realities, they would not have been enough for me: I should have imagined, dreamed, desired still more. Within myself I found an inexplicable void which nothing could have filled—a certain yearning of the heart for another kind of enjoyment of which I had no idea and yet of which I felt the need" (I, 1140). He is careful to add that this craving for the unattainable was not a painful experience, since it contained "a very lively feeling and an alluring sadness which I should not have wanted to be without." At the same time he felt himself being transported beyond the domain of language and reflection to the contemplation of "all the beings of nature, the universal system of things and the incomprehensible Being who encompasses everything." Just as he had refused to rest content with the dreams of his own inner world, so was he now unable to limit himself to the physical world, however entrancing its form. "I was stifling in the universe, I should have liked to soar up into the infinite." The mood culminated in an attitude of speechless adoration before the majesty of God and his creation. In "the excitement of his transports" he could do nothing but exclaim: "O great Being! O great Being!"

Since unsatisfied longing thus gave way to ecstatic delight, Jean-Jacques considered that days such as these formed "his life's true happiness—happiness without bitterness, without tedium, without regrets, to which I should willingly have confined the happiness of my whole existence" (I, 1142).

The occasional experience of an "inexplicable void" thus did not create a serious problem for Rousseau, for such moments were absorbed into a more fundamental religious mood. It will be recalled that the last parts of *La Nouvelle Héloïse* were written at a time when he was becoming increasingly preoccupied with religious questions and was already feeling the inadequacy of his efforts to achieve mere earthly happiness. Yet so great was the power of immediate feeling and the need to enjoy the reality of personal experience that, even in a specifically spiritual form, his dream of happiness still retained its essential human characteristics, and, in particular, the desire for perfect inner unity and plenitude. In a sense Julie welcomes death as a mere prelude to complete and unalloyed bliss in the next world; the Vicaire too, as we have seen, relates his hope of immortality to his dream of personal fulfilment. It would seem, therefore, that Rousseau tended to consider the religious aspect of his search for happiness as an extension and completion of his most precious moments of earthly bliss.

The presence of this religious element also explains the strongly contemplative aspect of his most rapturous moods. His greatest delight was to lose himself in an ecstatic contemplation that enabled him to enjoy his own existence and at the same time feel an intimate, if mysterious personal affinity with the spiritual aspects of nature and its incomprehensible Creator. At such times Rousseau seems to have attained an absolute felicity, beyond which it was not possible for him to go as long as he was still tied to his mortal body.

This exalted view of a happiness that culminated in contemplative ecstasy was not powerful enough to give Rousseau a permanent sense of inner security during his last years, for he was becoming increasingly aware of the difficulty of reconciling his idealism with the grim reality of everyday existence. He might indeed look beyond this mortal life to the enjoyment of perfect bliss in the next world, but in the meantime he had to reckon with the influence of circumstances which threatened to destroy his inner peace. In spite of the glowing terms in which he described his dream of perfect bliss, his high hopes of realising it on this earth did not sustain him until the very end. In the first paragraph of the *Rêveries* he clearly indicated one of the main obstacles which lay in his path. His longing for the full enjoyment of his personal being was constantly frustrated by the nagging thought that he had to prove himself worthy of this experience; it was not enough for him to be a "good and innocent" man; he had to know that he was one "whose heart had never known any reprehensible inclination." The search for happiness could never be satisfactorily completed until he had answered the question which appears in the first paragraph of the *Rêveries*, "What am I myself?"—a question which seems all the more surprising when we recall the hundreds of pages already devoted to answering it in previous works. Anxious reflection constantly impelled him to re-examine the basis of his happiness at the very moment when he seemed to have attained it. Within himself he still had to ward off the insidious influence of secret guilt, whilst in the outer world he was constantly aware of the menacing gaze of his relentless enemies. His "devouring need to love and be loved" made him both seek and fear another's presence and, in the last resort, his reaction to other people was inseparable from his desire to know himself as an innocent man. At the same time the overwhelming need to protect the image of his innocence and goodness led him to exaggerate the malevolence of his persecutors, so that, to the very end of his life, his need to become the object of his own reflection not only conflicted with his equally strong desire to enjoy the unsullied sense of his personal existence, but also helped to create a fatal rift between himself and other men. Moreover, since this antithesis between good and evil was too extreme to be permanently acceptable to his tormented mind, he felt a recurrent need to find a new basis for his happiness. Still ardently longing for the enjoyment of an existence that was "without admixture or obstacle," he was none the less exposed to disturbing inner pressures which made its attainment either hazardous or impossible.

Apart from the influence of this persistent self-questioning, Jean-Jacques was faced with a difficulty of a more mundane and physical kind. He recognized that with advancing age he could not recapture the ecstasies of his former years; his imagination was growing weaker, his sensibility more blunted. He could no longer "plunge headlong into the ocean of nature" and "identify himself with the universal system"; likewise, the reveries of his old age were less ecstatic than the rarefied moods of his earlier years. "My imagination which is already less lively, is no longer fired by the contemplation of the object inspiring it; I am less intoxicated by the ecstasy of reverie; there is more reminiscence than creation in what it produces henceforth; the spirit of life is gradually being extinguished in me; my soul leaps out only with difficulty from its decrepit envelope" (I, 1002). The same theme reappears in the ninth Promenade: "My soul, obfuscated and obstructed by my organs, grows feebler every day and, under the weight of these heavy masses, no longer has enough vigour to leap forth, as formerly, from its old envelope" (I, 1075). Even memory, in spite of its fascination, was too fitful to provide the "solid basis" Rousseau so desperately needed. However entrancing his idealistic aspirations might be, he realised that he would henceforth have to rely on the pleasures of sense experience. "My soul, dead to all great movements, cannot be affected by anything but the objects of the senses. I now have nothing but sensations, and it is only through them that I can be affected by pain or pleasure here below." "My ideas," he had already affirmed in the same Promenade, "are almost nothing but sensations, and the sphere of my understanding does not go beyond the objects by which I am immediately surrounded" (I, 1066).

As this last remark shows, the earlier ecstatic contemplation of nature, which made him lose contact with "all particular objects" through a mood in which he "felt and saw only in the whole," had been replaced by a humbler but perhaps more stable relationship with the physical world.

After trying to find happiness in diverse ways, Rousseau suddenly resumed a former hobby, botany. He considered this to be an innocent pastime which not only took him away from his enemies' hostile gaze, but allowed him to come into close contact with the nature he loved. Henceforth he proposed to examine nature "in detail" rather than *en masse*. As well as providing "delightful recreation for his eyes," his botanical excursions would be commemorated by a herbarium of flowers and plants which would serve as a far more satisfactory "journal" of his lonely walks than the impersonal medium of the written word. Freed from the anxious reflection which usually accompanied his literary self-analysis, he hoped to possess a speedier and more effective means of recovering happy memories and elaborating new dreams. Botany, therefore, would not be a scientific pursuit, but the leisurely activity of an innocent man who was delighted by the "chain of accessory ideas."

Yet this seemingly harmless pastime did not allow Rousseau completely to overcome the ambiguity of his attitude towards "sensations," which involved not only the contemplation of physical nature but reactions to living people. Sense experience could never be quite simple for Rousseau, because it was related to the feelings of his "heart." It thus brought him anxiety as well as pleasure. On the days when he saw nobody he was "happy and content without division, without obstacle," but as soon as he encountered a "sinister look" or heard an "envenomed word," he knew that "the influence of his senses upon his heart constituted his life's sole torment" (I, 1082). "Always too much affected by physical objects and especially by those which bear a sign of pleasure or pain, benevolence or aversion, I let myself be carried along by these external impressions without being able to avoid them except by flight. That is my only trouble; but it is enough to spoil my happiness" (I, 1068).

Disturbing though these experiences might be, Rousseau in his last years was increasingly eager to enjoy the "happy, gentle life for which he was born" (I, 1081). At times he even felt himself to be the "happiest of mortals" living in "the earthly paradise." Although he sporadically acknowledged his need to achieve greater "virtue," he tended to long more and more for the spontaneous "goodness" of an "old child" who was also a "man of nature."

In spite of its attractions, Rousseau did not consider

that this way of life offered an example that ought to be imitated by other men, for he saw his own position as unique: nobody but himself, he believed, could become the victim of "the most iniquitous and absurd system ever devised by an infernal spirit." Only his particular circumstances justified the pursuit of such a simple existence. No doubt this new way of life still expressed certain principles which had already been prominent in his didactic writings, but they had constituted only one part of a complex pattern involving "virtue" as well as "goodness." Whereas the unsophisticated individual living in rural solitude could trust the "goodness" of his natural feelings, most men were compelled to transform their "natural" freedom into the "moral" and "civil" freedom suited to social and political life. Far from denying the importance of this moral development, Rousseau had given it considerable emphasis, as a work like the *Contrat Social* abundantly testifies; but his advocacy of virtue had never been able to conceal his own predilection for "goodness," even in those works which affirmed the moral superiority of the former. In the very *Discours* which extolled the merits of "virtue" he could not forbear from evoking "the simplicity of early times" and regretting the growing remoteness of "the beautiful shore adorned by nature's hands alone" (III, 22), whilst *Emile* concluded, as we have seen, with a curious juxtaposition of civil morality and rural idyll. In later years, as he moved further and further away from social life, he described, in the first of the *Dialogues,* the "ideal world which was like ours and yet quite different" (I, 668 f), a world whose inhabitants were privileged to know the "beautiful" and "harmonious" delights of "immediate enjoyment" as they abandoned themselves to the "gentle primitive passions" derived from true *amour de soi.* A life such as this did not need the virtue which made men "combat and conquer nature" (I, 670). Occasionally, it is true, Rousseau would admit with surprising frankness that he was excessively prone to extol his virtue when he was merely following his natural "inclinations" (I,

1052); he admitted that the "sensitive and good Jean-Jacques" might be required to leave life "not better, for that was not possible, but more virtuous than when he entered it" (I, 1023). Yet these sporadic avowals were not powerful enough to divert him from the pursuit of "a happiness" for which he felt himself to be made; he believed that both by temperament and circumstances, he was freed from the moral obligations imposed upon other men by their continued acceptance of social and political values.

Yet Rousseau's defiant determination to be happy "in spite of them" could not completely overcome his uneasiness; not only the involuntary intrusion of the ambiguous feelings already examined, as well as his recognition that "virtue" required a kind of happiness which differed in important ways from that of the merely "good" man, but also his restless exploration of new ways of achieving inner peace betrayed a secret dissatisfaction with his chosen ideal. His final decision to abandon writing for botany seems to indicate the renunciation of all his efforts to present a fixed reflective account of perfect happiness. Anxious thought about this problem might still continue to exert some kind of peripheral influence on his psychological life, but he was determined to subordinate it henceforth to the more palpable satisfactions of an activity that accorded priority to experience over reflection. It was, therefore, perhaps appropriate that the *Rêveries* should have been left unfinished and that, on the eve of his death, Rousseau was not engaged on literary work but on a botanising expedition that gave him his last experience of "peace and rest" amid the nature he loved so much.

INDIVIDUAL IDENTITY AND SOCIAL
CONSCIOUSNESS IN ROUSSEAU'S PHILOSOPHY

JOHN CHARVET

At the beginning of *Emile*, Rousseau contrasts and opposes two modes of existence, existing as a man according to nature and existing as a citizen against nature.[1]
But he immediately goes on to suggest that, if we consider what it is to bring up a man according to his true
nature, we may perhaps find the two modes reconciled
in one type of existence, the existence of a natural man
educated to live in cities. But while the rest of *Emile*
confidently assumes that this reconciliation is being effected, the initial hesitancy with which it is proposed
reflects a recurrent doubt in Rousseau's thought as to
whether the two modes are reconcilable, as to whether
the good citizen can be created without first destroying
nature in him. In this essay I shall consider these issues
as they constitute for Rousseau a problem about man's
consciousness, about the way in which individual men
identify themselves in relation to other men, and I shall
show why it is that Rousseau can and should be unclear
in his own mind as to whether he has or has not brought
about the desired reconciliation between nature and
society.

In the brief characterization of these two modes with
which *Emile* begins, natural man is described as existing as an absolute and independent whole, as possessing a complete individual existence in himself,
whereas the citizen is said to exist merely as a fraction
of a larger whole, namely, the political community, to
exist merely relatively to and dependent on the com-

This essay was especially written for this volume by John Charvet,
Lecturer in Political Science, London School of Economics.
[1] *Emile*, ed. Garnier (Paris: 1961), pp. 9–11.

munity, and this appears to deny his natural completeness as an individual. To understand this problem as a problem of man's consciousness, I shall begin with Rousseau's fuller account of natural man's existence in the *Discourse on the Origins of Inequality* (the *Second Discourse*).

In reading the first part of the *Second Discourse* it might be thought that natural man's absolute and independent existence consists in the fact that he is supposed by Rousseau to be leading a solitary material life, and so pursues his well-being independently of other members of his species. But this would be a merely contingent fact about man's original condition, which could have been otherwise; he could, that is to say, have existed in co-operating groups which would have made his good for himself dependent on his relations with other members of the group. If the sense in which man's natural existence is said to be absolute and independent were merely this contingent supposed fact about his original material condition, it would be without the moral significance that Rousseau quite clearly wishes to attach to it. For if he formerly pursued his good independently of others, but now does so in co-operation with them, this seems no sort of problem at all.

More than this must be involved in Rousseau's meaning, and the more that is involved concerns the nature of what Rousseau calls man's natural self-love, or the principle of *amour de soi*, which governs man's actions in the state of nature. Rousseau wants to say that man's natural self-love is absolute, in the sense that it involves no reference to beings other than himself. Whether a man is well or ill with himself depends only on how he stands to himself and not on how he stands relatively to other beings. But this again might be thought merely to arise out of the fact of his supposed solitary material mode of existence. That this is not the case, however, can be seen from a consideration of the following passage, in which Rousseau is concerned to distinguish man's natural self-love, *amour de soi*, from another form of self-love, *amour-propre*.

One must not confuse *amour-propre* with *amour de soi,* two passions which are very different both with regard to their nature and their effects. *Amour de soi* is a natural sentiment which inclines every animal to watch over his own preservation, and which, directed in man by reason and modified by pity, produces humanity and virtue. *Amour-propre* is only a relative and artificial sentiment, which is born in society and which leads every individual to make more of himself than every other. It inspires in men all the evils they perpetrate on each other, and is the true source of honour. If this is well understood, I maintain that in our primitive condition, which is the true state of nature, *amour-propre* does not exist; *for each man considering himself as the sole observer of himself, the only being in the universe who takes any interest in him, as the sole judge of his own merit, no sentiment which depends on comparisons which he is not in a condition to make, could take root in his soul* [my italics].[2]

The contrast in this passage is between *amour de soi,* which is absolute, and *amour-propre,* which involves making comparisons between oneself and others, so that one's well-being for oneself comes to depend on the results of these comparisons. The assertion is that man naturally does not make such comparisons, and the question is why he does not do so. Rousseau's answer seems to be that natural man is unable to make comparisons, because he sees himself as the sole observer and judge of himself. But this cannot be right, for there is no reason why natural man, given this, should yet not compare, say, his own strength or swiftness of foot with that of another man, as indeed Rousseau says elsewhere that he will do when engaged in a temporary contest with another over some object of desire.[3] Rousseau's point should be that any such comparison would not affect the

---

[2] *Political Writings,* ed. Vaughan (Oxford: 1962), Vol. I, p. 217. (The translation here as in subsequent passages is my own.)
[3] Ibid., p. 203.

status of his self-love as absolute and not relative. For while he may see another as stronger than himself, and bear this in mind in deciding whether to engage in a fight for the common object of desire, his being well with himself will not be affected by the mere fact that the other is stronger than himself; he will not feel depressed merely because he sees himself in this respect as inferior to the other. I say that this should be Rousseau's point because the reason Rousseau offers for the impossibility of natural man's making comparisons only makes sense on this supposition. For to say that natural man sees himself as the *sole* observer and judge of himself is to say that he does not see other men as his observers and judges. He cannot then be aware of being present to the consciousness of other men as anything at all, and so cannot see himself as *being estimated by them* as superior or inferior. He cannot, that is to say, be concerned with the status he occupies in the eyes of others, and so cannot be worried about status at all. It would thus follow that whether he sees himself in particular instances as superior or inferior to other men could of itself make no difference to his well-being.

We can now see that natural man's existence is absolute and independent in a sense more significant than its merely material isolation, and at the same time we can begin to see the source of Rousseau's later problems. Natural man exists for himself alone, not simply by pursuing his good independently of others, but, according to Rousseau, because he does not make comparisons between himself and other men; and yet, as we have seen, Rousseau's point expressed more clearly should be that natural man exists for himself alone, because he does not make comparisons in a context in which he sees himself as existing for others, as having an identity for them. Thus the primary fact, which ensures the absoluteness and independence of natural man's existence, is that this man is for himself the only person that exists in the world, the only observing and judging consciousness. Other men, Rousseau says, he sees "almost as he regards animals of another species".[4] Natural man exists for himself in a radically different way from the way in which others exist for him, for he possesses an identity for himself and yet does not recognize other men as similarly endowed with self-consciousness. Natural man, in not being aware of others as centres of consciousness in the world, cannot be aware of having an existence in their consciousness, of being somebody for them. But it follows from this that the natural state of man's consciousness, understood in this way as living for himself alone, does not merely happen contingently to be non-social, while it could be social, but is *necessarily* non-social, for it is defined in such a way as to be incompatible with a social consciousness. For a social consciousness must involve an awareness of the conscious existence of others, together with an awareness of one's own existence for others in their consciousness, both of which are necessarily excluded by this understanding of nature. In these terms, society could never be based on nature, for nature and society are mutually exclusive.

However, while Rousseau's own argument requires this development in order to complete its own sense, the fact that Rousseau himself does not express it clearly is of great importance for his later position. For by talking as if it is in the first place the comparing or the not comparing of oneself with others that separates man's natural self-love, *amour de soi,* from its social form, *amour-propre,* and so natural man's consciousness from social man's, rather than the making of such comparisons in a context in which the individual is conscious of existing only for himself or of existing for others as well, Rousseau is enabled to introduce these two elements into his story of human corruption in a way which profoundly misconstrues the relations between them, and so subsequently to pursue his task of reconciling nature and society, while concealing from himself the incoherence, in his own terms, of such an enterprise.

---

[4] Vaughan, Vol. I, p. 217.

I now turn to the second part of the *Second Discourse*, in which Rousseau develops his idea of the corruption of human nature in society, for it is only in relation to this corruption that the problem of *Emile* and its proposed solution can properly be understood. The process is introduced in the following passage:

> As ideas and feelings succeeded one another, and the mind and the heart were developed, men continued to become less wild; their relations were extended, and their ties contracted. They accustomed themselves to assemble before their huts or around a large fire; the song and the dance, true offspring of love and leisure, became the amusement or rather the occupation of men and women thus idly gathered together. Each one began to consider the rest, and to wish to be considered in turn, and public esteem came to acquire a value. Whoever sang or danced the best, whoever was the most handsome, the strongest, the most skilful, or the most eloquent, came to be of most consideration; and this was the first step towards inequality and vice at the same time. From these first distinctions arose on the one side vanity and contempt, on the other shame and envy; and the fermentation caused by these new leavens finally produced combinations fatal to innocence and happiness.[5]

In this passage the crucial element in the process, which finally destroys human happiness and innocence, is that men come to have for themselves, not as in Rousseau's nature a purely private identity, but a public identity, the identity created for them by public opinion, to which they attach value. The question is, however, how this creation of and attachment to a public identity comes about? I do not think that Rousseau is here attending very closely to this question, but nevertheless this passage implies an answer, which, although it must be a false account of the process, is, as I shall try to show,

---

[5] Ibid., p. 174.

at the same time the account that Rousseau must hold if his problem and solution in *Emile* is to make any sense. The answer to my question which this passage implies, then, is as follows: Rousseau says that in the context of their common activities each man begins to consider, in a manner which we may understand as involving appreciation or judgement of, others. Others come to have for him an identity as good singers, dancers, etc., and as a result he comes to desire to be appreciated as such in his turn by others. Hence the opinion of others becomes important for him, and he comes to have and desire a public identity. In this account, then, the public identity appears as a result of a process which begins with the appreciation or judgement by the individual of the qualities and performances of others. And this, as I shall argue, must be false. We would have to suppose, for this account to be true, that, to begin with, each man does not see himself as having an identity for others, as being observed and judged by others, for if this were the case he would already have a public identity. Consequently we must suppose that each man is not aware of others, but, as in nature, only of himself, as being a source of judgement and appreciation in the world. He cannot therefore be aware that, when he is doing his appreciation of someone, others also are appreciating this person, so as to constitute already a public appreciation of him. The appreciation must be purely private to himself. We now have to suppose that having appreciated the other, he wishes to be appreciated in turn, but the question is how could he have such a desire unless he already attached value to the opinion that others might have of him, and so was already aware of having an identity for them? For seeing another as a good something or other, a good fighter or swift runner, was something he was quite capable of doing, as we saw, in mere nature, without producing in him any desire to be appreciated in his turn, because he did not see others as observers and judges of himself, and so did not see himself as having an identity for them. Hence if this desire to be appreciated by others is to be plausible, it presupposes what is obvious in the situation Rousseau describes, that men have already become aware of having an identity for others. It is when men become aware of being observed and judged by others in the common activities they carry on that they come to have each for themselves this public identity which then becomes the object of their concern and so transforms the nature of their self-love. And it is only then that Rousseau's process of corruption can begin. Insofar, then, as Rousseau presents the creation of and concern for this public identity as a consequence of comparing oneself with others and desiring to be judged well by others, he has reversed the true state of the relationship between them.

The corruption which Rousseau discusses is manifested in the first place in an intense competitiveness, for a man is now only well with himself insofar as he achieves the positions of public honour accorded by public opinion, so that his good for himself becomes dependent on defeating others in the struggle for public recognition. This competition for the necessarily scarce positions of honour not only brings each man's interests into contradiction with every other man's, but generates also all the peculiarly human vices; envy, malice, vanity, pride, contempt, etc., are all passions which inflame men against each other, arising out of the fundamental passion of *amour-propre*, since they all presuppose that the individual's primary self-identification is in terms of his appearances for others. While of course Rousseau has much else to say about this corruption and the stages of its development, the consequence is that although men have acquired a social consciousness, in that they no longer exist for themselves absolutely without reference to others, but exist for themselves in their relations to others, they have nevertheless not become good for others, but on the contrary have become the enemy of their fellow men and perpetually dissatisfied with themselves.

Rousseau suggests that in order to understand the

mess that social man has got himself into, and consequently the differences between this man and natural
man, we must understand that:

> there is a sort of men who value the opinion of the rest
> of the world, who are happy and content with them-
> selves on the testimony of others rather than on their
> own. This is in effect the true cause of all these dif-
> ferences: the savage [natural man] lives within him-
> self; social man, always outside himself, knows how
> to live only in the opinions of others; and it is, so to
> speak, from their judgement alone that he derives the
> sense of his own existence.[6]

We have here an account of the transformation of natural man into a social being together with a related account of the emergence of this social being's corrupt
existence. This corrupt social existence of man is constituted by his living in the opinions of others, by which
a man exchanges his natural self-sufficient existence for
a personal dependence on others. This form of social
existence is thus quite clearly against nature, so that the
project to reconcile nature and society, by refounding
society on nature, requires the conception of a new social
consciousness, which excludes this personal dependence.
In terms of the understanding of nature presented above,
however, this must be an impossible undertaking. And
yet because the new element in man's existence, which
transforms him from a natural into a social being, is identified as the making of comparisons, out of which the
corrupt consciousness develops, so that the corrupt consciousness is not itself the transforming agency, this impossibility is potentially concealed from Rousseau's view.
For the making of comparisons is not necessarily, in
terms of Rousseau's nature, anti-natural; as we have seen,
natural man could make such comparisons between himself and other men, without altering Rousseau's conception of nature. Thus, while Rousseau sees natural man

---

[6] Vaughan, Vol. I, p. 195.

in the *Second Discourse* as incapable of making such comparisons, when we find in *Emile* that the new social consciousness, which is to be founded on nature, depends also for its generation on the making of comparisons, we cannot say that for this reason the new consciousness is contrary to nature. It is this possibility which Rousseau in proposing his solution in *Emile* exploits, and to a consideration of this I now turn.

The solution in *Emile* is presented in terms of an education that is in accordance with nature. The point in this education at which the social problem of the *Second Discourse* as discussed above directly arises, and thus the point at which Rousseau's solution is required, is Emile's adolescence, for it is at this age and not before that Emile is supposed to acquire a social consciousness. To understand how this can be so it is necessary to understand the nature of the education that Emile the child has received; but since this cannot be entered into here, it must suffice to emphasize that Rousseau requires that the child's education should be such that his consciousness will be like natural man's, absolute and not relative, and hence not a social consciousness at all. Thus he says of his Emile immediately prior to his adolescence:

> He considers himself without relation to others, and is content that others do not think of him. He demands nothing of anybody and believes he owes nothing to anybody. He is alone in human society.[7]

Like natural man, then, the child, if properly educated, exists for himself alone, and it is because this non-social consciousness is attributed to the child that Rousseau can present the social problem as arising only at an age when his solution can be brought to bear on it.

The problem is introduced thus:

> My Emile, having up till now considered only himself, the first observation that he makes of his fellow men

---

[7] *Emile*, p. 244.

leads him to compare himself with them; and the first sentiment that this comparison arouses in him is the desire to obtain the first place. Here is the point at which *amour de soi* transforms itself into *amour-propre* and at which all the passions that depend on the latter begin to grow. But to determine whether those passions which will predominate in his character will be humane and gentle or cruel and evil, whether they will be the passions of benevolence or pity, or envy and covetousness, it is necessary to know what position he will feel himself to occupy in relation to others, and what sort of obstacles he will think he will have to overcome in order to obtain it.[8]

This passage reintroduces in part the story of the *Second Discourse*. Emile begins to observe others, compare himself with them, and comes to desire to be superior to them. But whereas this point in the *Second Discourse* led straight on to the generation of a corrupt social consciousness and the vicious passions, we are now offered the alternative of the good passions of pity and benevolence arising from the same source. Here, then, we have the new social fact of making comparisons leading to the creation of a consciousness of one's relations to others informed by the co-operative rather than the competitive passions. What we need to know is what these comparisons are that produce these desirable consequences. In the above passage we are told that *amour de soi* is transformed into *amour-propre*, so that *amour-propre* appears to have become the form of self-love which now guides Emile's conduct and relations. And in respect of *amour-propre* Rousseau says this:

Extend *amour-propre* over others, we will transform it into virtue, and there is no human heart in which this virtue does not have its root. The less the object of our concern relates immediately to ourselves, the less the illusion of particular interest is to be feared; the more

---

[8] *Emile*, p. 279.

we generalize this interest, the more equitable it becomes; and the love of the human race is in us the love of justice.[9]

There is a problem here as to what extending *amour-propre* over others means, but in view of the identity of interests it is supposed to produce, it would appear to mean extending our desire for precedence for ourselves and our interests over others, which itself would mean, by granting the same precedence to others, acknowledging an identity or equality of all interests. But if the identification of one's interests with the interests of others is the aim and end product, it is unclear how this is to be arrived at. For insofar as it depends on the comparisons one makes between oneself and others, it is obvious that to produce the above result, the content of comparisons must be equality between oneself and others, which this passage does not explain.

How this identification of oneself with others is arrived at has, however, already been explained in the account that Rousseau gives of the way in which Emile is introduced to other men. After his lonely and isolated childhood, Emile is introduced to others through their suffering and is required through the sentiment of pity to identify himself with them.[10] Suffering here is presented as the essence of humanity, that which reveals the truly human,[11] so that Emile, in relating himself to others through pity for their suffering, is identifying himself with others in respect of his and their essential humanity. This identification is the product of comparing oneself with others, for pity is said to be a relative sentiment, while the identification involves feeling oneself to exist in the other, so that one finds oneself in the other, and the other and oneself become the same. It is this emotional identification with others through love and pity that Rousseau claims is the basis of a truly moral

---

[9] Ibid., p. 303.
[10] Ibid., pp. 259 ff.
[11] Ibid., p. 260.

consciousness. His explanation of this is contained in a note of great importance, but he begins in the main text by saying that if this were the place, he would show how the moral conscience derives from these first movements of the heart towards others that Emile is experiencing, and how the notions of justice and goodness are not merely abstract words, but the affections of the soul enlightened by reason; and that reason alone, independently of conscience, could not establish any natural law, which on the contrary must be founded on a natural need of the human heart.[12] The note to this passage elaborates his meaning thus:

> The precept itself, to act towards others as one wishes that others act towards oneself, has no true foundation other than in conscience and sentiment; for what precisely is the reason for acting, being oneself, as though I were another, especially when I am morally certain of never finding myself in the same situation? And who will reply that in following this maxim very faithfully, I will get others to follow it in the same way with me? The evil man gains his advantage from the honesty of the just and his own injustice; he is quite content that all the world should be just except himself. That arrangement, whatever one may say, is not very advantageous for good men. But when the force of an expansive soul identifies me with my fellow man, and when I feel myself so to speak in him; it is in order not to suffer myself, that I wish him not to suffer; I interest myself in him for the love of myself, and the reason of the precept lies in nature itself, which inspires in me the desire for my well-being wherever I may feel myself to exist. From which I conclude that it is not true that the precepts of natural law are founded on reason alone, they have a more solid and certain base. The love of men derived from the love of self [*amour de soi*] is the principle of hu-

---

[12] *Emile*, p. 278.

man justice. The essence of all morality is given in the Gospel by that of the law.[13]

The moral relation for Rousseau is founded on this capacity, through love and pity, to identify oneself in the other so that one loves the other as oneself. Morality itself or virtue involving the love of all men, requires the generalization or extension of this identification to all, so that we arrive back by these means at the equality or identity of all interests which was said to be produced in the first place by the extension of *amour-propre* over others.

The answer to the question as to what comparisons between oneself and others are required in order both to generate relations with others informed by the co-operative passions, and to produce the capacity to treat all interests equally, is, then, that they should be comparisons relating to the human essence of suffering with the required conclusion that all men share in this respect the same essential identity. The new social consciousness is constituted by the acknowledgement of this identical nature, and the new social relations are based on the equality of all selves and their real interests that follows from it. This social consciousness, then, is dependent for its realization on the emergence in the adolescent Emile of what is not present for Rousseau in original nature, namely, his making comparisons between himself and others; but, as I have argued, it cannot for that reason be held to be contrary to nature, nor of course does Rousseau now wish to see these comparisons in this way. But this new consciousness is supposed to be based on nature also, and we must now consider how this is so.

In the last quoted passage the love of men, which this new consciousness involves, is said to be derived from the love of self in its natural form as *amour de soi*. But this *amour de soi* as it is expressed in the new consciousness cannot remain unchanged, for it requires modifica-

---

[13] Ibid., pp. 278–79.

tion through the comparisons one makes between one's self and other selves in order to produce the necessary identification of selves. Nevertheless while this modification intervenes to separate society from nature, it does not involve the destruction or denial of nature, but on the contrary builds upon nature. If this is so, it will appear that Rousseau has achieved his object. But how is this so? *Amour de soi* in nature was absolute, involving no reference to others, while through this modification a reference to other selves becomes implicit in one's own self-love. This occurs because as a result of the comparisons one makes one identifies oneself as having the same essential identity as other selves, characterized by suffering. But this self, in constituting the human essence, remains the same self that exists in nature, and not a new self that is the product of artificial social relations. Hence to acknowledge the shared identity of one's self with other selves is to come to an awareness through the socializing comparative faculties of only what is implicit in nature. Through reason, on which the relevant comparisons are dependent, one comes to see that the natural love of oneself is completed in the love of others. Thus the new social consciousness is founded on nature, but at the same time completes it.

In terms of my claim that Rousseau's conception of nature was that of a necessarily non-social human existence, so that the project to refound society on nature was an incoherent undertaking, what appears to have been achieved should have been impossible. However, all is not well with Rousseau's argument above. In the first place, the new consciousness does not simply require an acknowledgement of a shared identity between men, but a positive identification of one's individual existence with the existence of others. It requires the generation of feelings of love and pity towards others that no mere acknowledgement of a similar nature could of itself produce. We need some reason why men should be drawn to this positive identification with others. But we can immediately see that this attraction to others cannot be derived from nature as hitherto understood, for in nature each individual man is self-sufficient and has no need of others. Now, when Rousseau leaves Emile's isolated childhood behind in order to undertake to introduce the adolescent Emile to others through the conception of suffering humanity, we find Rousseau giving a completely new account of nature, which is incompatible with the old, without, however, any recognition on his part of this incompatibility. He says this:

> It is man's weakness which makes him sociable; it is our common miseries which carry our hearts to humanity; we would owe it nothing if we were not men. Every attachment is a sign of insufficiency: if each one of us had no need of others, he would hardly dream of uniting himself to them. Thus from our very infirmity is born our fragile happiness. A truly happy being is a solitary one; God alone enjoys an absolute happiness; but which of us has any idea of it? If some imperfect being could be sufficient for himself, what could he enjoy in our terms? He would be alone, he would be miserable. I do not conceive that he who has no need of anything can love anything. I do not conceive that he who loves nothing can be happy.
>
> It follows from this that we attach ourselves to our fellow men less by the sentiment of their pleasures than by the sentiment of their suffering; for we see much better in that the identity of our nature and the guarantee of their attachment to us.[14]

It is through this natural individual insufficiency, then, that we are drawn towards others, and that the required positive identification with them is produced. But this natural need for others, arising out of our common suffering, contradicts Rousseau's previous account of human nature in two fundamental respects: first, that man in nature had no need of others, but in living for himself alone was entirely self-sufficient, and second, that

---

[14] *Emile*, p. 259.

these natural men were not miserable sufferers but, on the contrary, contented in their self-sufficiency.[15] By not acknowledging the trace of a difficulty, let alone a contradiction, Rousseau assumes that the old conception is still in being, for society to be founded upon it, while proceeding on the basis of the new conception to account for what is unaccountable in the old, namely, the need for others, and doing so in terms of naturally suffering humanity, which is also incompatible with the old idea. What facilitates the retention of these contradictory elements is the fact that the new natural need for others is expressed in the sentiment of pity, while this sentiment was identified in the *Second Discourse* as natural to man. But this in no way helps to avoid the incoherence, for pity is presented in *Emile* as the positive identification of oneself with other men, and it is quite incoherent for Rousseau to suppose that this sentiment could be experienced by man in nature, since man in nature did not recognize other men as men at all. We cannot then say that the new social consciousness is founded on Rousseau's nature as originally understood, for it is dependent on a need of the individual for others, which is in contradiction with that nature. Man cannot be said naturally both to live for himself alone, and need the presence of others. The love of others derives from a need for others, which is not present and could not be present in *amour de soi*.

The new social consciousness is said to be founded on nature insofar as the love of others follows from and is a completion of one's natural self-love (*amour de soi*). It involves the identification of others and oneself as sharing the same essential nature, and in terms of this nature as having the same interests. This nature has been characterized as the common experience of suffering, but Rousseau does not consistently hold to this idea, and in the "Profession of Faith of the Savoyard Vicar," identifies the essential self of human beings with the will that

---

[15] Vaughan, Vol. I, p. 158.

is free. But here it is not the content that Rousseau gives to the idea of the essence or nature which all men share that is so important, but the form and implication of the argument that the notion is used to support. For insofar as the idea of the new social consciousness and the new social relation which is based on it consists in identifying men in terms of their essential nature alone, it involves a radical distinction and opposition between the essence or nature of men, which all have in common on the one hand, and the particular characteristics and qualities of individuals, which differentiate them from each other, on the other. The new consciousness of oneself and others must be a consciousness of that alone in respect of which one is the same as others or shares the same identity as them, and one is not the same in respect of one's particular characteristics or qualities, but only in respect of one's essence or nature. And the new social relation must be a relation between persons in respect of their essences and not their differentiating particularity. Essence and particularity are here opposed to each other, for one must exclude from this new consciousness all idea of the particularity of oneself and others. To the extent that this particularity of oneself and others enters into one's social consciousness and one's social relations, it contradicts the requirements of the new consciousness.

It is this opposition between one's essence and one's particularity, contained in Rousseau's purported solution to his nature-society problem, that produced the opening paradox of *Emile*, with which I began this paper, and also constitutes the reason for Rousseau's recurrent doubt as to whether in fact he has fully reconciled nature and society. The paradox arose because nature and society, man and citizen, were at first radically opposed to each other, only for the reader to be promised immediately a future reconciliation between them. In the original formulation of the opposition, man in nature was said to exist for himself as a complete individual, whereas the citizen had to deny this individuality and exist only as a partial being. The reconciliation, however, in this new consciousness and the new relations based on it merely develops the paradox, for on the one hand nature appears to be preserved in society, insofar as the new social man completes his nature identified in terms of his essential self, but on the other nature appears to be denied in society insofar as this new man has to deny his differentiating individuality in order to be himself.

Rousseau then cannot and should not be satisfied with his solution to the problem, while his solution creates the further problem of an internal division and opposition in each man between his essential and particular self. This, however, only arises because of his supposition that it is possible to exist in the world and have relations with others in terms of one's essential self alone. And this is incoherent because one's essence, however defined, does not of itself constitute an individual existence in the world. The essence of a thing identifies certain characteristics of an individually existing thing in virtue of which it is held to be the sort of thing it is. That is to say, they are characteristics which all members of a certain class of thing have in common, and which distinguish them as members of that class and not another. Thus, in respect of human beings, if the free will is said to be the essence of human beings, then free will is a characteristic of individually existing things, human beings, which all have in common, and which distinguishes them as human beings and not another thing. But human beings do not exist in the world as free will alone, but possessing other characteristics and qualities which identify them as particular differentiated human beings. Their essence as free will, by which they share the same identity, and their particular characteristics and qualities, by which they are differentiated from each other, cannot be opposed to each other, for they complement each other as all characteristics of the individually existing things they are. The opposition between them only arises if it is held that men should exist in respect of their essence only, and not in respect of their differentiating particularity.

Why, then, does Rousseau require men to exist as essence alone and to deny their particular individuality? Because for men to exist in society in their full particularity would be to reintroduce the old corrupt consciousness analyzed in the *Second Discourse*. For insofar as one exists in one's social relations in one's particularity, one will have to take account in these relations of the particularity of others and of oneself, as others in respect of oneself will also do. Hence how one is in these relations will be determined by judgements both of oneself and others of the particular qualities of persons, so that one's relations and the well-being that is dependent on them will be governed by one's particular appearances for others, and the particular appearances of others for oneself. In this way, one becomes again dependent for one's social well-being on the opinions of others, which itself will lead to the dangers of the competitive consciousness and competitive passions, which it is the aim of the new social consciousness to avoid altogether. For to the extent that the latter involves an existence in respect only of an individual's essence, men exist for each other as undifferentiated, and so no judgements concerning the particular qualities of persons can be made. But since this existence as pure undifferentiated essence is merely the abstraction from an individual's totality of qualities, of one which is not found alone, it is to attempt to exist as a pure abstraction, and to attempt to found relations with others on this basis is to attempt to have purely abstract relations, relations, that is, that could have no particular content, and so could not be social relations between men at all.

Rousseau's solution to his problem about the opposition between nature and society only involves a paradox because the central idea in the solution, a social relation based on the abstract essence of men, is an incoherent idea. This incoherence derives fundamentally from the attempt to conceive society and social relations in terms of nature that is defined in such a way as to be necessarily non-social. For this nature is not to exist for others, but only for oneself, whereas the social condition of man is an existence for others. But since this existence for others in society is in Rousseau's conception a purely abstract existence, which denies the particularity of oneself and others, nature is preserved at least negatively insofar as one thereby succeeds in not existing as a particular individual for others. If one is to remain a particular individual for oneself, this must be outside the social relation altogether and for oneself in one's self-communion alone. Since the social existence of man is an existence for others, which can only be an existence comprising his particular qualities, Rousseau's social philosophy involves the denial of the essence of social man.

This conclusion can be supported by a consideration of Rousseau's confusing use of the term *amour-propre*. Whenever he uses it, *amour-propre* is the social form of self-love, and is thus distinguished from *amour de soi* as the natural form of self-love. Despite this consistency there are two radically contrary valuations of *amour-propre*. When we first meet the term in the *Second Discourse*[16] it is treated as essentially contrary to nature, the artificial product of society, and inherently vicious. This valuation is maintained throughout the *Second Discourse* and at times in *Emile*.[17] But in *Emile* we also get a different valuation at the point at which its accommodation in the new social consciousness becomes necessary.[18] *Amour-propre* ceases to be identified as inherently vicious and becomes the basis for the generation of the good and co-operative social passions. It is no longer necessarily contrary to nature, but becomes the way in which nature is to be modified, although at the same time preserved, in society. The reason for these different valuations is that the self that is loved in the two cases is not the same self. In the former case it is the self in its particularity that is loved, and in the latter case it is

---

[16] To be found in the passage quoted above, p. 464.

[17] See in particular *Emile*, p. 249.

[18] To be found in the passage quoted above, pp. 471–72.

the essential self sharing the same identity as others. In both cases, however, *amour-propre* as the distinctively social form of self-love is a love of self, which, unlike the self in *amour de soi,* is identified as it is related to others. Where *amour-propre* is vicious, the self identified in its relations is the particular self, and is vicious because it involves a dependence on the appearances of this self to others, while where *amour-propre* is good, the self identified is the essential self without particularity and is good because it involves no dependence on others. The apparent contradiction between the two valuations of *amour-propre* reflects the opposition in Rousseau's system between the essential and particular self. But since the essential self is an abstract idea without possible individual existence, the only meaningful content to be given to the self that is loved in *amour-propre* is the self that, in possessing its general nature or essence as free will, possesses this in the particular way defined by its particular differentiated qualities. It is the love of this self in its relations, and thus as it appears to and is dependent on others, that must be the essential form of *amour-propre.* But at the same time it is this form which Rousseau's system requires to be destroyed, so that Rousseau's system involves the denial of the essential form in which social man expresses his self-concern.

ROUSSEAU'S THEORY OF THE FORMS OF GOVERNMENT

BERTRAND DE JOUVENEL

Rousseau had a profound impact upon the way of life of the late eighteenth century: thanks to him many parents became aware of and attentive to their children; he fostered enjoyment of natural beauties and contributed to a change in the style of gardening; he was instrumental in shifting the manner of personal relationships from polite restraint to excessive demonstrativeness; with a lag of a generation his political views fired Robespierre; with an even greater lag his Socinian religiosity was to pervade the nineteenth century. It would be hard to find another writer whose suggestions have proved effective so extensively.

Strangely enough, however, the very core of Rousseau's doctrine has been almost entirely disregarded. But is it so strange? In this respect, Rousseau was not only intellectually ahead of his day, but he was also affectively in direct opposition to the trend of his time, which has developed into the ruling spirit of our own: so much so that his attitude is puzzling to us.

Rousseau is the first great exponent of social evolution. His was the first attempt to depict systematically the historical progress of human society: here he precedes Condorcet, Saint-Simon, Comte, Marx-Engels and all those who sought to systematize views of social evolution. His concern to mark out stages of social development and to bring out the factors which he deemed crucial in the process is impressive against the background of contemporary writings. Everybody was then talking about

Reprinted, by permission of the author and publishers, from *Western Political Philosophies*, ed. M. Cranston. Bodley Head, London, 1964.

Progress but in a very loose manner, and Rousseau was the only one who thought of it as a process to be understood. Now the first author who offered an understanding of what everybody talked about should have been praised to the skies on that score. This, on the contrary, is what brought Rousseau the enmities which made the last part of his life a misery.

Rousseau attempting to place the manuscript of the *Dialogues* on the master-altar of Notre-Dame, because that then seemed to him the only way of ensuring that his protest against his persecutors should reach posterity. . . . Rousseau balked in his attempt and wandering through the streets of Paris, clutching his justification, in despair because there is no one he can trust to procure its posthumous publication. . . . Rousseau standing at street-corners, distributing leaflets copied in his own hand, which are spurned by passers-by . . . here are images which move us to pity, yet at the same time we feel that such conduct is pathological.

Again when we read the *Dialogues,* we feel that Rousseau is mainly the victim of his disordered imagination. I said 'mainly', not 'solely'. However much he exaggerated it, the evidence seems to me convincing that there was a continuing systematic attempt on the part of the *Philosophes* to discredit him. A war of derisive *bons mots* and ridiculous anecdotes was waged upon him which his own disposition made easy and which his sensitivity made effective. It will not do to plead that the *Philosophes* reacted without wilful malice to his being a 'difficult' person: they treated him as a dangerous man, and took advantage of his being difficult, making him ever more so by their expert teasing, finally driving him to desperate isolation.

But why did these lovers of Progress regard as dangerous the first systematic exponent of social evolution? For a solid and weighty reason: because Rousseau, while sketching evolution with a keen pencil, also painted it in dark colours. The *Philosophes* fought the Church, which they regarded as a restraining hand upon Progress, but an ever weakening hand. What if they now found in their path, coming from their own ranks, a new enemy, a voice warning against the dangers of Progress? To this challenger applied *a fortiori* the war-cry: *"Écrasons l'infâme!"* Rousseau points out that the *Philosophes*, having proved powerful enough to drive the Jesuits out of France, found it child's play to get rid of a single inconvenient individual.

In a concise recapitulation of his doctrine, Rousseau provides the key to the enmity of the *Philosophes*. A speaker is supposed to sum up the lessons he has drawn from a second painstaking reading of all Rousseau's works: 'I saw throughout the development of his great principle that nature has made man happy and good but that society corrupts him and causes his misery. Take the *Emile*, much read but much misunderstood; it is nothing other than a treatise on the spontaneous goodness of man, meant to show how vice and error, foreign to his constitution, invade it from outside and deteriorate it progressively.

'In his first writings, he is more concerned to destroy the delusive prestige which causes us to admire stupidly the very means of our misery, and he seeks to correct this false valuation which causes us to honour mischievous talents and to despise beneficial virtues. Everywhere he shows us mankind better, wiser and happier in its primitive constitution; blind, miserable and nasty as it moves away from it. His goal is to correct the error of our judgments in order to check the progress of our vices.'

It is easy to understand how exasperating the *Philosophes* must have found so pessimistic a view of Progress. It is also easy to understand that, during two centuries of accelerating Progress, admirers of Rousseau were prone to cast Noah's mantle upon what they regarded as an absurdity of their hero. But whether absurd or not, a doctrine which a great author explicitly states to be the essence of his message cannot be glossed over without a consequent misreading of his works. The respect due to the author requires that his books be read in the light of what he himself names as his central conception.

This dawned upon me many years ago, while studying the *Social Contract*, when I found it to be, not a hopeful prescription for a Republic to come, but a clinical analysis of political deterioration. In the *Social Contract*, Rousseau offered no recipe for turning the government of a large and complex society into a democracy: on the contrary, he offered a demonstration that great numbers and growing activity of government called for by increasing complexity of relationships, inevitably led to the centralisation of political authority in a few hands, which he regarded as the opposite of democracy. Quite early, Rousseau had expressed alarm about plans for the radical reconstruction of the French political system, and in the *Dialogues* designed for posthumous publication he complained bitterly:

> His object could not be to bring back large populations and big states to the initial simplicity but only to arrest, if possible, the progress of those small and isolated enough for their preservation from the perfection of Society and the deterioration of the species. . . . But the bad faith of men of letters and that silly vanity which for ever persuades everyone that he is being thought of, caused great nations to apply to themselves what was meant for small republics; and, perversely, one wished to see a promoter of subversion and troubles in the man who is most prone to respect national laws and constitutions, and who has the strongest aversion for revolution, and for *ligueurs* of all kind, who return the compliment.[1]

The subject of the *Social Contract* is not the social contract, but social affection. Under government man must necessarily be ruled—which is painful, and no one felt

---

[1] *Troisième Dialogue*, XXI, 129–30. The word *ligueurs* refers of course to the Ligue under Henri III, and to the violent agitation caused by the faction which then brought disorder to France.

this more than Jean-Jacques Rousseau. But the experience is the less painful as the rule to which a man is subject is less alien to him. Such rule does not cease to be alien, Rousseau insists, merely as a result of being authorised by a general mandate of the subjects. Each man must have participated personally in the formulation of the rule: the one who is 'administered' must himself be the 'legislator'.

The only form of association that Rousseau regards as legitimate is that where the associates 'take collectively the name of *people*, and are called specifically *citizens* in that they participate in the sovereign authority, and *subjects* in that they are under the rule of the laws of the state'. The word 'participate' is essential; and such participation must be real. For Rousseau, the assertion that the people is sovereign has a concrete meaning; it is not the case of a fiction from which one might as easily derive the unlimited power of a Bonaparte as that of a single elected body; he is saying that the laws may not be enacted except by a general assembly of the citizens, an assembly which has the legislative power, or, which, rather, *is* the legislative power, in the sense that, by definition, its power cannot be delegated. The distribution of roles between the people, which is sovereign, and the government, which executes a commission, is elaborated in the following passage:

> We have seen that legislative power belongs to the people, and can belong to nobody else. On the other hand, it is easy to see, on the basis of the principles already set forth, that the executive power cannot belong to the generality as a legislative or supreme body, because the executive is concerned with particular acts which do not fall within the province of law, or, consequently, of the sovereign, whose actions are purely legislative actions.
>
> The force of the public body can only be exerted through an agent who puts it into effect according to the directions of the general will, an agent who serves as a medium of communication between the state and

the sovereign, and who, in a way, brings about in the public person that which is brought about by the union of body and soul in the individual man. This is the reason for the existence within the state of a government that is often confused with the sovereign, of which, in fact, it is only the minister.

What then is the government? It is an intermediary body established between the subjects and the sovereign for their mutual communication, a body charged with the execution of the laws and the maintenance of freedom, both civil and political.[2]

Thus, according to Rousseau, the individuals who are citizens exercise their sovereignty collectively whenever they meet in the general assembly, which is called together from time to time; and they are habitually subject to a government, which is a permanent body, charged with the execution of the laws and of day-to-day administration. So we see two relationships of subordination: subordination of the government to the citizens as a body, and subordination of the subject to the government.

Rousseau admits only one sovereignty—that of the people, in other words, the body of citizens which has reality only in so far as it exercises legislative power. He explains:

The legislative power consists of two inseparable things: making the laws and maintaining them; that is to say, having supervision over the executive power. There is no state in the world where the sovereign has not this supervision. Without it, every association, every subordination, must fail between the two powers; the one will cease to depend on the other; the government will have no necessary connection with the laws; and law will become a mere word—a word signifying nothing.[3]

---

[2] *The Social Contract*, Book III, chap. 1.
[3] *Letters From the Mountain*, Part II, letter 7.

If the supervision by the body of citizens over the executive becomes less and less vigilant; if this executive power becomes more and more independent of the body of citizens, then there will be what Rousseau calls a 'slackening of sovereignty'.

Let us look more closely at this government, of which the members are 'absolutely nothing but a commission, a staff' or 'simple officers of the sovereign'. The government is itself a body of magistrates, and Rousseau admits that it may take various forms, identified according to the classical formula as 'democracy, aristocracy, monarchy'. On this subject he writes:

> The various forms that the government may take can be reduced to three main ones. After comparing their advantages and disadvantages, I would give preference to the one which is intermediate between the two extremes, and which bears the name of aristocracy. One must remember here that the constitution of the state and that of the government are two entirely distinct things, and must not be confused. The best kind of government is aristocratic; and the worst kind of sovereignty is aristocratic.[4]

If *The Social Contract* were merely a doctrinal work, there would be no more to say. The legislative power belongs to the whole body of citizens, who cannot delegate it; and there are commissioned magistrates, less numerous than the body of the citizens, but still numerous, who exercise the executive power. And that is that.

However, it is at this point that we touch on Rousseau's dynamic theory of the forms of government. To give, provisionally, a very crude account of it, I should put it thus: to the extent that the body of citizens becomes enlarged, participation becomes less real, less active, and, at the same time, the subject becomes less docile. This diminished docility prompts the government to use a greater force of repression, which itself entails

---

[4] *Letters From the Mountain*, Part I, letter 6.

the centralisation of a government, faced with the disaffection of the body of citizens; and so the government, evolving towards the power of one, evolves, in relation to the sovereign, towards the usurpation of sovereignty. I beg the reader not to judge the theory by this summary analysis; for I shall examine it now in greater detail.

To appreciate Rousseau's originality, it is worth while referring to Montesquieu. Montesquieu argues that a republic can only sustain its existence if its territory is small; and the reason he gives is geographical. In Montesquieu, the words 'distance' and 'remoteness' are key words: the author is plainly thinking in terms of communication and transport. Republican government cannot function if the people are too widely scattered for that rule to be enforced. How different is Rousseau's theory, which is founded on the human sentiments. The obedience of the citizen presents no problem, if it is a case of a citizen who holds himself responsible for the decisions of which the government is merely the minister.

It may be worth illustrating this moral situation with a familiar example. If I, as a convinced and devoted member of a voluntary society, receive from its executive secretariat a letter reminding me that I must do something or other in virtue of a decision taken at a meeting in which I have taken part, it may well be that this reminder will be unwelcome at the moment when it reaches me, but I should nevertheless think myself wrong not to comply with it. I should feel myself the more obliged, the more actively I had taken part in the meeting; and correspondingly, the less obliged the more purely nominal my membership of the society. This, I think, is the *affective* sense in which one must understand the following in *The Social Contract*:

> Suppose the state is composed of ten thousand citizens. The sovereign exists only collectively and as a body. But every member, as a subject, must be considered as an individual. Thus the sovereign stands

to the subject in the proportion of ten thousand to one; that is to say, each individual has for his share only one ten-thousandth part of the sovereign authority, though he must obey it entirely. If the size of the population is increased to a hundred thousand, the situation of the subject does not change, for each subject is equally with the rest subordinate to the empire of the laws, while his own single voice, reduced to a hundred-thousandth part, has ten times less influence in the formulation of those laws. Hence, since the subject is always one individual, the proportion in which the sovereign stands to him always increases in relation to the size of the population. From this it follows that the more the state increases, the more liberty diminishes.[5]

Reflect on this passage. Rousseau recognises that the 'empire of the laws' *weighs* on the subject. 'And this is a pressure which is painful for me if I want to move in a direction other than that in which the government presses me; though it is not in the least painful if my own free movement is in the same direction. I am the more ready to acknowledge my own impulsion in the government's pressure, the more lively a memory I have of having myself contributed to set it in motion. And this memory will be the more lively, the greater my contribution has been; and it will certainly be very much less lively if I have been lost in a great crowd. When I am thus lost, I no longer recognise my own impulsion behind the pressure I feel, but only the pressure of other people.

The same edicts seem to me the more oppressive, the less I have participated in their formulation; and my goodwill as a subject becomes correspondingly less. Hence there will be a need for more and more means of coercion if the government is to secure my obedience.

For Rousseau, two propositions are closely connected: 'the more the state enlarges, the more liberty diminishes'

---

[5] *The Social Contract*, Book III, chap. 1.

and 'government, to be any good, must be relatively stronger to the extent that the people are more numerous'. These are not two different expressions of the same idea, but two stages of Rousseau's reasoning. In the first place, the individual, lost in a greater crowd of citizens, feels less intensely his pride and sense of responsibility in participating, and when, as a subject, he receives his orders, they weigh heavily on him. He feels himself less free. Then, as this change of feeling makes him less well disposed towards the orders he is given, 'the repressive force must be increased': this is at the same time a consequence of his diminished feeling of freedom, and a positive factor of diminished freedom.

Exploring the consequences of the weakening of the sense of participation, Rousseau comes to the idea that 'the repressive force must be increased'. This entails a change in the form of the government.

> Since the total power of the government is always that of the state, it does not vary. From this it follows that the greater the strength which is spent by government on its own members, the less does it have left to exert on the people as a whole. Hence the more numerous the magistrates, the weaker the government.[6]

Rousseau adds: 'As this *maxim is fundamental,* let us apply ourselves to making it clearer'. So this maxim is fundamental. Rousseau says so; and it is curious that his best commentators have made so little of the matter. The reason why the government weakens if the magistrates are increased in number is that this introduces a diversity of wills into the body of the government, and the more friction there is within the government itself, the less energetically it can act on the subjects.

Now, if I am right in regarding Rousseau as thinking in terms of affective dispositions, one might translate his argument in the following way: To the extent that the subject finds himself less of a citizen, because his share

---

[6] *The Social Contract,* Book III, chap. 2.

of sovereignty has been too diluted, he is less and less disposed to obey the orders of the government, and the government needs more strength—not only coercive, but also psychological strength. Its edicts are the less compelling the more they appear to be the product of a compromise between the several elements that compose the government, and when the subject feels that such edicts might have been different if the balance of forces within the government had been even a little altered.

Therefore, not only does the same edict meet less and less goodwill in the subject, as the subject feels himself less and less a citizen, with the result that the edict requires more repressive enforcement; but an edict which seems to originate from a single steady will of the government requires less coercion in practice to effect obedience than the same edict which seems to originate from a government divided within itself. This means that a divided government in a state with a large population would need a greater amount of repressive force than it would in fact command.

Whatever may be said of this reading of Rousseau, there can be no denying that Rousseau insists on the practical necessity of a concentration of governmental authority wherever the population is large.

I have just proved that the government becomes weaker in proportion to the increase in the number of the magistrates; and before that, I proved that the greater the population of a state, the greater must be the repressive force of the government. From this it follows that the relative number of magistrates to the government, should be in inverse proportion to that of subjects to the sovereign. That is to say, the larger the state the more concentrated its government must be, so that the number of magistrates diminishes as the size of the population increases.[7]

Those who think of Rousseau merely as a master of

---

[7] *The Social Contract*, Book III, chap. 2.

sensibility and as a creator of powerful images should read again the first chapter of Book III of *The Social Contract*. One cannot fail to admire the rigour of the argument, or to remark the precision with which the author moves, by logical steps, towards his conclusion; a conclusion which Rousseau regarded as a law, what we should call today 'a positive law of political science'.

A positive law: thus one to be justified by empirical evidence; and how are we to explain that no research has been done to see whether the evidence validates or invalidates this law of so celebrated an author? Rousseau himself attached great importance to it; and we find it set out again in his *Letter from the Mountain*:

> The principle which determines the various forms of government depends on the number of members of which each is made up. The smaller the number, the stronger the government; the greater the number, the weaker the government, and since sovereignty tends always to slacken, government tends always to increase its power. Thus the executive body must always in the long run prevail over the legislative body; and when the law is finally subordinate to men, there remains nothing but slaves and masters, and the state is destroyed.

> Before this destruction, the government must, by its natural progress, change its form, and pass by degrees from a greater number to a lesser number.[8]

Note in the second paragraph of this quotation, the wording: 'the government *must*, by its *natural* progress'. The 'must' which I have italicised is clearly not an ethical 'must', but a scientific 'must'. Rousseau is not saying 'It is good that . . .' but 'It will come about that . . .'. We must look more closely at this introduction of the scientific 'must' into a work which was written, and which is read, in terms of the ethical 'must'. It is significant that Rousseau declares so very forcefully as what is 'going to

---

[8] *Letters From the Mountain*, Part I, letter 6.

happen' the very reverse of what, at the doctrinal level, he has proclaimed 'ought to happen'. In other words, Rousseau the social scientist predicts the destruction of what Rousseau the moralist recommends.

Each one of us, if he reflects a little, must distinguish what he considers desirable from what he considers probable. One might define optimism as the belief that the real will approach the desirable, and pessimism as the belief that the real will diverge from the desirable. Political pessimism is very marked in Rousseau. Consider the following words, addressed to the citizens of Geneva —the relevance will be clear if one remembers that the general council of the Genevan republic, where all the citizens met, corresponded to Rousseau's idea of the sovereign:

> What has happened to you, gentlemen, is what happens to every government like yours. In the first place, the legislative power and the executive power which constitute sovereignty are not separate. The sovereign people will for themselves, and by themselves they do what they will. Soon the inconvenience of this struggle of each against all forces the sovereign people to appoint some of their members to execute their will. These officers having fulfilled their commission, and given an account of it, return to the common equality. Little by little these commissions become more frequent; and finally permanent. Imperceptibly the commissioners form a body which is always active. A body which is always active cannot give an account of every single deed; it gives an account only of the principal ones; and soon it gives an account of none at all. And the more the power which executes is active, the more it enervates the power which willed its existence. The will of yesterday is supposed to be equally that of today; although the act of yesterday does not exempt one from acting today. Finally the inactivity of the power that wills makes it subordinate to the power that executes; the latter becomes gradually more inde-

pendent in its action, and soon in its volition also; and in place of acting for the power that wills, it acts on it. Thus there remains in the state only one active power, that of the executive. Executive power is only force; and where force alone rules, the state is dissolved. And that, gentlemen, is how all democratic states perish in the end.[9]

Notice that Rousseau does not say: 'This may happen', but 'This must happen'. Already we have remarked on the wording 'the government must, by its natural progress' and we have emphasised the 'must'; equally we may stress the expression 'natural progress'. The same adjective 'natural' occurs in this passage:

A government contracts when it passes from the hands of the many to those of the few, or, in other words, when it changes from democracy to aristocracy, and by one further remove, to royalty. This is its natural tendency. If the process were reversed, and a movement took place from smaller to greater, government might be said to slacken: but such a reversed process is impossible.

In fact, a government never changes its form except when its springs are too worn out for it to maintain its form. For if a government eased its severity while extending its dominion, its power would become null, and it would be even less able to conserve itself. So a government must wind up and strengthen the spring as it expands, for otherwise the state it holds up, would collapse in ruins.[10]

Such is Rousseau's 'scientific' theory of the evolution of the forms of government.

---

9 *Letters From the Mountain*, Part II, letter 7.
10 *The Social Contract*, Book III, chap. 10.

A. *Bibliography*:

MACDONALD, H., and HARGREAVES, M. *Thomas Hobbes: A Bibliography*. New York and London: The Bibliographical Society, 1952.

B. *Complete Works*:

English Works of Thomas Hobbes of Malmesbury (A reprint of the 1839 edition of Sir William Molesworth), 11 vols. Germany: Scientia Verlag Aalen, 1962. 2d reprint, 1966.

Opera Philosophica Quae Latine Scripsit Omnia (Complete Latin Works), 5 vols. Germany: Scientia Verlag Aalen, 1951.

C. *Selections*:

In *British Moralists 1650–1800*, 2 vols. Oxford: Clarendon Press, 1969. Edited and selected by D. D. Raphael. Vol. I—*Human Nature; Leviathan; Of Liberty and Necessity; De Cive; De Corpore Politico.*

Hobbes: Selections. New York: Scribners, 1958. Edited by F. J. E. Woodbridge. (This is a reprint of the 1930 edition.)

Body Man & Citizen. New York: Collier Books, 1962. Edited and with an Introduction by R. S. Peters.

The Metaphysical System of Hobbes, etc. New York: Open Court Publishers, 1958. Edited by M. W. Calkins, 2d edition.

D. *Leviathan*:

Edited, introductory essay, and notes by Michael Oakeshott, Basil Blackwell. Oxford, 1957. The same, but with an introduction by R. S. Peters, for New York: Collier Books, 1962.

Introduction by A. D. Lindsay. New York: Dutton, 1959. This is a reprint of the 1914 Everyman Edition, Dent.

Parts I & II. Introduction by H. W. Schneider. Indianapolis: Bobbs-Merrill, 1958.

Introduction by John Plamenatz. London: Collins, 1962. The same, Cleveland: World Publishing Co., 1963.

Abridged, edited, and introduced by F. B. Randall. New York: Washington Square Press, 1964.

Part I. Introduction by R. Kirk. Chicago: Regnery, 1956.

Introduction by W. G. P. Smith. Oxford: Clarendon Press, 1958.

E. *Other Works:*

Elements of Law, Natural & Politic. Introduction by M. M. Goldsmith, 2d edition. New York: Cass, 1969.

De Cive. Edited and abridged by S. P. Lamprecht. New York: Appleton, 1949.

Behemoth (A reprint of William Molesworth's Edition). New York: Franklin, 1963.

An Historical Narration Concerning Heresey & the Punishment Thereof. Stanford: Academic Reprints, 1954.

A SELECTION OF BOOKS ON HOBBES

BOWLES, J. *Hobbes and His Critics: A Study in Seventeenth Century Constitutionalism.* Oxford, 1952.

BRANDT, FRITHIOF. *Thomas Hobbes' Mechanical Conception of Nature.* London, 1928.

CATLIN, G. E. G. *Thomas Hobbes as Philosopher, Publicist, and Man of Letters.* Oxford, 1922.

GAUTHIER, DAVID P. *The Logic of Leviathan.* London: O.U.P., 1964.

GOLDSMITH, M. M. *The Political Philosophy of Hobbes: The Rationale of the Sovereign State.* Columbia, 1966.

———. *Hobbes' Science of Politics.* Columbia, 1966.

HOOD, F. C. *The Divine Politics of Thomas Hobbes.* Oxford, 1964.

LAIRD, JOHN. *Hobbes.* London, 1934.

MACPHERSON, C. B. *The Political Theory of Possessive Individualism.* Oxford, 1964.

MINTZ, SAMUEL I. *The Hunting of Leviathan.* Cambridge, 1962.

PETERS, RICHARD S. *Hobbes,* 2d ed. London, 1967.

ROBERTSON, A. C. *Hobbes.* London, 1886.

STRAUSS, LEO. *The Political Philosophy of Hobbes: Its Basis and Its Genesis,* tr. E. M. Sinclair. Oxford, 1936, and Chicago, 1952.

WARRENDER, H. *The Political Philosophy of Hobbes: His Theory of Obligation.* Oxford, 1957.

WATKINS, J. W. N. *Hobbes' System of Ideas: A Study in the Political Significance of Philosophical Theories.* London & New York, 1965.

A COLLECTION OF ESSAYS

BROWN, K. C., ed. *Hobbes Studies.* Oxford & Harvard, 1965.

ESSAYS IN COLLECTIONS, GENERAL WORKS, ETC., A SELECTION

GOOCH, G. P. "Hobbes," printed in his *Studies in Diplomacy and Statecraft.* London, 1942.

MINOGUE, K. R. "Thomas Hobbes and the Philosophy of Absolutism," in *Political Ideas,* ed. David Thomson. London, 1966.

OAKESHOTT, MICHAEL. "The Moral Life in the Writings of Thomas Hobbes," in his *Rationalism in Politics & Other Essays.* London, 1962.

PLAMENATZ, JOHN. "Hobbes," Ch. 4, in his *Man and Society,* Vol. I. London, 1963.

SABINE, G. H. "Thomas Hobbes," Ch. XXIII, in his *A History of Political Theory,* revised ed. New York and London, 1960.

WATKINS, J. W. N. "Hobbes," in *Western Political Philosophers*, ed. Maurice Cranston. London, 1964.

ARTICLES ON HOBBES

BERLIN, I. "Hobbes, Locke & Prof. Macpherson," *Political Quarterly*, 35 (1964), 444–68.

GERHARD, WILLIAM A. "The Epistemology of Thomas Hobbes," *The Thomist*, 9 (1946), 573–87.

JACOBY, E. G. "Hobbes and the Contract: A Study in Development," *Political Science*, 4 (1952), 3–11.

KAPLAN, M. A. "How Sovereign is Hobbes' Sovereign?", *Western Political Quarterly*, 9 (1956), 389–405.

MC NEILLY, F. S. "Egoism in Hobbes," *Philosophical Quarterly*, 16 (1966), 193–206.

MORRIS, BERTRAM. "Possessive Individualism and Political Realities," *Ethics*, 75 (1965), 207–14.

NAGEL, THOMAS. "Hobbes' Concept of Obligation," *Philosophical Review*, 68 (1959), 68–83.

PITKIN, H. "Hobbes' Concept of Representation," *American Political Science Review*, 58 (1964), 328–40 & 902–18.

PLAMENATZ, J. "Mr. Warrender's Hobbes," *Political Studies*, 5 (1957), 295–308.

ROSHWALD, M. "Leviathan after Three Hundred Years," *Plain View*, 9 (1954), 150–69.

SCHOCHET, G. J. "Thomas Hobbes on the Family and the State of Nature," *Political Science Quarterly*, 82 (1967), 427–45.

SKINNER, Q. "The Ideological Context of Hobbes' Political Thought," *Historical Journal*, 9 (1966), 286–317.

———. "Hobbes on Sovereignty: An Unknown Discussion," *Political Studies*, 13 (1965), 213–18.

STAUFFER, R. B., and VINACKE, W. E. "Hobbes Revisited: An Analysis of the Compatibility of the Theories of Human Nature and of the State in the Leviathan," *Journal of Social Psychology*, 48 (1958), 61–73.

STEWART, J. B. "Hobbes among His Critics," *Political Science Quarterly,* 73 (1958), 547–65.

WARRENDER, H. "The Place of God in Hobbes' Philosophy: A Reply to Mr. Plamenatz," *Political Studies,* 8 (1960), 48–57.

WATKINS, J. W. N. "The Posthumous Career of Thomas Hobbes," *Review of Politics,* 19 (1957), 351–60.

———. "Philosophy and Politics in Hobbes," *Philosophical Quarterly,* 5 (1955), 125–46.

WILLIAMSON, C. "Contradiction in Hobbes' Analysis of Sovereignty," *Canadian Journal of Economics and Political Science,* 32 (1966), 202–19.

WORKS IN FRENCH

Oeuvres Complètes. Paris, 1959 continuing.

LEIGH, R. A., ed. *Correspondance de Jean-Jacques Rousseau.* Geneva, 1965 continuing.

VAUGHAN, C. E., ed. *The Political Writings of Jean-Jacques Rousseau.* 2 vols. Oxford & New York, 1962.

WORKS IN ENGLISH

BEATTIE, A. H., trans. *Creed of a Priest of Savoy.* New York, 1956.

BLOOM, ALLAN, trans. and ed. *Politics and the Arts: Rousseau's Letter to d'Alembert.* Glencoe, Illinois, 1960.

CRANSTON, MAURICE, trans. and Intro. *Social Contract.* London & Baltimore, 1968.

FOXLEY, BARBARA, trans. *Emile.* London, n.d.

KENDALL, WILLMOORE, trans. *Considerations on the Government of Poland.* Minneapolis, 1947.

MASTERS, R. D. AND J. R., ed. and trans. *The First and Second Discourses.* New York, 1964.

WATKINS, FREDERICK, trans. and ed. *Political Writings.* Edinburgh & New York, 1953.

COMMENTARIES ON ROUSSEAU

Books

BROOME, J. H. *Rousseau: A Study of His Thought.* London, 1963.

CASSIRER, ERNST. *The Question of Jean-Jacques Rousseau,* trans. and ed. Peter Gay. New York, 1954.

COBBAN, ALFRED. *Rousseau and the Modern State.* London, 1934; reprinted Hamden, 1961.

GREEN, F. C. *Jean-Jacques Rousseau: A Critical Study of His Life and Writings.* Cambridge, 1955.

GRIMSLEY, RONALD. *Jean-Jacques Rousseau: A Study in Self-Awareness.* Cardiff, 1961.

HENDEL, C. W. *Jean-Jacques Rousseau: Moralist,* 2 vols. London, 1934; reprinted New York, 1962.

MASTERS, ROGER D. *The Political Philosophy of Rousseau.* Princeton, 1968; London, 1969.

SHKLAR, JUDITH N. *Men and Citizens: A Study of Rousseau's Social Theory.* Cambridge, 1969.

Articles

ALLERS, ULRICH S. "Rousseau's Second Discourse," *Review of Politics*, 20 (1958).

COBBAN, ALFRED. "New Light on the Political Thought of Rousseau," *Political Science Quarterly*, 66 (1951).

CROCKER, LESTER G. "The Relation of Rousseau's Second Discourse and the Contrat Social," *Romantic Review*, 51 (1960), 33–44.

GOSSMAN, LIONEL. "Rousseau's Idealism," *Romantic Review*, 52 (1961), 173–82.

HOFFMAN, STANLEY. "Rousseau on War and Peace," *American Political Science Review*, 57 (1963).

PLAMENATZ, JOHN. "Pascal and Rousseau," *Political Studies*, 10 (1962).

COMMENTARIES ON ROUSSEAU IN FRENCH
Books

BURGELIN, PIERRE. *La Philosophie de l'Existence de J. J. Rousseau.* Paris, 1952.

DERATHÉ, ROBERT. *Le Rationalisme de Jean-Jacques Rousseau.* Paris, 1948.

———. *Jean-Jacques Rousseau et la Science Politique de Son Temps.* Paris, 1950.

POLIN, RAYMOND. *Jean-Jacques Rousseau.* Paris, 1970.

STAROBINSKI, JEAN. *Jean-Jacques Rousseau, le Transparence et l'Obstacle.* Paris, 1957.

Articles

JOUVENEL, BERTRAND DE. "Essai sur la Politique de Rousseau," his introduction to *Du Contrat Social.* Geneva, 1947.

COLLECTIONS OF ESSAYS
English

"Jean Jacques Rousseau" in *Yale French Studies*, 28 (1961–62).

French

"Presence de Jean-Jacques Rousseau," *Annales de la So-cieté Jean-Jacques Rousseau*, Vol. 35. Paris, 1963.

"Rousseau et la Philosophie Politique," *Annales de la Philosophie Politique*, Vol. 5. Paris, 1965.